THE PRAEGER HANDBOOK OF
FAITH-BASED SCHOOLS IN THE UNITED STATES, K–12

THE PRAEGER HANDBOOK OF
FAITH-BASED SCHOOLS IN THE UNITED STATES, K–12

VOLUME 2

Thomas C. Hunt and James C. Carper, Editors

PRAEGER

AN IMPRINT OF ABC-CLIO, LLC
Santa Barbara, California • Denver, Colorado • Oxford, England

Library of Congress Cataloging-in-Publication Data

The Praeger handbook of faith-based schools in the United States, K–12 / Thomas C. Hunt and James C. Carper, editors.
   p. cm.
Includes bibliographical references and index.
ISBN 978–0–313–39139–2 (pbk. : alk. paper) — ISBN 978–0–313–39140–8 (ebook) 1. Church schools—
United States. 2. Church and state—United States. I. Hunt, Thomas C., 1930- II. Carper, James C. III. Title:
Handbook of faith-based schools in the United States, K–12.
LC427.P64   2012
371.070973—dc23   2012002308

ISBN: 978–0–313–39139–2
EISBN: 978–0–313–39140–8

16 15 14 13 12   1 2 3 4 5

This book is also available on the World Wide Web as an eBook.
Visit www.abc-clio.com for details.

Praeger
An Imprint of ABC-CLIO, LLC

ABC-CLIO, LLC
130 Cremona Drive, P.O. Box 1911
Santa Barbara, California 93116-1911

This book is printed on acid-free paper (∞)

Manufactured in the United States of America

This work is dedicated to the members of our immediate families and to all friends of faith-based schools.

Contents

Preface

As we noted in *The Praeger Handbook of Religion and Education in the United States* (2009), religion has not disappeared from American life. As the United States has become more secular and more religious simultaneously, the place of religion in the public square and the public school has remained a matter of intense, and sometimes rancorous, discussion. Americans have certainly expressed strong opinions about the place of religion in schools operated by the government since the genesis of modern public education in the mid-1800s. Debates and litigation continue regarding, among other issues, religion in the public school curriculum and the rights of students to exercise their faith in public schools. The recent controversies surrounding the Pledge of Allegiance, Intelligent Design/Evolution, and religious references during graduation addresses are cases in point.

Faith-based schools have also been part of the ongoing debate over the place of religion in our public life and education of the young. Although our 2009 *Handbook* included entries on faith-based schools, it dealt primarily with religion and public schooling. We developed *The Praeger Handbook of Faith-Based Schools* as a companion to the earlier work. It focuses solely on schools that are extensions of communities of faith. We hope that it will be a valuable resource for parents, legislators, journalists, educators, and citizens as well as scholars interested in this part of the American educational landscape.

Faith-based schools have endured periods of open hostility in the past, e.g., Catholic and Lutheran schools in the early twentieth century, and even today they remain the object of suspicion and criticism in some quarters, e.g., faith-based homeschooling. We hope that this *Handbook* will help critics and friends of faith-based schools arrive at a better understanding of these schools and their contribution to the common good as well as the preferences of families whose faith-commitments obligate them to seek a kind of education that cannot (and should not) be provided by the government. Pursuant to this goal, the *Handbook* includes an introductory essay that provides a general overview of faith-based schooling from the colonial period to the present; 49 chapters on schools, support organizations, and significant issues involving faith-based schools; and appended tables summarizing state and U.S. Supreme Court decisions affecting faith-based schools.

The *Handbook of Faith-Based Schools in the United States* is our tenth joint effort as editors/authors of books in the field of religion and education. As has been the case with previous work, this ambitious project would not have been possible, however, without the efforts of others. Forty-four scholars and practitioners contributed their time and talent to this *Handbook*. Though he did not contribute an entry, the late Warren Nord of the University of North Carolina, one of the top scholars in the area of religion and education, offered sage advice regarding content. We were also favored by John Witte of the Emory University Law School, who graciously granted us permission to use an edited version of his valuable summary of Supreme Court decisions dealing with religion.

We also recognize all of the editors at Praeger who saw the project through to completion. Beth Ptalis deserves our special thanks. We are grateful for their backing of this work.

Finally, we thank a number of persons who provided us with much-needed production and proofreading assistance, including Karen Hunt, Janet Hawkins, Chelsie Berry, and Lauren Flynn.

Thomas C. Hunt
James C. Carper

Part III

CATHOLIC SCHOOLS

31

Catholic Schools in the United States from Colonial Times to Vatican II

Thomas C. Hunt

THE COLONIAL ERA

Religious motives were the primary reason for the founding of Catholic schools in Florida and Louisiana in the seventeenth century, as missionaries attempted to spread the faith. These schools predated those established in the Massachusetts Bay Colony. The teaching force of Catholic schools included lay teachers, Franciscans, Capuchins, Carmelites, Jesuits, and Ursulines. There were schools at all levels—some were for boarders and others were day schools; some were racially integrated and some were solely for white children; and others were separate for free African American youth, taught by African American religious order personnel, as in New Orleans (McDermott and Hunt 1991, 46–50). In colonies under English (Protestant) rule, conflict with civil authorities occurred with some regularity (Buetow 1970, 23–36).

THE REVOLUTIONARY PERIOD

As the Revolution approached, the Catholic population in what was to become the United States of America was small and sometimes beset by religious bigotry. This prejudice took the form of limitations on rights of citizenship, restrictions on worship, and other measures that limited the practice of the faith, including in education. Slogans in several states, such as "No Popery," represented the general attitude towards Catholicism that prevailed in much of the land (Billington 1938, 9). It was this environment in which John Carroll was consecrated the fledgling nation's first Bishop on August 15, 1790 (Guilday 1922, 369).

Following the first American Synod in 1791, Carroll issued his first "Pastoral" in which he wrote of "The Advantages of a Christian Education," stating that "the principles

An earlier analysis of the same historical period can be found in the chapter, "Selected Episcopal and Papal Documents on Catholic Education (1792–1962)" by Thomas Hunt, which appears in the Alliance for Catholic Education Press publication, At the Heart of the Church: Selected Documents of Catholic Education.

instilled in the course of a Christian education, are generally preserved throughout life." He instructed Catholic parents that they should never cease attempting to instill the "habits of virtue and religion" in their children. In so doing, he asserted, their children "will remember with gratitude, and repay with religious duty, your solicitude for them" (Guilday 1954, 3–4). Carroll described the "virtuous and Christian instruction of youth" as a "principal object of pastoral solicitude" and emphasized the "necessity of a pious and Catholic education of the young to insure their growing up in the faith" (Buetow 1970, 45).

The First Amendment to the federal constitution required that no church could be established nor could the free exercise of religion be prohibited. Nonetheless, discrimination against Catholics, who constituted a distinct minority in the American population, did occur in the early years of the nation's history. Catholic bishops were deeply concerned with preserving the faith of their flocks and viewed the establishment of Catholic schools as a vital means to protect the faith of the young, which was a highly sought-after goal. Their efforts to provide schools for this purpose were many in the nineteenth century.

THE FIRST HALF OF THE NINETEENTH CENTURY

Catholics in the United States remained a distinct minority in the early years of the nineteenth century. That demographic situation was to change as the century progressed, due overwhelmingly to immigration. In 1820 the Catholic population was estimated at 195,000; in 1840 at 663,000 and in 1850 at 1,606,000 (McCluskey 1959, 27). At the beginning of the century, schooling in the United States was conducted for the most part in rural schools, most often under local auspices. Statesmen such as Thomas Jefferson had linked schooling to the republic and consequently sought to focus it on citizenship for a republican society. The country was heavily Protestant and its schools, in texts such as the *McGuffey Readers*, in practices such as the devotional reading of the King James Version of the Bible, and in leadership (Protestant ministers often served as superintendents of schools), reflected the dominant Protestant climate. Conflicts with Catholics in school practice occurred rather regularly and led to the development and spread of Catholic schools. As the number of Catholics increased, and the frequency of clashes with American institutions such as schools grew, Catholic policy for dealing with these encounters was formulated under the leadership of the Catholic hierarchy gathered in council as well as individually by local bishops, influenced at times by policies that emanated from the Vatican.

The Provincial Councils of Baltimore

Baltimore was the first Catholic diocese in the United States and had become its first metropolitan see. The Catholic population had grown to approximately 500,000 by 1829, in a total American population that had reached about twelve million (Buetow 1970, 112). In response at least in part to the urging of Bishop John England of Charleston, South Carolina, the American bishops met in council in Baltimore on October 1, 1829, in their first such gathering. Educational concerns were among the items the bishops were to look at, namely the "best method of counteracting the pernicious influence of the anti-Catholic groups in the country, of regulating the instruction of Catholic youth, and of encouraging and supporting religious communities, especially of women devoted to educational work" (Guilday 1932, 85). The Council Fathers also enacted two decrees that bore directly on education. In the 34th Decree they adjudged that it was "absolutely necessary that schools be established in which the young may be taught the principles of faith and morality, while being instructed in letters," and the 35th Decree called for textbooks that would "accurately communicate Catholic doctrine and worship and Catholic history" (Guilday 1932, 94–95).

Bishop England's call for religious communities, especially of women, who would teach in the Catholic schools the Council called for, began to be realized in the wake of the Council. Orders of vowed religious women, of both native origin and those who came from Europe, played an indispensable role in the existence and spread of Catholic schools throughout the nineteenth and well into the twentieth century. Only four years (1829–1833) separated the first two Provincial Councils of Baltimore, yet several events occurred in that brief period that had a considerable impact on the life of Catholic schools. Anti-Catholic bigotry remained and in some places intensified. The American Protestant Association, a fiercely nativist and anti-Catholic body, was founded in New York City in 1830 (Guilday 1932, 100–103). Meeting in 1833 in the Second Provincial Council of Baltimore, the Council Fathers addressed educational issues in their "Pastoral." They wrote that the education of the "rising generation" was a "subject of the first importance." Their concern for education included seminaries and colleges as well as parish schools, with the goal of providing young Catholics with the "best opportunities of literature and science united to a strict protection of their morals and the best safeguards of their faith" (Guilday 1954, 74).

Anti-Catholic bigotry was on the rise in the 1830s in American society and this bigotry affected Catholic schools. For instance, the Ursuline convent in Charlestown, Massachusetts, was burned and "revelatory" books such as Rebecca Reed's *Six Months in a Convent* and Maria Monk's *Awful Disclosures* were published. Meeting in 1837 in the Third Provincial Council of Baltimore, the American Church's leaders called on the Catholic laity to make Catholic educational institutions "as perfect as possible" (Guilday 1954, 115).

Horace Mann and the Common (Free) School Movement

In 1836, Horace Mann, a Whig politician who was named secretary of the State Board of Education in Massachusetts by then-Governor Dwight, spearheaded the drive for a common (for all, rich and poor, boys and girls) school movement in Massachusetts. His fellow educator, Henry Barnard, followed suit in neighboring Connecticut, and eventually the movement spread across the country, leading Horace Mann to be termed the "father" of the American public school. Basically, Mann argued for a tax-supported, state-regulated school that was "nonsectarian." (In reality, it was pan-Protestant.) The common school featured the teaching of "common-core Christianity," that is, all the truths accepted by Christians, such as the Fatherhood of God, and the devotional reading, without note or comment, of the King James Version of the Bible, defined by Mann as the "acknowledged expositor of Christianity," which, in his view, made the common school religious (Cremin 1957, 105). Arguing that private schools, especially those of a sectarian nature, were socially divisive, and that the common school idea had never been tried anywhere before, Mann looked to the common school to produce social harmony in the state, which was experiencing an influx of immigrants (many Irish and Catholic), migrants from rural areas, and a rise in industrialization, consequent urbanization, and extreme differences of wealth among its citizens. Mann, and his disciples, led the successful crusade to implement his common school model in American society.

In the Wake of the Common School

The spread of the common school posed a threat to the faith and morals of Catholic children in the eyes of many Catholics, including the bishops. Meeting in 1840 for the Fourth Provincial Council of Baltimore, the Church's leaders took note specifically of the dangers to the faith of Catholic children posed by the common school and addressed their responsibility in safeguarding the faith of the children enrolled in these schools.

Schools occupied a prominent place in the "Pastoral" of the bishops, who referred to providing Catholic schools for Catholic children as "one of their most pressing obligations" (Guilday 1954, 124). Catholic parents came in for criticism by the bishops for not financially supporting the schools as they should. The failure to provide schools, the bishops charged, deprived the children of the teaching of religion, which could lead to the "total abandonment of their religious practices" (Guilday 1932, 125). The bishops criticized the "indiscriminate use" of the Bible, brought about by its daily reading in public schools, and averred that the popular practice of reading the Bible in that fashion would likely lead to "more contempt than veneration" (McCluskey 1964, 60). The Council Fathers also inveighed against the textbooks used in the common schools, stating that many of those in "general use" in public educational institutions made "covert and insidious efforts" to "misrepresent our principles, to distort our truths, to vilify our practices and to bring contempt upon our Church and its members" (Guilday 1932, 128–29).

Nativist-inspired attacks on Catholicism and Catholic schools continued unabated as the decade of the 1840s progressed. The Church was identified as the enemy of the Bible and the opponent of the recently established common schools. The Church was described as "one vast brothel" and the Pope of being the anti-Christ (Billington 1938, 166–68). The Fifth Provincial Council of Baltimore met in 1843 in this charged atmosphere. Very forceful in their criticism of the common schools, the bishops warned Catholic parents of the dangers inherent in attending these schools, dangers brought about by the sectarian use of the Bible and the "offensive and dangerous matter" in the textbooks used. Parents were warned of their responsibility for the welfare of the souls of their children in such an environment and were enjoined to see that no threats to the faith of their children be tolerated in the common schools (McCluskey 1964, 63).

Religious Strife in Philadelphia and New York City

Nativist-inspired violence flared up in Philadelphia in the early 1840s in the Bible riots. The Philadelphia School Board accepted Bishop Kenrick's request in 1844 that Catholic children in the Philadelphia public schools would be allowed to read the Catholic (Douay) Version of the Scriptures instead of the King James Version. The resulting Nativist riots led to the destruction of Catholic buildings, including churches, and many homes of the Irish American Catholics. The rioting took the lives of 13 persons, and more 50 fifty were wounded befoe the violence was quelled. After the riots, Nativist sentiment over the situation was expressed in statements such as "The Papists deserve this and much more" and "It were well if every Popish church in the world were leveled with the ground" (Billington 1938, 220–37).

A conflict of a different sort erupted in New York City in the early 1840s. There, the aggressive Bishop, John Hughes, sought the Catholics' "share" of the school fund, obtained through taxation. Hughes's actions led to a clash between him and the New York City Free School Society, a private group of wealthy Protestants, who were funded by the State of New York to conduct schools for the poor children of New York City, who were, in the main, Irish-American. Hughes, and his Catholic supporters, pointed to the devotional reading of the King James Version of the Bible in the public schools and to the presence of textbooks that were offensive to Catholics. One such book, *An Irish Heart*, stated that if Irish immigration to the United States continued on the same scale as it had, the United States would be "appropriately styled the common sewer of Ireland" (Ravitch 1974, 51).

Hughes was unsuccessful in his efforts to obtain public tax funds for his people, but he did unify them in the process and started a Catholic school system in New York City that served as a model to successive generations of American Catholics. In her book, *The Great School Wars in New York City, 1805–1973*, educational historian Diane Ravitch has identified this conflict as the first "great school war" (Ravitch 1974, 3–76).

The remaining years of the first half of the nineteenth century experienced no lessening of tension over the issue of Catholic schools in the United States. Books such as the *History of the Papacy in the United States* called on all loyal Americans to oppose the "man of sin," the Pope (Guilday 1932, 144). The continuing flood of European immigrants, many of them Catholic, had been steady since the 1820s. Now, in the 1840s, it increased, and along with it came a large growth in the Catholic presence in the United States, a phenomenon that caused fear in the minds and hearts of some of their fellow Americans, especially those of a nativist orientation.

In 1846, the year of the Sixth Provincial Council of Baltimore, there were 21 suffragan dioceses to Baltimore; 675 Catholic churches; 26 bishops; 709 priests, of whom 508 were diocesan; 22 seminaries; 15 colleges; over a million Catholics; and 14 Catholic publications, weekly or monthly, in the United States (Guilday 1932, 144–45). The Provincial Council held that year did not specifically address Catholic schools, nor did the council that followed in 1849.

THE SECOND HALF OF THE NINETEENTH CENTURY

As mentioned above, massive Catholic immigration in the last three decades of the first half of the nineteenth century struck fear into the hearts of many Protestant Americans. In that 30-year period almost 2.5 million immigrants, many of whom were Catholic, entered the country, with 1.7 million arriving in the 1840s (*Report on Population of the United States at the Eleventh Census, 1890* 1895, lxxx). The Catholic population numbered almost two million by 1852, the year of the First Plenary Council of Baltimore, as a result of this influx of immigrants (Guilday 1932, 171). Often retaining their ties to the "old country" in their faith, culture, and language, many of these recent arrivals looked to their parish school to transmit these loyalties to their children and were looked on as "un-American" by some of their fellow citizens. An essential entity in this process was the parish school, established to teach the Catholic faith "in its entirety" (Burns 1917, 15). Aware of the difficulties to faith presented by the pan-Protestant common school, the American hierarchy accepted their responsibility to protect and sustain the faith of Catholic children and resolved to do what they could to build schools in every parish to meet their apostolic duty (Guilday 1954, 187–90). Catholic parents were exhorted to do their best to give their children a Christian education, one which was always "subordinate to religious influence," and they were warned not to be "led astray" by "false and delusive theories which are so prevalent, and which leave youth without religion," including those that would "separate religion from secular education." Instead, the bishops advised, parents should heed their voices and bring up their children as they were brought up by their own "pious parents" (Guilday 1954, 187–89). Parents were instructed that no sacrifice was too great to provide their children with a Catholic education, one that would protect their children from "all the evils of an uncatholic education," which emanated from the very "system" of public education (Guilday 1954, 189–91). The Council Fathers called on all the nation's bishops to build schools in those parishes that did not as yet have them in order that all Catholic children could attend a school that was "directed by religious motives" (Guilday 1932, 178–79).

The German Influence—the Story of Cincinnati

The Catholic Church, abetted by the huge influx of immigrants, mainly German and Irish, continued to grow as the nineteenth century reached the halfway mark. As the nation expanded to the west, the Catholic Church set up new dioceses, for instance in Cincinnati, Milwaukee, and St. Louis, each of which was heavily populated by German-Americans. They formed what was known as the "German triangle." These immigrants, many of whom were Catholic, brought with them a dedication to maintaining German culture, which included a commitment to their respective faith and language, and looked to their parochial schools to preserve and foster both.

The German Catholic presence was especially noticeable in Cincinnati at this time, and it manifested itself in the Catholic population's devotion to Catholic schools. The German-American Catholics had set up their first school in Cincinnati in 1834. Enrollment increased, and by 1841 they had established their second school. Several years later there were six German parish schools in the city with over 1,800 students (Walch 1996, 51). The First Provincial Council of Cincinnati met in 1855 and the assembled bishops directed parish pastors to do all they could to avoid having their children attend schools that endangered their faith. They called on Catholic parents to "aid and sustain" Catholic schools, which was their "solemn obligation" (Guilday 1932, 144–45). "Religion," they wrote, was the "very foundation of all sound education." Consequently, they held that the building of Catholic schools was as important as "building new churches" (Lamott 1921, 275). The Council Fathers then set forth the German parishes as a model for the English-speaking ones to follow:

> Our excellent German congregations leave us nothing to desire on this subject. The children attend Mass every morning, they sing with one accord the power of God. They go from the church to the school. They are accustomed to cleanliness and neatness of dress, to diligent and affectionate respect for their parents, the reverend Clergy and their teachers. We have nothing more at heart than that the pupils of our English schools should imitate their example.
>
> Burns and Kohlbrenner 1937, 138

The Cincinnati prelates followed up their espousal of Catholic schools in the Second Provincial Council three years later when they instructed pastors of parishes in their Province "under pain of mortal sin" to see that their parishes had schools "whenever conditions warranted" (Burns 1912, 186).

The public schools did not escape the bishops' comments unscathed. In 1861 they described the public school system of Cincinnati as "plausible, but most unwise," and declared it was accountable for the "rising generation" being schooled without firm principles or with "false, at least, more or less, exaggerated and fanatical principles."

This educational system, they maintained, "if carried out according to its alleged intent of abstaining from any definite religious instruction is well calculated to raise up a generation of religious indifferentists, if not of practical infidels, and . . . its tendency is to develop false or very defective, if not dangerous principles" (Jenkins 1866, 34).

The Know-Nothing Party

The 1850s witnessed the arrival on the American scene of another Nativist movement, the Know-Nothing Party. Started in response to what was said to be the growing political influence of Roman Catholics, the Party's agenda was aimed at eliminating the influence of Catholics and curbing immigration. Membership was limited to native-born Americans and featured religious bigotry. The Party's name was derived from the required response to an inquiry about it: "I know nothing." Couched in secrecy, the Party reached the pinnacle of its political influence in the mid-1850s. In 1856 it shed its cloak of secrecy and changed its name to the American Party, and that year elected seven state governors. One of its aims was to prevent Catholics from being elected to office. Members of the Party took part in election-day riots in 1854 and 1855. Catholic priests were at times insulted and vowed religious women (nuns) sometimes found it unsafe to wear their religious habits in public due to possible Know Nothing harassment.

The Party was active in school matters, supporting Protestant values and practices in the public schools, such as the reading of the King James Version of the Bible; opposing public financial support for Catholic schools, which were deemed disloyal; and advocating inspection of Catholic schools. Catholicism in general, with its growing population due to immigration, and Catholic schools in particular, were perceived to be a national threat.

The Know Nothing Party disappeared from the national scene as quickly as it had arisen as the issue of slavery replaced immigration as the leading national concern. Opposition to Catholic schools, some of it couched in patriotic terms, remained well into the twentieth century, however.

The "Syllabus of Errors"

Mid-nineteenth century Europe was a scene of turmoil and revolution. Currents of nationalism and rationalism were rampant, as the "old order" was frequently challenged on a widespread scale. Pope Pius IX confronted those strains, including the movement toward unification in Italy, which threatened to strip the Church of the Papal States, considered a sacred trust by Pius IX.

The "modernist" tendency enveloped education as well, and the Pope was pressed to defend the Church's traditional role in schooling. Shortly before he issued the "Syllabus," he outlined the Church's position on education in a letter to the Archbishop of Fribourg in which he staunchly defended the God-given right of the Church in schooling and stated that schools that denied the rightful role of the Church in education "cannot in conscience be frequented" (Conway 1884, 667). The Pontiff followed that letter up with the controversial "Syllabus" on December 8, 1864 in which he condemned "errors" such as attributing the control of schooling to the "civil power," and that Catholics could approve a "system of instruction" that separated schooling "from the Catholic faith and from the power of the Church" (Helmreich 1964, 2–5).

The Pope directed that the "Syllabus" be sent to all the Catholic bishops of the world so they would know what doctrines he had "repudiated and condemned" (Hales 1962, 266–67). Catholics, he asserted, had no alternative but to accept his authoritative teaching, because Jesus had given Peter and his successors the "supreme power of shepherding, ruling, and governing the Church" (Clarkson 1955, 85–86). It was not possible, he maintained, for Catholics to reject this teaching "without sinning and without departing in the least bit from the profession of the Catholic faith" (Helmreich 1964, 2–5).

Catholic Education in post-Civil War America

The Civil War had an enormous impact on life in the United States. One of its consequences was the intensification of a national spirit in the northern states, which included a growth in the attitude that the public schools were the bulwark of the republic. Pan-Protestantism remained influential in a number of areas, especially in the citizenship context. Private schools came to be more readily seen as socially divisive.

This was the atmosphere in which the Second Plenary Council of Baltimore opened in 1866. Opposition from the Know-Nothing Party notwithstanding, the Church's membership had increased from 1,980,000 to 3,842,000 since 1852 (Guilday 1932, 193–94). In the Council's "Pastoral," the bishops approved a section on the "Education of Youth," which included a quotation from a statement of the First Plenary Council that "religious teaching and religious training should form part of every system of school education," advised parents that they should inculcate in their children "habits of obedience, industry, and thrift" from the very beginning of their lives, and asserted that "true happiness" must be placed in submission "to the dispensations of Providence" (Guilday 1954, 215–16).

The clashes with civil authorities over school issues became both more frequent and acerbic in the United States as the century progressed. Some Catholic bishops inveighed against the "secular" or "godless" public school and questioned the Catholicity of parents who sent their children to these schools. Archbishop Elder of Cincinnati, for instance, held that Catholic parents were bound to obey their bishop on the school question, or else renounce their religion (Jenkins 1886, 82–83). Meanwhile, his fellow Ohioan, Bishop Gilmour of Cleveland, insisted that there could be "no division" on the school question (Jenkins, 1886, 84–85). Bishop Rosecrans of Columbus, Ohio went so far as to equate in terms of Catholic doctrine support of Catholic schools with belief in the Real Presence of Christ in the Eucharist and the Divinity of Jesus Christ (Jenkins, 1886, 86). James Gibbons, at the time (1873) Bishop of Richmond, Virginia, soon to become Cardinal Archbishop of Baltimore, claimed that religious and secular education could not be separated. Without Catholic schools, Gibbons feared that in the future it would be "much easier to find churches for a congregation, than a congregation for the churches" (Jenkins 1886, 212–22).

There existed at the time, however, internal disagreement over Catholic schools among the members of the Catholic hierarchy. This dissension reached the press. James A. McMaster, a convert and editor of the *Freeman's Journal* in New York, used the pages of his paper to promote Catholic schools and attack public schools, often referring to them as "pagan" and "godless" (Walch 1996, 55). He was a forceful advocate of getting Church authorities to speak out on behalf of Catholic schools and attack public schools. Some Catholic writers, most notably Orestes Brownson, disagreed with McMaster's castigation of public schools. Brownson felt that some parish schools were of poor quality. He also argued that Catholic children from good homes would not be hurt by attending public schools and that they might have a positive impact on those schools (Walch 1996, 56–57).

Enter the Vatican

The Vatican, in response at least in part to McMaster's prodding, inquired of the American archbishops about American public schools. The archbishops opposed setting a policy of denying the sacraments to parents of Catholic children who did not send their children to Catholic schools, instead sending them to public schools. The Vatican, through the Congregation of the Propagation of the Faith (the United States was officially a missionary territory throughout the nineteenth century in the official view of the Catholic Church, hence the country came under the Propagation's jurisdiction), in 1875 issued an "Instruction" that strongly supported attendance at Catholic schools and seriously warned against frequenting public schools. If attendance at public schools caused the danger of loss of faith, parents who ignored Catholic teaching in this matter, and allowed their children to go to schools "in which the ruin of their souls is inevitable," were not to be absolved in Confession (McCluskey 1964, 122–26). The Instruction was accurately seen as favoring the position of those American bishops and that of James McMaster, who strongly supported Catholic schools and the necessity of Catholic children to attend them.

Church and State in American Policy

There was internal dissension over the necessity of attending Catholic schools; that dissension was paired with the external hostility and tensions swirling around the issue. State legislatures increasingly passed legislation dealing with the certification of teachers, compulsory school attendance, and school accreditation and became involved in setting curricula. Public schools were increasingly seen in some quarters as the bedrock of American citizenship and of the Republic itself (Tyack 1974). Leading government figures added to this view. For example, President Ulysses S. Grant, in a speech to his former troops in Des Moines, Iowa, on October 29, 1875, urged them to "encourage free schools" and not to allow any money "to the support of sectarian schools." Such aid might destroy the public schools, Grant contended, which served as the "promoter of that intelligence which is to preserve us as a nation." Grant predicted that if the nation were to experience another "contest in the near future of our national existence, . . . the dividing line will not be Mason and Dixon's, but between patriotism and intelligence on the one side, and superstition, ambition and ignorance on the other." Grant's audience understood that "superstition" referred to the Catholic Church (McGreevy 2003, 91).

Grant's position was supported by the proposed amendment to the federal Constitution authored by Representative James G. Blaine of Maine, which stated that, among other things, no public funds could be used to support any religious sect or its activities (which would include schools). The amendment passed the House of Representatives by the whopping margin of 180 to 7, but fell just short of the required two-thirds margin for congressional approval in the Senate due to a 26 to 16 vote (Johnson 1934, 21). However, the climate in which Catholic schools existed between 1877 and 1917 is revealed by the fact that during those years 29 states incorporated some form of the Amendment into their state constitutions (Walch 1996, 63).

The Third Plenary Council of Baltimore

In the mid-nineteenth century, America Protestantism had constituted the major threat to Catholic schools, with its influence evident in textbooks, the devotional reading of the King James Version of the Bible and other school practices, and by its personnel.

After the Civil War the civil, or secular, state had replaced Protestantism as the major adversary for Catholic education. Concerned over the American Catholic school question, the Vatican summoned three American archbishops to Rome in 1883 in preparation for what was to become the Third Plenary Council of Baltimore. The Council Fathers addressed the school question in their Pastoral, noting that the secular public schools had "shut religion out" of the schools, thus constituting "a more false and pernicious notion" than could be imagined (Guilday 1954, 245). After an appeal to Catholic pastors and parents to "multiply our schools and perfect them," the bishops enacted the following decrees:

"I. That near every church a parish school, where one does not yet exist, is to be built and maintained *in perpetuum* within two years of the promulgation of this council, unless the bishop should decide that because of serious difficulties a delay may be granted.

IV. That all Catholic parents are bound to send their children to the parish school, unless it is evident that a sufficient training in religion is given either in their own homes, or in other Catholic schools, or when because of a sufficient reason, approved by the bishop, with all due precautions and safeguards, it is licit to send them to other schools. What constitutes a Catholic school is left to the decision of the bishop" (McCluskey 1964, 83–94).

The decrees, threats of spiritual penalties and pleas notwithstanding, resulted in modest growth in the years that immediately followed the Council. In 1884 there were 6,613 Catholic parishes in the United States, 2,532 of which had parish schools. Three years later, in 1887, the number of parishes had increased to 6,910 and the schools numbered 2,697 (Burns and Kohlbrenner 1937, 144). A spurt in institutional and enrollment growth was soon to come.

Anti-Catholic school sentiment received a boost in the wake of Baltimore III with the founding of the American Protective Association (APA) in 1887. Established to defend American institutions against foreign aggression, the APA opposed the growing presence of Catholics and their influence in American society, abetted by immigration. It focused some of its attention on Catholic schools, opposing their attempts to gain public financial aid (Buetow 1970, 168).

Teaching Orders of Religious Women and Men

Edicts and pleas of councils and bishops along with sacrifices of Catholic parents on behalf of Catholic schools would have come to naught were it not for the teaching orders of vowed religious women and men. Some orders of religious women hailed from Europe and had been recruited for American schools, usually by bishops. Buetow notes that the first community of religious women of American origin was the American Visitation Nuns, followed closely in 1812 by the Sisters of Charity established in Emmitsburg, Maryland by Mother Elizabeth Bayley Seton (Buetow 1970, 60). Buetow lists 44 orders of "non Diocesan Teaching Communities of Religious Women" that were founded between 1829 and 1884 as well as 11 orders of "Teaching Brotherhoods" during those years (Buetow 1970, 115–17). The remarkable story of Catholic schools in the United States would not have been possible without the indispensable contributions of these dedicated women and men over the years.

Conflict in Wisconsin

The State of Wisconsin was the site of two major conflicts involving education in the later years of the nineteenth century that describe the embattled position of Catholics and their position in the nation. The first of these was between the Catholic Church and pan-Protestantism and the second was between the Church and the civil state. The first tilt was over the place of the Bible in the public schools of the state. Wisconsin was admitted to the Union in 1848 with a constitution that forbade sectarian instruction in public institutions and prohibited the civil state from engaging in or supporting worship. Originally, devotional Bible-reading of the King James Version was viewed as a religious, but not sectarian, practice; it was looked on as constitutional and was supported by a clear majority of the state's inhabitants and practiced in the state's public schools. Immigration into the state, which included a considerable number of Catholics, led to changed attitudes toward the practice. Ultimately, the Wisconsin Supreme Court, responding to a suit brought by Catholic citizens in the town of Edgerton, reversed a decision by the Circuit Court, in the first of its kind decision on March 17, 1890, in which the Court adjudged that the practice constituted sectarian instruction, was worship, and consequently was unconstitutional (Hunt 1981, 589–619).

The second major clash between the Catholic Church, this time joined by Lutherans, was with the civil state over the Bennett Law. Enacted in 1889 by the Wisconsin legislature, the offensive portions of this Law to the Catholic and Lutheran leaders focused on the planks that defined a school as one in which the subjects were taught in the English language and required school attendance in the public school district in which the students lived. The state's Catholic bishops issued a "Manifesto" in which they charged that the Law was "unnecessary, unjust, and offensive" (Heming 1896, 283). A fierce struggle erupted that lasted throughout 1890 and resulted in the defeat of the Republican governor, William Dempster Hoard, the chief supporter of the Bennett Law, in his bid for reelection, resulting in the Catholics and Lutherans emerging victorious. The Bennett Law was repealed by the legislature in 1891 and replaced by the so-called Desmond Law, one that met with the approval of Catholic and Lutheran leaders, thus giving the churches a substantial amount of control over the schooling of their members and limiting the authority of the civil state over their education (Hunt 1981, 69–93).

The Teaching of Leo XIII
Pope Leo XIII took an active role in matters that dealt with church–state relations, including those that bore on educational matters, an issue on which both the state and the Church had rights and duties. He insisted on the presence of religion in schools and called on governments to respect the primary rights of parents, who were endowed by God with the right to direct the education of their children, a right that no civil authority could preempt or morally interfere with. Author of a number of encyclicals (letters to the Church that were issued with the teaching authority of the Pope and were to be accepted by all Catholics), Leo's most important encyclical in this area, "Sapientiae Christianae," which that dealt with basic control issues in education, was issued in January of 1890. In this authoritative letter, the Pontiff taught that Catholics were bound in conscience to follow the teaching of the Church over all other agencies in matters such as education. Parents, he contended, were to follow God's plan for educating their children, a plan that was communicated by the Church. They were bound in conscience to imbue their children with the "principles of Christian morality, and absolutely oppose their children from frequenting schools where they were exposed to the fatal poison of impiety" (Husslein 1940, 156–58, 162).

The School Controversy

Daniel Reilly has written a book devoted to that topic, *The School Controversy, 1891–1893*. The controversy within the American hierarchy over the school issue had been simmering for some time, and it boiled over as a result of the ongoing struggle, especially following Archbishop John Ireland of St. Paul's talk at the 1890 meeting of the National Education Association (NEA). Ireland, a leading liberal prelate, called an "Americanizer" by some, was asked to address the NEA gathering in St. Paul. Ireland upheld the primary rights of parents in overseeing the education of their children, but in the course of his remarks he recognized the right of the civil state to see that its citizens were being appropriately educated and highlighted the role of the public schools in that task:

> Free Schools. Blest indeed is the nation whose vales and hillsides they adorn, and blest the generations upon whose souls are poured their treasure. No tax is more legitimate than that which is levied for the dispelling of mental darkness and the building up within a nation's bosom of intelligent manhood and womanhood.
>
> *National Education Association Journal of Addresses and Proceedings* 1890, 179–80

Ireland went on to propose that while the government should not teach religion, it should subsidize denominations for the secular education they provided as a service to good citizenship (*National Education Association Journal of Addresses and Proceedings* 1890, 180).

Ireland's remarks were considered by ecclesiastical and civil leaders. Two of his fellow bishops, Micahel A. Corrigan, Archbishop of New York City, and Bernard McQuaid, Bishop of Rochester (New York), registered complaints with the Vatican about the orthodoxy of some of his points. Ireland defended himself in a letter to Cardinal Gibbons, asserting that the public schools were not "hot beds of vice" and that the state had the right to educate and to enact reasonable compulsory attendance laws in that process (McCluskey 1964, 148). Evidently, complaints from his fellow bishops continued to reach the Vatican, in sufficient number and strength to lead Cardinal Gibbons to write to Pope Leo in defense of Ireland in which he told the Pope that Americans were proud of their public schools and that a condemnation of Ireland would have a "disastrous effect" on the Church in the United States (Reilly 1969, 242–46).

The internal struggles were far from over. Ireland, faced with financial difficulties in maintaining parochial schools, turned the schools in Faribault and Stillwater, Minnesota, over to local school authorities for the sum of $1.00, roughly following a procedure that had been previously employed in Lowell, Massachusetts; Savannah, Georgia; and was being employed at that time in Poughkeepsie, New York (Reilly 1969, 74–75). The plan generally called for the teaching of religion after school hours and required the civil authorities to cover the operating costs of the school. The facilities were available to the parishes after school hours. Some members of the American hierarchy regarded his plan as a "sell-out." One, Archbishop Katzer of Milwaukee, who had led the Catholic fight against the Bennett Law, said Ireland's action was a "surrender of a Catholic school to state authorities" (Reilly 1969, 138). Members of the Protestant clergy criticized the plan from a different viewpoint, opposing the state subsidy of Catholic schools.

The tensions escalated with the appearance of Dr. Thomas Bouquillon's pamphlet, entitled *Education - to Whom Does It Belong?* in which Bouquillon, a faculty member at the Catholic University of America, wrote that the state, as well as the family and church, had the right to educate (Bouquillon 1891). Bouquilllon's thesis was quickly challenged by Rene Holaind, SJ, who said Bouquillon had given civil governments, especially a non-Christian one, too much authority in education (Holaind 1891). Ireland, in Rome to defend his Faribault-Stillwater plan took up Bouquillon's cause and defended Bouquillon's loyalty to the Church to the Propagation of the Faith. He deplored what he thought was the unjust condemnation of public schools on the part of some American Catholics, including bishops. He warned of a substantial backlash against the Catholic Church in the United States if such tactics continued (Reilly 1969, 267–70).

The internal "warfare" among the American bishops over the issue of Catholic schools raged on. The indirect intercession of Pope Leo, via the Fourteen Propositions of his personal representative, Archbishop Francesco Satolli, failed to end the dispute (Reilly 1969, 271–76). One of Satolli's propositions, which incurred the wrath of the conservative faction of bishops, forebade pastors or bishops from excluding from the sacraments both parents who failed to send their children to Catholic schools and the children themselves. Indeed, Satolli instructed the clergy that they should not "show less love for the children that attended the public schools than for those that attend the parochial schools" (McCluskey 1964, 158).

The Ethnic Issue

The majority of Catholic schools were located in urban areas in the nineteenth century, often in ethnic neighborhoods, with a pastor of the parish and the nuns who taught in the school being of the same ethnic background as the students. Prior to the latter years of the century many of these schools, rural as well as urban, were peopled by German-Americans who were committed to the cause of parochial education and received financial support from the Leopoldine Association in Austria on their behalf. The German-American prelates in Wisconsin, for instance, had led the Catholic fight against the despised Bennett Law. There were also many Irish American Catholics in Catholic schools, but overall the Irish did not have the same devotion to parochial education that the Germans had. Both groups, as well as those immigrants who came to the United States between 1890 and 1920, usually from southern and eastern Europe, notably the Poles, Italians, and Slovaks, also experienced prejudicial treatment at the hands of American Nativists. Catholic schools in general, and especially those that featured the values and customs of the "old country," were looked on as "un-American" by Nativists, who regarded them as socially divisive and loyal to a foreign power. In 1887 another Nativist group, the American Protective Association, had been formed to combat the so-called Catholic menace, with considerable animus directed at Catholic schools that were allegedly "un-American" and loyal to a foreign potentate, the Pope. Internally, Catholicism was plagued with intense strife in the years immediately preceding the turn of the century over allegations that the failure to adopt ethnic schools, even ethnic dioceses, had led to the loss of faith for a huge number of Catholic children (Shaughnessy 1969). Some individuals, such as Peter Cahensly, had unsuccessfully sought the appointment of national bishops by Pope Leo XIII in the United States as a "solution" to the problem (Reilly 1969, 72). The divisions over the "school question" between and among the American Catholic hierarchy, sometimes exacerbated by ethnic issues, were so deep that it took the direct intervention of Pope Leo himself to achieve peace, which he accomplished in a letter to Cardinal Gibbons in 1893 in which he wrote that Catholic schools were to be "sedulously promoted" and that public schools were "not to be entirely condemned." The judgment of the bishop of the diocese would determine "when it is lawful and when it is unlawful to attend public schools." He concluded his letter with a plea to the bishops to end their bitter fraternal dispute and to forge a spirit of unity and cooperation (Reilly 1969, 228–29).

Catholic School Growth

External hostility and internal bickering notwithstanding, Catholic schools had experienced a remarkable growth in the waning years of the nineteenth and the early years of the twentieth century. They numbered 2,246 in 1880 with an attendance of 405,234. A decade later there were 3,194 schools with 633,238 students. By 1900 the numbers had grown to 3,811 schools and 854,323 pupils, and by 1910 there were 4,845 schools with an enrollment of 1,237,251 (Buetow1970, 279). The increase in Catholic population continued as the twentieth century progressed. By 1917 there were 5,687 parishes with schools, with Catholic school students numbering 1,537,644 out of a total Catholic population of 17,022,879 (Buetow 1970, 225).

THE TWENTIETH CENTURY

The World War I Era

Despite their phenomenal growth, the challenges for American Catholic schools were far from over. At no time in the nineteenth century, for instance, were more than one-half of the eligible Catholic children in attendance at Catholic schools (Buetow 1970, 216). Two national organizations were added to the Catholic roster in the early years of the twentieth century. The first was the Catholic Educational Association (CEA), a voluntary professional association, that was founded in 1904 (its name was changed to the National Catholic Educational Association (NCEA) in 1928). Formed to provide a forum for the exchange of educational ideas, the CEA had to overcome the long-standing and firmly held tradition that Catholic education was a parish and diocesan matter. The second was the National Catholic Welfare Conference (NCWC), established in 1919. It succeeded the National Catholic War Conference and was the policy-making arm of the American bishops (Walch 1996, 104–5).

The codification of the laws of the Church, assembled in 1918, contained a number of decrees that dealt with Catholic schools. Canon 1113 held parents accountable for the education of their children and stated that education that failed to recognize the attainment of the child's "supernatural destiny, is not education" (Bouscaren and Ellis 1945, 539). Canon 1374 reiterated the point made in the Third Plenary Council of Baltimore that it was up to the local bishop to determine if a Catholic child could attend a "mixed" school, and Canon 1375 proclaimed the right of the Church to establish schools. Canon 1379 held the bishop of the diocese responsible for establishing schools and called on Catholics to contribute to the support of the schools. Canon 1381 said it was the "right and duty" of the bishop to make certain that nothing occurs in the schools for which they are responsible that is "contrary to faith or morals," including supervision of personnel and texts (Woywood and Smith 1952, 136–40).

The Code was followed a year later in 1919 by the Pastoral Letter of the American bishops in which they observed that the worldwide war had consequences for education, which included religion and morality. They went on to praise the commitment of those Catholics who had dedicated their lives to the cause of Catholic education as a "holy work" and commended those whose assistance had aided in building up "our schools" (Huber 1952, 14–16).

Legislation requiring Catholic parents to send their children to Catholic schools endured decades past the issuance of the Code of Canon Law. For instance, McCluskey observes that as late as 1958–59, 55 of 104 dioceses polled in a survey required attendance at Catholic schools either through diocesan statute or episcopal decree. Failure to observe such requirements could result in denial of absolution to parents in 12 of the 55 (McCluskey 1959, 118).

Meanwhile, Catholic school enrollment had increased during the decade that included World War I to 1,701,219 in 5,852 schools in an overall Catholic population of 17,735,553 in 1920 (Buetow 1970, 179). Charges were levied by some Americans against the loyalty to the United States of Catholicism in general and its schools in particular in the wake of the war. These accusations, which had strong support in a number of states, led to the enactment by the state of Oregon of a law, passed with the support of the Ku Klux Klan, that required attendance at public school by all children between the ages of 8 and 16 on the grounds that such attendance was necessary for good citizenship, with the corollary that private schools were divisive. The United States Supreme Court denied Oregon's claim, held that the child is not the mere creature of the state, supported the right of parental choice in the schooling of their children, and ruled the law unconstitutional under the Fourteenth Amendment (*Pierce v. Society of Sisters* 268 U.S. 510, 1925).

A Settled System

Catholic schools, guaranteed their legal right to exist, settled into their role of educating children as the twentieth century progressed. They met the growing activity of the civil state in certifying educational personnel and accrediting schools. In 1929, in the midst of increased claims of totalitarian nations in education, Pope Pius XI issued his famous encyclical, *Divini Illius Magistri* ("Christian Education of Youth"), in which he set forth the Catholic policy on education, supporting the primary rights of parents in the education of their children and the "God-centeredness" of Catholic schools. Attendance at "neutral" schools could at best be tolerated. The goal, the Pontiff averred, was "Catholic education in Catholic schools for all the Catholic youth" (Pius XI 1939, 60–65).

The Progressive Era

Catholic education moved into the progressive period in American education in the twentieth century, beginning with the efforts of Thomas Edward Shields and later with his pupil, George Johnson. Shields gained prominence as a member of the faculty of the Catholic University of America, and Johnson served in leadership capacities as secretary general of the National Catholic Educational Association and as head of the National Catholic Welfare Conference Department of Education (Walch 1996, 119–27). Shields's efforts were focused on the psychology of education, including how to teach, and Johnson's on "bridge building," both within and without Catholic education (Walch 1996, 118–33). Among Johnson's many accomplishments was his leadership in serving on the Commission on American Citizenship, established at the Catholic University of America, which centered on the role of Catholic education in democratic citizenship (Walch 1996, 130–33).

The period also witnessed the increased activity on the part of the civil state towards accreditation of schools and programs and certification of teachers. Catholic schools successfully met these challenges. The various orders of vowed religious women accepted the responsibility for the academic preparation of their nun-teachers. They had traditionally focused their programs on the religious preparation, including emphasis on the particular traditions of their order, when the young women were in postulancy and novitiate. They relied on the craft system when the sisters were first sent out to teach, in response to the calls from bishops and pastors, depending on veteran teachers to assist the beginning teachers. Walch observes that the number of teaching sisters taking summer and extension courses skyrocketed during this period (Walch 1996, 150).

Catholic schools struggled mightily during the Depression. They survived mainly through the services of the many Catholic nun-teachers who ministered for a pittance and the loyalty of many of the Catholic faithful. In the 1935–36 school year there were 1,945 secondary schools with 16,784 professional staff, of whom 14,121 were religious, enrolling 284,736 students and 7,929 elementary schools with a student enrollment of 2,102,889 and a professional staff of 55,467 religious and 3,436 lay (Buetow 1970, 226). A majority of Catholic leaders, episcopal and educational (including Johnson), opposed the policy of general federal aid to education that was proposed by some during the 1930s and 1940s, arguing that education should be left in the hands of state and local authorities and fearing government control if enacted. The American hierarchy, as well as George Johnson, were unsuccessful in their efforts to get public funding for Catholic schools (Walch 1996, 129–30).

The Courts and Catholic Education

Catholic schools, with considerable economic travail, survived the Depression years of the 1930s. They joined in the cooperative efforts on the part of American schools during the war years in the early 1940s. A new era, one of litigation, was ushered in during the 1940s. In 1930, the United States Supreme Court had upheld a Louisiana practice of providing textbooks to pupils of private as well as public schools in that state, on the basis of the aid going to the child, not the school, a practice known as indirect aid and utilizing the "child benefit" principle (*Cochran v. Louisiana State Board of Education* 281 U.S. 320, 1930). Then, in 1940, the United States Supreme Court made the First Amendment applicable to the states through the Fourteenth in *Cantwell v. Connecticut* 210 U.S. 296 (1940). In 1947 the Supreme Court ruled on a case from New Jersey that dealt with busing of pupils to nonpublic schools, *Everson v. Board of Education* 330 U.S. 1 (1947). It was the first of a number of Court decisions that had a major impact on Catholic schools throughout the remaining years of the twentieth century. New Jersey had authorized its local school districts to be responsible for the transportation of its students to schools. Ewing Township had included parents of nonpublic schools among those to be reimbursed for the cost of this busing. Everson, a citizen in the district, filed suit, contending that the payments to parents of church-affiliated school students violated the establishment clause of the First Amendment. The Court, by the narrowest of margins (5-4), ruled in favor of the township, on the grounds of the child benefit principle, that is, it was the children, not the church, who were served by the practice and that the civil state had the responsibility for their safety. While it upheld the practice, the Court laid down the Everson Dicta, which proved to be very troublesome in the future for proposals that would provide public aid to patrons of faith-based schools. These Dicta stated, among other things, that "Neither a state nor the Federal Government can set up a church. Neither can pass laws that aid one religion, aid all religions, or prefer one over another. . . . In the words of Jefferson, the clause against establishment of religion by law was intended to erect 'a wall of separation between church and state' " (*Everson v. Board of Education* 330 U.S. 1, 1947).

The Teaching Force

Two major phenomena that dealt with Catholic school teachers surfaced mid-century. The first of these was the Sister-Formation Movement, which related to the preparation of religious women as teachers, nurses, and social workers. Speaking to the National Catholic Educational Association (NCEA) in 1956, Sister Mary Emil, I. H. M., the first chairperson of the National Sister-Formation Committee, said that when it came to teaching, the program was designed to make a Sister "a better religious and a better professional person" by formal academic education and informal influences, "spiritual and intellectual," in her training, both pre-service and in service (Buetow 1970, 251). The impetus for the movement may be said to have gained support from the words of Pope Pius XII, who, when speaking to school sisters in 1951, stated, "Many of your schools are being described and praised" as being very good—"[b]ut not all." The Pontiff exhorted his audience to see that the teaching Sisters were well trained and met the requirements of the State. The NCEA, responding to the Pope's speech, arranged conferences that addressed the implementation of the Pontiff's words (Buetow 1970, 251–52).

The second phenomenon was the growing number of lay teachers in Catholic schools. By 1950 the number of lay teachers had increased to 20,075 out of a faculty 116,073 (Buetow 1970, 249–50). Their number had increased by 156 per cent between 1946 and 1956, compared with 22.5 per cent for vowed religious (McCluskey1959, 105). The Church had to address the issue of providing these teachers with a living wage and appropriate job security. Their presence added to the financial pressure on Catholic schools, due to the greater expense the schools incurred with their salaries and benefits, compared to the costs of the vowed religious (Buetow 1970, 249–50).

The Rise of the Coinstitutional High School

Mid-century also saw the rise of the coinstitutional high school, which peaked in the early 1960s. These schools actually dated back to the nineteenth century in several American cities when some pastors arranged for religious brothers to teach the boys and religious sisters to teach the girls in schools. Coinstitutional high schools had a renaissance of sorts following an "Instruction" of the Congregation of Religious in 1957. Pope Pius XI had referred to coeducation as "false" and "harmful" in his encyclical "Christian Education of Youth" (Pius XI 1939, 56). There were 61 central Catholic high schools in existence in 1925, but their number had increased to over 400 by 1958–59, when they constituted the majority of Catholic secondary educational institutions and enrolled 500,304 students, compared with 310,464 for private high schools, which were usually operated by religious orders and more likely to be single gender (McCluskey 1964, 100). Coinstitutional high schools were generally founded in communities that did not have sufficient enrollment for separate gender high schools, which had been in the majority of Catholic secondary schools into the twentieth century. The coinstitutional high schools had common laboratories and a gymnasium but featured separate instruction for boys and girls, especially in physical education.

Hierarchical Support for Catholic Schools

Catholic schools received support during this period from the American bishops with their 1950 document, "The Child: Citizen of Two Worlds," and from Pope Pius XII, who frequently addressed their importance during mid-century. The American bishops' message proclaimed that Catholic schools offered the young the opportunity for a

God-centered education here on earth, one which met both their eternal and temporal needs, and which teaches them that their fulfillment is to live "with God in eternity" (McCluskey 1964, 193–205). Pius XII, meanwhile, identified the primary goal of education as "collaboration with divine grace for the formation of the true and perfect Christian" (Yzermans1957, 174–78). As educators, the Pontiff declared, teachers had the duty of motivating their youthful charges to have "devotion to duty, family, and country" and as Catholic educators they had the responsibility of making every student a "good Christian" (Yzermans 1957, 170–71).

American Catholic Schools at Mid-Century

Catholic schools, and their private counterparts, had experienced phenomenal growth in the mid twentieth century. In 1959 Catholic schools enrolled 4,101,792 students in elementary schools and 810, 768 in secondary schools (McCluskey 1959, 100). Catholic and other private schools had experienced a growth rate of 118 percent since 1940, compared with 36 percent in public schools (McCluskey 1959, 107). The Catholic school population, which accounted for about 14 percent of the total elementary and secondary school population in the United States was heavily concentrated in the nation's cities. For instance, McCluskey notes that half of the school population in Green Bay, Wisconsin, and 52 per cent of that in Manchester, New Hampshire, was enrolled in Catholic schools. Percentages of Catholic school enrollment were 16 in New York; 34 in Chicago; 39 in Philadelphia; 23 in Detroit; 24 in Hartford; 28 in Cincinnati; 30 in Boston; 33 in Milwaukee and New Orleans; 40 in Buffalo; and 42 in Pittsburgh (McCluskey 1959, 46). Walch points out that especially in large cities such as Chicago, New York, and Philadelphia, the huge enrollment gains had put tremendous strain on the resources of the Catholic Church (Walch 1996, 170–73). Attempts to gain public financial support—although not all Catholic bishops were in favor of such aid, fearing government control would result—had been unsuccessful, and the first Catholic president of the United States, John F. Kennedy, had declared that any such aid, except for "fringe matters such as busses, lunches, and other services," would be unconstitutional (Walch 1996, 209). The formation of activist groups, such as the Citizens for Educational Freedom (CEF), under the leadership of Father Virgil C. Blum, SJ., a political scientist, had achieved some success in several states. Blum et al. argued for aid to the student based on his/her Fourteenth Amendment rights, but they were unsuccessful overall in their efforts to obtain significant financial aid for Catholic schools (Hunt 1985, 123–34).

The impressive statistical growth notwithstanding, on the eve of the Second Vatican Council, American Catholic schools, as well as the entire Church, were about to undergo earth-shaking developments with the convening of the Second Vatican Council by Pope John the 23rd in October of 1962.

REFERENCES AND FURTHER READING

Abell, Aaron L. (ed.). *American Catholic Thought on Social Questions*. Indianapolis, IN: Bobbs-Merrill Co. 1968.

Baast, P. A. "Our Catholic Schools." *Catholic World* XLVI, 275 (February 1888): 603–9

Barry, Colman J. *The Catholic Church and German Americans*. Milwaukee: Bruce Publishing Co., 1953.

Billington, Ray A. *The Protestant Crusade, 1800–1860*. New York: Macmillan, 1938.

Blanshard, Paul. *Catholicism and American Freedom*. Boston: Beacon Press, 1963.

Blum, Virgil C. *Freedom in Education*. Garden City, NY: Doubleday and Company, 1965.

Bouquillon, Thomas J. *Education: To Whom Does It Belong?* Baltimore: John Murphy, 1892.

Bouscaren, T. Lincoln and Adam C. Ellis. *Canon Law: A Text and Commentary.* Bruce Publishing Co., 1945.

Brann, H. A. "The Improvement of Parochial Schools." *The American Catholic Quarterly Review* IX, 34 (April 1884): 238–53.

Buetow, Harold A. *Of Singular Benefit: The Story of U.S. Catholic Education.* New York: Macmillan, 1970.

Buetow, Harold A. *The Catholic School: Its Roots, Identity, and Future.* New York: Crossroads, 1988.

Burns, James A. *Catholic Education: A Study of Conditions.* New York: Longmans, Green and Co., 1917.

Burns, James A. *The Growth and Development of the Catholic School System in the United States.* New York: Benziger Brothers, 1912.

Burns, James A., and Bernard J. Kohlbrenner. *A History of Catholic Education in the United States.* New York: Benziger Brothers, 1937.

Butts, R. Freeman. *The American Tradition in Religion and Education.* Boston: Beacon Press, 1950.

Cantwell v. State of Connecticut. 310 U.S. 296 (1940).

Carper, James C., and Thomas C. Hunt. *The Dissenting Tradition in American Education.* New York: Peter Lang, 2007.

Carper, James C., and Thomas C. Hunt eds. *Religious Schooling in America.* Birmingham, AL: Religious Education Press, 1984.

Cassidy, Francis P. "Catholic Education in the Third Plenary Council of Baltimore." *The Catholic Historical Review* Part I, XXXIV (October 1948): 275–305.

Cassidy, Francis P. "Catholic Education in the Third Plenary Council of Baltimore." *The Catholic Historical Review* Part II, XXXIV (January 1949): 414–36.

Clarkson, John F., et al. eds. *The Church Teaches: Documents of the Church in English Translation.* St. Louis: B. Herder Book Co., 1955.

Cochran v. Louisiana State Board of Education, 281 U.S. 370 (1930).

Conway, James. "The Rights and Duties of Family and State in Regard to Educaton." *The American Catholic Quarterly Review* IX, 33 (January 1884): 105–26.

Conway, James. "The Rights and Duties of the Church in Regard to Education." *The American Catholic Quarterly Review* IX, 36 (October 1884): 650–69.

Cremin, Lawrence A. ed. *The Republic and The School: Horace Mann On the Education of Free Men.* New York: Teachers College Press, 1957.

Cross, Robert D. "Origins of the Catholic Parochial Schools in America." *The American Benedictine Review* 16 (1965): 194–209.

Cross, Robert D. *The Emergence of Liberal Catholicism in America.* Cambridge, MA: Harvard University Press, 1958.

Culver, Raymond B. *Horace Mann and Religion in the Massachusetts Public Schools.* New Haven, CT: Yale University Press, 1929.

Desmond, Humphrey J. *The A.P.A. Movement.* Washington, DC: The New Century Press, 1912.

Dohen, Dorothy. *Nationalism and American Catholicism.* New York: Sheed and Ward, 1967.

Dolan, Jay P. *The American Catholic Experience.* Garden City, NY: Doubleday and Company, 1985.

Dolan, Jay P. *The Immigrant Church.* Notre Dame, IN: University of Notre Dame Press, 1983.

Ellis, John Tracy. *A Guide to American Catholic History.* Milwaukee: Bruce Publishing Co., 1959.

Ellis, John Tracy. *American Catholicism.* Chicgo: University of Chicago Press, 1969.

Ellis, John Tracy. "American Catholics and the Intellectual Life." *Thought* 30 (Autumn 1955): 351–88.

Ellis, John Tracy. ed. *Documents of American Catholic History.* 3 vols. Wilmington, DE: Michael Glazier, 1987.

Ellis, John Tracy. ed. *The Life of James Cardinal Gibbons.* 2 vols. Milwaukee: Bruce Publishing Co., 1952.

Gabel, Richard J. *Public Funds for Church and Private Schools.* Washington, DC: Murray and Meister, 1937.

Gibbons, James. "The Necessity of Religion for Society." *The American Catholic Quarterly Review* IX, 36 (October 1884): 670–92.

Glenn, Charles L. *The Myth of the Common School.* Amherst, MA: The University of Massachusetts Press, 1988.

Gmeiner, John. *The Church and Foreignism*. St. Paul: Brown, Tracy and Co., 1891.

Grant, Mary A., and Thomas C. Hunt. *Catholic School Education in the United States*. New York: Garland Publishing, 1992.

Greeley, Andrew M., and Peter H. Rossi. *The Education of Catholic Americans*. Chicago: Aldine Publishing, 1966.

Guilday, Peter. *A History of the Councils of Baltimore (1791–1884)*. New York: Macmillan, 1932.

Guilday, Peter. *The Life and Times of John Carroll*. New York: The Encyclopedia Press, 1922.

Guilday, Peter. ed. *The National Pastorals of the American Hierarchy, 1792–1919*. Westminster, MD: The Newman Press, 1954.

Hales, E. E. Y. *Pio Nono*. Garden City, NY: Doubleday and Co., 1962.

Helmreich, Ernst. ed. *A Free Church in a Free State?* Boston: D.C. Heath and Co., 1964.

Heming, Harry H. *The Catholic Church in Wisconsin*. Milwaukee: T.A. Sullivan, 1896.

Hennessey, James. *Amrican Catholics: A History of the Roman Catholic Community in the United States*. New York: Oxford University Press, 1981.

Herberg, Will. *Protestant- Catholic- Jew: An Essay in American Sociology*. Garden City, NY: Doubleday and Co., 1955.

Higham, John. *Strangers in the Land: Patterns of American Nativism 1860–1925*. New York: Atheneum, 1970.

Hodge, Charles. "Common Schools." *Biblical Repertory and Princeton Review* 5 (April 1833): 217–29.

Holaind, R. I. *The Parent First: An Answer to Dr. Bouquillon's Query, "Education: to Whom Does It Belong?"* New York: Benziger Brothers, 1891.

Huber, Raphael M. ed. *Our Bishops Speak: National Pastorals and Annual Statements of the Hierarchy of the United States, 1919–1951*. Milwaukee: Bruce Publishing Company, 1952.

Hunt, Thomas C. "Citizens for Educational Freedom." *Religious Education 80, 1 (Winter 1983):* 123–34.

Hunt, Thomas C. "Labor Strife in Catholic Schools: Some Historical Considerations." *Intrernational Review of History and Political Science* XXV, 2 (May 1988): 1–13.

Hunt, Thomas C. "The Bennett Law of 1890: Focus of Conflict between Church and State." *Journal of Church and State* 23, 1 (Winter 1981): 69–93.

Hunt, Thomas C. "The Edgerton Bible Decision: The End of an Era." *The Catholic Historical Review* LXVII, 4 (October 1981): 589–616.

Hunt, Thomas C. "The Impact of Vatican Teaching on Catholic Educational Policy in the United States during the Late Nineteenth Century." *Paedagogica Historica* 80, 1 (Winter 1985): 1–13.

Hunt, Thomas C., Ellis A. Joseph and Ronald J. Nuzzi. eds. *Catholic Schools in the United States: An Encyclopedia*. 2 vols. Westport, CT: Greenwood Press, 2004.

Hunt, Thomas C., Ellis A. Joseph and Ronald J. Nuzzi. eds. *Handbook of Research on Catholic Education*. Westport, CT: Greenwood Press, 2001.

Husslein, Joseph. ed. *Social Wellsprings*. 2 vols. Milwaukee: Bruce Publishing Co., 1940.

Jenkins, Thomas J. *The Judges of Faith: Christian vs. Godless Schools*. Baltimore: John Murphy and Co., 1886.

Johnson, Alvin W. *The Legal Status of Church-State Relationships in the United States*. Minneapolis: The University of MInnesota Press, 1934.

Johnson, George. "The Need of a Constructive Policy for Catholic Education in the United States." *Catholic Educational Review* 23 (1925): 385–94.

Jorgensen, Lloyd P. "The Oregon School Law of 1922: Passage and Sequel." *The Catholic Historical Review* LIV (October 1968): 455–68.

Justice, Benjamin. *The War that Wasn't*. Albany, NY: State University of New York Press, 2005.

Kane, John J. *Catholic-Protestant Conflicts in America*. Chicago: Regnery Co., 1955.

Katz, Wilber G. *Religion and American Constitutions*. Evanston, IL: Northwestern University Press, 1963.

Kinzer, Donal L. *An Episode in Anti-Catholicism: The American Protective Association*. Seattle: University of Washington Press, 1964.

Kliebard, Herbert M. ed. *Religion and Education in America: A Documentary History*. Scranton, PA: International Textbook Company, 1969.

Kraushaar, Otto F. *American Nonpublic Schools: Patterns of Diversity*. Baltimore: Johns Hopkins University Press, 1972.

Kraushaar, Otto F. *Private Schools: From the Puritans to the Present*. Bloomington, IN: Phi Delta Kappa Educational Foundation, 1976.

Kuzniewski, Anthony J. *Faith and Fatherland: The Polish Church War in Wisconsin, 1896–1918*. Notre Dame, IN: University of Notre Dame Press, 1973.

Lannie, Vincent P. *Public Money, Parochial Education, Bishop Hughes, Governor Seward and the New York School Controversy*. Cleveland: Case Western Reserve, 1968.

LaNoue, George R. *Public Funds for Parochial Schools?* New York: National Council of Churches, 1963.

Lazerson, Marvin. "Understanding American Catholic Education History." *History of Education Quarterly* 17, 3 (Fall 1977): 277–317.

Lee, James Michael. *Catholic Education in the Western World*. Notre Dame, IN: University of Notre Dame Press, 1967.

Malbin, Michael. *Religion and Politics: The Intentions of the Framers of the First Amendment*. Washington, DC: American Enterprise Institution for Public Policy Research, 1978.

McAvoy, Thomas T. *A History of the Catholic Church in the United States/* Notre Dame, IN: University of Notre Dame Press, 1969.

McAvoy, Thomas T. *The Americanist Heresy in Roman Catholicism 1895–1900*. Notre Dame, IN: University of Notre Dame Press, 1963.

McAvoy, Thomas T. *The Great Crises in American Catholic History, 1895–1900*. Chicago: Henry Regnery Company, 1957.

McCluskey, Neil G. *Catholic Viewpoint on Education*. Garden City, NY: Hanover House, 1959.

McCluskey, Neil G. ed. *Catholic Education in America: A Documentary History*. New York: Teachers College Press, 1964.

McDermott, Monica, and Thomas C. Hunt. "Catholic Schools: A First in Louisiana." *Momentum* XXII, 4 (November 1991): 46–50.

McGlynn, Edward. "The New Know-Nothingism and the Old." *The North American Review* CXLV, 370 (August 1887): 192–205.

McGreevy, John T. *Catholicism and American Freedom: A History*. New York: W. W. Norton and Company, 2003.

McSweeney, Patrick F. "Heartless, Headless and Godless." *Catholic World* XLVI, 274 (January 1888): 433–37.

Mead, Edwin H. *The Roman Catholic Church and the Public Schools*. Boston: George H. Ellis, 1890.

Meiring, Bernard J. *Educational Aspects of the Legislation of the Councils of Baltimore*. New York: Arno Press and the New York Times, 1969.

Meyer v. Nebraska, 262 U.S. 390 (1923).

Michaelsen, Robert S. *Piety in the Public School*. New York: Macmillan 1970.

Moynihan, James H. *The Life of Archbishop John Ireland*. New York: Harper and Brothers, 1953.

Muller, Michael J. *Public School Education*. New York: B. J. Sadlier and Co., 1872.

Murphy, John F. "Thomas E. Shields: Religious Educator." *Notre Dame Journal of Education* 5 (1974): 358–69.

Myers, Gustavus. *History of Bigotry in the United States*. New York: Random House, 1943.

National Education Association: Journal of Proceedings and Addresses 1890. Topeka, KS: Clifford C. Baker, 179–80.

O'Connor, James. "Anti-Catholic Prejudice." *The American Catholic Quarterly Review* I, 1 (January 1876): 5–21.

Onahan, William J. "The Catholic Church and Popular Education." *The American Catholic Quarterly Review* VIII, 29 (January 1883): 264–81.

Pfeffer, Leo. *Church, State and Freedom*. Boston: Beacon Press, 1953.

Pierce v. Society of Sisters, 268 U.S. 510 (1925).

Pius XI, "Christian Education of Youth." In *Five Great Encyclicals*, 36–75. New York: The Paulist Press, 1939.

Preston, Thomas S. "What the Catholics Want." *Forum*. I (April 1886): 161–71.

Putz, Louis J. ed. *The Catholic Church, U.S.A.* Chicago: Fides Publishers Association, 1956.

Ravitch, Diane. *The Great School Wars: New York City, 1805–1973*. New York: Basic Books, 1973.

Redden, John D., and Francis A. Ryan. *A Catholic Philsophy of Education*. Milwaukee: Bruce Publishing Co., 1956.

Reilly, Daniel F. *The School Controversy, 1891–1893*. New York: Arno Press and The New York Times, 1969.

Report on Population of The United States at the Eleventh Census: 1890. Vol. I, Part I. Washington, DC: Government Printing Office, 1895.

Ross, William G. *Forging New Freedoms: Nativism, Education, and the Constitution, 1917–1927*. Lincoln: University of Nebraska Press, 1994.

Ryan, Mary Perkins. *Are Parochial Schools the Answer? Catholic Education in the Light of the Council*. New York: Guild Press, 1963.

Sanders, James W. *The Education of an Urban Minority: Catholics in Chicago, 1833–1965*. New York: Oxford University Press, 1977.

Shaughnessy, Gerald. *Has the Immigrant Kept the Faith?* New York: Arno Press and The New York Times, 1969.

Shaw, Richard. *Dagger John: The Unique Life and Times of Archbishop John Hughes of New York*. New York: Paulist Press, 1977.

Shea, John Gilmary. "Catholic Free Schools in the United States—Their Necessity, Condition and Future." *The American Catholic Quarterly Review* IX, 36 (October 1884): 713–25.

Shea, John Gilmary. "The Progress of the Church in the United States from the First Provincial Council to the Third Plenary Council of Baltimore." *The American Catholic Quarterly Review* IX, 35 (July 1884): 471–97.

Sheedy, Morgan M. "The School Question: A Plea for Justice." *Catholic World* XLIX, 293 (August 1889): 649–55.

Stewart, George C., Jr. *Marvels of Charity: History of American Sisters and Nuns*. Huntington, IN: Our Sunday Visitor Publishing Division, 1994.

Stokes, Anson Phelps. *Church and State in the United States*. 3vols. New York: Harper Brothers, 1950.

Sweeney, David F. *The Life of John Lancaster Spalding*. New York: Herder and Herder, 1965.

Tyack, David B. "The Kingdom of God and the Common School." *Harvard Educational Review* 36, 4 (Summer 1966): 447–69.

Tyack, David B. *The One Best System: A History of American Urban Education*. Cambridge, MA: Harvard University Press, 1974.

Walch, Timothy. *Parish School: American Catholic Parochial Education from Colonial Times to the Present*. New York: Crossroad Publishing Company, 1996.

Woywood Stanislaus, revised by Callistus Smith. *A Practical Commentary on the Code of Canon Law*. New York: Joseph F. Wagner, Inc., 1952.

Yzermans, Vincent A. ed. *Pope Pius XII and Education*. St. Meinrad, IN: Grail Publications, 1957.

Zwierlein, Frederick J. (ed.). *The Life and Letters of Bishop McQuaid*. 2 vols. New York: The Art Print Shop, 1926.

32

Catholic Schools in the United States from Vatican II to Present

Ronald J. Nuzzi, James M. Frabutt, and Anthony C. Holter

It is difficult to overestimate the significance of Catholic schools in the United States, situated as they are as bastions of temporal gifts and spiritual riches. Catholic schools are no less than a vital, historically rich social institution on one hand and an earthly shepherd for salvation on the other. As the single largest sector of the private school market with approximately 7,000 schools and 2.1 million students, Catholic schools' centrality in the social fabric of the nation is manifest in numerous ways. First, there is a decades long unbroken chain of academic scholarship focused on Catholic education—both how it is constituted and what impacts it delivers. Second, there has been and continues to be a vigorous and pertinent policy discourse surrounding the contributions of Catholic schools to the public good, as well as whether and to what extent parents can utilize public funding to support their children's education at Catholic schools. Third, Catholic schools serve not only as powerful vehicles for deepening students' academic understanding but also as incubators of the social conscience of the young, doing so with efficiency and faithfulness for generations of students and citizens.

Building on the historical foundations that undergird Catholic schools' emergence and sustenance during the years prior to the Second Vatican Council (see Hunt, this volume), this chapter carries forth the saga of Catholic education to the present day. Touching upon governance models, shifting demographics, financial stress, Catholic identity, student achievement, public policy, and Church documents, the chapter describes the changes, challenges, and developments germane to Catholic schools since Vatican II. The chapter closes with a look forward, suggesting several strategies for the ongoing and future success of Catholic schools.

THE CHANGING LANDSCAPE OF AMERICAN CATHOLIC SCHOOLS

The past five decades have been witness to drastic changes in the landscape of American Catholic education. In his commentary on the state of Catholic education, Frank Bredeweg stated that "if [Catholic schools] have become accustomed to anything, it is change" (1982, 17). Descriptive data from the past 50 years of Catholic schools and schooling certainly confirm this quip.

Since 1960, the number of Catholic schools has decreased from 12,893 to 7,094, and the number of students served in those schools has decreased from 5.25 million to 2.12 million (McDonald and Schultz 2010). This drastic decline represents a net loss of roughly 50 percent of both the total student population and total number of schools in just five decades. The composition of the Catholic school workforce has also undergone significant reconfiguration. In 1960, approximately 74 percent of all Catholic school teachers and leaders were priests, religious sisters, or religious brothers. As of 2010, less than 4 percent of the Catholic school workforce was consecrated religious.

While shocking to consider, these general statistics only tell part of the story of significant and substantial changes to Catholic education in the last half century. To develop a more nuanced understanding of the myriad changes to American Catholic education since the Second Vatican Council, this section will investigate the following core change areas: (1) enrollment, facilities, and staffing, and (2) school governance and finances.

School Enrollment

It is no secret that the trend line for Catholic school enrollment has decreased dramatically over the past five decades. With the exception of a few years at the end of the twentieth century, there has been a net loss of students enrolled in Catholic schools each of the past 50 years. Annual data collected by the National Catholic Educational Association (NCEA) indicate that Catholic school enrollment has declined by 3.5 million students from the peak enrollment of 5.6 million in 1964–1965 (Brigham 1989; McDonald and Schultz 2010). This tidal loss of students means that 1.5 million more students have left or been displaced in the last half-century than are currently enrolled in Catholic schools.

Catholic school enrollment data from the most recent decade (2000–2010) highlight the contemporary regression of Catholic schools and Catholic school enrollment. The NCEA reported that since 2000 nearly 20 percent (~1,600) of all Catholic schools have been closed or consolidated, and over 20 percent (~500,000) of all students have left or been displaced from the Catholic school system (McDonald and Schultz 2010). These most recent declines in Catholic schools and Catholic school attendance followed modest growth in enrollment between 1990 and 2000 where, despite continued school closure, "there was a steady enrollment increase (1.3%)" (McDonald and Schultz 2010, 16).

Despite the overall downward trend in Catholic school enrollment, several interesting student-level shifts have occurred in Catholic student religious affiliation and ethnicity. Although the total number of both Catholic and non-Catholic students has decreased considerably since the 1970s, the percentage of non-Catholic students has risen dramatically. Non-Catholic student enrollment has increased as a percentage of total enrollment from 2.7 percent in 1970 to 14.5 percent in 2010 (Bredeweg 1985; McDonald and Schultz 2010). These percent totals represent changes in the overall number of non-Catholic students from approximately 120,000 in 1970 to 307,000 in 2010, which is slightly less than the total number of non-Catholic students enrolled during the peak year 1982 (n = 320,000) (Bredeweg 1985; McDonald and Shultz 2010).

Since the desegregation of Catholic schools in the 1940s, Catholic schools have continued to enroll "significant numbers of students who are members of racial or ethnic minorities" (Convey 1992, 42). Currently, approximately 30 percent of Catholic school students are racial and ethnic minorities (McDonald and Schultz 2010). Although the percentage of minority students continues to rise, the total number of students in key demographic categories has faltered over the last decade. For example, over the past 10 years Hispanic students have remained the second largest ethnic group among Catholic school students. In fact, their percentage of the total enrollment has grown from 11 percent in 1999 to just under 13 percent in 2010 (McDonald and Schultz 2010). Although the percentage increased slightly, there are fewer total Hispanic children in Catholic schools today (n = 272,203) than there were in 1999 (n = 283,827). The current number of Hispanic children enrolled in Catholic schools is the lowest it has been in the past 10 years, despite the fact that 35 percent of all practicing Catholics are Latino (Pew Hispanic Center 2007).

The Staffing of Schools

The most dramatic change in the Catholic school workforce over the past five decades has been the near complete changeover from religious to lay teachers and leaders. In 1960, approximately 74 percent of all Catholic school educators and leaders were priests, religious sisters, or religious brothers, and as of 2010, less than 4 percent of the Catholic school workforce was consecrated religious. This transition to lay teachers and leaders "currently does not seem to present academic or administrative problems," but this had not always been the prevailing opinion (Bredeweg 1982, 17). In *Parish School*, Timothy Walch quoted Edward O'Reilly—then Superintendent of Catholic Schools in the Archdiocese of Chicago—who in 1960 stated that "the more lay teachers we have, the less effective will be our schools" (Walch 2003, 172).

Contemporary scholars of Catholic education have echoed the sense of loss expressed at the heart of Superintendent O'Reilly's commentary. Out of sincere appreciation, and maybe even some nostalgia, for the immeasurable contribution of so many men and women religious, scholars have written about the "living endowment" (Walch 2003, 134) and "strategic subsidy" (Grace 2002, 87) afforded to Catholic schools and Catholic school children through their sacrifice and dedication to the apostolate of Catholic education.

The Number of Schools in Operation

It is not surprising that the trajectory of Catholic schools since Vatican II has mirrored trends in enrollment and religious staffing. The total number of Catholic schools peaked during the 1965–1966 academic year at 13,292: 10,879 were elementary schools and 2,413 were secondary schools (Brigham 1989). Since that time, the numbers for each of these school categories is currently less than half of what they were in the mid-1960s. As of the 2009–2010 school year, there were just 5,889 elementary and 1,205 secondary schools across the United States (McDonald and Schultz, 2010).

Perhaps more troubling than overall loss of schools is the disproportionate loss of Catholic primary schools—especially those in the urban core. Recent data confirm that since the 2000 academic year, 98 percent of all Catholic school closures have been Catholic elementary schools (McDonald and Schultz, 2010). The most current data from the National Center for Education Statistics Private School Universe Survey (PSS) indicate a net loss of 1,417 Catholic schools between the years of 1989 and 2006 (NCES 2008). When considered by location of school community, central city accounted for the largest portion of school closures (1,181 schools or 65% of school closures) followed by rural/small town (648 schools or 35% of school closures). These school closures were offset by a modest increase of 412 schools located in the "urban fringe/large town" sector—a 14% increase from the 1989 urban fringe/large town school population.

The NCEA uses slightly different terms to describe the location categories of Catholic schools, but the data they have been collecting since 1968 on school location confirms

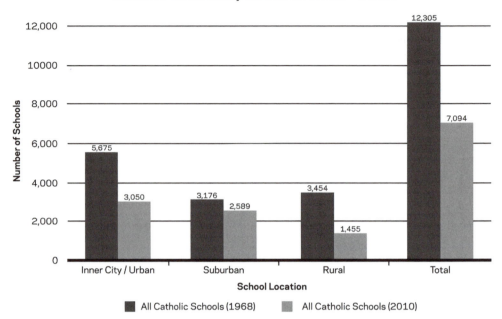

Figure 32.1   Catholic schools by school location and total for the years 1968–2010.

the shifts present in the more recent NCES data. Figure 32.1 depicts the overall loss of Catholic schools in urban and rural locales and the relative stability of suburban schools between 1968 and 2010.

NCEA and NCES data highlight a general trend of Catholic school closure in the urban core and relative stability, even growth, in suburban communities that sociologist Andrew Greeley first discussed in *The Church and the Suburbs* (1963). In this seminal text, Greeley reminded readers that prior to the 1950s, most Catholics were working-class Americans who lived in large, urban cities. Consequently, the majority of Catholic parishes and schools could also be found in large, urban cities. According to Greeley, the mass migration of Catholics to suburbia represented "a decisive turning point in the history of American Catholicism"—one that continues to affect Catholic schools to this day (Greeley 1963, 53).

National demographic shifts also affect the health and viability of American Catholic schools. In 1950, over 75 percent of the Catholic population in the United States lived in either the Northeast or the Midwest. By 2008, only 52 percent of U.S. Catholics lived in either the Northeast or the Midwest (Center for Applied Research in the Apostolate 2009). Although the Catholic population may have migrated from the North and East to the South and West, the brick-and-mortar institutions of the Church have been slow to follow. A report published by the Notre Dame Task Force on the Participation of Latino Children and Families in Catholic Schools highlighted the enormity of this demographic shift and its impact on Catholic schools in recent years. According to the Task Force, "the Diocese of Pittsburgh has one Catholic school for every 6,400 Catholics while the Diocese of Brownsville has one for every 64,000" (Notre Dame Task Force on the Participation of Latino Children and Families in Catholic Schools 2009, 53).

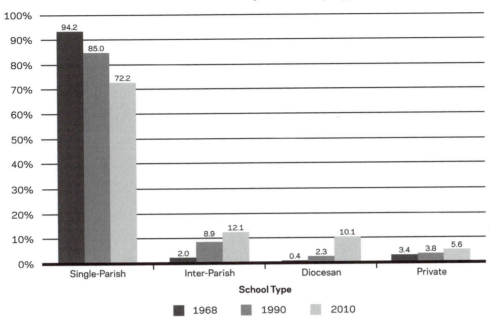

Figure 32.2   Percent of total elementary school population by school type for the years 1968, 1990, and 2010.

SCHOOL GOVERNANCE AND FINANCES

Changes in the number of schools and the number of students enrolled in them has precipitated changes in the way schools are organized, governed, and financed. Claude Harris succinctly captured the overall trajectory of this shift when he wrote, "Catholic schools have evolved from a church-funded endeavor managed by professed religious to a system of largely parent-funded programs for a diminishing portion of the Catholic school population" (Harris 2000, 56).

Despite radical changes in the landscape of Catholic education, four primary categories of Catholic school governance have remained: single-parish, inter-parish, diocesan, and private (see Figures 32.2 and 32.3). Both ecclesial authority (i.e., Canon law) and civil authority (i.e., local, state, and federal laws) shape each of these models of Catholic school governance. For the purposes of this chapter, the term governance is used to describe the general framework that dictates the establishment, management, and financing of Catholic schools (see Haney, O'Brien, and Sheehan, 2009 for a more detailed discussion of the *Code of Canon Law* and Catholic school governance). The following section presents the salient features of each governance model, addresses changes over time, and highlights innovative changes within each of these traditional governance categories.

Single-Parish Schools

The term "parish school" refers to any Catholic school that is "sponsored by a single parish church community" (McDonald and Schultz 2010, 10). As such, parish schools operate under the authority of the pastor, though he may choose to delegate certain managerial, educational, or financial responsibilities to the appropriate council, board, or individual.

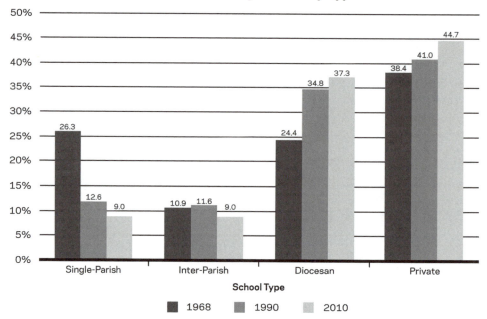

Figure 32.3 Percent of total secondary school population by school type for the years 1968, 1990, and 2010.

The first Catholic school in the Unites States was technically a parish school (Saint Mary's Parish School—1783, Walch 2003), and remained the dominant model for school governance for the next 225 years. In fact, as late as the 1970s, "over 90 percent of the elementary schools in the nation were parish schools" (Convey 1992, 37). Despite their historical prominence, Figures 32.2 and 32.3 illustrate the steady decline in the percentage of parish elementary school (1968, 94.2%; 2010, 72.2%) and secondary school (1968, 26.3%; 2010, 9.0%) sponsorship.

Inter-Parish Schools

As the name suggests, inter-parish schools are schools sponsored by more than one parish or by a regional association of parishes. Pastors from the sponsoring parishes often share responsibilities for managing the schools and will elect a representative to chair or sit on a board that governs the inter-parish school (Haney, O'Brien, and Sheehan 2009). The inter-parish model of school governance has increased dramatically in the last five decades as demographic and financial factors have forced the consolidation or regionalization of many traditional parish schools. In 1968 only 2.0 percent of all elementary schools and 10.9 percent of all secondary schools were considered inter-parish schools. Today, 12 percent of elementary schools and 11.6 percent of secondary schools are considered inter-parish schools.

Despite the financial and managerial sponsorship of multiple parish communities, there is some fear that the increase of inter-parish or regional schools actually heightens a sense of separation between the life of the parish and the life of the Catholic school. In reflecting on how this could be so, Haney, O'Brien, and Sheehan stated that "often the parish that physically houses the interparish school looks on it as its own while the other parishes have lesser feelings of ownership" (2009, 36). These diminished feelings of ownership and connectedness can lead to declines in financial contribution and even student enrollment.

Diocesan Schools

All Catholic schools in a given diocese are under the pastoral care and authority of the bishop, but schools that are classified as "(arch)diocesan schools" are also administered by the diocese or by a diocesan board that reports to the bishop (Haney, O'Brien, and Sheehan 2009). Diocesan elementary schools were virtually unheard of prior to the 1960s. In 1968 less than 1 percent of all Catholic elementary schools were classified as diocesan, compared to over 10 percent during the 2010 academic year. There was also considerable growth in the percentage of diocesan secondary schools between 1968 (24.4%) and 2010 (41.0%). Some contend that the increase in diocesan administration of schools over time is related to the increasing financial burdens of single-parish sponsorship (Convey 1992).

In an effort to offset some of the costs associated with single-parish sponsorship or a cluster of struggling diocesan schools, several dioceses have developed a "consortium" model of school governance. A consortium of Catholic schools often operates within the diocesan structure, but has a centralized governing board with administrative responsibility only for the schools in the consortium. This hybrid model of governance has gained popularity in dioceses where the urban schools have been especially hard hit. The Consortium of Catholic Academies (www.catholicacademies.org) in Washington, D.C., and the Mother Theodore Catholic Academies (www.archindy.org/mtca/index.html) in Indianapolis, IN, are two examples of the consortium model designed to provide efficient and effective guidance to Catholic schools that may not be viable on their own.

Private Catholic Schools

Private Catholic schools are those that are "owned or sponsored by religious congregations or by boards of trustees" (Haney, O'Brien, and Sheehan 2009, 43). Private sponsorship of Catholic secondary schools has remained the most common form of secondary school governance over the past five decades (1968 = 38.4%, 2010 = 44.7%), with the majority of these secondary schools owned or sponsored by religious congregations (Buetow 1970; Convey 1992). Private sponsorship of Catholic elementary schools has remained relatively low, but constant over the same time period (1968 = 3.4%, 2010 = 5.6%).

Perhaps the largest growth area within the private school governance model are the Catholic schools that have been established to serve the poor and marginalized—often in the urban center of major cities. San Miguel, Nativity, and Cristo Rey are just a few examples of the new urban Catholic school—one that is often sponsored by a religious congregation and managed by a board of directors. Since these schools do not charge tuition to cover the cost to educate each child, they rely heavily on private benefaction, grant support, and other innovative funding mechanisms such as the corporate work study program at Cristo Rey in which students job-share at local businesses to help pay for the cost of their education. A sign of their growing numbers, and growing needs, The NativityMiguel Network of Schools was established in 2006 to "to guide and strengthen the development of a growing network of schools across the country that are designed to provide families struggling in impoverished neighborhoods with a high quality education" (http://www.nativitymiguelschools.org/).

The four primary categories of Catholic school governance have remained relatively stable over the past half-century, but subtle and innovative changes within each model represent an "adaptive response" to the myriad financial and managerial challenges facing Catholic schools (James 2005, 287).

School Finances

Whereas Catholic education was practically free to families and students five decades ago, nearly all contemporary Catholic schools rely on some form of tuition payment or private benefaction to offset the full cost to educate each child. Tuition payments alone represent 80 percent of the total school income for the average contemporary Catholic school (Gautier, Buck, and Cidade 2009). Some researchers argue that the increased reliance on tuition as the primary funding mechanism for Catholic education has precipitated the "eliting" of Catholic schools and priced many families out of the market (Baker and Riordan 1998). According to Baker and Riordan (1998), there has been a seismic shift in the family wealth of contemporary Catholic schools students compared to those who attended Catholic schools five decades ago. Today, "almost one-half (45%) of all Catholic secondary students attending Catholic schools are living in households in the top quarter of the income distribution" (19).

In the past decade alone, both the average tuition charged and average annual cost to educate each child have increased, but not in equal strides. In 2000, the average tuition charge at a Catholic elementary school was $1,787 while the national average cost to educate a child was $2,823, meaning that tuition covered 63 percent of the total cost of education. In 2009, the average tuition charged at a Catholic elementary school had increased to $3,159, but the average cost to educate a child had more than doubled to reach $5,870, meaning that current tuition covered only 54 percent of the total cost of education (McDonald and Schultz 2000, 2010).

The growing differential between tuition charged and the actual cost of education has troubling financial implications for Catholic schools. Under the current tuition metrics, an administrator at a typical Catholic elementary school with an enrollment of 200 students must raise or otherwise account for an additional $500,000 each year to cover the gap between tuition charged and the actual cost to educate each student. It is no wonder, then, that in a recent national study of pastors of parishes with schools, priests named finances as one of the top two challenges currently facing their schools and Catholic education more broadly (Nuzzi, Frabutt, and Holter 2008).

Describing the changing landscape of Catholic education over the past five decades has proven easier than explaining the reasons for the decline itself. Many researchers and practitioners have posited that a constellation of factors have, over time, made Catholic schools a less accessible and even less desirable educational option for parents and their children. It is beyond the scope of this chapter to provide a detailed description of the many social and ecclesial factors affecting these changes; however, the following provides a brief overview of and suggested resources for further exploration of the major contributory factors.

Among the reasons for the decline in American Catholic education, researchers and theorists cite demographic shifts in the Catholic population specifically (Convey 1992; McGreevy 1996), and declining birthrates among U.S. families in general (Convey 1992). They cite the drastic loss of women religious and increasing costs associated with hiring competent lay teachers and leaders to replace them (Grace 2002; Harris 2000; Walch 2003; Wittberg 1994). They cite increased competition from other private and alternative public schools (McLellen 2000) paired with weakening anti-Catholic bigotry in both the public square and the public school (Dolan 2002; Greeley 1963; Ryan 1964). Finally, and perhaps most perniciously, some scholars cite the lack of support and vision from the American Catholic Bishops as a central cause of the challenges and decline facing Catholic education in the United States (Greeley, McCready, and McCourt 1976; Walch 2003).

In many ways, the story of American Catholic schools over the last half century has come full circle. The Catholic school system was strained nearly to the limits in the 1960s due to rapidly increasing demand and decreases in the space and religious men and women available to meet the demand. Now, 50 years later, the American Catholic school system is again strained, but for much different reasons.

While the changes to American Catholic education pose increasing challenges, they also represent important opportunities to restructure and revitalize individual schools and even the Catholic educational system itself (Brown and Greeley 1970; Koob and Shaw 1970). In a compelling conclusion to *S.O.S. for Catholic Schools*, Albert Koob and Russell Shaw reminded Catholics that even in adversity, "the opportunity is there and where there is opportunity, there is also duty" (Koob and Shaw 1970, 150). The next section of this chapter delves deeper into the financial and spiritual challenges facing Catholic schools and Catholic education, and the opportunities present therein.

CHALLENGES FACING CONTEMPORARY CATHOLIC EDUCATION

Catholic schools have been under tremendous pressures that have threatened their survival and at times, compromised their record of success. Although socially complex organizations such as schools present a variety of operational and strategic opportunities for improvement and change, pastors recently reported a strong focus on two primary challenges that demanded immediate attention, new and creative thinking, and some dramatic changes in the business-as-usual approach (Nuzzi, Frabutt, and Holter 2008). These two challenges were (1) finances—a broadly construed category that included tuition and enrollment management, long-range planning, marketing, capital improvements, and accessibility of Catholic schools to the poor and middle class and (2) faith—a similarly general way to designate all of those matters that touch on the unique contribution of the Catholic school: its Christ-centered, Gospel values; the participation of school families in the sacramental life of the Church; the teaching of religion as a part of the formal curriculum; and the overall Catholic identity or ethos of the school itself.

Finances

The financial challenges facing Catholic schools have their origin in history and the unprecedented commitment to teaching and administration made by vowed religious women and men (Buetow 1970, 1985, 1998). For decades, religious sisters, brothers, and priests, inspired by their personal faith in Jesus, which they lived out in the context of a faith-based community, provided free professional services to Catholic schools. These contributed services allowed Catholic schools to grow and prosper, free of charge to families, and provided an effective vehicle for the enculturation and socioeconomic advancement of generations of immigrant Catholics (Walch 2003).

It is only with the gradual departure of these dedicated personnel that Catholic schools began to hire lay men and women to teach, and with that change came the need to charge an ever-increasing tuition. No single factor has influenced the financial challenges facing Catholic schools today as much as this monumental shift in the origin and status of its human resources (Cook 2002).

The budgetary status of many Catholic schools today is delicate. Operational costs are rising with inflation, and the demands associated with technology seem perennial. The need to pay a competitive and just wage to teachers and administrators also places Catholic schools in competition with nearby public and private schools for the best teachers, and salary can be a highly attractive differential. Financial management has rightfully become a primary challenge, one that impacts every other dimension of school life.

An often ignored fact about Catholic schools is that 100 percent of students receive some form of financial aid. As noted earlier, tuition charges, while rising steadily, do not approach the true per-pupil cost to educate a child. In most cases, the difference between the charged tuition and the per-pupil cost is generated by direct financial support from a parish, diocese, or religious community and by extensive institutional advancement efforts, development programs, benefaction, and fundraising. These funds, often referred to as subsidy in the literature, amount to billions of dollars a year, and provide a means of support for every student in Catholic schools in the United States.

Because of the various sources of revenue for the typical Catholic school, financial management involves the balancing of a variety of revenue streams. Raising tuition too sharply in an effort to increase revenues can result in an overall enrollment decline and have a negative effect on the budget. Securing a large philanthropic gift can create complacency and an unwillingness to pursue more extensive development efforts or fundraising opportunities. Some dioceses have undertaken sophisticated statistical analyses to predict such trends and anticipate financial constraints. For example, the Diocese of Arlington, Virginia, has calculated a series of algorithms based on census data including the socioeconomic status of parishioner-stakeholders in Catholic schools. The algorithm predicts how overall school enrollment will rise or fall based on corresponding movement in the tuition charged. Using this calculation, principals and pastors can predict with a reasonable level of accuracy how many students will be lost by increasing tuition at varying amounts. The process allows administrators to identify the optimal level of tuition increase that will support revenue growth and avoid either the departure of a large number of students or the undercharging of a population that could afford to pay more (Daniel J. Ferris, Assistant Superintendent of Education, Diocese of Arlington, unpublished data).

The Archdiocese of St. Louis, one of the largest Catholic school systems in the United States, has studied recently closed Catholic schools in an effort to better understand factors associated with long-term viability (James, Tichy, Collins, and Schwob 2008). Using a path analysis tracking dozens of indicators, researchers identified a set of variables that typically have preceded school closings. By clearly describing and measuring these predictor variables, administrators are able to plan strategic interventions and to begin them before the fiscal situation becomes critical.

These revenue concerns are manifested in the Catholic school primarily through three interrelated experiences of fiscal constraint: enrollment management, financial management, and the need to maintain affordability (Nuzzi, Frabutt, and Holter 2008). The balance between these themes is obviously precarious, for it is "impossible to talk about enrollment management without citing financial concerns" (Nuzzi, Frabutt, and Holter 2008, 33). Similarly, there is a "symbiotic relationship of enrollment and finances"

(Nuzzi, Frabutt, and Holter 2008, 33), creating a need for a concomitant realization on parents' part of the value of a Catholic education.

The theological and social justice challenge related to enrollment and financial management is the concern of affordability and the need to keep tuition within reach of middle-class and even low-income families. This challenge has been coined "the eliting of the Catholic school," indicating that students come from increasingly higher socioeconomic classes (Baker and Riordan 1998, 16–23; Greeley 1998, 24–25; Greeley 1999, 463). The general fear is that by setting tuition based on school budgetary needs without regard for the population of potential students and stakeholders, Catholic schools will increasingly become the province of the economically affluent and perhaps even exclusively so. Because of the Gospel imperative to care for the poor and the marginalized, forever enshrined in the example of Jesus, such a result is morally unacceptable and theologically suspect to many, ultimately questioning whether such schools can authentically embrace a Catholic identity if they are unaffordable for and inaccessible to all those of any status other than wealthy.

Capital improvements, including standard maintenance projects, major renovations, expansions, and new construction constitute another major focus in the category of finances. It is not uncommon for a Catholic parish to have several major buildings on the property—church, school, parish hall, gymnasium—all constructed at different times and all containing an array of age-related depreciation and deterioration in need of attention. The average Catholic elementary school operating today was established in 1936, with more than half built before 1950 and 17 percent built before 1900 (White House Domestic Policy Council 2008). Thus, even if the operational costs and annual budgetary shortfalls would come into balance dramatically and immediately, longer term capital projects would present themselves and require fiscal support.

Faith

The second major challenge facing Catholic schools is in the area of faith, namely the need to strengthen the overall Catholic ethos of the school, giving it a clear and compelling Catholic identity in such a way that the personal holiness and human development of the students is the final outcome. Accomplishing these dual aims of Catholic education—holiness and human development—in an empirical, observable way remains a constant concern for Catholic educational leaders (Nuzzi 2002).

This challenge also has its historical origin in the declining numbers of vowed women and men religious serving in the schools as teachers and principals. In addition to working free of charge, they also brought their religious formation and education with them into classrooms and offices, helping to imbue schools with a strong Catholic liturgical and sacramental life, a spirituality rooted in the particular charisms of sponsoring religious communities, and a singular dedication to the mission of the Church (Gabert 1973). This personal and living witness is difficult to replace and impossible to replicate. Catholic colleges and universities now find themselves faced with the relatively new responsibility of preparing professionals for service in Catholic schools while attempting to recreate what the vowed religious did by personal example, namely enact a solid professionalism in the context of a faith-based, Gospel-inspired, mission-driven educational institution. This means that professional preparation programs now combine the knowledge bases of teacher education and educational administration with spiritual and pastoral formation previously found in religious life. Over the past several decades, dozens of programs have been created nationwide to meet this growing need (Smith and Nuzzi 2007, 2008).

An additional complicating factor in the ongoing effort to maintain and strengthen the Catholic identity of Catholic schools emanates from the lack of general agreement surrounding the constitutive elements of Catholic identity. The term itself means different things to different people and a variety of rubrics have been developed in recent years to help measure the construct of Catholic identity in ways that might be helpful to church leaders, accrediting agencies, religious formators, and consumers. Among the recent tools for the assessment of Catholic identity are the Catholic Education Foundation's Catholic Identity Assessment from Buffalo, NY; the Western Catholic Education Association's Catholic Identity Standards; the Minnesota Catholic Education Association's Standard for Catholic Identity; AdvancedEd's Standards-Based Indicators of Catholic School Identity; Standards for Excellence in Catholic Elementary and Secondary Schools from Loyola University Chicago; and the University of Notre Dame's Catholic School Identity Inventory (CSII). Each of the instruments and protocols has a particular lens through which Catholic identity is viewed.

The Catholic Church has had a record of robust participation in the philosophy of education (Joseph 2001; Maritain 1943) and in broader theories of epistemology and ontology (Aquinas 1945). Official Church documents and pronouncements, dating back to the 1500s and continuing into the modern and post-modern era, articulate a somewhat comprehensive view of Catholic education and a consistent emphasis on such essentials as the unity of faith and reason, the integration of faith and culture, and education of the whole person (*The Catholic School* 1977; *Divini Illius Magistri*, 1929; *Fides et Ratio* 1998; *Immensa* 1588; *Veritatis Splendor* 1993). The unity of knowledge and of knowing that is the goal of the authentically Catholic school means that there can be no separation between learning and religious development. There are no secular subjects, in as much as all learning helps one to understand and appreciate the overarching order of all creation, the intrinsic goodness of the universe, and one's place and vocation within it (*Gravissimum Educationis* 1965; *The Religious Dimension of Education in a Catholic School* 1988).

This integration of faith and knowledge is essential to the proper understanding of Catholic identity and results in an educational program that sees mutuality between the pursuit of academic excellence and the pursuit of holiness. In fact, the quest for excellence in academics is accurately portrayed as a means to operationalize the quest for holiness in an educational environment, by using one's God-given gifts to full capacity and by contributing to society in meaningful and life-giving ways. Thus, academic excellence is not a separate and distinct goal for Catholic schools in addition to the pursuit of holiness. It is, rather, an essential avenue for the pursuit of holiness in the educational community of the school. The religious purposes of the school—its sacramental and liturgical life, religious instruction, and feast days—advance and serve the academic purposes of the school by reinforcing the values of the community, extolling honorable and virtuous behavior, highlighting positive role models, and uniting all stakeholders in a common and uplifting mission. The academic endeavors of the school—its rigorous curriculum with high standards for all—advance and serve the religious goals of the school by teaching the central mysteries of the faith, the Scriptures, and the common moral value system of the community, and especially by building an educational community in the school focused on high achievement and hard work, supported by the spiritual and liturgical practices central to Catholicism. The ultimate purpose of a Catholic school education is perhaps singular.

It is salvation, eternal life. All classes and teaching, all prayer and worship, all grades and activities, ultimately serve that end. A school may be considered Catholic where these dual purposes of holiness and human development experientially merge into this one, singular goal.

DEVELOPMENTS IN CATHOLIC EDUCATION

Amidst the aforementioned dual challenges of finances and faith, several positive developments in Catholic education have transpired since the 1960s, each one markedly increasing our understanding of the dynamics within and surrounding Catholic schools. Three such developments chronicled here include heightened attention to student achievement data; continued reinforcement—via several Church documents—of the vital and saving mission of Catholic schools; and the evolving and increasingly complex public policy debates surrounding parental choice of schools.

Academics

In the decades immediately following the Second Vatican Council, there was a heightened interest in the state of education in general, and in the academic, social, and religious outcomes of Catholic education specifically. A series of studies commissioned by secular and religious organizations, and administered by leading sociologists and educational researchers, confirmed the positive impact of Catholic education on its students that has come to be known as the "Catholic school effect." These early studies conducted by Andrew Greeley, James Coleman, and others brought both heightened interest in Catholic schools as a novel educational environment and increased skepticism in the purported academic and social benefits they confer. The following section highlights foundational and contemporary research on Catholic education and the Catholic school effect.

Prior to the 1960s, rigorous empirical research on Catholics schools was scant. However, by the end of that decade, major strides had been made to both describe and evaluate the impact of Catholic schools across the United States. One of the first and most ambitious research projects of this period was *Catholic Schools in Action* (Neuwien 1966). Although criticized by some for its methodological limitations, this report launched a debate on Catholic school effectiveness that continues to this day.

Catholic Schools in Action was conducted by researchers at the University of Notre Dame and sponsored by several secular and religious organizations. Over a four-year span, researchers surveyed elementary and secondary schools from nearly every diocese in the United States and conducted rich case study analyses "to bring to the citizens of this country a deepened awareness of their opportunities and responsibilities" (Neuwien 1966, 24). Results of the study covered school structure and enrollment, finances, religious outcomes, and academics and highlighted that, on average, Catholic school students excelled on standardized tests, exceeded national norms, and attended college at high rates (Neuwien 1966). Despite some methodological concerns, *Catholic Schools in Action* was "truly a pioneering study of Catholic schools" (Convey 1992, 12).

Several important studies of Catholic schools and their effect followed the groundbreaking study published in *Catholic Schools in Action*. Throughout the 1960s and 1970s, Andrew Greeley conducted two major studies investigating the religious and social effects of Catholic education (Greeley and Rossi 1966; Greeley, McCready, and McCourt 1976) that, in combination with the Notre Dame study, would set the stage for a more sophisticated assessment and more contentious debate of the primary effects of Catholic schooling.

Interest in the social, religious, and academic outcomes of Catholic school students surged in the 1980s, and once again spawned vigorous debate about the merits of the "Catholic school effect" and the caliber of the educational inquiry used to support such claims. It should be noted that the growing interest in Catholic schools and Catholic education throughout the 1980s was set against the backdrop of increasing dissatisfaction with the public school system. Reports such as *A Nation at Risk* (National Commission on Excellence in Education 1983) used images of war and foreign siege to warn against the lagging academic performance of U.S. students compared to their international peers.

One year before the publication of *A Nation at Risk*, Coleman, Hoffer, and Kilgore published *High School Achievement: Public, Catholic, and Private* (1982), in which their analysis of the High School and Beyond (HS&B) data indicated that Catholic school students outperformed their public school peers in mathematics, reading, and vocabulary. Additionally, the researchers noticed that certain background factors—namely parent education and student minority status—had less impact on students attending Catholic schools than they did on students attending public schools. Said another way, the personal background factors that typically compromise academic achievement "were smaller and appeared to diminish as the student progressed through Catholic school" (Hoffer 2000, 104). Furthermore, these findings were upheld in subsequent studies conducted on longitudinal HS&B datasets (Coleman and Hoffer 1987; Hoffer, Greeley, and Coleman 1985).

Similar conclusions were reached in an independent study conducted by Andrew Greeley entitled *Catholic Schools and Minority Students* (1982). Greeley used the same HS&B data that Coleman and associates had used, but focused exclusively on the impact of school attendance on academic achievement for minority students. Greeley's analysis, which also controlled for background factors likely to impact academic achievement, confirmed that minority students who attended Catholic schools outperformed their minority peers who attended public schools (Greeley 1982). Additionally, Greeley's analysis suggested that "Catholic schools were especially effective for multi-disadvantaged students: minority students from home backgrounds of low educational achievement" (Convey 1992, 19).

The assertion of a Catholic school effect supported by these and other studies throughout the 1980s inspired subsequent researchers to identify the specific school-level factors responsible for such academic advantages. A series of independent research initiatives highlighted challenging curriculum, strong focus on discipline, a supportive school community, high rates of school attendance, and core religious values as key components to the academic success of Catholic school students (Bryk, Holland, Lee, and Carriedo 1984; Bryk, Lee, and Holland 1993; Coleman and Hoffer 1987).

The primary findings and conclusions presented in each of these studies ignited both fierce debate and criticism throughout the education community over concerns about methodological limitations of the study and the implications of its findings (Manno and Graham 2001). Despite the fact that advanced statistical techniques allowed the researchers to control for many potentially confounding background factors, critics still faulted the inquiry for not going far enough to control for selection bias (Noell 1982)—the absence of random assignment to school—and student motivation (Keith and Page 1985). Others were alarmed that "Catholic schools more nearly approximated the 'common school' ideal of American education than did public schools" since they asserted that Catholic schools "were beneficial not only to students from advantaged backgrounds, but also to those from disadvantaged backgrounds" (Convey 1992, 17). As Convey (1992) noted, this debate was taken to the public square in separate special issues of the *Harvard Educational Review* and *Sociology of Education*, the implications of which have shaped educational inquiry on the topic some 20 years later.

Recent scholarship has added to the back-and-forth debate over the existence and extent of the Catholic school effect. An analysis of advances in Catholic educational research indicated that between 2005 and 2010, nearly 20 percent (*n* = 54) of all books and articles on Catholic educational research addressed the academic impacts associated with the Catholic school effect (Hunt, Frabutt, Holter, and Nuzzi 2010). Each publication that addressed academic and sector effects either "challenged" (e.g., Reardon, Cheadle, and Robinson, 2009) or "confirmed" (e.g., Carbonaro and Covay 2010) the academic advantages associated with Catholic school attendance.

Nearly 50 years after the first systemic assessment of K–12 Catholic schools in *Catholic Schools in Action*, and over two decades since the seminal work by Andrew Greeley, James Coleman, and associates, the empirical study of the academic preparation provided in Catholic school has become more sophisticated, but no less engaging. Despite some disconfirming reports and more modest effects than were presented nearly 30 years ago, the preponderance of evidence suggests that the Catholic school effect is indeed a Catholic school advantage. Students who attend Catholic schools are more likely to excel academically, graduate from high school, and attain a post-secondary education when compared to their public school peers. Over 20 years since it was first suggested, the advantage of Catholic school attendance on students' academic achievement remains strong and at the forefront of Catholic educational research.

Church Documents on Catholic Schools[1]

Since the Second Vatican Council, Church documents about Catholic schools have forcefully articulated the Church's vision for and esteem toward these places of evangelization, for "Catholic schools proceed *ex corde Ecclesiae*, from the very heart of the Church" (Miller 2006, vii). Although a succession of documents pertaining to Catholic schools have issued from a variety of authors—popes, councils, the Roman curia, and national bishops' conferences—this review centers on some of the most prominent and juridically powerful. Table 32.1, however, provides a chronological listing of Church documents since Vatican II that either directly or indirectly address Catholic education. Each of these documents, it should be noted, builds upon several foundational documents on Catholic education that pre-date Vatican II (e.g., *Spectata Fides* 1885; *Divini Illius Magistri* 1929).

Universal Church Documents

Documents emanating from the Vatican are addressed to the universal Church and thus have the most force and reach. *Gravissimum Educationis* [Declaration on Christian Education] (1965) is a cornerstone ecumenical document promulgated by Vatican II, and as such carries significant import. In addition to the *Code of Canon Law*, which contains specific sections that speak directly to Catholic schools, six major documents have been published by the Congregation for Catholic Education since Vatican II:

---

[1]The authors acknowledge Ms. Amy Grinsteinner for her significant contributions to earlier drafts of this section.

Table 32.1 Comprehensive Listing of Church Documents Related to Catholic Education Since the Second Vatican Council (Frabutt, Holter, and Nuzzi 2010)

Catechetical Documents

1997	*Catechism of the Catholic Church*	

Encyclicals and Other Papal Documents

1975	Paul VI	*Evangelii Nuntiandi* [On Evangelization in the Modern World]
1979	John Paul II	*Catechesi Tradendae* [On Catechesis in Our Time]
1981	John Paul II	*Familiaris Consortio* [The Role of the Christian Family in the Modern World]
1994	John Paul II	*Gratissimam Sane* [Letter to Families]
1999	John Paul II	*Ecclesia in America* [The Church in America]

Documents of the Second Vatican Council

1965	Vatican II	*Gaudium et Spes* [On the Church in the Modern World]
1965	Vatican II	*Gravissimum Educationis* [Declaration on Christian Education]

Documents from the Roman Curia

1977	Sacred Congregation for Catholic Education	*The Catholic School*
1982	Sacred Congregation for Catholic Education	*Lay Catholics in Schools*
1988	Congregation for Catholic Education	*The Religious Dimension of Education in a Catholic School*
1998	Congregation for Catholic Education	*The Catholic School on the Threshold of the Third Millennium*
2002	Congregation for Catholic Education	*Consecrated Persons and Their Mission in Schools*
2004	Pontifical Council for Justice and Peace	*The Compendium of the Social Doctrine of the Church*
2007	Congregation for Catholic Education	*Educating Together in Catholic Schools*

Documents from the United States Bishops

1972	National Conference of Catholic Bishops/United States Catholic Conference (NCCB/USCC)	*To Teach as Jesus Did*
1976	United States Catholic Conference	*Teach Them!*
1990	NCCB/USCC	*In Support of Catholic Elementary and Secondary Schools*
1995	United States Catholic Conference	*Principles for Educational Reform in the United States*
1999	NCCB/USCC	*Our Hearts Were Burning Within Us*
2005	United States Conference of Catholic Bishops	*Renewing Our Commitment to Catholic Elementary and Secondary Schools in the Third Millennium*

From *No Greater Work: Meditations on Church Documents* (2010), edited by James M. Frabutt, Anthony C. Holter, and Ronald J. Nuzzi, pp. xi–xii. Used by permission of the Alliance for Catholic Education Press at the University of Notre Dame.

The Catholic School (1977); *Lay Catholics in Schools: Witnesses to Faith* (1982); *The Religious Dimension of Education in a Catholic School* (1988); *The Catholic School on the Threshold of the Third Millennium* (1997); *Consecrated Persons and Their Mission in Schools* (2002); and *Educating Together in Catholic Schools* (2007).

As a group, these documents cover a broad range of topics concerning Catholic education. Each document exhibits a unique character, but several common themes are evident among them. First, these documents emphasize that true education is one that forms the whole person. Second, they assert that teachers in Catholic schools must be qualified both in the subjects they teach and in their knowledge of religious doctrine. Third, each document foregrounds the important role that parents play in the education of their children. Finally, these documents stress that states and governments must provide parents with the right to choose a Catholic education. Further examination of these themes below elucidates a consistent narrative about what the Church believes and articulates about Catholic schools.

Educating the whole person. According to the Second Vatican Council, a true education is one that "aims at the formation of the human person in the pursuit of his ultimate end and of the good of the societies of which, as man, he is a member, and in whose obligations, as an adult, he will share" (*Gravissimum Educationis* 1965, §5). Likewise, several other documents raise the notion that education must benefit both the personal salvation of students and the common good of society. Catholic schools should develop the physical, moral, and intellectual abilities of students. They also should train them to be civically engaged; both during their school years and after graduation students should take an active part in the social life of their communities, thereby promoting the common good. However, schools must be always be cautious of focusing solely on the academic and social aspects of education, for a "[c]omplete education necessarily includes a religious dimension" (*The Catholic School* 1977, §19).

Teachers and the religious dimension of education. Because a religious dimension is necessary for a true education, the Church asserts that teachers in Catholic schools must be qualified not only in their subject area but also in their sound knowledge of religious doctrine. Catholic schools, like other private schools, are unique in that they are able to include religious themes in every area of study. If students raise questions that explore religion across subjects outside their formal religion class, their teachers "should be adequately prepared to deal with such questions and be ready to give them the attention they deserve" (*The Religious Dimension of Education in a Catholic School* 1988, §64). If teachers are not adequately trained and therefore cannot include a religious dimension in their classes, they have failed to provide their students with a complete education.

Parents as the primary educators. Teachers are not the only ones responsible for ensuring that children receive a complete education. In fact, they are secondary in this role. The Church designates parents as the primary and principal educators of their children (Frabutt and Rocha 2009; Frabutt et al. 2010). Several obligations are inherent in this role. First, parents must raise their children in a Christian environment. It is vitally important that parents "create a family atmosphere animated by love and respect for God and man, in which the well-rounded personal and social education of children is fostered" (*Gravissimum Educationis* 1965, §9). Second, whenever possible parents must send their children to schools that provide Catholic education. Finally, parents must realize that their duty as educators does not end upon their children's enrollment in school. Instead, they must "cooperate closely with the teachers of the schools to which they entrust their children to be educated" (Canon Law 796, §2). The Church states that parents should be heavily involved in their children's education beginning at birth and continuing throughout their lives.

Parental choice of schools. Church documents recognize that it is often financially difficult for parents to send their children to Catholic schools. Because of this, the documents put forth the claim that "[p]arents also have the right to that assistance, to be furnished by civil society, which they need to secure the Catholic education of their children" (Canon Law 793, §2). The Church argues that, because we live in a pluralistic society, it is of great importance that children are not required to be educated in a system that constitutes a school monopoly. By offering an alternative to public schools, Catholic schools provide a valuable and necessary service toward this end. However, if parents are not able to choose to send their children to Catholic schools because of financial concerns, many of these schools are ultimately faced with economic hardship. Some may be forced to close, thereby further decreasing the number and kind of alternative schooling options that are so important in a pluralistic society. Part of states' responsibility in allowing for parental choice is offering subsidies to parents so they can exercise true liberty in choosing which school their children will attend.

Documents on Catholic Schools: The Church in the United States

Just as the Vatican has consistently clarified and reinforced its message concerning Catholic schools, since the Second Vatican Council, so too has the American Catholic Church. Authored by a national bishops' council, these statements are specifically intended for the American audience (see Table 32.2). Although they do not carry as much weight as documents released by the Vatican, they are still pertinent because they offer special clarification and guidance for Catholic schools in a specifically American context. Several examples of these documents are *To Teach as Jesus Did* (1972), *Teach Them! A Statement of the Catholic Bishops* (1976), and *Renewing Our Commitment to Catholic Elementary and Secondary Schools in the Third Millennium* (2005). These documents largely echo the themes set forth in the Vatican documents. In addition, the United States Conference of Catholic Bishops (USCCB) has recognized that "[t]he educational mission of the Church is an integrated ministry embracing three interlocking dimensions" (*To Teach as Jesus Did* 1972, §14). The first dimension holds that the Church must proclaim the message revealed by God and teach doctrine. Second, a sense of fellowship and a building of community must be present. Finally, there must be an element of service to the Christian community and to the whole world.

The USCCB noted that "Catholic schools afford the fullest and best opportunity to realize the threefold purpose of Christian education" (*To Teach as Jesus Did* 1972, §101). This affirmation of Catholic schools is only one example of many found throughout the documents of both the USCCB and the Vatican. While differing somewhat in focus, Church documents released since Vatican II have consistently noted the centrality of and unwavering support for Catholic schools, most decidedly because they "form part of the saving mission of the Church, especially for education in the faith" (*The Catholic School* 1977, §9). The Church recognizes the important and salvific role Catholic schools play in society today, and through these teachings and writings Church leaders hope that the entire Catholic community and the rest of the world will do the same.

PUBLIC POLICY

Parental Choice of Schools

Since Vatican II, parental choice of schools—often referred to as school choice—represents the most seminal public policy development in relation to Catholic schools. The issue of school choice is set on the cornerstone of parents' personal liberty—the unfettered

Table 32.2   Selected Church Documents on Catholic Schools: Content Summary (Left Column) and Commentary (Right Column)

Gravissimum Educationis (1965)

In *Gravissimum Educationis*, the council laid out principles that are fundamental to Christian education, particularly in schools (Massucci, 2004). The document is consisted of 12 sections: (1) the meaning of the universal right to an education; (2) Christian education; (3) the authors of education; (4) various aids to Christian education; (5) the importance of schools; (6) the duties and rights of parents; (7) moral and religious education in all schools; (8) Catholic schools; (9) different types of Catholic schools; (10) Catholic Colleges and Universities; (11) faculties of sacred sciences; and (12) coordination in scholastic matters.

As a Conciliar document issued from an ecumenical council, *Gravissimum Educationis* holds the greatest force among Church documents. The document was released at a time when Catholic schools were flourishing; however, by issuing this document the Second Vatican Council recognized the continuing need to educate all individuals in order that they might actively participate in social, economic, and political affairs (Massucci, 2004).

The Catholic School (1977)

The document represents the first document released in the 400-year history of the Congregation for Catholic Education that focuses its attention on K–12 Catholic schools. As such, it is the anchor document for a steady line of publications concerning Catholic schools that have come from the Congregation since. This document can be read as a response to the Second Vatican Council's placement of renewed emphasis on the Church (Nuzzi, 2004a).

Highly theological, this document moves beyond the common pedagogical and academic arguments for Catholic education and ties the mission of these schools to the ministry of Jesus, the salvific mission of the Church, and the common good of the community (Nuzzi, 2004a). The document is divided into seven sections: (1) the Catholic school and the salvific mission of the Church; (2) present difficulties over Catholic schools; (3) the school as a center of human formation; (4) The educational work of the Catholic school; (5) the responsibility of the Catholic school today; (6) practical directions; and (7) courageous and unified commitment. Each section is broken down into numbered paragraphs, totaling 97 in all.

The Religious Dimension of Education in a Catholic School (1988)

The Religious Dimension of Education in a Catholic School discusses the particular religious aspect or element of Catholic school culture (Nuzzi, 2004b). The document is divided into five sections, in addition to the introduction and the conclusion: (1) the religious dimension in the lives of today's youth; (2) the religious dimension of the school climate; (3) the religious dimension of school life and work; (4) religious instruction in the classroom and the religious dimension of formation; and (5) a general summary: the religious dimension of the formation process as a whole. These sections are all divided into subsections and numbered paragraphs, totaling 115 in all.

The Religious Dimension of Education in a Catholic School is another curial document written by a dicastery. This document marks only the third time the Congregation for Catholic Education released official material that exclusively focuses on K–12 Catholic schools. This document is also unique in that, while recognizing that there are many other types of primary and secondary education programs, it restricts its attention solely to Catholic schools. Its purpose is to highlight the function and the characteristics of the overall religious environment of Catholic schools (Nuzzi, 2004b).

(continued)

Table 32.2 (Continued)

Code of Canon Law (New English Translation, 1983)

The Code of Canon Law is the official law of the Church. As such, its precepts carry great weight within the universal Church.

Canon Law covers a great many areas within the Church. Title III of Book III (Canons 793-821) is entitled "Catholic Education." Most applicable to Catholic education are Canons 793–806. Canons 793–795 are concerned with some of the general precepts of Catholic education, and Canons 796-806 are directly concerned with Catholic schools. The remaining sections of the Catholic Education chapter focus on post-secondary education.

To Teach as Jesus Did (1972)

In addition to discussing Catholic schools, *To Teach as Jesus Did* articulates a broad view of education that includes education in all realms, such as adult education and education in family life (Nuzzi, 2004c). A section entitled "Catholic School" is broken down into four subsections: (1) Doctrine, community, service; (2) The crisis of Catholic schools; (3) Action needed now; and (4) Catholic schools called to reorganization. Like many of the Vatican documents, each of the subsections of *To Teach as Jesus Did* is divided into numbered paragraphs; the paragraphs concerned with Catholic schools are §101–126, 26 paragraphs in all.

To Teach as Jesus Did is a pastoral message authored by a national bishops' conference. While it does not officially carry as great a weight as a document released from the Vatican, it does give clarification and guidance for a particular national context. This document is the strongest statement in support of Catholic education released by the USCCB. It was the result of an extensive consultation process undertaken after Vatican II requested in *Gravissimum Educationis* that national bishops' conferences issue official statements pertaining to Catholic education (Nuzzi, 2004c).

Renewing Our Commitment to Catholic Elementary and Secondary Schools in the Third Millennium (2005)

In this document the bishops both reaffirmed their support of Catholic schools and revisited many of the issues discussed in "In Support of Catholic Elementary and Secondary Schools." In addition to the introduction and conclusion, the document has four main sections: (1) Why we value our Catholic elementary and secondary schools; (2) Catholic schools today; (3) The challenges of the future; and (4) Future action. The second section is further divided into two subsections—Overview Since 1990 and The Good News. The third section is also broken down into subsections: (1) The Face of our Church; (2) Personnel; (3) Finances; and (4) Advocacy.

Renewing Our Commitment can be viewed as a continuation of the USCCB's 1990 document "In Support of Catholic Elementary and Secondary Schools." The bishops noted that, while much of what was discussed in the 1990 document has been addressed, there was still much to be done in the field of Catholic education. "Renewing Our Commitment" offers both an update to and a continuation of the messages presented in 1990.

freedom to select the best educational opportunity for their child. Moreover, such freedom implies that parents should be able to select a school regardless of whether it is public or private, religious or secular, geographically close or distant. As Garnett (2010) highlighted:

> In our traditions and under our Constitution, it is not the case that education and its aims are exclusively the province and concern of the state. Private and religious schools are not

anomalies and outlaws, grudgingly tolerated; instead, they reflect our foundational commitments to freedom, pluralism, and limited government. Parental control and choice in education is, and should be framed as, the normative baseline, not the exception or novelty.

Garnett 2010, 94

In actual practice, school choice enables parents to select from a continuum of educational options, including intra- and inter-district transfer programs, homeschooling, magnet schools, charter schools, and faith-based schools.

School choice was thoroughly vetted at the federal level in the *Zelman v. Simmons-Harris* case (2002), which examined the constitutionality of a school voucher program in Cleveland, Ohio. Komer and Neily explained that "Rejecting a challenge under the Establishment Clause of the U.S. Constitution, the Court held that publicly funded K–12 voucher programs may include both religious and non-religious options, just as college aid programs like Pell Grants and the GI Bill have always done" (2007, 3). The justices' majority opinion centered on two important points. First, the voucher program exhibited religious neutrality, offering assistance directly to parents regardless of their religion and for use in an array of educational options, again without regard to religion (Friedman Foundation for Educational Choice 2010b; Komer and Neily 2007). Second, Cleveland's voucher program featured private choice, directing aid to parents, who then exert personal choice of school. In that way, parents may "... direct government aid to religious schools wholly as a result of their own genuine and independent private choice" (*Zelman v. Simmons-Harris* [00-1751] 536 U.S. 639 [2002]).

A Catholic perspective on parental choice of schools. From a Catholic perspective, as noted previously, numerous Church documents have long been especially clear about parents' right and duty to select the best educational option for their children: "Parents . . . must enjoy true liberty in their choice of schools" (*Gravissimum Educationis* 1965, §6). In fact, "from the earliest Church document on education, Pope Leo XIII highlighted the right of parents to choose Catholic schooling for their offspring, demonstrating the relevance of this issue from the infancy of Catholic education" (Frabutt and Rocha 2009, 16). Church documents underscore the responsibility of the state not to abrogate parental rights, such as when "a compulsory system of education is imposed by the State from which all religious formation is excluded" (Pontifical Council for the Family 1983, §5).

Major Parental-Choice Mechanisms Relevant to Catholic Education

School vouchers and program exemplars. School vouchers are one school-choice mechanism that directly impact Catholic schools. Through school vouchers, parents use portions of public tax funding[2] set aside for education to send their children to the school of their choice. The Alliance for School Choice noted that "in voucher programs, education dollars 'follow the child,' and parents select private schools and receive state-funded scholarships to pay tuition" (2010, 7). Currently, school voucher programs are constitutional in 34 states and are operative via nine programs (Friedman Foundation for Educational Choice 2010b; Komer and Neily 2007). Several types of voucher programs currently populate the U.S. school-choice landscape, and three of the most common are means-tested voucher programs, school/student failure programs, and special-needs programs.

---

[2]Most typically, but private funds of corporations or foundations can be used as well.

Children and families with income levels below a predetermined threshold, referenced to be at or around 185 percent of the federal poverty guideline, are eligible for means-tested voucher programs (Alliance for School Choice 2010, 24). Enacted in 1990, the Milwaukee Parental School Choice Program (MPSC) is the oldest and most prominent school voucher program for low-income families (Robinson, 2005; White House Domestic Policy Council, 2008). Kafer explained that

> after the program grew to include religious schools, the teachers union and other interest groups filed a lawsuit contending that the program violated both the First Amendment and the Wisconsin constitution. The Wisconsin Supreme Court, however, upheld the voucher program in 1998. (2009, 5)

Eligibility for MPSC extends to students living in the Milwaukee Public School District with a family income below 175 percent of the federal poverty guideline, which for 2010–2011 is set at $39,630 for a family of four (Wisconsin Department of Public Instruction [WDPI] 2010a). MPSC currently operates at 111 schools and has a total enrollment of 20,956 students (WDPI 2010b). Other examples of means-tested voucher programs include Louisiana's Student Scholarships for Educational Excellence Program and Ohio's Cleveland Scholarship and Tutoring Program (CSTP). Begun in 1996–97, the Cleveland Scholarship and Tutoring Program (CSTP) was the first in the nation to provide a publicly funded voucher for use in religious schools.

A second set of voucher programs—failing schools, failing students voucher programs—are expressly designed to provide school-choice options to parents whose children attend poorly achieving public schools (Alliance for School Choice 2010, 24). One example is Ohio's Educational Choice Scholarship (EdChoice) Program, enacted in 2005. Eligibility extends to "students from schools that have been in Academic Watch or Academic Emergency—the lowest categories on the state's school rating system—for two of the last three school years" (Ohio Department of Education 2010, 1). Families of these students, or students who would enter kindergarten at a low performing school, can use a scholarship to attend the participating private school of their choice. There is a current cap of 14,000 EdChoice Scholarships, each awarding $4,250 to elementary level students and $5,000 to high school students (Ohio Department of Education 2010, 2).

Special-needs voucher programs compose a third category, and via these programs, parents of children with special educational needs direct public funding to the school of their choice. Typically, children with an Individualized Education Program (IEP) meet the eligibility qualifications for special-needs voucher programs. Programs of this type operate in Ohio, Florida, Utah, Georgia, Oklahoma, and Louisiana. In Florida, for example, the John M. McKay Scholarship for Students with Disabilities Program is open to students with disabilities who have an Individualized Education Plan. These families have the opportunity to transfer to another public school or attend one of 926 participating private schools. For the 2009–10 academic year, $138.7 million was disbursed to 20,926 students, for an average scholarship payment of $7,144 (Florida Department of Education 2010, 1).

Scholarship tax credits and program exemplars. Of the 18 current school choice programs in operation across the United States, half of them are scholarship tax credit programs available in seven states, making such programs the other primary vehicle for parental choice of schools (Alliance for School Choice 2010, 19). These programs " . . . have received less press than vouchers but actually may have a better chance in many states"

(Kemerer 2009, 69). Tax credit scholarship programs are constitutional in 48states. Operationally, "Tax-credit-funded scholarship programs enable individuals or corporations to receive a tax credit for donating a portion of their state tax liability to private scholarship-granting organizations. Personal tax credits and deductions give parents a tax break for approved educational expenses" (Komer and Neily 2007, 3). Thus, individuals or corporations make donations to Scholarship Granting Organizations, which in turn direct scholarships to families exercising parental choice of schools. The Friedman Foundation for Educational Choice explained that

> in some states, students must meet certain income criteria to be eligible for scholarships. Scholarship Granting Organizations can be started by community groups, philanthropic organizations, or any other group that wants to extend school choice to children. Participating private schools are required to meet standards for safety, fiscal soundness, and non-discrimination. (2010a, 5)

For the 2009–10 school year, scholarship tax credit programs received total funding of just over $236 million, allowing 115,642 students to receive an average scholarship of $2,044 (Alliance for School Choice 2010, 17).

Arizona is a useful parental school choice context to consider as an exemplar, offering an individual school tuition organization tax credit and two types of corporate school tuition organization tax credits. First, enacted in 1997, is a personal scholarship tax credit that allows individual taxpayers to contribute to School Tuition Organizations (STOs; private, non-profit organizations) that support student scholarships (Arizona Department of Revenue 2010). Individuals receive a dollar-for-dollar credit of up to $500 and married couples filing jointly can claim up to $1,000. In 2006 a second tax credit, the Corporate School Tuition Organization Tax Credit, was enacted. This program provides a credit on corporate income taxes for corporations that donate to STOs. These scholarships, over 2,500 in 2009–10, are directed toward eligible families whose income does not exceed 185 percent of the federal poverty guideline (Alliance for School Choice 2010). Third, in 2009 the Arizona state legislature enacted an additional corporate tax credit scholarship serving special education students in public schools and students in foster care. Known informally as Lexie's Law, the scholarship program has a statewide cap of $5 million, and in 2009 it disbursed approximately $2.8 million in scholarships to 472 students (Alliance for School Choice 2010).

A More Prominent National Discourse, with Policy Implications

Given the various types of school choice mechanisms just reviewed, and their growing entrenchment across the country, developments in the school-choice arena are at or near the center of any dialogue about public policy and Catholic education in the United States. National thought leaders, academics, educational practitioners, and policy stakeholders continue to discuss school choice, including how and to what extent it impacts Catholic education. Consider three examples. A comprehensive, multidimensional academic treatment of school choice emerged in 2009's *Handbook of Research on School Choice* (Berends, Springer, Ballou, and Walberg). In addition to elucidating the empirical basis of various school choice experiments, the text provides the political (Hill and Jochim 2009), legal (Kemerer 2009), and social (Berends and Zottola 2009) groundings of the school choice debate. At the federal level, in 2008, the White House Domestic

Policy Council moderated a Summit on Inner-City Children and Faith-Based Schools. The subsequent report, "Preserving a Critical National Asset: America's Disadvantaged Students and the Crisis in Faith-based Urban Schools," trumpeted the role of vouchers as a public policy strategy to assist faith-based schools:

> Scholarships have long been a strategy of school reformers to expand the options and improve the academic performance of low-income students stranded in chronically low-performing public schools. A significant body of research testifies to the positive results of scholarship programs in areas such as graduation rates, competitive effects on public schools, parental satisfaction, and more. But scholarships also have the important subsidiary benefit of creating a sustainable stream of income for financially struggling schools.
>
> White House Domestic Policy Council 2008, 36

The report likewise extolled the value of tax credits, noting in reference to Pennsylvania's Educational Improvement Tax Credit (EITC) program that

> The positive impact on faith-based urban schools is striking. For example, despite the loss of population in Western Pennsylvania and the trend of enrollment declines in most faith-based urban schools, all 12 Catholic high schools in the Diocese of Pittsburgh have increased enrollments each year the EITC has been in place.
>
> White House Domestic Policy Council 2008, 39

Finally, dialogue and debate emerging from several national platforms has reiterated the potentially transformative role of school-choice legislation and continued advocacy for stemming the declining enrollment of Catholic schools (Hamilton, 2008; Notre Dame Task Force 2007; Saroki and Levenick 2009). The unifying thread behind each of these speaks to an imagined future of Catholic schools in which increased parental choice of schools plays a heightened role.

STRATEGIES FOR THE FUTURE SUCCESS OF CATHOLIC SCHOOLS

Given the remarkable successes that Catholic schools have enjoyed in the U.S.—from the enculturation of immigrant communities in the 1900s to the academic achievement of African American and Latino students today—they have few powerful advocates. Internally, the Catholic Church does not appear focused on preserving or growing its market share in K–12 education. The United States Conference of Catholic Bishops has not identified Catholic schools as a priority (http://www.usccb.org/priorities), and while individual dioceses and bishops may have created strategic plans, no national, comprehensive program exists that unites Catholic educators and parents in a single vision for the future (Piderit and Morey 2008). In fact, many of the strategic planning documents operationalized in recent years detail what might more accurately be called a strategic downsizing, i.e., the closing, consolidation, and merging of parishes and schools to cut costs, better utilize personnel, and make best use of extant facilities.

Downsizing, even if it is right-sizing, is not a vision. Catholic school education at the K–12 level in the United States would benefit operationally and strategically by the formulation of a comprehensive vision for the future of Catholic schools, outlining goals and the steps needed in order to achieve those goals. Such a vision statement would serve a variety of important purposes. First, it would help galvanize stakeholders within the Catholic community around a set of common goals. Second, it would help clarify priorities for external support such as philanthropy and benefaction. Third, it would draw the attention of the broader civic community to the positive social contributions that Catholic schools make to the common good and to the general civic order. Finally, it would set the stage for policy modifications and new legislation, at the state and national levels, that would help not only preserve Catholic schools, but eventually strengthen their contribution to the educational landscape and to the academic, social, and moral development of the next generation.

Short Term and Immediate Strategies for Success

The steady decline in both the numbers of Catholic schools and the number of students in Catholic schools in the period 1965–2010 merits serious attention and action (White House Domestic Policy Council 2008, 5–7). Moreover, the unbroken decline in the period 2002–2010 indicates that absent some new and creative interventions, the downward spiral will soon result in the existence of significantly fewer Catholic schools, and these will share a certain bimodality (Hallinan 2000, 201–220).

Specifically, the surviving Catholic schools will more than likely fall into one of two categories: schools serving a wealthier population, middle-upper class and above, who can afford the full cost of tuition as an out-of-pocket expense; and, schools serving the economically disadvantaged, mostly in an urban setting, with a governance and funding structure that allows for formidable external support. Schools in the middle—the neighborhood or parish school where children from different socioeconomic groups and ethnic and racial backgrounds might mix—will continue to close.

Four related but diverse strategies, if acted upon with haste, have the ability to temper this decline. While not offering a panacea for all that ails Catholic education, these four efforts, when taken together, address the immediate, short-term challenges facing Catholic schools in a way that offers some hope and promise for future, long-term viability. The four needed strategies are (1) aggressive advocacy for public policy changes in every state; (2) more successful accessing of federal Title funds that are already available; (3) benefaction for scholarship funds to serve as a bridge until new public policy is enacted; and (4) targeted recruitment of under-served racial and ethnic minorities for enrollment in Catholic schools, especially school-age Latinos and African Americans.

As noted previously, this is the age of parental choice in education. Every year, more and more districts and states adopt policies that fund a parent's choice, from tax credits and vouchers, to scholarships and lotteries (Alliance for School Choice 2010). While the total number of students attending private schools remains small compared to the overall number of students in public schools, nationwide support grows for parental choice, and the Catholic Church has long understood the role of the parent as primary in the education of their children. From a policy perspective, however, the Church has done little to advocate for legislation that would protect a parent's autonomy. Coupled with the relative monopoly enjoyed by public school education, this lack of concerted engagement in the arena of educational policy has left thousands of parents with no good choice for the education of their children and no access to any other type of schooling save the one endorsed and sponsored by the government. Support for the primacy of parental choice in education has taken on many forms, mostly varying legal strategies to allow for public funds to follow the child based upon the selection of school by the parent. The most common legislative vehicles in recent years have been tax credit programs for individuals and corporations and voucher plans (Florida Legislative 2008; Gottlob 2008). Whatever the legally permissible and constitutionally viable process, the nature and structure of these approaches have funded parental choice and created new options for children in low-performing schools.

Since this public policy angle is thoroughly consistent with official Catholic Church teaching, it presents no major obstacles to implementation other than the will to be focused and the determination to be engaged. In fact, in several states that have seen recent success in this arena, the deciding factor has been the public engagement of the Catholic Church. These efforts must continue and increase, and reach a national audience. While similar grass roots organizing may need to occur in all 50 states, such state level legislative debates often follow a similar pattern. As the Catholic Church is organizationally present in every state and operates schools in every state, the fundamental infrastructure needed to advance such policy changes is arguably already in place.

As previously noted, federal legislation already includes significant funds for private education in the form of Title funds, mostly pass-through funds distributed to states and then on to local school districts, who distribute them to private schools according to the guidelines given in law. Title funds are federal and are targeted by law to specific needs such as special education, professional development, teacher education, and free and reduced-cost school lunches. Private schools, including Catholic schools, have to make a documented case to receive such funds, and they must apply for them well in advance of actual need through the local school district in which they reside. For a variety of reasons, Catholic educational leaders have been sadly unsuccessful in accessing their fair and legally guaranteed share of these federal funds.

In a recent study of a large Catholic school system in the United States it was found that millions of dollars in Title funds that were available to Catholic educational leaders had not been accessed by them (Stephen Perla, Senior Director, ACE Consulting, unpublished data). Anticipating the 2011 reauthorization of some form of the No Child Left Behind Act, Catholic school administrators and indeed all private school administrators must strive for a just and proportionate share of Title funds, reasonably based on the numbers of students served. In 2010–2011, approximately 11 percent of school age children in the United States were educated in private schools (www.capenet.org). Were private school leaders successful in accessing a full 11 percent of federally appropriated Title funds, the acquired goods and services would be approximately $1 billion. Most recent estimates of current levels of access from private schools nationwide places the current number near $200 million (Stephen Perla, unpublished data). Securing these dollars and the support services they represent does not entail new legislation or time-consuming lawsuits. These funds are already available and indeed already distributed to local districts. What is needed is resolve and the human resources dedicated to securing them in a manner that meets the standard of law.

Because such public policy changes take time and the public school bureaucracy works slowly, it would be wise not to anticipate quick and immediate improvements in these first two arenas. While concerted action is needed for long-term viability, such large scale social changes develop over time, take root in a few key or targeted states, and spread nationwide as success becomes easier to demonstrate. For this reason, the third strategy of focused benefaction and philanthropy is essential in order to generate sufficient scholarship funds for families and children in need. Such funds would serve as a bridge mechanism, providing a temporary means of access to a high-quality education for those who might not otherwise be able to afford the cost of a private education. An additional benefit of these scholarships, if brought to scale, would be the stabilization of enrollments in the private sector and, concomitantly, higher faculty and student retention. This stabilization would be an important precursor to success in the public policy arena because parental-choice legislative mechanisms will not look appealing or politically viable in an ever-downsizing private school sector. In fact, scholarship opportunities, when freely offered and accessed, can be understood as a way to implement parental choice, albeit privately funded, and as a way to demonstrate the desirability of publicly funding parental choice in education.

An example of benefaction brought to scale for scholarships is the Children's Scholarship Fund (CSF). The CSF, which is not a Catholic or faith-based organization, has given away more than $400 million dollars in privately funded scholarships to 111,000 children in grades K–8 nationwide since 1999 (http://www.scholarshipfund.org/drupal1/). Every year, the CSF, in collaboration with many other philanthropic partners, raises $43 million to provide scholarships for 29,000 students. Since more than 80 percent of CSF parents choose Catholic schools for their children—largely in the inner cities—it is safe to say CSF has put $320 million into the Catholic schools serving the urban poor and in many cases a largely non-Catholic population. The success of an organization like the CSF is a strong testimony to the importance of scholarship funds, the manifest choices of parents for the education of their children, the need for funding parental choice more broadly, and the grassroots support that such programs enjoy. Benefaction, however, must be understood as a temporary sustaining mechanism while new legislation and public policy changes are undertaken. Private benefaction as a long-term solution to funding parental choice would gradually produce donor fatigue.

A fourth and final strategy is directed to the targeted recruitment of minority populations that have been historically well served by Catholic schools. Recent research has demonstrated that Catholic schools in the urban core do a remarkable job of educating minority students, especially African American and Latino students (Jeynes 2007; Neal 1997; York 1996). This documented success should be the first step in attracting more students from minority groups to enroll in Catholic schools using one or more of the strategies discussed above. Moreover, with success on the public policy front, students from racial and ethnic minorities stand to benefit from enrolling in Catholic and private schools and would likely do so in significant numbers.

The success of Catholic schools at closing the proverbial achievement gap is an attractive and compelling phenomenon. However, it is not the only reason that Catholic schools would be considered by parents from under-represented minority groups. In the case of Latino immigrants, the attraction runs deeper because most of these families are traditionally and culturally Catholic. While the number of Latinos in the United States has skyrocketed in recent years, the number of Latinos in Catholic schools has remained stagnant since 1995. Catholic leaders have recognized this serious under-representation of Latinos in Catholic schools and have begun a nationwide effort to address the situation within the next 10 years (Notre Dame Task Force on the Participation of Latino Children and Families in Catholic Schools 2009). While a parallel strategy to recruit African American students has yet to materialize, recent studies have chronicled the extraordinary success of African American students in inner-city Catholic schools (McCloskey 2008; Mincy 2006).

CONCLUSION

Catholic schools have been a vital part of the American educational landscape for several centuries. They have enjoyed extraordinary success as instruments of enculturation, faith transmission, and academic attainments. Their success has been well documented in ongoing research that has consistently demonstrated that Catholic schools produce engaged citizens and animated Catholics. Catholic schools have thus proven themselves to be a wise investment both for the Catholic Church and the republic.

Notwithstanding such success, K–12 Catholic schools have experienced significant and steady decline through the past several decades, related to multiple internal and external realities, that has resulted in major shifts in staffing, governance, finances, and Catholic identity. The social context of education and schooling has changed radically and the place of the Catholic Church within the overall American experience continues to undergo serious challenges. Fiscal problems dominate the discourse in Catholic education today, threatening the mission by increasingly limiting accessibility to those who can pay their own way. The nationwide downsizing of Catholic education continues unabated.

In order to preserve, strengthen, and expand this great national and ecclesial asset, broad inter-religious and ecumenical collaboration is needed among all participants in the private school sector. Catholic parents, leaders, and educators need to partner with colleagues in other faith traditions who operate schools and begin concerted lobbying and advocacy efforts to make parental choice the law of the land. The Catholic voice is largely unheard in this debate and that is regrettable. As the single largest player in the private school sector, Catholics ought to be leading the way to reform. State and federal educational policies, Blaine Amendments, voucher programs, tax credits—these are all issues that should occupy Catholic and private school leaders' attention.

The Catholic school system in the United States was born and prospered largely as the result of great sacrifice by those who were highly committed to its mission. No less a sacrifice is called for today by those who are similarly committed to educating the next generation in a tradition that is decidedly Catholic and American. It is difficult to envision an America or a Catholic Church without Catholic schools.

REFERENCES AND FURTHER READING

Alliance for School Choice. *Fighting for Opportunity: School Choice Yearbook 2009–10*. Washington, DC: Author, 2010.

Aquinas, Thomas. *Basic Writings of Saint Thomas Aquinas*. Edited by Anton C. Pegis. New York: Random House, 1945.

Arizona Department of Revenue. "School Tax Credits, Publication 707." http://www.azdor.gov/ LinkClick.aspx?fileticket=lyMlhtowOpw%3d&tabid=114 (accessed December 10, 2010).

Baker, David P., and Cornelius Riordan. "The 'Eliting' of the Common American Catholic School and the National Education Crisis." *Phi Delta Kappan* 80 (1998): 16–23.

Berends, Mark, and Genevieve C. Zottola. "Social Perspectives on School Choice." In *Handbook of Research on School Choice*, edited by Mark Berends, Matthew G. Springer, Dale Ballou, and Herbert J. Walberg, 35–53. New York: Routledge, 2009.

Berends, Mark, Matthew G. Springer, Dale Ballou, and Herbert J. Walberg, eds. *Handbook of Research on School Choice*. New York: Routledge, 2009.

Bredeweg, Frank. *United States Catholic Elementary and Secondary Schools 1981–1982*. Washington, DC: National Catholic Educational Association, 1982.

Bredeweg, Frank. *United States Catholic Elementary and Secondary Schools 1984–1985*. Washington, DC: National Catholic Educational Association, 1985.

Brigham, Frederick H. *United States Catholic Elementary and Secondary Schools 1988–1989. A Statistical Report on School, Enrollment, and Staffing*. Washington, DC: National Catholic Educational Association, 1989.

Brown, William E., and Andrew M. Greeley. *Can Catholic Schools Survive?* New York: Sheed and Ward, 1970.

Bryk, Anthony S., Peter B. Holland, Valerie E. Lee, and Rueben A. Carriedo. *Effective Catholic Schools: An Exploration.* Washington, DC: National Catholic Educational Association, 1984.

Bryk, Anthony S., Valerie E. Lee, and Peter B. Holland. *Catholic Schools and the Common Good.* Cambridge, MA: Harvard University Press, 1993.

Buetow, Harold A. *A History of United States Catholic Schooling.* Washington, DC: National Catholic Educational Association, 1985.

Buetow, Harold A. *Of Singular Benefit: The Story of Catholic Education in the United States.* New York: Macmillan, 1970.

Buetow, Harold A. *The Catholic School: Its Roots, Identity, & Future.* New York: Crossroad, 1988.

Carbonaro, William, and Elizabeth Covay. "School Sector and Student Achievement in the Era of Standards Based Reforms." *Sociology of Education* 83 (2010): 160–82.

Center for Applied Research in the Apostolate. *Special Report: Parish Life Today.* Washington, DC: Author, 2009.

Coleman, James S., and Thomas Hoffer. *Public and Private Schools: The Impact of Community.* New York: Basic Books, 1987.

Coleman, James S., Thomas Hoffer, and Sally Kilgore. *High School Achievement: Public, Catholic, and Private Schools Compared.* New York: Basic Books, 1982.

Congregation for Catholic Education. *Consecrated Persons and Their Mission in Schools.* London: Catholic Truth Society, 2002.

Congregation for Catholic Education. *Educating Together in Catholic Schools: A Shared Mission Between Consecrated Persons and the Lay Faithful.* Strathfield, NSW, Australia: St. Paul's, 2007.

Congregation for Catholic Education. *The Catholic School on the Threshold of the Third Millennium.* Boston: Pauline Books and Media, 1998.

Convey, John J. *Catholic Schools Make a Difference: Twenty-Five Years of Research.* Washington, DC: National Catholic Educational Association, 1992.

Cook, Timothy. "Teachers." In *Catholic Schools Still Make a Difference: Ten Years of Research 1991–2000,* edited by Thomas C. Hunt, Ellis A. Joseph, and Ronald J. Nuzzi, 57–72. Washington, DC: National Catholic Educational Association, 2002.

Dolan, Jay P. *In Search of an American Catholicism: A History of Religion and Culture in Tension.* New York: Oxford University Press, 2002.

Florida Department of Education. "McKay Scholarship Program, July 2010." http://www.florida schoolchoice.org/Information/McKay/files/Fast_Facts_McKay.pdf (accessed December 10, 2010).

Florida Legislature, Office of Program Policy Analysis & Government Accountability. "The Corporate Income Tax Credit Scholarship Program Saves State Tax Dollars, Report No. 08-68." http://www.oppaga.state.fl.us/reports/pdf/0868rpt.pdf (2008, accessed December 10, 2010).

Frabutt, James M., Anthony C. Holter, and Ronald J. Nuzzi. *No Greater Work: Meditations on Church Documents for Educators.* Notre Dame, IN: Alliance for Catholic Education Press, 2010.

Frabutt, James M., Anthony C. Holter, Ronald J. Nuzzi, Heidi Rocha, and Laura Cassel. "Pastors' Views of Parents and Their Role in Catholic Schools." *Catholic Education: A Journal of Inquiry and Practice* 14 (2010): 24–46.

Frabutt, James M., and Heidi Rocha. *Entrusted in Faith: Parents, Children, and Catholic Schools.* Notre Dame, IN: Alliance for Catholic Education Press, 2009.

Friedman Foundation for Educational Choice. *Is School Choice Constitutional?* Indianapolis, IN: Author, 2010b.

Friedman Foundation for Educational Choice. *The ABCs of School Choice, 2009–10 Edition.* Indianapolis, IN: Author, 2010a.

Gabert, Glen. *In Hoc Signo: A Brief History of Catholic Parochial Education in America.* Port Washington, NY: Kennikat Press, 1973.

Garnett, Richard W. "School Choice and the Challenges That Remain: A Comment on Richard D. Komer's 'School Choice and State Constitutions' Religion Clauses.'" *Journal of School Choice* 4 (2010): 93–99.

Gautier, Mary L., Anna C. Buck, and Melissa A. Cidade. *Dollars and Sense: Catholic schools and Their Finances 2008–2009*. Washington, DC: National Catholic Educational Association, 2009.

Gottlob, Brian. *The Fiscal Impact of Tax-Credit Scholarships in Georgia*. The Friedman Foundation for Educational Choice, 2008.

Grace, Gerald. *Catholic Schools: Mission, Markets, and Morality*. London: RoutledgeFalmer, 2002.

Greeley, Andrew M. *Catholic High Schools and Minority Students*. New Brunswick, NJ: Transaction Books, 1982.

Greeley, Andrew M. "More Assertions not Backed by Data." *Phi Delta Kappan* 80 (1999): 463.

Greeley, Andrew M. *The Church and the Suburbs*. New York: Paulist Press, 1963.

Greeley, Andrew M. "The So-Called Failure of Catholic Schools." *Phi Delta Kappan* 80 (1998): 24–25.

Greeley, Andrew M., William C. McCready, and Kathleen McCourt. *Catholic Schools in a Declining Church*. Kansas City, KS: Sheed and Ward, 1976.

Greeley, Andrew M., and Peter B. Rossi. *The Education of Catholic Americans*. Chicago: Aldine Publishing Company, 1966.

Hallinan, Maureen T. "Conclusion: Catholic Education at the Crossroads." In *Catholic Schools at the Crossroads: Survival and Transformation*, edited by James Youniss and John J. Convey, 201–20. New York: Teachers College Press, 2000.

Hamilton, Scott, ed. *Who Will Save America's Urban Catholic Schools?* Washington, DC: Thomas B. Fordham Institute, 2008.

Haney, Regina, Stephen O'Brien, and Lourdes Sheehan. *A Primer on Educational Governance in the Catholic Church*. Washington, DC: National Catholic Educational Association, 2009.

Harris, Joseph, C. "The Funding Dilemma Facing Catholic Elementary and Secondary Schools." In *Catholic Schools at the Crossroads: Survival and Transformation*, edited by James Youniss and John J. Convey, 55–71. New York: Teachers College Press, 2000.

Hill, Paul. T., and Ashley E. Jochim. "Political Perspectives on School Choice." In *Handbook of Research on School Choice*, edited by Mark Berends, Matthew G. Springer, Dale Ballou, and Herbert J. Walberg, 3–17. New York: Routledge, 2009.

Hoffer, Thomas B. "Catholic School Attendance and Student Achievement: A Review and Extension of Research." In *Catholic Schools at the Crossroads: Survival and Transformation*, edited by James Youniss and John J. Convey, 87–116. New York: Teachers College Press, 2000.

Hoffer, Thomas B., Andrew M. Greeley, and James S. Coleman. "Achievement Growth in Public and Catholic High Schools." *Sociology of Education* 58 (1985): 74–97.

Hunt, Thomas C., James M. Frabutt, Anthony C. Holter, and Ronald J. Nuzzi. "What You Need to Know: Advances in Catholic Educational Research." Paper presented at the annual meeting of the National Catholic Educational Association, Minneapolis, Minnesota, April 6–8, 2010.

James, John T. "Changes in Funding and Governance of Catholic Elementary Education in the United States." *British Journal of Religious Education* 29 (2005): 287–301.

James, John T., Karen L. Tichy, Alan Collins, and John Schwob. "Developing a Predictive Metric to Assess School Viability." *Catholic Education: A Journal of Inquiry & Practice* 11 (2008): 465–84.

Jeynes, William H. "Religion, Intact Families, and the Achievement Gap." *Interdisciplinary Journal of Research on Religion* 3 (2007): 1–24.

John Paul II. *Fides et Ratio* [On the Relationship Between Faith and Reason]. Washington, DC: United States Catholic Conference, 1998.

John Paul II. *Veritatis Splendor* [The Splendor of Truth]. Boston: St. Paul Books and Media, 1993.

Joseph, Ellis A. "The Philosophy of Catholic Education." In *Handbook of Research on Catholic Education*, edited by Thomas C. Hunt, Ellis A. Joseph, and Ronald J. Nuzzi, 27–64. Westport, CT: Greenwood Press, 2001.

Kafer, Krista. *A Chronology of School Choice in the U.S.* Golden, CO: Independence Institute, 2009.

Keith, Timothy Z., and Ellis B. Page. "Do Catholic High Schools Improve Minority Student Achievement?" *American Educational Research Journal* 22 (1985): 337–49.

Kemerer, Frank R. "A Legal Perspective on School Choice." In *Handbook of Research on School Choice*, edited by Mark Berends, Matthew G. Springer, Dale Ballou, and Herbert J. Walberg, 55–77. New York: Routledge, 2009.

Komer, Richard D., and Clark Neily. *School Choice and State Constitutions: A Guide to Designing School Choice Programs*. Arlington, VA: American Legislative Exchange Council and The Institute for Justice, 2007.

Koob, Albert C., and Russell Shaw. *S.O.S. for Catholic Schools: A Strategy for Future Service to Church and Nation*. New York: Holt, Rinehart, and Winston, 1970.

Leo XIII. "Spectata Fides" [On Christian Education]. http://vatican.va/holy_father/leo_xiii/encyclicals/documents (1885, accessed December 10, 2010).

Manno, Bruno V., and Heather Graham. "Research on Catholic School Effectiveness." In *Handbook of Research on Catholic Education*, edited by Thomas C. Hunt, Ellis A. Joseph, and Ronald J. Nuzzi, 281–97. Greenwich, CT: Information Age Publishing, 2001.

Maritain, Jacques. *Education at the Crossroads*. New Haven, CT: Yale University Press, 1943.

Massucci, Joseph D. "Declaration on Christian Education, The." In *Catholic Schools in the United States: An Encyclopedia*, Vol. 1, edited by Thomas C. Hunt, Ellis A. Joseph, and Ronald J. Nuzzi, 211–13. Westport, CT: Greenwood Press, 2004.

Miller, J. Michael. *The Holy See's Teaching on Catholic Schools*. Atlanta, GA: Solidarity Association, 2006.

McCloskey, Patrick J. *The Street Stops Here: A Year at a Catholic High School in Harlem*. Los Angeles: University of California Press, 2008.

McDonald, Dale, and Margaret M. Schultz. *The Annual Statistical Report on Schools, Enrollment and Staffing: United States Catholic Elementary and Secondary Schools 2009–2010*. Arlington, VA: National Catholic Educational Association, 2010.

McGreevy, John T. *Parish Boundaries: The Catholic Encounter With Race in the Twentieth-Century Urban North*. Chicago: University of Chicago Press, 1996.

McLellan, Jeffrey A. "Rise, Fall, and Reasons Why: U.S. Catholic Elementary Education, 1940–1995." In *Catholic Schools at the Crossroads: Survival and Transformation*, edited by James Youniss and John J. Convey, 13–31. New York: Teachers College Press, 2000.

Mincy, Ronald B. *Black Males Left Behind*. Washington, DC: Urban Institute Press, 2006.

National Conference of Catholic Bishops. *To Teach as Jesus Did*. Washington, DC: United States Catholic Conference, 1972.

National Commission on Excellence in Education. *A Nation at Risk: The Imperative for Educational Reform*. Washington, DC: United States Department of Education, 1983.

National Center for Education Statistics. *Private School Universe Survey (PSS) 1989–90 Through 2005–2006*. Washington, DC: U.S. Department of Education, 2008.

Neal, Derek. "The Effects of Catholic Secondary Schooling on Educational Achievement." *Journal of Labor Economics* 15 (1997): 98–123.

Neuwien, Reginald A., ed. *Catholic Schools in Action*. Notre Dame, IN: University of Notre Dame Press, 1966.

Noell, J. "Public and Catholic Schools: A Reanalysis of 'Public and Private Schools.' " *Sociology of Education* 62 (1982): 123–32.

Notre Dame Task Force on Catholic Education. *Making God Known, Loved, and Served: The Future of Catholic Primary and Secondary Schools in the United States*. Notre Dame, IN: Alliance for Catholic Education, University of Notre Dame, 2007.

Notre Dame Task Force on the Participation of Latino Children and Families in Catholic Schools. *To Nurture the Soul of a Nation: Latino Families, Catholic Schools, and Educational Opportunity*. Notre Dame, IN: Alliance for Catholic Education Press, 2009.

Nuzzi, Ronald J. "Catholic Identity." In *Catholic Schools Still Make a Difference: Ten Years of Research 1991–2000*, edited by Thomas C. Hunt, Ellis A. Joseph, and Ronald J. Nuzzi, 9–20. Washington, DC: National Catholic Educational Association, 2002.

Nuzzi, Ronald J. "Catholic School, The." In *Catholic Schools in the United States: An Encyclopedia*, Vol. 1, edited by Thomas C. Hunt, Ellis A. Joseph, and Ronald J. Nuzzi, 113–14. Westport, CT: Greenwood Press, 2004a.

Nuzzi, Ronald J. "Religious Dimension of Education in a Catholic School, The." In *Catholic Schools in the United States: An Encyclopedia*, Vol. 2, edited by Thomas C. Hunt, Ellis A. Joseph, and Ronald J. Nuzzi, 552–54. Westport, CT: Greenwood Press, 2004b.

Nuzzi, Ronald J. "To Teach as Jesus Did." In *Catholic Schools in the United States: An Encyclopedia*, Vol. 2, edited by Thomas C. Hunt, Ellis A. Joseph, and Ronald J. Nuzzi, 663–65. Westport, CT: Greenwood Press, 2004c.

Nuzzi, Ronald J., James M. Frabutt, and Anthony C. Holter. *Faith, Finances and the Future: The Notre Dame Study of U.S. Pastors*. Notre Dame, IN: Alliance for Catholic Education Press, 2008.

Ohio Department of Education. "Ohio EdChoice Scholarship Program Fact Sheet." http:// www.ode.state.oh.us/GD/Templates/Pages/ODE/ODEDetail.aspx?page=3&TopicRelationID=667 &ContentID=46154&Content=94301 (accessed December 10, 2010).

Pew Hispanic Center and Pew Forum on Religion and Public Life. *Changing Faiths: Latinos and the Transformation of American Religion*. Washington, DC: Pew Research Center, 2007.

Piderit, John J., and Melanie M. Morey. *Renewing Parish Culture: Building for a Catholic Future*. Lanham, MD: Sheed & Ward, 2008.

Pius XI. *Divini Ilius Magistri* [Christian Education of Youth]. Washington, DC: National Catholic Welfare Conference, 1929.

Pontifical Council for the Family. *Charter of the Rights of the Family*. Washington, DC: United States Catholic Conference, 1983.

Reardon, Sean F., Jacob E. Cheadle, and Joseph Robinson. "The Effect of Catholic Schooling on Math and Reading Development in Kindergarten Through Fifth Grade." *Journal of Research on Educational Effectiveness* 2 (2009): 45–87.

Robinson, Gerard. *Survey of School Choice Research*. Milwaukee, WI: Institute for the Transformation of Learning, Marquette University, 2005.

Ryan, Mary Perkins. *Are Parochial Schools the Answer?* New York: Holt, Rinehart, and Winston, 1964.

Sacred Congregation for Catholic Education. *Lay Catholics in Schools: Witnesses to Faith*. Boston: St. Paul Editions, 1982.

Sacred Congregation for Catholic Education. *The Catholic School*. Washington, DC: United States Catholic Conference, 1977.

Sacred Congregation for Catholic Education. *The Religious Dimension of Education in a Catholic School*. Washington, DC: United States Catholic Conference, 1988.

Saroki, Stephanie, and Christopher Levenick. *Saving America's Urban Catholic Schools: A Guide for Donors*. Washington, DC: The Philanthropy Roundtable, 2009.

Sixtus V. "Immensa" [On the Roman Curia]. In *Bullarium Romanum a Pio Quarto Usque ad Innocentium IX* [Papal bulls from Pius IV to Innocent IX], Vol. 11, 615–22. Rome: The Vatican, 1588.

Smith, Paige A. "The University Consortium on Catholic Education (UCCE): A Response to Sustain and Strengthen Catholic Education." *Catholic Education: A Journal of Inquiry & Practice* 10 (2007): 321–42.

Smith, Paige A, and Ronald J. Nuzzi. "Beyond Religious Congregations: Responding to New Challenges in Catholic Education." In *International Handbook on Catholic Education: Challenges for School Systems in the 21st Century*, edited by Gerald R. Grace and Joseph O'Keefe, 103–25. Dordrecht, The Netherlands: Springer, 2008.

United States Catholic Conference. *Teach Them!* Washington, DC: Author, 1976.

United States Conference of Catholic Bishops. *Renewing our Commitment to Catholic Education in the Third Millennium*. Washington, DC: Author, 2005.

Vatican Council II. *Gravissimum Educationis* [On Christian Education]. Washington, DC: National Catholic Welfare Conference, 1965.

Walch, Timothy. *Parish School: American Catholic Parochial Education from Colonial Times to Present*. Washington, DC: National Catholic Educational Association, 2003.

White House Domestic Policy Council, The. *Preserving a Critical National Asset: America's Disadvantaged Students and the Crisis in Faith-Based Urban Schools*. Washington, DC: U.S. Department of Education, 2008.

Wisconsin Department of Public Instruction. "MPSC Facts and Figures for 2009–2010." http:// www.dpi.state.wi.us/sms/choice.html (accessed December 10, 2010b).

Wisconsin Department of Public Instruction. "The Milwaukee Parental Choice Program: Information for Parents." http://www.dpi.state.wi.us/sms/pdf/mpcp_brochure_2010–11.pdf (accessed December 10, 2010a).

Wittberg, Patricia. *The Rise and Decline of Catholic Religious Orders: A Social Movement Perspective.* Albany: State University of New York Press, 1994.

York, Darlene E. "The Academic Achievement of African Americans in Catholic Schools: A Review of the Literature." In *Growing Up African American in Catholic Schools*, edited by J. J. Irvine and M. Foster, 11–46. New York: Teachers College Press, 1996.

33

Catholic Homeschooling

Amy S. McEntee

Catholic parents teaching their children in their own homes is not a new educational practice. The 1917 Code of Canon Law underscores the responsibility of parents to educate their children, stating, in the English translation, "Parents are bound by the most grave obligation to take care as far as they are able for the education of children, both religious and moral, as well as physical and civil, and of providing them with temporal goods" (Peters 2001, 383). Providing this education within the home was commonplace in the United States, regardless of religious tradition, prior to the establishment of common school systems in the nineteenth century (Carper and Hunt 2007, 239; Carper and Ray 2002, 228). The establishment of the common school and subsequent development of the Catholic parochial school system in the mid-nineteenth century made home education nearly nonexistent (Carper and Hunt 2009, 8; Ray 2001, 406).

MODERN HOMESCHOOLING MOVEMENT

The resurgence of Catholic homeschooling in the mid-1970s to early 1980s coincides with two separate, but influential, events: the larger homeschooling movement in the United States led predominantly by evangelical Protestants, and the decline of the Catholic school system.

Protestant Homeschooling Carves the Path

The public school system in the United States, at its inception, was highly reflective of the predominantly evangelical Protestant culture of the mid-nineteenth century. Carper and Hunt note, "Most Americans at the time believed that religion, Protestant Christianity in particular, should play a central role in education of the young" (2009, 4). They continue, " . . . most Protestants supported the common school movement of the mid-1800s . . . "(Carper and Hunt 2009, 4). The decline of evangelical Protestantism as the major religious influence in the late nineteenth and early twentieth century and the establishment of secular humanism found many evangelical Christians dissatisfied with public education (Carper 2000, 15–16). One response to the secularization of schools was a return to home-based education, beginning in the mid-1970s and exploding in the 1980s (Carper 2000, 15; Ray 2001, 406). It is important to note that the homeschool movement simultaneously garnered support in the late 1960s and early 1970s as a pedagogical movement through the work of education reformers such as John Holt (Stevens 2001, 35–38; Carper and Hunt 2009, 28). The number of homeschooled students grew from an estimated 12,500 in 1978 to approximately 93,000 in 1983 (Ray 2001, 405). The parents of these homeschooled students, predominantly evangelical Christians, advocated for public policy changes and the legal right to homeschool. In 1980, only three states specifically recognized homeschooling. Through the extensive advocacy of parents, homeschooling was legal in all states by the early 2000s (Carper and Hunt 2007, 245). If it were not for the early collaboration among the various religious traditions, it is not likely that the homeschooling movement would exist as it does today.

Private Catholic Schools and Homeschooling

At the same time that evangelical Christians were becoming dissatisfied with public education, the Catholic parochial school system was also experiencing decline. In the mid-1960s, Catholic schools in the United States were losing their sense of mission. In the time of uncertainty, it was Mary Perkins Ryan's book, *Are Parochial Schools the Answer? Catholic Education in the Light of the Council*, published in 1963 that seemed to "crystallize" the doubts. Noting that Catholic schools had done well to serve the Church population of the nineteenth century—predominantly poor immigrants—the Church could better serve the population by focusing its resources elsewhere, while parents take responsibility for religious education (Carper and Hunt 2009, 27). Enrollment in Catholic schools began declining in 1967–68 and continued to decline through the next several decades (Carper and Hunt 2009, 27–28).

The decline in Catholic school enrollment and subsequent increase in Catholic homeschooling is understood to be a response to the Second Vatican Council, though what kind of response is not clear. Some parents expressed concerns about the academic and doctrinal decay in Catholic schools, while some reacted to the changes that resulted from the Second Vatican Council. As a result, parent-run private Catholic schools were opened. Dr. Mary Kay Clark writes in her book *Catholic Home Schooling: A Handbook for Parents*, "By 1971, we in the Catholic Parents of Columbus organization felt our energies were being wasted in trying to change the schools and/or educators. So the organization changed its approach completely. We decided to form our own school, Mater Dei Academy in Columbus, Ohio" (Clark 1993, xxviii). Clark notes that several other parent-run schools were started in many cities across the United States in the same time frame, including Seton School, which was founded by Dr. Anne Carroll in Manassas, Virginia, in 1975 (Clark 1993, xxviii). Seton would eventually develop the most widely used Catholic home-study program in the country.

For other parents, homeschooling was a result of fully embracing their parental rights and duties, as reiterated by the council fathers. In the Declaration on Christian Education, it states, "Parents who have the primary and inalienable right and duty to educate their children must enjoy true liberty in their choice of schools" (*Gravissimum Educationis* 1965, §6). Further, the Pastoral Constitution on the Church in the Modern World, declares that "[p]arents should regard as their proper mission the task of transmitting human life and educating those to whom it has been transmitted" (*Gadium et Spes* 1965, §50). In a 2008 informal survey, Laurie Gill, editor of *Homefront* newsletter, commented, "By activating the laity and awakening us to our baptismal call, the Second Vatican Council paved the way for Catholic homeschooling" (Warren 2008, 25).

Initially, the number of Catholic families leaving the parochial school system in favor of homeschooling was not significant enough to gain the attention of the bishops. Eventually, as the number of Catholic homeschoolers increased, the bishops would take note, though, and the relationship of homeschoolers to the local bishop would become a point of contention as both parties wrestled with their roles and responsibilities in educating children.

CATHOLIC HOME-STUDY PROGRAMS

In 1977, William Bowman established Our Lady of Victory School, a non-profit organization based in Post Falls, Idaho, which was the first to offer complete Catholic home-study program. In 2011, Our Lady of Victory reported an enrollment of 1,500 students (Our Lady of Victory website http://www.olvs.org 2011, "About Us"). In 1980, Dr. Anne Carroll started Seton Home Study School, a branch of Seton Junior and Senior High School, in Manassas, Virginia. The home study program was created in response to the request from parents for correspondence courses. Dr. Mary Kay Clark became the director of Seton Home Study in 1985, leading the division as it moved to Front Royal, Virginia, and expanded its services, becoming one of the largest Catholic book publishers in the country. Seton is reported to be the most-used home-study program in the United States, with nearly 10,000 students (Seton Home Study School website 2011, "Our Story"). Our Lady of the Rosary School was founded in 1983 in Bardstown, Kentucky. Of the three earliest home-study programs, it is the only one to specifically claim to be organized as a response to the "heresy or half-truths being taught by Modernists" (sic) (Our Lady of the Rosary school website 2002, "History of OLR").

While not all Catholic homeschoolers use home-study programs, these programs played an important role in the early days of homeschooling. They provided parents with a course of study based on the traditional curriculum that was commonly found in Catholic schools prior to the 1960s, utilizing traditional Catholic textbooks. They provide what some parents feel is lacking in Catholic schools. A 1997 article in the *National Catholic Reporter* gives credence to this, quoting one Catholic homeschooling parent as saying, "Our main reason for homeschooling is that we want our children to be educated in their Catholic faith. This was not happening in the local Catholic school" (Marrin 1997, 3). In the same year, a study by the National Home Education Research Institute found that approximately 24 percent of all homeschooling families utilized complete curriculum packages, such as the home-study programs (Farris 1997, xxvi–xxvii). Throughout the 1990s and into the twenty-first century, complete Catholic curriculum programs would increase, as was the case in 1993 when Kolbe Academy in Napa, California, added a home-study component (Kolbe Academy website http://www.kolbe.org 2011, "Kolbe's History"). To further legitimize their efforts on behalf of Catholic homeschooling families, many of the home study programs have become accredited through various organizations.

DIOCESES TAKE NOTE

The early 1990s saw the publication of several books on Catholic homeschooling, which worked to further expand the movement. In 1993, *Catholic Home Schooling: A Handbook for Parents* by Mary Kay Clark, director of Seton Home Study program, was published. The following year, *Designing Your Own Classical Curriculum* by Laura Berquist was published by Bethlehem Books (subsequent editions were published by Ignatius Press). In 1996, Kimberly Hahn and Mary Hasson's book, *Catholic Education: Homeward Bound* was published by Ignatius Press. These books are understood to have helped promote homeschooling among Catholic families, increasing the overall number of Catholic homeschoolers. Writing in 2009, Brian Ray notes, "[M]ost studies show that since the mid-1990s roughly three-fourths of home-educating parents are clearly religious in the conventional sense, and the large majority of these are self-proclaimed Bible-believing Christians (e.g., evangelical, fundamentalist, or reformed Protestants) or, as a much smaller portion, Roman Catholics" (Ray 2009, 241). In the first half of the decade, the number of homeschooled children more than doubled, numbering more than one million in 1995 (Carper and Hunt 2007, 244–45).

The explosive growth in homeschooling finally captured the attention of Catholic educators on the national level in the early 1990s. With the number of Catholic homeschooled children being estimated at 70,000, the National Catholic Educational Association Department of Elementary Schools sent a 10-question survey to superintendents in 175 arch/dioceses to assess the extent and impact of Catholic homeschooling. The memorandum from Sr. Antoinette Dudek, OSF, who was then the assistant executive director for Early Childhood and Special Educational Services, summarizing the findings of the survey, which was published in the October 1995 issue of the *San Diego News Notes* (Holman 2000, "October 1995 articles"). The survey resulted in the 1996 study that confirmed that a "small and widely dispersed" number of parents were opting for home education (Marrin 1997, 3). At the time, Dr. Brian Ray of the National Home Education Research Institute estimated that Catholic homeschooling was growing at a rate of about 15 percent per year (Marrin 1997, 3). In 1997, as a result of the 1996 study, the Diocese of Pittsburgh published the document "Faith Education in the Home," which is believed to be the first set of diocesan guidelines for homeschooling (Marrin 1997, 3). The document, now in its second edition, sets out to establish the responsibilities of the Church and parents as co-educators in the faith, because "catechesis is the work of the whole Church" (Diocese of Pittsburgh 2006, 7). Other dioceses followed with their own guidelines for selecting religious education materials and preparing for reception of Sacraments.

CONTROVERSY ERUPTS

Having already done battle with state educational leaders regarding their right to homeschool, some parents felt the bishops and dioceses were now impeding their canonical right and obligation to educate their children. What ensued is a controversy that remains unclear to this day.

In the late 1980s and early 1990s, Catholic homeschooling families had begun to organize themselves into local, state, and national groups separate from the predominantly Protestant homeschooling groups. In 1989, the first national organization, Traditions of Roman Catholic Homes (TORCH), was formed (Warren 2008, 48). TORCH identifies itself as "an association of lay faithful established to promote homeschooling among Catholic families and to support those families who are engaged in providing their children's primary education at home" (TORCH website, undated, "About TORCH"). The National Association of Catholic Home Educators (NACHE) was formed in 1991 and maintained close ties to TORCH through the 1990s, with individuals often holding positions on both organizations' boards of directors (Warren 2008, 48). As advocates for homeschooling families, the organizations sought to build positive relationships between the families and Church leadership, where "our expression of faith through homeschooling enriches the Church and at the same time we benefit from the blessings of the wider Church" (TORCH website undated, "TORCH Philosophy"). Both organizations were supportive of the development of diocesan guidelines for homeschooling with at least one of their members, Kimberly Hahn, participating in the task force that wrote the Pittsburgh guidelines (Warren 2008, 49; "Faith Education at Home" 2006, 19).

In 1996, the Catholic Home School Network of America (CHSNA) organized in order to mediate between Catholic homeschoolers and diocesan leaders (Warren 2008, 49; Marrin 1997, 4). CHSNA believed that diocesan guidelines, especially those requiring parents to place their children in parish religious education sacramental preparation programs, undermined the right of parents to educate their children in matters of faith (Marrin 1997, 4). Further, CHSNA disapproved of NACHE and TORCH's support of diocesan guidelines, leading to controversy between the national organizations (Warren 2008, 49). In 1998, CHSNA printed its own position in *Rights and Responsibilities of Parents in Religious Education* (Warren 2008, 49). It does not appear that the controversy was ever resolved. In 2003, NACHE became the Catholic Family Expo, sponsoring a large convention in the Washington, D.C., area, while CHSNA was virtually defunct by 2008 (Warren 2008, 50).

AN INCOMPLETE PICTURE

What has been published in regard to Catholic homeschooling does not provide a complete representation of all Catholic families who choose to home educate. While it is difficult to estimate the exact number of Catholic homeschooled children, it is estimated between 1.7 and 2.35 million children were home educated in the United States in 2010 (Ray 2011, 3). Past research has estimated Catholics to make up approximately 5 percent of all homeschoolers, thus it is estimated that between 86,500 and 115,000 Catholic children were home educated in 2010 (Marrin 1997, 3). Based on enrollment estimates gathered from the home-study programs, the majority of home-educated Catholic children use curricula assembled from the variety of resources available, though there is no hard statistical data to support this claim. Further, the written history of Catholic homeschooling is heavily representative of parents who choose homeschooling out of concern for the orthodoxy of Catholic schools. It is reasonable to believe that, like the Protestant homeschooling movement, many parents also enjoy the freedom of choosing appropriate learning methods for their children. Although the home-study programs emphasize the classical or scholastic approach, it is likely that Catholic homeschooling families also utilize methods such as unschooling, Charlotte Mason, and Montessori. Though much is unknown about the Catholic homeschooling movement, it seems to be enjoying growth as a Catholic educational option.

REFERENCES AND FURTHER READING

Berquist, Laura. *Designing Your Own Classical Curriculum: A Guide to Catholic Home Education*, Third Edition. San Francisco: Ignatius Press, 1998.

Carper, James C. "Pluralism to Establishment to Dissent: The Religious and Educational Context of Home Schooling." *Peabody Journal of Education* 75, 1/2 (2000): 8–19.

Carper, James C. *The Praeger Handbook of Religion and Education in the United States, Volume One A-L.* Westport: Praeger Publishers, 2009.

Carper, James C., and Brian D. Ray. "Religion, Schooling, and Home Education: Past and Present." In *Religion, Education, and the American Experience*, edited by Edith L. Blumhofer, 223–42. Tuscaloose: University of Alabama Press, 2002.

Carper, James C., and Thomas C. Hunt. *The Dissenting Tradition in American Education*. New York: Peter Lang, 2007.

Clark, Mary Kay. *Catholic Home Schooling: A Handbook for Parents, First Edition*. Charlotte: TAN Books and Publishers, 2009.

Diocese of Pittsburgh, Secretariat for Education. *Faith Education at Home: Catholic Homeschooling, Second Edition*. Diocese of Pittsburgh, 2006.

Farris, Michael. *The Future of Home Schooling*. Washington, D.C.: Regnery Publishing: 1997.

Hahn, Kimberly and Mary Hasson. *Catholic Education: Homeward Bound: A Useful Guide to Catholic Homeschooling*. San Francisco: Ignatius Press, 1996.

Holman, Jim. "Bureaucrats Eye Homeschoolers," *San Diego News Notes*, October 1995, under "Inside Look at Diocese Memos." http://www.sdnewsnotes.com/ed/articles/1995/1095me.htm (accessed November 12, 2010).

Kolbe Academy. "About Us: Kolbe's History." http://www.kolbe.org/kolbe_s_history/ (accessed January 10, 2011).

Marrin, Pat. "Catholic Homeschooling: Parents Teach Their Kids for a Variety of Reasons." *The National Catholic Reporter*, August 29, 1997.

Our Lady of the Rosary School. "History of OLRS." http://www.olrs.com/History_of_OLRS/history_of_olrs.html (accessed January 10, 2011).

Our Lady of Victory School. "About Us." http://www.olvs.org/index_int.asp (accessed January 10, 2011).

Peters, Edward N. *The 1917 Pio-Benedictine Code of Canon Law in English Translation*. San Francisco: Ignatius, 2001.

Ray, Brian D. "The Modern Homeschooling Movement." *Catholic Education: A Journal of Inquiry and Practice*, 4. 3 (March 2001): 405–21.

Ray, Brian D. "Homeschool Population Report 2011." National Home Education Research Institute, January 3, 2011. http://www.nheri.org/HomeschoolPopulationReport2010.pdf. (accessed January 10, 2011).

Ryan, Mary Perkins. *Are Parochial Schools the Answer? Catholic Education in The Light of The Council*. New York: Guild Press, 1963.

Second Vatican Council. Declaration on Christian Education: *Gravissimum Educationis*. 28 October, 1965. Austin Flannery, ed. *Vatican II: The Conciliar and Post Conciliar Documents*, Vol. 1. New Rev. Ed. Northport, NY: Costello, 1998.

Second Vatican Council. Pastoral Constitution on the Church in the Modern World: *Gaudium et Spes*. December, 1965. Austin Flannery, ed. *Vatican II: The Conciliar and Post Conciliar Documents*, Vol. 1. New Rev. Ed. Northport, NY: Costello, 1998.

Seton Home Study School. "About Us." http://www.setonhome.org/ourstory.shtml (accessed January 10, 2011).

Stevens, Mitchell. *Kingdom of Children*. Princeton: Princeton University Press, 2001.

Traditions of Roman Catholic Homes, "About TORCH." http://www.torchhomeschooling.org/about_torch.php?page=philosophy (accessed January 11, 2011).

Warren, Draper J. "The History of Catholic Homeschooling: A Movement Preserving Order or A Rebellion Against It?" Thesis, Christendom College, 2008. Unpublished.

34

Catholic School Sponsorship

Brother John R. Habjan, S. M. and George J. Lisjak

The sponsorship of Catholic schools by religious congregations developed during the end of the twentieth and beginning of the twenty-first centuries as a means of preserving the congregations' charism within those schools. Developments in the Catholic Church and in society led to the need for a new model of religious presence and influence in Catholic schools.

THE PRE-SPONSORSHIP ERA

Born between 1946 and 1964, members of the baby boomer generation who attended Catholic elementary school, high school, or college have varied memories of their experiences. They do remember, however, that the majority of their teachers were Brothers, Sisters, and priests, most of whom were members of the religious congregations that assumed responsibility for the school and, in many cases, owned it. They can recall saying "Yes, Sister," "Thank you, Brother," and "I will not do it again, Father" and getting up from their seats when a Brother, Sister, or priest entered the classroom. Though some can remember painful experiences, the vast majority of the memories of Catholic education are of committed teachers who cared about their students (Scott 2003, 176).

These Brothers, Sisters, and priests carried with them, into classrooms, offices, and work areas, their commitment to, and lived expression of, the charism of their religious congregations. By virtue of their religious formation, and supported by their communal mission, their presence ensured that the charism was manifest in every aspect of the school.

In the relatively rare instances when they were joined by laypersons, there was no doubt that the religious nature of the school was of central importance. Religious congregations wanted to guarantee that those non-members working with them knew the charism of the congregation. For example, in 1933, one of the first laymen to teach at a Marianist high school in the Midwest was given a copy of the religious order's Constitutions at the end of his interview with the principal. When the prospective teacher asked the Brother Principal what he was to do with the book, he was told to read and memorize the material, and that there would be a quiz on its contents. There was a quiz; he passed it; and after nearly 40 years of service at the school, he retired, believing that the contents of the book positively affected his teaching ministry at the school. In 1980, he still had the Constitutions and still could recite passages.

This strong emphasis on the Catholic nature of Catholic schools as embodied in the physical presence of religious Brothers, Sister's and priests remained as long as the large numbers of religious remained. By the 1960s, several factors had contributed to lowering the number of religious present in the schools.

CHANGING DEMOGRAPHICS, CHANGING THOUGHT

The late 1950s and early 1960s saw an expansion of Catholic education throughout the United States as the population increased and Catholic families moved from cities to suburbs. By the mid-1960s, Catholic school enrollment stood at a peak of about 4.5 million for Catholic elementary schools and about 1 million for Catholic high schools (National Catholic Educational Association). The increased enrollment stretched the personnel resources of religious congregations and dioceses, whose leaders sought to maintain not only educational quality but also a high level of influence on the Catholic nature of the schools. "In 1962, Cardinal Joseph Ritter of St. Louis called a halt to new school construction until his pastors could organize schools with forty-nine or fewer students per classroom and a ratio of three religious to every lay teacher" (Walch 1996, 167). As the number of Catholic schools increased, so did the need for teachers. This resulted in more men and women who were not vowed religious or diocesan priests ministering in Catholic schools. The administration of the school, however, remained in the hands of vowed religious and priests (Grant and Vandenberg, 2004, 16).

Vatican Council II (1962–1965) profoundly changed the experience of Church for Catholics, raising questions and challenging familiar beliefs and practices. Among its many effects was the expansion of the opportunities for greater lay involvement in church ministries, including education, that were formerly the nearly exclusive domain of religious, while, at the same time, contributing to the need for an increase in that lay involvement.

In particular, the Council produced three documents that had a direct influence on the increased involvement of the laity in Catholic education. *Apostolicam Actuositatem* (1965), the Decree on the Apostolate of the Laity, clearly stated that the role of the laity was indispensable in the mission of the Catholic Church. "Our own times require of the laity no less zeal: in fact, modern conditions demand their apostolate be boarded and intensified" (Paragraph 1). *Perfectae Caritatis* (1965), on the renewal of Religious Life, challenged members of religious congregations to be faithful to their charism while adapting to changing times as they worked in their congregational ministries. *Gravissimum Educationis* (1965), on Catholic Education, stressed the importance of Catholic education and the need for it to be true to the Gospel message and charism of the religious congregation.

Collectively, these documents paved the way for an increased collaboration and shared responsibility in Church ministries, including education. However, they also embodied the seeds of a new way of thinking that further decreased the numbers of religious serving in Catholic schools.

At the same time as the decrees of Vatican II challenged Catholics, lay and religious, to live their faith in new ways for a new time, the United States experienced an upheaval of its own. Changing mores and changing lifestyles reflected a culture that was evolving in ways not imagined by an earlier generation.

A complete discussion of the interplay of these changes in the Catholic Church and in society, and of their effects, has generated many volumes and is beyond the scope of this work. It is sufficient to note that these changes were accompanied by a dramatic decrease in the number of religious vocations. Between 1958 and 1962, 32,334 women entered religious congregations of women; from 1962 to 1965, the number was 18,316; and from 1966 to 1970 the number was 8,699 (Ebaugh 1993, 48 and Neal 1990, 31). Similar declines occurred in the number of vocations of religious brothers and priests, leaving fewer religious available for all ministries, including education.

Perfectae Caritatis had an additional effect on those who did enter, or remained in, religious life. Members of religious congregations prayed and talked a great deal about how to adapt to the changing times in light of the call of Vatican II. One result was the acceptance of new ministry opportunities that sought to address societal needs and utilize the talents of members of the congregation. As members of religious congregations engaged in new ministries, the number of vowed religious available to serve in more traditional ministries, including Catholic schools, declined (Grant and Vandenberg 1998, 21).

It is true that the overall enrollment in Catholic schools eventually began to decline as well. Catholics whose own attendance at Catholic schools had been accepted as a matter of course by their parents did not always feel the same obligation in the education of their own children. Many factors, particularly increased personnel costs due to the hiring of more lay persons and the eventual extension of more comparably just compensation for religious, contributed to dramatic increases in the tuition charged in Catholic schools, making them unaffordable for some and a less attractive economic choice for others. However, the rate of decline in the need for educators in Catholic schools did not match the rate of decline in the number of religious available to fill this need. Catholic schools continued to exist and continued to be staffed by a growing proportion of lay persons.

A FOCUS ON CHARISM

Perfectae Caritatis instructed religious congregations that " . . . adaptation and renewal of the religious life includes both the constant return to the sources of all Christian life and to the original spirit of the institutes and their adaptation to the changing conditions of our time" (Paragraph 2). The word charism was beginning to be used by religious congregations in presenting the blending of the Gospel, Church teachings, and the inspiration of the congregation's founder(s). In the twenty-first century, the term *charism* is commonly used in discussions among members of a religious congregation and their colleagues in ministry in talking about what makes their schools unique among other Catholic educational institutions.

What is charism? St Paul in his first letter to the Corinthians (1 Cor. 12:4–6) states, "There are different kinds of spiritual gifts but the same spirit; there are different forms of service but the same Lord; there are different workings but the same God who produces all of them in everyone" (The New American Bible 1986, 1243). The Augustinian Recollects, building on St. Paul, define charism as referring "to that which makes a religious community unique; the particular faith vision of the founder that has left a lasting character on the life and work style of the community" (Augustinian Recollects). Charism is then a gift given to an individual or group by the Holy Spirit for the building of the Christian Community (Society of Mary [Marianists]).

Since Vatican II, members of religious congregations have spent time discerning the unique elements of their charism and of the appropriate ways to adapt it to the current times. This ongoing dialogue has created a shared understanding that has given a clearer direction to the ministries sponsored by most religious congregations.

For those congregations involved in Catholic school ministry, the means of implementing their particular charism within this ministry became an issue of significant concern. During the time when religious filled the classrooms and offices of Catholic schools, it had been assumed that non-vowed personnel at a school would learn from the example of the vowed religious what it meant to minister in a school administered by a particular religious congregation. The sheer numbers of religious ensured the charism would guide the school. Those non-vowed members of the school community would absorb through osmosis what it meant to be a Catholic school in the tradition of a particular religious congregation. In times when the numbers of religious had shrunk dramatically and would continue to do so, congregations could no longer rely on this approach.

One of the most significant effects of these Vatican Council II documents and new awareness was the realization of a response to the dilemma faced by religious congregations' recognition of the importance of enlivening charism within Catholic school ministries, knowing that the traditional means for doing so had become no longer viable.

THE ROOTS OF SPONSORSHIP

By the 1990s, members of most religious congregations involved in Catholic education had begun a serious dialogue about this situation. They worked to determine their charism's unique expression specifically in terms of educational ministry. In most cases, the dialogue involved not only the members of the religious congregations but also the lay collaborators who had become a much more significant part of the ministry. It was a process of reviewing foundational and historical documents in the light of Scripture and Church teachings, organizing the ideas of their predecessors in education, and recognizing the "signs of the times." The result was an articulation of the elements of the charism that characterized the congregation's educational ministry.

For example, the Society of Mary (Marianists) determined their educational characteristics as educating for formation in faith; educating in family spirit; providing an integral, quality education; educating for service, justice, and peace; and educating for adaptation and change (Society of Mary (Marianists) 1996). The Visitation Order determined that their school communities would (1) foster a personal friendship with God, which leads to a faith-filled vision of life; (2) integrate a strong academic course of studies with a Salesian spiritual dimension; (3) build faith communities that call their members to understand the value of diversity and to respect the dignity of each person; (4) and promote the development of liberty of spirit, which empowers students to make life-giving choices, model gospel values of peace and justice in order to be catalysts for positive change, and encourage an awareness of and care for the gifts of God's creating hand (Visitation Salesian Network 2004*)*. Other congregations have published similar formulations (e.g., the Society of the Holy Child Jesus in *Goals for Schools of the Holy Child Jesus* (Society of the Holy Child Jesus), the Society of Jesus in *What Makes a Jesuit High School Jesuit?* (The Jesuit Conference, 2000), the Brothers of Christian Schools in *Touching the Hearts of Students: Characteristics of Lasallian Schools* (Van Grieken, 2002), and the

Society of the Sacred Heart in *The Goals and Criteria for Sacred Heart Schools in the United States* (The Network of Sacred Heart Schools)).

Although the characteristics of education that have derived from different charisms are unique in their particular expressions and emphases, it is evident that they share a commitment to the Gospel message. Those particular expressions and emphases reflect the unique contribution to the educational ministry of the Catholic Church that is based in the charism of each of the religious congregations.

The term sponsorship became part of the vocabulary of religious congregations after the work of Sister Concilia Moran, R. S. M., in the late 1970s (Moran 1978, 53). "The varying degrees of influence sought by the founding congregations come under the rubric of 'sponsorship,' a term that has no official status in either civil or canon law but has evolved over the last thirty years to describe the different ways congregations or orders relate to the institution in mutual efforts to keep the founding charism alive. There is no universal model for how this is done ... " (*Mission and Identity* 2003, 97).

Although there is no single accepted methodology for the implementation of the sponsorship relationship, there is a generally accepted purpose. "Sponsors have various roles in the life of an institution. First and foremost, they are the interpreters of the institution's mission. ... Sponsors function as an institutional memory and conscience. They name the institution's ideals and articulate the implications of the founding charism in the midst of changing times" (Morey and Holtschneider 2001, 9).

The different language used by different religious congregations to define sponsorship illustrates the range of relationships that the term encompasses: "Mutually beneficial and dynamic relationship between the congregation and an organization in which the SSND charism and educational vision are defining characteristics of the organization" (School Sisters of Notre Dame); "Sponsorship represents a complex, mutually binding set of expectations and responsibilities freely embraced for the achievement of a common mission" (Society of Mary, Marianists); "Xaverian sponsorship is a complex of guiding principles, governance structures, formational programs, and networking opportunities. The Xaverian Brothers and their lay collaborators have come to ensure that the schools that have the name Xaverian live up to their mission 'to serve the Church in its work of evangelization, particularly through the ministry of education'" (Xaverian Brothers); "Sponsorship is the relationship between the Sinsinawa Dominican Congregation and the local institution. The relationships established are created to further the mission of the Sinsinawa Dominicans" (Sinsinawa Dominicans).

THE IMPLEMENTATION OF SPONSORSHIP

Despite differences in the particular definitions of sponsorship, there are elements typical to its implementation across some or all religious congregations engaged in it. These include a clear articulation of the meaning of sponsorship of schools for the particular congregation; ongoing dialogue to refine this meaning among members of the congregation themselves and with lay collaborators; attention to school leadership; formation programs for lay collaborators ministering in the schools at a variety of levels, including administrators, faculty and staff members, and board members; explicit education and formation of students in elements of the charism; networking among sponsored institutions; and a process of review for accountability.

The development of characteristics of education, discussed above, becomes a central element in the articulation of the meaning of sponsorship for a religious congregation. These characteristics help to concretize the charism as it is to be embodied in schools sponsored by the congregation. From them derive the actions and processes that then become part of the sponsorship relationship. These elements are typically expressed in a Sponsorship Agreement that delineates the responsibilities of both the sponsors and the sponsored school, the means for assessing the fulfillment of those responsibilities, and the time period for which parties commit to participate in the relationship. This agreement is typically signed by the leadership of a religious congregation, the head of school, and, where applicable, appropriate diocesan officials.

Sponsorship remains a relatively new concept. Those engaged in it recognize that all of its meanings and implications, both for sponsors and for sponsoring schools, are not yet evident. Members of religious congregations that sponsor schools continue to discuss these meanings and implications. Since the essence of sponsorship involves sharing educational ministry with lay persons who serve in sponsored schools, these lay persons are accepted as partners and so are actively invited into the conversation.

There is a general recognition of the importance of school leadership among sponsoring religious congregations. Some congregations tailor specific formational experiences for school leaders or prospective school leaders. In addition, sponsorship typically includes the sponsoring congregation having influence over the hiring of the CEO of the school. That influence may range from complete authority, in cases where the school is owned by the congregation, to, at the least, representation on search committees, for schools that are sponsored but not owned.

Most religious congregations have developed formation programs for personnel in sponsored schools. However, the formality and intended audiences of the programs vary. Typically, there are formation programs for administrators, faculty and staff, and board members. Programs may focus on orientation for those new to the school or on more in-depth experiences for those who have been with the school for some time. These programs include opportunities for learning about the charism and the education ministry of the congregation, developing commitment, and sharing ideas and experiences with those from other schools sponsored by the congregation.

Schools exist for the development of their students. Although students are formed in large measure by the adults who are the focus of the kinds of formation discussed above, providing instruction and formation in the charism directly for students is often part of sponsorship relationships. Programs for students typically involve faith formation, community building, social outreach, and interaction between students from various schools. These programs help students develop their faith life and share experiences of social service at their schools. Students are encouraged to use what they have learned to help their church communities and society at large. Some sponsorships include curricula that directly convey basic elements of the history and charism of the sponsoring congregation.

Religious congregations that sponsor schools typically provide for some means of networking among schools. This may occur through forums and meetings convened around a particular issue or through regular formation activities that bring together administrators, faculty, staff, or board members from all of the congregation's sponsored schools.

Sponsorship relationships include some means of assessing fidelity to the sponsorship agreement. The manner and frequency of this assessment varies considerably, however.

For some, periodic reviews of performance of heads of school are used to determine adherence to the charism, while in others, visiting teams of educators from other sponsored schools conduct a review. Regardless of the means, the assessment provides data useful in the decision to continue the sponsorship relationship.

Although there are common elements in the implementation of sponsorship, there is also considerable variety in sponsorship relationships. Each sponsoring congregation typically faces a variety of practical concerns that impact the sponsorship relationship. Among these are the following.

SCHOOL OWNERSHIP

The ownership of sponsored schools impacts the sponsorship relationship. Some schools are wholly owned by the religious congregations that minister in them. Others are owned by the local diocese or by their own boards of directors. Other relationships of partial or co-congregation ownership may also exist. Sponsorship may be implemented differently in these different situations.

As mentioned above regarding the hiring of the head of school, the ownership relationship impacts the expectations of influence of the sponsoring congregation. This impact may extend to other areas of the sponsorship relationship, including, for example, level of participation in formation programs or implementation of curricula. The degree of influence expected by a sponsoring congregation, and how much that expectation varies with the ownership relationship, is an important decision area for sponsors.

FINANCIAL COMMITMENT

Ownership of a school automatically involves financial commitment and liability. Regardless of ownership, sponsorship requires some additional commitment of resources by the sponsoring congregation. These include the provision of programming as well as personnel and other resources to manage the sponsorship relationship. Some sponsors also provide direct financial support, typically in the form of student financial aid. In addition, some sponsorship agreements include a financial contribution to be made by sponsored schools to help offset costs.

Personnel Placement

Although their numbers have decreased, sponsoring congregations typically have at least some religious personnel available for education ministry. Religious congregations may consider the availability and placement of these personnel, either directly in sponsored schools or in positions of management or oversight of sponsorship relationships, as more or less important.

These and other factors combine to nuance sponsorship relationships and increase their complexity. However, that these various situations have been successfully accommodated within functioning sponsorships is evidence that school sponsorship is a robust construct.

THE FUTURE OF SPONSORSHIP

Catholic schools have already come far from the days of nearly total staffing by Brothers, Sisters, and priests. Catholic education will continue to change. Can Catholic schools maintain not only their Catholicity but also the richness brought to that Catholicity through the embodiment of the religious charisms, which led to their founding and have continued to sustain them? While we cannot know the answer as this is being written, the development of the sponsorship movement provides a reason for hope that they can.

Sponsorship encompasses much complexity. As its history lengthens, more issues will continue to surface around its implementation. Beginning in the mid-1990s, a group of religious and lay persons who have some formal responsibility for managing the sponsorship of schools for religious congregations began meeting. This group, founded by Sister Eileen McDevitt, SHCJ, and known as Directors of Sponsorship, had grown by 2010 to include representation from approximately 30 congregations. The group meets annually to increase its understanding of the issues involved in sponsorship and to share ideas. This group represents the kind of cross-congregation learning and support that can move the overall understanding and implementation of sponsorship forward.

Sponsorship embodies a high level of intentionality about enlivening religious charism in Catholic schools in response to the signs of the times of the late twentieth century and ongoing developments of the twenty-first century. It involves continual critical assessment of mission effectiveness and integration. It provides a venue for genuine collaboration among religious and lay educators. As such, it represents both a faithful implementation of the Vatican II teachings regarding Catholic education and a sign of hope for its future.

REFERENCES AND FURTHER READING

Augustinian Recollects. "Glossary." Augustinian Recollects. http://www.augustianrecollects.org/glossary (accessed March 1, 2010).

Brothers of Christian Schools. http://www.brothersvocation.org/whatwedo (accessed June 7, 2010).

Bryk, Anthony, Valerie Lee, and Peter Holland. *Catholic Schools and the Common Good.* Cambridge, MA: Harvard University Press, 1993.

Carolyn, C. S. J., Sister. "Lay Teachers Have a Spiritual Role." *Catholic School Journal* 63, 1 (1963): 43–44.

Congregation for Catholic Education. "Consecrated Persons and Their Mission in Schools" (October 28, 2002). Congregation for Catholic Education. http://www.vatican.va/roman_curia/congregations/ccatheduc/ (accessed May 6, 2010).

Congregation for Catholic Education. "Lay Teachers in Schools: Witnesses to Faith" (October 15, 1982). Congregation for Catholic Education. http://www.vatican.va/roman_curia/congregations/ccatheduc/ (accessed May 6, 2010).

Congregation for Catholic Education. "The Catholic School (March 19, 1977)." Congregation for Catholic Education. http://www.vatican.va/roman_curia/congregations/ccatheduc/ (accessed May 6, 2010).

Congregation for Catholic Education. "The Catholic School on the Threshold of the Third Millennium" (December 28, 1997). Congregation for Catholic Education. http://www.vatican.va/roman_curia/congregations/ccatheduc/ (accessed May 6, 2010).

Deters, L. J. "Recruiting and Training of Lay Teachers." *National Catholic Educational Association Bulletin* 56, 3 (1959): 307 in Kozar, Albert. "The Catholic Lay Teacher." *Marianist Educator,* 17, 1 (1966): 52–57.

DiPietro, S. C., Melanie. "Sponsorship: A Word of Caution." *The Legal Bulletin* 78 (2004): 21–29.

Ebaugh, Helen Rose. *Women in the Vanishing Cloister.* New Brunswick, NJ: Rutgers University Press, 1993.

Frericks, Donald. "The Marianist Lay Teacher in the Catholic School System." *Marianist Educator* 17 (1966): 6–9.

Gitlin, Todd. *The Sixties: Years of Hope, Days of Rage.* New York: Bantam Books, 1993.

Grant, Mary Kathryn, and Patricia Vandenberg, C. S. C. *After We're Gone.* Mishawaka, IN: Ministry Development Resources, 1998.

Grant, Mary Kathryn, and Patricia Vandenberg, C. S. C. *Partners in the Between Time: Creating Sponsorship Capacity*. Mishawaka, IN: Ministry Development Resources, 2004.

Hession, Alice. "Current Topics in the Sponsorship of Schools." Xaverian Brothers. http://www.xbss (accessed May 23, 2010).

Hunt, Thomas C., Ellis Joseph and Ronald Nuzzi, eds. *Catholic Schools in the United States*. New York: Greenwood Press, 2004.

Hunt, Thomas C., and Timothy Walch, eds. *Urban Catholic Education: Tales of Twelve American Cities*. Notre Dame, IN: Alliance for Catholic Education Press, 2010.

Jesuit Conference. *What Makes a School Jesuit?* Chicago: Loyola Press, 2000.

Kaufman, Christopher. *Education and Transformation: Marianist Ministries in America Since 1849*. New York: Crossroad Publishing Co., 1999.

Kelley, S. M., Paul. "The Marianist Lay Teacher: His Role in the S. M. Apostolate of Education." *Marianist Educator* 17 (1966): 1–5.

Lee, S. M., Bernard. *The Beating of Great Wings*. Mystic, CT: Twenty-Third Publications, 2004.

Marist Brothers. http://www.maristbr.com (accessed April 10, 2010).

Mathews, S. M. Stanley. "Speaking Out: I." *Marianist Educator* 17 (1966): 14–21.

McCann, Patricia. "Catholic Identity, New Age and Women Religious." *America Magazine* 189:2 (July 21, 2004). http://www.americamagazine.org (accessed February 16, 2010).

McCloskey, Patrick. *The Street Stops Here: A Year at a Catholic High School in Harlem*. Berkeley, CA: University of California Press, 2008.

Mission and Identity: A Handbook for Trustees of Catholic Colleges and Universities. Washington, DC: ALCU, ACCU, and AGB, 2003.

Moran, R. S. M., Concilia. "Sponsorship: The Uneasy Question." *Hospital Progress* 59, 10 (November 1978): 52–5, 70.

Morey, Melanie and Dennis Holtschneider. "Today, Co-create with Lay Collaborators." *Current Issues in Catholic High Education* 21 (Fall 2001): 3–39.

Mueller, F. S. C. Frederick. "Sponsorship of Catholic Schools: Preserving the Tradition." In *The Catholic Character of Catholic Schools*, edited by James Youniss, John Convey, and Jeffrey McLellan, 38–61. Notre Dame, IN: University of Notre Dame Press, 2000.

Mueller, F. S. C. Frederick. *The Formation of New Teachers: A Companion on the Lasallian Journey*. Washington, DC: Christian Brothers Conference, 2008.

Munley, A. "Threads for the Loom." Paper presented at the Leadership Conference of Women Religious, Silver Spring, MD, 1992.

National Catholic Educational Association (NCEA). "A Brief History of Catholic Schools in America." http://www.ncea.org/p/articlesmi_qa3859/is_2004/ai_n9362627/ (accessed June 12, 2010).

Neal, Marie A. *From Nuns to Sisters*. Mystic, CT: Twenty-Third Publications, 1990.

Network of Sacred Heart Schools, The. "The Goals and Criteria for Sacred Heart Schools in the United States." Society of the Sacred Heart. http://www.sofie.org/index.php?option=com_content &task=view&id=165&Itemid=48 (accessed July 2, 2010).

The New American Bible. Iowa Falls, IA: World Bible Publishers, 1986.

Place, Michael. "Toward a Theology of Sponsorship." *Catholic Health Association of the United States* (Jan/Feb 2004) in the CBS Interactive Business Network, http://www.findarticles.com/p/arrticlesmi _qa3859/is_2004/ai_n9362627/ (accessed March 3, 2010).

School Sisters of Notre Dame. http://www.ssndmankato.org (accessed May 6, 2010).

Scott, Beverly Pangle. *Thank You, Sister!* Allen, TX: Thomas More, 2003.

Sinsinawa Dominicans. "Sponsorship." Sinsinawa Dominicans. http://www.sinsinawa.org /01_About_Us/03_What_We_Do/Sponsorship.htm (accessed April 10, 2010).

Sinsinawa Dominicans. *Cor ad Cor in Caritate et Veritate Loquitur (Heart Speaks to Heart in Charity and Truth.)* Sinsinawa, IL: Sinsinawa Dominicans, 2005.

Society of the Holy Child Jesus. "Goals of Holy Child Schools." Society of the Holy Child Jesus. http:// holychildschools.org/hcn.nsf/pages/goals (accessed July 2, 2010).

Society of Mary (Marianists). *Characteristics of Marianist Education*. Dayton, OH: Marianist Press, 1996.

Society of Mary (Marianists). "Sponsorship Program." Society of Mary (Marianists). http://www.marianist.com/mecResources (accessed January 22, 2010).

Society of Mary (Marianists). "A Glossary of Marianist Terms." Society of Mary (Marianists). http://www.marianist.com/ministries.php?pid=220 (accessed January 22, 2010).

United States Conference of Catholic Bishops. "Called and Gifted for the Third Millennium." 1995. United States Conference of Catholic Bishops. http://www.usccb.org/statements.shtml (accessed March 3, 2010).

United States Conference of Catholic Bishops. *Renewing Our Commitment to Catholic Secondary and Elementary Schools in the Third Millennium.* Washington, DC: United States Conference of Catholic Bishops, 2005.

United States Conference of Catholic Bishops. *To Teach As Jesus Did.* Washington, DC: United States Conference of Catholic Bishops, 1973.

Van Grieken, F. S. C., George. *Touching the Hearts of Students: Characteristics of Lasallian Schools.* Landover, MD: Christian Brothers Publications, 2002.

Vatican Council II. "Apostolicam Actuositatem (Decree on the Apostolate of the Laity)." November 18, 1965. Vatican Council II. http://www.vatican.va/archive/hist_councils/ii_vatican_council/index.htm (accessed March 3, 2010).

Vatican Council II. "Gravissimum Educationis (Declaration on Catholic Education)." October 28, 1965. Vatican Council II. http://www.vatican.va/archive/hist_councils/ii_vatican_council/index.htm (accessed March 3, 2010).

Vatican Council II. "Gaudium et Spes (Pastoral Constitution on the Church in the Modern World)." December 7, 1965. Vatican Council II. http://www.vatican.va/archive/hist_councils/ii_vatican_council/index.htm (accessed March 3, 2010).

Vatican Council II. "Perfectae Caritatis. (Adaptation and Renewal of Religious Life)." October 28, 1965. Vatican Council II. http://www.vatican.va/archive/hist_councils/ii_vatican_council/index.htm (accessed March 3, 2010).

Visitation Salesian Network. *Educating the Mind and the Heart in the Visitation Tradition.* Washington, DC: Visitation and Salesian Network, 2004.

Walch, Timothy. *Parish School.* New York: Crossroad Publishing, Co., 1996.

Xaverian Brothers. http://www.xbss.org/foundationdocument (accessed April 5, 2010).

Wittberg, Patricia. "Declining Institutional Sponsorship and Religious Orders: A Study of Reverse Impact." *Association for the Sociology of Religion* (Fall, 2000) in the CBS Interactive Business Network, www.findarticles.com (accessed March 5, 2010).

35

The Threshold of New Catholic and Faith-Based Learning Environments: The Advance of the Digital Culture

Angela Ann Zukowski, MHSH

The digital age has ushered in a radical new way for thinking about education in the twenty-first century. The Internet Generation treats technology differently than their parents or teachers ever thought about or used technology. It is expanding more quickly in students' immediate milieu than within our present learning environments. The Internet has initiated a new sense of place where people communicate, collaborate, and create diverse communities via social networking. It is here that students are spending significant amounts of quality time that is informing, forming, and transforming their sense of self and community. Expanding educational research is demonstrating these shifting realities, calling for "re-imagineering" the profile of teaching and learning in the decades ahead. We are only beginning to witness the digital era offering a new sense of power to students.

iTunes, iPhoto, GarageBand, iGoogle, iMovie, iDVD, iWEB, blogs, twitter, Facebook, and Web 2.0 are only a few of the digital tools at our creative disposal. The virtual landscape is an escalating new frontier for quality education. It is fluid, dynamic, and growing every minute, even every nanosecond. The higher education landscape is metaphorically crossed with fault lines, those fissures in the landscape creating potential areas of dramatic change and is more "seismic" than it has been in decades (Staley and Trinkle 2011). We can no longer generalize from the traditional needs of students 10 to 23 years old. This tectonic shift will compel many new conversations and directions at all levels of education (Staley and Trinkle 2011). Technology is not only changing—it's doing so at quantum speed. It took radio over 35 years before its audience reached 50 million users; cable TV about 13 years; Facebook 3 years; and YouTube 3 months! Yes, one day educators awoke, and the dawning of a new digital era created a landscape within which cultures were redefining the meaning of borders, contexts, relationships, and even what it means to be human. A number of new factors are emerging that challenge our perception of education: (1) digital-age students who are entering our schools with intensive digital skills and habits; (2) gesture-based computing; (3) sourcing and cloud computing (Bristow, Dodds and Plungge 2010, 14–15) and what these mean for our schools; and (4) how information technology (IT) is transforming instruction and learning, moving away from teaching as the medium of knowledge delivery to instruction as facilitating discovery(Koester 2011, 36).

A new culture with an evolving new language, psychology, and techniques is embracing us. Marc Prensky, to describe the generation that is right at home with the new culture, coined the term "digital natives." Those who continue to find the new digital terrain unfamiliar and uncomfortable were identified as "digital immigrants." *Born Digital: Understanding the First Generation of Digital Natives* (Palfrey and Gasser 2008) explores the coming of age of the new generation and how our world soon will be reshaped in their image. It is obvious from observing most young people particularly within our campuses that digital media attention consumes a demanding portion of their day. They are always connected, or, wired! We only need observe students in study halls, walking on campus, playing on ball fields, or simply sitting at home in their rooms. There is seldom a moment when some form of media is not connected to their ear, occupying their vision, or both as digital multitasking is the order of their day. E-music, cell phones, texting, iPads, iPods, Facebook and evolving e-applications are consumed by the iGeneration with accelerating speed. The yeasting of new digital media with a perceived urgency to be on top with the newest and latest is creating a culture of high digital consumption and addiction. The research of Larry Rosen and others is clearly demonstrating this paradigm cultural media shift. As educators, we cannot ignore it! We are faced with a series questions and concerns. What is the direct impact on the meaning of being a human person within a digital culture? Does creating dozens of online profiles, avatars and second life situations accelerate a radical new way of human understanding of communication and relationships? Do digital media entrepreneurs have a moral responsibility for critically reflecting on how their digital creations impact the essence and existential reality of being human? What is the world that the digital media entrepreneurs are creating and the iGeneration is absorbing predicating onto traditional human values? Finally, how does the response to these questions impact and discovering new learning styles within our various learning communities?

In the seminal book: *Flow: The Psychology of Optimal Experience*, Mihaly Csikszentmihalyi (1990) argued that people are happiest when they can reach a state of "flow." If we consider what it means to be "in flow" in an information landscape defined with social networking media, we come to appreciate that Web 2.0 has led us into "the flow," a channel for being tuned in, attentive to where the information is, which is everywhere. The swelling media landscape is capturing the attention of younger generations with a sense of their being "in the flow" of information—the urgency of being connected all the time (Zukowski 2011, 15).

Amidst the copious changes and challenges that Catholic education faces in the twenty-first century, the Medici Effect is one that makes the most sense for these times. The Medici Effect refers to the creative explosion in Florence when the Medici family brought together people from a wider range of disciplines. It is believed that by connecting individuals with differing fields new ideas emerged. In effect, it prepared the ground for the Renaissance, the most innovative era in history (Dyer, Gregersen and Christensen 2009, 63). The dilemmas facing current Catholic and faith based schools in terms of architecture, learning spaces, learning styles, standardization, curriculum design, and the constant evolution of digital technology and resources indicate that education has reached a tipping point. The clustering, merging and dissolving of Catholic schools signals that entrepreneurial thinking is not a luxury, or an option but an essential ingredient for crossing the twenty-first century threshold. It calls for Catholic educational leaders who can imaginatively embrace the concept of disruptive innovation (Christensen, Horn and Johnson 2008). Innovation in education requires leaders who can imaginatively embrace the disruptive innovation theory uninhibited by the spiraling down conversations that frequently paralyzes creative thinking. Catholic educational leaders have the responsibility to be unfettered by the constant shifts projected into new learning environments and motivate their faculty and staffs to become entrepreneurs, imagineers, or innovators of a new learning future design.

Innovators consistently ask questions that challenge the status quo, or common wisdom. To question effectively, it means walking around and asking "Why," "Why not?" and "What if?" Every existing assumption is challenged opening the door for options and opportunities that may always have been present but were untapped because the right questions were not posed. This is why Catholic and faith based education has frequently ended up in the spiraling down educational crises we have stumbled into in the late twentieth and early twenty-first centuries. Some educational leaders may have employed what Christensen calls sustaining innovation that is comfortable when disruptive innovation ought to have been encouraged, or at least entertained. There are others who perceive that constraints triggered by resource allocations, or technology restrictions prevent innovative thinking when in fact "great questions" an be generated by the constraints to spark off innovative insights for experimenting with new ideas. A prerequisite for tomorrow's Catholic and faith based educational leadership is to be enthusiastically engaged in encouraging their faculties to create prototypes and launching pilot initiatives that re-imagine their education in a digital era.

While consulting in a Catholic urban school a principal said: "These ideas sound great but it is risky business when we are in a survival mode! We could fail! Furthermore, the stress in these times is too great to imagineer! Already my faculty's spirit and energy is maxed out!" However, this is exactly the time when we should be innovative piloting initiatives that spiral our conversations up and down the continuum. We need new pathways into the future. Catholic and faith based educational leaders are called to encourage, mentor, recognize and celebrate experimentation at every level of the system. This is the foundation needed for an innovative culture that will make the difference for education to succeed in the twenty-first century.

A new renaissance in Catholic and faith based education necessitates entertaining the *Medici Effect* in order to cross the threshold. Connecting and networking with diverse related and unrelated educational personnel and community partners to ask "great questions" and pioneering with new digital technologies and resources is the portal for new educational discoveries. An article in the *Harvard Business Review* entitled *Change for Change's Sake* (Vermeulen, Puranam and Gulati 2010, 71) indicated that "Restructuring gets people to start forming new networks, making the organization as a whole more creative. It also disrupts all the routines in an organization that collectively stifle innovation and adaptability." The question is how can Catholic education survive through change and still maintain its sense of hope and vision. Every day new discoveries are emerging from the least expected places within the Catholic educational culture. Though innovative thinking may be innate to some, it can also be developed and strengthened through practice. I am observing cohorts of Catholic educators who meet regularly with community entrepreneurs to speak about their approach to innovation and have them respond to the teachers' dreams and visions for alternative solutions. Perhaps the words of Steve Forbes may inspire Catholic and faith based school educators for the future: "The real source of wealth and capital in this new era is not material things. It is the human mind, the human spirit, the human imagination, and our faith in the future" (Trilling and Fadel 2009, 151).

EDUCATIONAL TRENDS INFLUENCING CATHOLIC AND FAITH BASED LEARNING

Today there are educational trends yeasting in every corner of the system. They are stirring the ideas of teaching and learning both within and without the traditional classroom. We have experienced a great deal of change in such a short time in our lives. Most Catholic and faith based learning environments maintain a fairly good set up of classroom computers that are networked and have Internet access. Digital projectors, SmartBoards, or Promethean Activboards are permanently installed in classrooms. In addition, Activotes, or Student Performance System, handheld assessment tools (clickers, or similar tools), are being used in the classroom. The state-of-the-art learning managements system called Blackboard is frequently found in schools, allowing teachers to post online content and students to interact in an online learning environment. These devices allow teachers the opportunity to receive immediate feedback on student learning acquisition in order to determine when students have mastered a skill, or need re-teaching. While computer labs continue in schools the desk top or portable computer is being enhanced by use of Netbooks and iPads. This will evolve quickly; thus transforming the design space of our learning environments.

The plethora of tools—blogs, Wikis, podcasts, social media networking (SKYPE, Twitter, and Facebook) can be intimidating for some. Eleven years ago Google was launched. Today the global dominant media company is Google, and the verb "to Google" has entered the English language. IPhones, iPads, and Apple iPhone are the "must have" global consumer items and are being woven into educational environments with copious applications. Hardware ranges from the iPod Touch to super smartphones like the iPhone, Android, Microsoft and BlackBerry devices, to tablet computers like the iPad or Netbook, and includes phone/tablet hybrids (Meloni 2010). All of these devices include an operating system, some sort of connectivity method to the Internet (be it Wi-Fi, 3 G, or otherwise), the ability to download and run applications, and store transfer data. But even in countries where access to basic communications is still difficult, the new landscape is taking shape. Africa, for example is the fastest growing mobile phone market in the world and both China and India are adding more than seven million new mobile subscribers a month. Accordingly, our world media connectors are intensifying and creating new gateways for comprehending understanding people and the world from first hand virtual experiences of meaning, culture and values. For Catholic educators these tools keep on forming the basis of new approaches to, and means of interacting with students, each other and information. There is a new GPS navigational system for education and Catholic educators are accelerating speed for implementation each day.

During a recent National Catholic Educational convention educators expounded on the reality that their students are multimedia sponges. They spend significant time out of school hours filled with images, video, sound, music and animation. Can we realistically think that walking through the doors of our Catholic schools with traditional lesson plans, exercises and techniques can alter our digital native's way of being engaged within such a context? Catholic educators are discovering ways that digital tools and resources are improving learning and higher order thinking. They can provide students with multiple angles to get at the same material, thus facilitating project-based work that enables them to dig further and deeper. This idea of in-depth research is a kind of virtual information archeology adventure that is sparking the attention, imagination, critical thinking skills and collaborative learning among our students. Educators are spending much more time thinking about their learning goals, mapping curriculum, pedagogy and professional development within a digital culture. They realize it is necessary to think carefully about the instructional software they purchase and the peripherals they choose to support learning within a quality educational environment. I agree with those Catholic educators who believe that we need to first focus on learning to think critically and technology later; and second focus on the curriculum, instructing and assessment to be effective. It is true that it is not sufficient for students to simply discover and communicate information via digital tools and resources. We have to demonstrate to students how to evaluate the information's veracity, how to reason logically, how to come to evidence—based decisions, how to create relevant knowledge, and how to apply this learning to new situations (Burns 2005). The latest trend may or may not be the most effective learning style for particular students but when Catholic educators keep their minds open to the rich deposit of growing digital resources then they are discovering alternative opportunities for advancing the quality of Catholic education in the twenty-first century.

PATHWAYS THROUGH DIGITAL LEARNING EXPERIENCES

Digital expressions are changing how we listen and speak today (Ohler 2009). Digital fluency is much more of a perspective than a technical skill set. Teachers who are truly digitally fluent blend creativity and innovation into lesson plans, assignments, and projects and understand the role that digital tools can play in creating meaningful learning experiences that engage the whole student.

Currently I am teaching a course entitled *Vocation and the Arts*. Students have been encouraged to apply their world digital skills to many class assignments and exercises to demonstrate their new learning. One assignment focused on Encounters with Great Artists: Musicians and Painters. The first group selected music as the focus of their presentation entitling it *"Woodstock 2010."* Based upon a popular exercise called The Meeting of Great Minds the students assumed the character of one of their favorite musicians, e.g., Bono, Mozart, etc. They dressed into the character and cleverly entertained the other students with anecdotes of the character's life and artistic contributions to culture. Video clips from www.YouTube.com offered virtual experiences of particular musical selections from YouTube's vast archives. Multimedia PowerPoint backgrounds created a visual historical cultural setting for contextualizing their characters' stories. The student audience assumed the roles of journalists interviewing each musician in light of the musician's contribution to culture. The assignment was to compose an e-news release for publication on our course Isidore website for students' critique.

The second group focused on major artists. For the project entitled *"Capturing Our World,"* the project students asked all the students to bring their computers to class. The students applied Facebook for their digital experience. The week before class everyone was sent an e-invitation to accept one of the designated world famous artists (role played by one of the students) as a friend on the group's Facebook site. During class costumed, students in character narrated a brief review of their life story and significant contributions to the world of art. Using the Smart Board and Internet the students googled clips of the artist's work. The student audience was required to follow along on their computers by sending spontaneous e-questions and comments to each of the historical characters on their Facebook page either on the designated all, discussion board, or chat room. Each student could see all the questions being posted animating their own personal e-postings to build a robust selection of comments and questions around the artist's work. These were all addressed as a wrap up of the session. The interactivity and enthusiasm among the students was vibrant and dynamic. This was demonstrated in the individual summary multimedia assignments posted in their e-portfolio. What is significant is that students are fearless at adopting digital communication resources into the learning experiences in ways that manage information in a creative, entertaining and inspiring way.

There is a growing consensus that much of our students' learning lives is and will be spent interacting in online, ritual networks, forming groups with others on the basis of their passions and their need to learn (Ohler 2009). It is a shift that challenges the relevance of the traditional classroom in some fundamental ways.

BEST PRACTICES

Mount DeSales Academy in Macon, Georgia has been leading the way by integrating Web 2.0 tools into their planning and teaching in faith formation. Through the program Moodle teachers are creating online learning communities with tools such as journals, forums, testing Moodle, blogs, and class resource pages. Moodle is an Open source Course Management System (CMS) also known as a Learning Management System (LMS), or a Virtual Learning Environment (VLE). It is popular among educators as a tool for creating online websites for student learning. Dr. Gabe Germann uses Moodle for his Social Justice class as an opportunity for students to express their opinions on difficult topics and respond to their classmates' thoughts, leading to deeper engagement. Kathryn Kane incorporates online journals to engage students on topics within her Foundations of Faith course. She has discovered students are more reflective and delve deeper into their subject matter through the computer and internet applications. Sue Hinderlider offers students alternative assignments in her New Testament class, including posting the results of student research. Catholic educators are learning to use the many activity modules (such as e-Forums, Wikis, Databases, etc) to build richly collaborative communities of learning around their subject matter. The resources are rich, varied and plentiful.

The FLIP video camera has become the easiest tool for video recording, creation, messaging and editing. The tool helps students to be the center of learning and makes it even easier for parents to witness learning achievement. As an example, a kindergarten class created Mother's Day greetings with the FLIPs sending not a card made of construction paper but a video-taped personalized message within an e-mail to their mother, which included a segment of the entire class singing a song in tribute to mothers.

DIGITAL STORYTELLING: A MEANS OF CAPTURING STUDENT'S COLLECTIVE IMAGINATION AND EXPERIENCES

It is amazing how simple or sophisticated the process of digital storytelling can be for teachers and students. A recent convocation of Catholic educators shared personal accounts of how they are effectively applying digital storytelling into the curriculum which is demonstrating that it has strengthened critical thinking, writing and media literacy skills. Digital stories are an engaging methodology for animating the learning environment. The immense quantity of e-resources available to cultivate imaginative digital stories is constantly expanding. Educators are communicating how digital story telling can be integrated into every dimension of their curriculum. Furthermore, the practice of composing digital stories is demonstrating an enhancement of students writing skills across the board.

There are basic techniques that an educator, or students can manipulate to creatively construct a meaningful digital story. It is imperative to commence with a well defined story board which presumes a basic understanding of story mapping and skills with written and oral storytelling techniques. Brooks and Young (2010) define the basic parameters for creating a digital story. "A digital story is a digital video clip, told in the author's own voice, illustrated mostly with still images, with an optional music track added for emotional effect, and/or a voice over." They recommend a few key elements to animate an attractive digital story: (1) commence the digital story with an imaginative lead slide; (2) identify a full-bodied plot, problem-issue, or, e-experience that can engage the viewer; (3) present a strong case for identifying one, or more alternative solutions to initiate a response; and, (4) wrap up the story with a resilient concise conclusion. Educators indicate that e-sources located at www.reports.razfish.com, www.jasonoher.com and www.educause.edu/eli offer continues updates of relevant resources and ides to amplify one's digital story knowledge and skills.

UP ANOTHER NOTCH FOR SAMPLE BEST PRACTICES

I observed an excellent demonstration of this dynamic when a junior high class was assigned to design a contemporary creative interpretation of the Beatitudes. The enthusiasm with which the students embraced the exercise incorporating all the elements of quality digital storytelling along with critical biblical reflection and discernment stimulated an enlightening academic conversation for Beatitude Living both within the learning environment and their local community, as the production was posted on the school's website. The fact that the overall experience stirred the minds and hearts of the students and local community into a specific plan of action for the community that continues until today demonstrates the effectiveness of the new media approach.

Christ the King School (Richmond, VA) using skills learned in their Advanced Technology Class created a "Traveling through Space" virtual tour which illustrates another form of digital storytelling. Students used computer technology combined with advanced film editing techniques and music soundtrack scoring to produce a movie that explored our solar system, starting with the sun, taking us to the edge of the solar system. The goal was to aid seventh grade students in their awareness of space education. The objective was to use technology in the classroom through integrating the media resources of their broadcast studio with the use of digital image manipulation of iMovie, iDVD, and GarageBand.

Educators at St. Pius V Catholic School (Buena Park, California) were looking for ways to supplement their elementary math curriculum. Dealing with differences in student skill levels has always been a challenge, particularly in math. But SmartMath's adaptive platform builds differentiation into each question by adjusting materials and content difficulty based on each student's practice performance. In this way, teachers reach all students, even those who are falling behind and those who are well ahead. The result is that students achieve success in math and move through each topic at their own pace until the material is mastered.

In keeping with the twenty-first Century Skills Initiative, St. Matthew Parish School (Akron, Ohio) introduced a robotics unit into the curriculum. The experience offered an opportunity for community outreach, as well as an opportunity to develop St. Matthew's students' interest in robotics. A summer week-long Robotics Camp exposed students to the excitement of building and programming a robot via the LEGOS robotics curriculum.

Students collecting water samples for analysis may not be an unusual project. But a class of second graders confidently using sophisticated scientific equipment and integrating high-tech media elements into the project certainly is. Students began a day at Old Dominion University's Center for Coastal Physical Oceanography by collecting water samples while classmates videotaped and took digital photos of students at the various scientific stations. Students used SMART Boards to present demonstrations related to the samples. All of these activities were filmed by class members. Students next used the video and photos they had collected, as well as still shots from the digital microscopes, to create iMovies and what they had learned. They added text and music, edited their work, burned the final products to DVDs and even created labels. Finally, the students wrote a science broadcast script describing—and thus teaching—what they had learned. It was produced in the school's broadcast studio.

Saint Augustine of Canterbury School (Kendall Park, NJ), has been operating a school television station, KTN (Knights Television Network). When a group of students asked "Where is the 'good news'?" It dramatically changed both the broadcasts and the school's atmosphere. Now the school's Channel 98 has been transformed into the *Channel of Hope* which shares good news daily throughout in-school broadcasts, as well as podcasts that can be enjoyed by anyone, on and off campus, through the school's website. The Word of the Day is no longer a vocabulary word from the newspaper but a word such as compassion, courage, or beliefs, displayed on a PowerPoint slide along with a meaningful visual and a suggested practice for the day. KTN features student broadcasts and scrolling Power Point slide presentations, all focused on the topic of good news. All aspects of this communication are designed and maintained by 10-, 11-, and 12- year-old students who are self-motivated, innovative and spirited. The steady stream of hopeful news broadcast by these students helps mute the negativity of the public media that all students are exposed to every day.

St. Rose of Lima Academy (Short Hills, NJ) has implemented the borderless classroom. Eighth-graders are working with scientists to investigate seals in Antarctica, while seventh-graders collaborate with university-based science mentors to study seedling growth, all made possible through current and emerging technology. New technological tools have expanded learning beyond the science lab, creating a borderless classroom for a global education experience. The curriculum was designed by teacher Cristina Wage. Using webcasts, email, and blogs, students share findings and questions with other students and scientists worldwide. Students engage in hands-on plant investigations through *Planting Science*, a collaborative learning resource supported by scientific societies and universities. They also participate in the *National Geographic Jason Project*, which applies research data from *NASA, NOAA*, and others as it connects students with scientist explorers through live events and message boards. These and other high-tech programs have noticeably increased student engagement. The school has taken a step toward going green as they move toward a paperless classroom. Curriculum materials are shared online and students use collaborative applications to share homework and class requirements. Participation platforms make collaborative writing possible for group projects and peer review without the constraints of time or paper.

The innovation application of iPods within the learning environment is a stellar initiative of Pensacola Catholic High School (Pensacola, Florida). The *iPod Pals Project*, a collaborative initiative with another Catholic School (St. John the Evangelist Catholic School) combined technology and religion to create lessons that are animating and effective. By preparing podcasts on themes related to the Corporal Works of Mercy, a richer appreciation and understanding is imbedded in the students' life and memory of how to translate discipleship into the twenty-first century. The iPod initiative includes the raising of social consciousness through original music composition on the Seven Works of Mercy and how they make a difference in both students and general contemporary life.

E-SOCIALIZATION: GIFT OR THREAT

Several times during the academic year I meet with select groups of elementary and secondary Catholic school students to discuss how their learning is enhanced, or challenged by accessible digital tools and resources that are introduced into the learning environment. The conversation is lively as a flood of ideas flow around the room.

The millennial generation is surfing the Internet exploring, designing and actively engaging in new ways of communication and social networking. The ease with which students K though 12 navigate the Internet portals is far beyond the imagination most Catholic and faith based educators would ever have imagined three years ago. As one Catholic educator said to me following a presentation: "Oh that the students would spend such quality time with their academic studies!" Personally, I think what we are experiencing are clues for approaching alternative new realities for discovery learning in a digital culture.

As educational theorist Marc Prensky speaks about the "Digital Natives," who are well versed in the uses and etiquette of computers, digital cameras, cell phones, text messaging, Weblogs, Facebook and related social media networks, we begin to sense the inevitable systemic digital changes influencing discovery learning in the coming decades. These students have been born into a world filled with gadgets and online community, and to most of them it's a way of life (Prensky 2001). Included in our conversation is the iGeneration's reliance on speed and multitasking via their digital tools. We observe that they are never doing only one task at a time but use the rapid pace of technology to enable them to be connected to family, friends and school. Students are craving the same speed they get from the digital world for classroom learning. Catholic educators are facing the facts that a new digital democracy is emerging and expanding with quantum leaps and our students are the primary citizens of this democracy. Often they cannot understand why we current educators are making such a "big issue" of a culture that is so transparent and functions with ease. On the Web, anyone with a digital camera has the power to change history (Poniewozik 2006, 63). While some educators may continue to question whether the Internet offers any real socialization experiences or opportunities—chat rooms, Instant Messaging, YouTube, Facebook and more are nurturing a new communications culture for self-expression and relationships. These relationships are not "light of nature" either! User generated content is revolutionizing the media landscape. It is reported that users upload over 70,000 new videos to the YouTube site every day. Over 100 million YouTube videos are viewed every day. Video-sharing sites are changing the flow, style, format and flood of information. All one needs is a combination of an iPhone, or digital camera and a website and one is contributing to the new media landscape, as well as sense and experience of history. It is easy, cheap recording and free distribution—that makes it both potent and complex. We have yet to understand the "tip of this iceberg" of what are significantly developing here and the difference it will continue to make on humanity's socialization processes for years to come.

Facebook is the second-most-visited Internet site, after Google, and it claims more than 400 million active users as of February 2010 (Kirkpatrick 2010). More than 20 percent of the 1.7 billion people on the Internet worldwide now regularly use Facebook. Kirkpatrick indicates that if the growth rates of both Facebook and the Internet remain steady, by 2013 every single person online worldwide will be on Facebook. Facebook operates in 75 languages, and about 75 percent of its active users are outside the United States. Facebook's vice president for product puts it this way: "We want to give everyone the same power that mass media has had to beam out a message." Isn't this what we are experiencing today? Simply pay attention to your television news, iPhones and Social Networking sites. The proof is in our existential situation.

Weblogs (blogs) are the new medium that has risen out of the web culture. While it may appear to be similar to discussion boards it is a relatively new technology that has emerged out of the youth web-culture. People maintained blogs long before the term was coined, but the trend gained momentum with the introduction of automated publishing systems, most notably Blogger at www.blooger.com. A blog is an online journal or diary, which reflects the personality of the author. Applied within a learning environment blogs can motivate students to read and critically reflect on one another's contributions and can enhance the quality of their own academic studies and personal perspective in light of the e-community's conversation. It is considered a discourse tool for web-based learning.

Researchers are indicating that growing self-expression is manifested in blogs. As attempts are being made to create a sense of online community through discussion boards, sometimes with, or without limited success, blogging is cultivating the desired sense of on-line community. Research indicates that since it (blogging) has evolved out of the normal stream of e-culture it has become a democratic medium for all involved. Blogs are creating pathways for faculty and students to ask questions, define inquiry, process and synthesize data and information, draw conclusions and develop action plans based on new found knowledge with likeminded people.

The shift in the learning paradigm from an objectivistic to constructivist perspective within the learning environment seems to be the key for understanding blogging (Dickey 2004, 280). Constructivist perspective is that knowledge is constructed not transmitted. The learner is active in the process. In order for blogging to be effective it requires an attitude of exploration, interaction and manipulation within the learning environment by bloggers (Dickey 2004).

Creating blogs is a dynamic for building bridges among Catholic school administrators/faculty, parents, and students. Blogs create opportunities for asynchronous e-conversations with select constituents on a particular Catholic school issue or concern. By establishing a blog on changes in a Catholic school ethos, customs, directives, new curriculum, service projects, or technical infrastructure, Catholic school administrators and faculty glean a collective response from parents as one of the means for creating a healthy dialogic process. Yet, blogs offer fast feedback and often Catholic school administrators indicate they may not always be able to handle the flood of information and/or the expectations created by opening the door to share insights. In these situations administrators are delegating a staff or faculty member to monitor the flow of information and immediate feedback.

Teachers are creating blogs to share their interests, concerns, research, new ideas and frustrations with other teachers in similar venues across the country. Whether it is lesson plans, curriculum designs, seeking collaborative student projects, seeking new resources, etc. blogs are breaking new ground for teacher interaction. www.weblogged.com is a site dedicated to discussions about the use of Web-related technologies in K–12 education and is a resource frequently mentioned by educators to collect rich web links, best practices and related information. www.fieducation.blogspot.com, www.typebad.com and www.schoolblogs.com offer links to other bloggers and advocacy organizations to support curriculum enhancement.

Twitter, a free micro-blogging service, is advancing social networking capabilities for learning. Tweaking is no longer a pastime adventure but essential for being connected all the time! Users sign up, create a profile and begin sending short messages to both select individuals and everyone within their signature radar. Known as tweets, all within your range or preferred company come to know all about what you are doing and thinking at the moment. Transparency is the rule of the moment. All other users may read one's updates unless the sender gives access only to specific people. More than 1,000,000 people followed President Barack Obama on Twitter throughout his campaign. Learning environments are beginning to demonstrate the potential of Twitter through the Twitter website, or by SMS, RSS, email and a host of other applications. Yes, it is considered a social media for personal and informal communication and learning, as well as linking school programs, special school networks, notices and urgent messages with faculty, parents and students. With Catholic and faith based school administration and faculty seeking ways to have more instant communication with parents for more participative engagement, Twitter is becoming an excellent distribution system.

Recently the world has observed the power and potential of digital tools and Internet access and distribution with world events. The Chilean mine disaster (2010), the political upset in Egypt and the Middle East (2011) and rapidly expanding independent iNews reporting indicates that our textbooks (as such) are becoming obsolete as history, geography, religion, demographics are rapidly evolving today.

Clearly, social networking sites can create and maintain relationships that wouldn't have existed otherwise. But can they sustain relationships? What kind of relationships are they? Are these expanding e-socialization sites only a way to avoid dealing with people face to face? Or, as one of my students wrote in a final paper, "The intensification and demands of social networking is one more factor strengthening a culture of distraction. It holds us prisoner from coming to know our authentic selves." Her reflections centered on the constant demand of being connected all the time, multitasking through a diversity of applications while lacking the courage to be attentive to contemplation and silence. Is it possible that our youth, in particular, can lose the limited interpersonal communication skills they currently have by ignoring, encouraging or affirming their time in these "places"? There is still much research demanded here. We have only begun a very, very long frontier journey.

Educators need to be cognizant of their responsibility for monitoring and determining the ethical factors that influence the lives of our students from time spent online. Just as social-networking sites and Internet communications can accelerate and amplify the adolescent's normal sexual explorations, they can do the same with another time-honored teenage tradition: bullying. Furthermore, the Internet allows impersonation of another, something that's nearly impossible to do in a school hallway (*U.S. News and World Report* 2006, 55–66). This can, as we are seeing today, have dangerous ramifications for the lives of unsuspecting students. The examples are numerous and I am sure that each of us has an experience or story to tell. Thus, establishing ethical and moral principles and standards is essential for our students to navigate through the Internet cyberterrain!

Rome Catholic School (Rome, New York) has taken a lead in the world of Internet security by creating and teaching the first high-school Cyber Security course in the nation. Students learn about data protection, firewalls, data hiding, wireless security, and more. The class was created in partnership with the Rome Air Force Research Laboratory, Syracuse University, and ITT (Information Technology) industry. From the class the school has formed a cyber forensic team of expert students who investigate internet agreement and student handbook violations concerning damaged computes and cyber bullying. In addition to technical education, the cyber education program provides lectures on cyber ethics into which Christian values and the universal moral code are incorporated. Several websites mentioned by educators for addressing concerning ethical use of digital tools and internet resources are Digital Dossier (www.youtube.com/watch?v=791VLA) which describes all the digital resources that accumulate about a typical person; Connectsafely (www.connectsafely.org) which includes social network safety tips for students and parents; WoogieWorld website (www.woogiworld.com/educators), offers games that teach cybersafety, cyberethics, cybersecurity and cyberhealth. Parents are educated through guest speaker initiatives and from the school's website on how to keep their children cyber safe. Catholic and faith based educators are refining ways to work with students in shaping this emerging online democratic culture grounded in solid ethical principles which define the dignity of the human person and quality of life.

Blogging, Facebook MySpace, Twitter, texting, etc. are here to stay. They are part of American culture. But that which is useful can also be dangerous. We, who have been entrusted by God with the education of His children, have a grave obligation to keep them safe and to keep ourselves safe as examples of gospel living for young people to follow. Today's Catholic and faith based educator should understand that the personal behavioral boundaries between adult and young person extend to the world of cyberspace, as well as the physical world of school and extra-curricular activities (Shaugnessy 2010, 38). Every effort we endeavor to pursue in this regard can work toward creating an alternative countercultural dimension to this exploding online existential reality. Our intentional engagement can make all the difference for enhancing the dignity of persons in an expanding cyber culture. Vast numbers of e-resources are emerging to aid parents for managing social networking time and addictions in their children's lives. A few of the most frequently mentioned aids are www.BlogSafety.com, www.GetNetWise.org, www.MySpaceWatch.com and www.SafeSpacers.com.

GROWTH OF VIRTUAL WORLDS FOR PROFESSIONAL DEVELOPMENT OPPORTUNITIES

Integrating an e-mentoring program to support students working on projects having special needs, with curriculum mapping and ongoing education among faculty is a growing phenomenon. E-mentoring is recognized as an expanding development for enhancing quality learning communities that are making a difference in the digital age. Exposing more and more teachers to an e-mentoring program both fosters a culture of mentoring and supports the development of talented and motivated teachers. How specifically does e-mentoring support Catholic and faith based schools? Several evolving praxis have been identified by teachers: (1) gaining, or providing valuable knowledge, skills, and experience from another person; (2) building and expanding a network of teachers and experts in the field within and beyond the school or region to nurture innovative learning environments; and, (3) helping to explore alternative perspectives for considering what Catholic, or faith based learning environments need to look like in the future! A number of Catholic and faith based schools have indicated that getting started with webinars each month, hosted by an e-mentoring facilitator (a local teacher, or expert in the field) who reviews lesson plans, curriculum mapping, or strategies for strengthening teaching and learning skills has been an effective e-mentoring opportunity.

Trinity High School's IT Department (CSTA 2011) has used Moodle to create a variety of educational experiences, assessment and resources for teachers' professional development. A Moodle site called the "Staff Portal" embeds critical school functions such as maintenance and professional development requests, field trip forms, departmental forms, attendance reporting, school newsletters, and so on so that faculty can be connected and engaged day by day. Over the past few years Moodle, as a tool for everyday tasks and curriculum development, is now sponsoring a total of 317 courses housed on the Rockspace site including 13 training courses to help teachers revising scope and sequence documents, using Smartboard technology and to help in understanding Open Source options in the classroom.

There is a vast amount of curriculum content on line in a variety of formats, including text, audio and video clips. Resources for IT Best Practices can be discovered at Discovery Educational's Lesson Plan Library (http://school.discoveryeduction.com/lessonplans); Teachers Helping Teacher (www.pacificnet.net/!mandel/index.html); Teachers First (www.teachersfirst.com/index.cfm); Thinkfinity (www.thinkfinity.org/lesson-plans).

DIGITAL LIBRARIES: WORLD ACCESS TO KNOWLEDGE PAST AND EVOLVING

Libraries have been considered culturally sustaining initiatives of society. They are essential for academic life. Over the last 10 years, a new place and strategy for imaging libraries in the digital age have been evolving before our eyes. Libraries had been seen as a repository of vast print and media knowledge with authored works of cultural and academic contributors in a single place. Today we see libraries struggling to place much of their content online. Librarians are purchasing e-journals, e-magazines, e-books and alternative sources of e-knowledge to enrich students' lives to include the rapidly shifting knowledge and information concerning the world, politics, religion, science, economics, literature, peoples and more. However, digital culture is demonstrating that physical libraries are not the essential hubs of knowledge anymore. In the digital world, we are experiencing that people change knowledge and transform the information every nano-second. They are accessing the information from a vast array of portals of social networking sources and applications. Our Catholic and faith based schools are discovering that both libraries and IT must develop new policies and shared understanding for the more communal technological paradigms (via the digital age) that users are beginning to expect.

Ecological and financial concerns are ushering in the e-publishing field requiring our faculty and students to be able to access e-textbooks, e-learning exercises and e-opportunities with greater ease. E-books can be read digitally on a computer screen, a special e-book reader, a personal digital assistant (PDA), or even a mobile phone. The e-book is not limited to static pictures; it can also integrate video, audio, animation, and even interactive simulation. In other words, e-books are consumed on a screen rather than on paper. We begin to save a vast number of trees and forests while preserving our ecological system for the future. Thus, we are beginning to see e-Notebooks and iPads becoming a normal tool for effective learning across most middle to upper grades. Kindle e-readers are being used for special needs students with exceptional success. As we are moving in this direction, educators are beginning to work in close collaboration with publishers as we re-imagine what the book itself might look like in a networked and interactive future. Organizations such as the Institution for the Future of the Book http://www.future ofthebook.org are expanding our literary horizons.

Electronic portfolios have become an essential academic graduation requirement within Catholic High Schools. Notre Dame High School (New Haven, Connecticut) established their e-portfolio's detailed requirements in concert with students. The purpose of the electronic portfolio is to showcase the work students completed during their four years at Notre Dame. The purpose is to prove that students have successfully satisfied the stated outcomes Notre Dame has established for graduation. It is available for review by students, parents, teachers, prospective colleges, and even potential employers. Students create a portfolio containing examples of their work that demonstrate understanding and mastery of various subjects. It is stored on the school's local computer network. Their goal is to illustrate student growth over time by demonstrating an understanding of their own work. An outgrowth of their student electronic portfolio is a faculty portfolio used to evaluate teacher performance on a yearly basis. The electronic portfolio system has become a very innovative use of technology at Notre Dame High School to encourage effective teaching, learning, and growth on the part of both students and faculty.

DISTANCE LEARNING: BLENDED, OR HYBRID

What is the future of the e-classroom? This question continues to oscillate as educators ponder the virtual realities and opportunities that seep into our traditional educational environments. Academic conversations are expanding on the benefits and complementary elements of face-to-face, online, and blended-learning formats. A growing number of higher learning institutions are requiring undergraduate students to participate in alternative learning modes that include online courses. The numbers of online academic degrees are proliferating particularly as the present economic situation is becoming a barrier for residential studies for many. High school students are given opportunities to participate in accelerated academic online courses to acquire undergraduate credits prior to entering college. A deluge of e-certificate and e-in-service programs offer a wide menu of opportunities without the student leaving the office or home.

The focus on online learning requires just as much attention on the instructor as the student. The formation of online instructors is a key component for successful e-learning experiences. The idea that a teacher can simply step right into an online environment from the traditional classroom is not necessarily the case. Perhaps this is where some of the misunderstandings are emerging regarding the effectiveness of e-learning. A new learning context requires that teachers (instructors) are initiated into the practice of new digital skills that enable a quality e-experience to be meaningful and successful. Internally run e-training courses, formal and informal mentoring rank high among most institutions for preparing educators for the e-dimension of discovery learning. Some institutions of higher learning offer a common comprehensive training program for all e-instructors across the board. A review of several institutions profiles a few common denominators that prepare online instructors. These elements are: (1) asynchronous participation in a three to four-week e-seminar for e-instructors; (2) synchronous online conversations regarding grading, class preparation, or specific e-learning themes; (3) teaching an e-course with mentors shadowing and providing guidance; (4) occasional online faculty meetings for information on new e-learning methodologies, or course design; and (5) requirement to participate in an instructor refresher seminar every three to four years to rejuvenate, or refresh one's e-instructor skills.

The long-term impact of online learning whether totally online, blended, or hybrid is yet to be determined. I do not think it is an either/or but a both/and future reality. However, the potential of online learning for offering a rich panorama of e-courses across disciplines that could not be offered in the past because of the lack of available specialized faculty due to financial resources, or space, is being altered. Schools are designing hybrid learning environments that bring in distance resources, faculties and student cohorts to study world religions, social justice concerns and expanding language awareness and skills. E-courses benefit students who request specialized courses when only three to four students are interested. E-courses are enhancing home schooling at all levels. E-courses and programs are building new professional and academic bridges among higher education, professional communities, and elementary and secondary education.

CONCLUSION

While educators and IT leaders celebrate the seamless accessibility of technology for many students, we still discover poverty is present in pockets around the country. We continue to hear reports of the "haves and have nots" regarding IT in one form or another. We face further challenges with students with limited English proficiency (ESL) who are at a disadvantage in using computers for creative and problem-solving activities (Schrum and Levin 2009). Many times, equipment is not available to ESL programs, but even if the hardware exists, software and Web sites use academic English (Zehr 2001). Educators need to be equipped to combine their technology and ESL skills in order reach a growing population in our educational environments.

Educators, course designers and IT leaders cannot ignore this reality without coming up with creative solutions for a digital-access balance as a matter of social justice in the twenty-first century. While not every student is coming to our classes with digital devices accessible to them 24/7, their numbers are rapidly growing for several reasons: digital and mobile devices are proliferating and are available at lower costs; the amount and quality of digital content for learning is exploding; and interactive environments online are becoming easier to use and more useful. The International National Educational Technology Standards and Performance Indicators for Teachers and Students (2007, 9–12) set the tone and pace for IT in our learning environments; however, it is time to revisit these standards in light of an evolving iGeneration and Digital culture. Catholic and faith-based school administrators and faculties need to find positive and creative ways to work with students in shaping this emerging online democratic culture. We may not alter it dramatically, but we can demonstrate to our students that we can create a countercultural dimension to the expanding digital reality that could make a difference in enhancing the dignity of persons in a cyberworld.

We perceive only the sensations we are programmed to receive, and our awareness is further restricted by the fact that we recognize only those for which we have mental maps or categories (Zanders 2000). It is time to re-shape our educational mental maps and categories for learning in the twenty-first century. Educators are leaders in effecting this transformation so that is becomes woven into the very fabric of our lives. Educators need to understand it and have it work for the good of humanity, nurturing a quality of life while creating a culture of justice and peace throughout the world supported by assessable and evolving digital culture.

REFERENCES AND FURTHER READING

Bristow, Rob, Ted Dodds, Richard Northam and Leo Plugge. "Computing and the Power to Choos." *EDUCAUSE Review.* (May–June 2010): 14–15.

Brooks—Young, Susan. "Telling a Story, Web 2.0 Style." *Today's Catholic Teacher.* March 2010, 10.

Catholic Schools of Tomorrow Award for Innovation Entries. Sponsored by Peter Li, Inc.

Catholic Schools of Tomorrow Award for Innovation Entries. Christ the King Catholic School—Norfolk, Virginia. 2011.

Catholic Schools of Tomorrow Award for Innovation Entries. Mount DeSales Academy—Macon, Georgia. 2009.

Catholic Schools of Tomorrow Award for Innovation Entries. Notre Dame High School. West Haven, Ct. 2011.

Catholic Schools of Tomorrow Award for Innovation Entries. Pensacola Catholic High School. Pensacola, Florida. 2011.

Catholic Schools of Tomorrow Award for Innovation Entries. Roman Catholic School. Rome, New York. 2008.

Catholic Schools of Tomorrow Award for Innovation Entries. St. Augustine of Canterbury School. Kendall Park, New Jersey. 2010.

Catholic Schools of Tomorrow Award for Innovation Entries. St. Matthew Parish School—Akron, Ohio. 2010.

Catholic Schools of Tomorrow Award for Innovation Entries. St. Rose of Lima Academy. Short Hills, New Jersey. 2010.

Catholic Schools of Tomorrow Award for Innovation Entries. Trinity High School. Louisville, Ky. 2011.

Christensen, Clayton, Michael B. Horn and Curtis W. Johnson. *Disrupting Class.* New York. McGraw Hill, 2008.

Dede, C., J. P. Honan, and L. C. Peters, (eds.). *Scaling Up Success: Lessons from Technology Based Educational Improvement.* San Francisco: John Wiley & Sons, 2005.

Dickey, Michele. "The Impact of Web-logs (Blogs) on Student Perceptions of Isolation and Alienation in a Web-based Distance—Learning Environment." *Open Learning* 19: 13 (2004): 280.

ISTE (International Society for Technology in Education. Washington, D.C. (2007): 9–12.

Kirkpatrick, David. *The Facebook Effect. The Inside Story of the Company that Is Connectingthe World.* New York: Simon & Schuster. 2010.

Koester, Jolene. "Information Technology and Tomorrow's University." *EDUCAUSE Review.* (January–February 2011): 36.

Meloni, Julie. "Hardware and Software: Tools for Online and Hybrid Learning." *The Chronicle for Higher Education.* November 5, 2010, 13–22.

Ohler, Jason. "Orchestrating the Media Collage." *Educational Leadership* (March 2009): 9.

Palfrey, John and Urs Gassar. *Born Digital: Understanding the First Generation of Digital Natives.* New York: Basic Books Press, 2008.

Poniewozik, James. "Technology." *Time* December 26, 2006. 63.

Poniewozik, James. "Products and Services that Work for Catholic Education." *Today's Catholic Teacher,* November–December 2010, 28.

Rosen, Larry. *Rewired: Understanding the iGeneration and the Way They Learn*. New York. Palgrave MacMillan, 2010.

Rosen, Larry. "Teaching the iGeneration." *Educational Leadership*. March 2009). 9.

Rossini, Carolina. "The Open World: Access to Knowledge as a Foundation for an Open World" Colorado. *EDUCAUSE Review*. July-August (2010): 60–68.

Schrum, Lynne and Barbara B. Levin. *Leading 21st Century Schools: Harnessing Technology for Engagement and Achievement*. Thousand Oaks, California. A SAGE Company (Corwin): 2009.

Schultze, Quentin J. *Habits of the High-Tech Heart: Living Virtuously in the Information Age*. Michigan: Baker Book House Company 2002.

Shaughnessy, Sr. Mary Angela. "Social Media: Legal Issus for Teachers." *Today's Catholic Teacher*. January-February (2010): 38.

Staley, David J. and Dennis A. Trinkle. "The Changing Landscape of Higher Education." *EDUCAUSE Review*. (January-February 2010): 16.

Tapscott, Don. *Growing Up Digital*. New York. McGraw-Hill Books, 2009.

Trilling, Bernie and Charles Fadel. *21st Century Skills: Learning for Life in Our Times*. San Francisco: Jossey-Bass, 2009.

Vermeulen, Freek, Phanish Puranam and Ranjay Gulati. "Change for Change's Sake." *Harvard Business Review* (June 2010): 71.

Zander, Ben and Rosamund Stone Zander. *The Art of Possibility: Transforming Professional and Personal Life*. Boston: Harvard Business School Press, 2000.

Zehr, M. "Technology Counts 2011: Language Barriers." *Education Week*. 20, 35, 2001, 28–29.

Zukowski, Angela Ann. "Reframing Religious Presence in a Digital Culture." *Horizon* (Winter 2011): 15.

36

Catholic Independent and Unaffiliated Schools

John J. White

Independent and unaffiliated Catholic schools are schools that have arisen since the close of the Second Vatican Council outside of diocesan or parochial control and often without episcopal approbation. Founded by lay persons concerned about a perceived lack of fidelity in existing Catholic schools, independent Catholic schools are one manifestation of the restorationist impulse in American Catholicism that is also expressed in Catholic publishing and media as well as in the growth of movements and groups like Opus Dei, the Legionaries of Christ, and Catholics United for the Faith (Varacalli 2005, 51–52).

Unlike schools operated by canonically established lay movements like Opus Dei, these independent schools have no defined legal status under canon law, and as such they do not enjoy structural or institutional support from the Church. In order to create a system of support, independent Catholic schools formed the National Association of Private Catholic Independent Schools (NAPCIS) in 1995. NAPCIS accredits independent schools, it offers a form of teacher certification, and it provides advice and professional development to new and existing schools. NAPCIS stresses fidelity to the Pope and to the magisterium of the Church while resisting administrative control by diocesan departments of education, which they believe to have been compromised by adherence to educational fads arising out of the public schools. While some individual independent schools have received episcopal approval, others have not, and are therefore not permitted to use the term *Catholic* in their names.

Catholic education in the United States underwent a seismic shift in the aftermath of the Second Vatican Council. The number of lay faculty grew enormously as priests and religious left the schools and as new vocations decreased. Lay teachers tended to have received their training in schools of education, where even in Catholic colleges there was no distinction made in the preparation of public or Catholic school teachers (Weinig 2007). Changes were made to the curriculum, particularly in the area of catechesis, where what was perceived as an overly intellectual approach to religious education was replaced by what its proponents believed to be a more holistic and experiential approach to religious education. This "new paradigm" reflected openness to the contemporary world and a willingness to collaborate with and utilize the pedagogical innovations found in the secular educational community (Shimabukuro 1998, 35). To liberals or progressives, the changes after Vatican II represented a maturation of American Catholicism as the Church was cleansed of antiquated ideas, while to conservatives the changes were viewed as a dangerous secularization of the structures of Catholic life (Carlin 2003, 36–38; Varacalli 2005, 41–42). As the number of students fell and as schools began to be closed, tuition rose to cover the cost of lay faculty and staff, which to conservatives represented a further secularization of the schools as the market increasingly came to drive decisions about schools (Carlin 2002, 56–57). Catholic schools soon directed their marketing efforts toward those who could pay, which meant the schools increasingly sought to meet the needs of upper middle class Catholics, whose aspirations did not necessarily translate into authentically Catholic ends (Varicalli 2010, 22). Those Catholic schools that thrived into the 1990s were those that served an elite social and economic class (Baker & Riordan 1998, 17).

THE FIRST INDEPENDENT SCHOOLS

Some parents reacted to this perceived secularization of Catholic schools by removing their children from parochial schools and homeschooling them or establishing small independent schools with other like-minded parents. Independent Catholic schools began to develop as early as 1969, when Holy Innocents School opened in New Jersey. By the mid 1970s schools had also been founded in Louisville, Kentucky (Holy Angels), Post Falls, Idaho (Our Lady of Victory), and Wheat Ridge, Colorado (Colorado Catholic Academy). Parents who founded these schools were often concerned about issues of what it meant to be "faithful" Catholics and which literary, theological, and cultural elements should be emphasized in the curriculum, while others sought to escape innovations like the new child-centered pedagogy, sex education, and reformed catechetical doctrine (Guernsey & Barott 2008, 487). As the number of teachers and administrators trained in schools of education primarily designed to train public school teachers increased, the public school model began to dominate in Catholic school administration as well as in classrooms. Eileen Cubanski, the founder of St. Maria Goretti School in Loomis, California, and a founder and executive director of NAPCIS, described the frustration that motivated many parents who became involved in founding independent schools. Parents who were "scandalized and dismayed" at what was taking place in parish schools brought their complaints to the priest only to discover that he had lost control of his school to the "centralized bureaucracy that had taken hold in every diocese in the name of the Catholic School Department." The diocesan education department, which had been "established to be an advisory body to the pastor, became the policy-setting authority for Catholic schools. Once parish schools became diocesan schools, bureaucrats, not parents, became the primary educators of children" (Cubanski 2007, 13). Parents who challenged the new system found themselves labeled as troublemakers, and appeals to the local bishop usually resulted in the bishop siding with the school and/or diocesan administrators (Spencer 1996).

This experience was repeated all over the United States, and schools began to be set up as non-profit, 501(c)(3) corporations on the initiative of individuals or groups of lay Catholics. In California three schools were either founded or mentored in the 1980s by Francis Crotty, a retired highway patrol officer. Kolbe Academy in Napa became the most well known of these schools. Crotty designed the curriculum of his schools around the 1599 *Ratio Studiorum* of the Society of Jesus. Kolbe's curriculum emphasized classical languages and the development of mnemonic and oratorical skills imparted through the traditional Jesuit practices of prelection, imitation, repetition, and emulation. Approached by homeschooling parents for help in designing their curricula, Crotty produced several pamphlets and guidebooks, the most well known of which is his *Implementation of Ignatian Education in the Home* (1995). This small book has brought Ignatian educational principles to homeschoolers and to independent Catholic schools throughout the United States and has played a significant role in making traditional Ignatian education the basis of many independent and homeschooling curricula. Today, Kolbe continues to operate a K–12 independent school called Kolbe Academy and Trinity Grammar and Preparatory School, after the former school merged with the latter in 2008. The school also operates the Kolbe Homeschool Academy, a distance-learning school that can either supplement or be the basis of a Catholic homeschooling curriculum.

THE FOUNDATION OF NAPCIS

Although it is impossible to determine the actual number of independent Catholic schools operating at any given time, by 1995 it was estimated that there were over 100 schools in existence, and most of them had fewer than 100 students (Cubanski 2007, 14). In the summer of 1995 Crotty, Cubanski, and the administrators of two other schools were making a retreat at "Sweetwater," the California home of Fr. Joseph Fessio, SJ, the founder and editor in chief of Ignatius Press and one of the spiritual leaders of the Catholic restoration movement. Crotty saw the need for an association that would assist schools in preserving their Catholic identity and which would also assist new schools that wished to remain faithful to Catholic teaching. From this retreat, NAPCIS was born. The four founding member schools were Kolbe Academy, Manresa Academy of Reno, NV; St. Thomas Aquinas School of Tahoe City, CA; and Cubanski's St. Maria Goretti Academy. A foundational document of NAPCIS came to be called "The Sweetwater Statement," a name consciously chosen to stand in opposition to the 1967 "Land of Lakes" statement in which U.S. Catholic colleges and universities asserted their institutional independence from any authority external to the academic community itself. Although it was directed toward higher education, to the founders of NAPCIS the Land of Lakes statement was a major source of the secularization in Catholic secondary and elementary schools as those ideas percolated through the Catholic educational establishment, "trickling down" to the lowest and most local levels of Catholic schooling. The Sweetwater Document was a clear rejection of the principles of Land of Lakes, stating that the purpose of NAPCIS would be "to provide for the spiritual and academic welfare of our nation's Catholic schoolchildren, directed to the greater glory of God and the growth of His Church on earth. Fulfillment of this purpose will come from strict adherence to the Magisterium of the Roman Catholic Church and from the implementation of reasonable and demonstrated practices of education" (quoted in Cubanski 2007, 14).

The other issue with which NAPCIS had to deal at the time of its foundation was the use of the word "Catholic." The Code of Canon Law (Canons 803.3 and 808) says that no school or university can call itself Catholic without the consent of the competent ecclesiastical authority. In other words, a school is Catholic only if the bishop says that it is Catholic. As a result of this, all official NAPCIS documents have an asterisk after the C in NAPCIS, thus: NAPC*IS. Originally, this asterisk directed the reader to a statement that pointed out that, in accordance with c.803.3, a school can only refer to itself as Catholic if it has been approved by the Ordinary, and that while some NAPCIS schools have received such approbation, episcopal approval is not a prerequisite for NAPCIS membership. (Today the asterisk remains but the explanation is buried deep within the NAPCIS website.) A lay-operated non-profit corporation established as a private school teaching the Catholic Faith is not required to obtain the bishop's permission to open, nor is episcopal approval or recognition necessary so long as that school does not call itself a Catholic school. NAPCIS has always recommended, however, that schools should seek to establish a respectful and good working relationship with the local ordinary.

ACCREDITATION

One of the problems that independent schools faced was a lack of what Cubanski referred to as "gravitas"; as each school stood on its own there was no way to determine the quality of education offered, nor was it possible to determine to what extent the school was faithful to Catholic educational and spiritual principles. In 1998 NAPCIS created a set of six criteria for accreditation as well as 15 "Standards of Excellence" by which schools might be accredited. While many of these standards address the same issues of professional competency of faculty and staff and the quality of curriculum and facilities as would a secular accrediting organization, the first four standards (available at the NAPCIS website) all address the issue of the personal fidelity of the faculty and staff to the Pope and to the teaching authority of the Church, a fidelity that is expected to be expressed in the mission, educational philosophy, and curriculum and in the teaching methods of the school as well. The accreditation process takes up to three years and requires a self-study and a school visit by a NAPCIS visiting committee that evaluates on-site performance based upon information submitted in the self-study. Accreditation lasts for six years, during which the school must submit an annual report to NAPCIS. Accreditation is not a requisite for NAPCIS membership. As of December, 2010, NAPCIS's website reported that 15 of its 66 member schools were accredited, with another 8 schools in the review process at that time.

TEACHER CERTIFICATION

Peter Steinfels wrote that Catholic schools experienced a "near death experience" as they shifted from religious to lay control. The old system of school governance, staffing, and administration was disrupted without sufficient thought being given to its replacement (2003, 203–4). The secularization of schools of education in Catholic colleges and universities occurred at the same time that lay teachers were coming to predominate in Catholic classrooms, creating something of a perfect storm for those who wished to preserve traditional Catholic forms of pedagogy and curriculum. Watzke corroborates Steinfels's assertion, pointing out that not only was there no plan for the development of a cadre of teachers trained in Catholic curriculum and instruction, but Catholic schools of education adopted a "one-size-fits-all" approach that viewed specific training for Catholic schools as somehow limiting or inadequate (Watzke 2002, 145; 2005, 463–66). Catholic colleges with a reputation for orthodoxy and conservatism have not been much help. Kenneth Weinig (2007) noted that none of the Catholic colleges most closely associated with the restoration movement prepare candidates specifically for Catholic pedagogy. Thomas Aquinas (California), and St. Thomas More and Magdalene colleges (New Hampshire) have no teacher-preparation programs, and Weinig found that the Franciscan University of Steubenville, OH made no distinction between public and Catholic teacher preparation (30–31).

Independent Catholic schools generally avoid hiring state licensed teachers because they wish to avoid compromising the integrity of their school with "a teacher contaminated with the prevalent attitudes and dangerous theories being offered in teacher preparation courses in colleges and universities" (Cubanski 2009, 11). As a result, few teachers come into independent Catholic school classrooms with any pedagogical training. Schools tend first to hire for Catholic mission, and then for content knowledge, and finally for expertise in pedagogy. In 2002, NAPCIS introduced its own Teacher Certification Program. It is not a pre-service teacher-preparation program, but a school-based induction and mentoring program intended to help form teachers who already are employed in independent schools. It is based upon the Five Magisterial Principles of Education drawn from Pius XI's 1929 encyclical on Christian education, *Divini Illius Magistri*. With a mentor teacher, the candidate for certification follows a one-year curriculum based on NAPCIS's Standards of Excellence for Teachers that leads to a Provisional Certificate. These standards cover the principles of Catholic education; the essential truths of the Catholic faith and moral life; the principles of professionalism and responsibility; methods of teaching and evaluating students; methods of mentoring and motivating; and methods of classroom management and discipline. After this is completed a certification examination is given, and it is sent with supporting materials from the mentor teacher and the school administrator to NAPCIS for certification. After five years and further professional development the teacher may apply for Master Teacher status. NAPCIS does not mandate a pedagogical format; each school is free to develop its own or to teach according to Ignatian, Dominican, Lasallian, or other established Catholic principles. The NAPCIS TCP assists schools in articulating and strengthening their own pedagogical and educational philosophy while adhering to that which is distinctively Catholic (Cubanski 2009, 11).

NAPCIS AND INDEPENDENT SCHOOL GOVERNANCE

NAPCIS is governed by a board of trustees, which includes Francis Crotty and Eileen Cubanski as well as founders or principals of three other schools. NAPCIS is also supported by a Council of Scholars, many of whom are the leading intellectual lights of the American Catholic restorationist movement. Finally, NAPCIS's episcopal advisor is Raymond Cardinal Burke, Cardinal Prefect of the Supreme Tribunal of the Apostolic Signatura, who previously served as Archbishop of St. Louis. Burke is known as the leading American conservative prelate, and he is a supporter of traditional Catholic education. Although Cardinal Burke's association with NAPCIS might be intended to compensate for the lack of canonical status for member schools, his association with NAPCIS serves to confirm many liberals' belief that independent Catholic schools are a divisive element in the Church.

Because most independent schools have been founded in the last 30 years and are the product of the vision of a single parent/founder or a small group of founders, the transfer of power or of school administration from the founding generation to the succeeding generation has often been difficult and has sometimes resulted in an already small and struggling school splitting in two. Trinity Prep in California was founded in 1995 as a result of a split with Kolbe Academy; the two schools merged again in 2008 (Zehnder 1999). Guernsey & Barott (2008) examined the phenomenon of conflict within independent Catholic schools and noted that managerial conflicts between founders and successors or new stakeholders were exacerbated by the schools' operating without the structures of the Church, and that NAPCIS recognizes that this is a frequent phenomenon among schools (496).

INDEPENDENT SCHOOLS AND THE INSTITUTIONAL CHURCH

There is a certain irony between NAPCIS's insistence on loyalty to the magisterium of the Church and the poor relations that many independent schools have with their local diocesan officials, something that critics of independent Catholic schools are quick to point out. Diocesan superintendents, Catholic schools of education, and leaders of the National Catholic Educational Association (NCEA) equate legitimacy with existing diocesan educational structures, and they use the independence of these schools as a way to dismiss them. In a 1998 interview with John Allen of the *National Catholic Reporter*, Robert Kealey of the National Catholic Educational Association (NCEA) pointed out that "When people say the doctrine being taught [in Catholic schools] is not Catholic, well obviously what is being taught is what the bishop believes should be taught, so there's a contradiction here. . . . What is being taught is what has been approved by the superintendent of schools as the representative of the bishop." In that same article, Jerome Porath, superintendent of the Los Angeles Catholic school system noted that it is contrary to the magisterium of the Church to claim loyalty to the Holy Father but to be disloyal to the local bishop.

It does not appear that independent or NAPCIS member schools will be welcomed into the mainstream of Catholic education by those at the university level, either. In May of 2010, Patricia Weitzel-O'Neill, former superintendent of schools in the Archdiocese of Washington and currently executive director at the Center for Catholic Education at Boston College's Lynch School of Education, termed independent schools "faux Catholic schools" because they do not have episcopal approval (Pattison 2010). In its 2006 landmark study *Making God Known, Loved, and Served: The Future of Catholic Primary and Secondary Schools in the United States* The Notre Dame Task Force on Catholic Education listed several "internal challenges" that Catholic schools are likely to be facing. The report cited the need for academic excellence and increasing Catholic identity as two of the challenges, but it did not suggest that there are specific Catholic pedagogies that are distinguishable from best practices in public schools or that Catholic identity could be uncovered and made manifest through a Catholic curriculum based in the trivium, quadrivium, classical languages, and the humanities or that the absence of these elements from today's Catholic school represents a problem (7–8). In essence, NAPCIS sees major problems where the American Catholic educational bureaucracy does not even see questions, and vice versa.

NAPCIS assumes that there will be an adversarial relationship between independent schools and diocesan education officials. It has produced a 26-page position paper designed to assist member schools in dealing with their local bishop, urging schools to attempt to make polite and regular contact directly with the bishop and to avoid any contact with his diocesan department of education or the diocesan superintendent of schools (NAPCIS). This is because most member schools see the centralization of Catholic schools under the control of secular educationists as one of the core problems facing Catholic education.

INDEPENDENT SCHOOLS AND THE CATHOLIC RESTORATION

Independent and unaffiliated Catholic schools are a part of a restorationist impulse that has gained strength in recent years. Restorationists do not seek a return to some imagined golden era of Catholicism; they seek to bring a dynamic Catholic orthodoxy back into the Church, institutionalizing a strong Catholic presence in the public square. They are a product of these times and not some other time, and they are comfortable utilizing the technological, cultural, and scientific tools of twenty-first-century life in order to accomplish those goals (Varacalli 2006, 50). Allen (1998) sees evidence of this when he writes that NAPCIS schools are a Catholic manifestation of the general trend in American education toward school choice. They are often infused with the same spirit as that found in Mother Angelica's EWTN television network; *The Wanderer* Forum; Women for Faith and Family; and Catholics United for the Faith, whose *Faith and Life* elementary school catechetical series, while being criticized by superintendents in several dioceses as too "intellectual and dogmatic" or "extremely cognitive," has become the standard set of texts for independent schools and homeschoolers (Sullivan 1999, 127–31). Several teachers and administrators in NAPCIS schools are involved in the Catholic Schools Textbook Project, which has produced five history and geography textbooks published by Ignatius Press.

With their emphasis on solid academics, classical languages, and the great works of the western canon, many NAPCIS members have established themselves as excellent schools. Each year since 2004, the Acton Institute has recognized 50 schools in its Catholic High School Honor Roll, with up to 10 NAPCIS schools appearing in the list in any given year (Cubanski 2007, 15; Schmiesing 2007, 16–17). The Honor Roll recognizes excellence in academics, Catholic identity, and civic education. The adaptation of medieval and early modern Catholic pedagogy to meet twenty-first century needs is in itself a fascinating development in Church history; when one considers that this is being accomplished with little funding in the twenty-first century version of the Irish hedge school it becomes remarkable. Finally, when one learns that these schools are operated by lay men and women who for the most part have had little exposure in their own educational experiences to traditional Jesuit pedagogy or to grammar, logic, and rhetoric, and who in most cases have received little or no formal teacher training, it makes this new movement worthy of notice by all those who have an interest in the religious and humanistic education of Christian children.

REFERENCES AND FURTHER READING

Allen, John. "New independent schools strike a 'less is more' stance—except on Catholic doctrine." *National Catholic Reporter*, (September 11, 1998).

Baker, David P., and Riordan, Cornelius. "The 'Eliting' of the Common American Catholic School and the National Education Crisis." *The Phi Delta Kappan*, 80, 1 (Sept. 1998): 16–23.

Carlin, David. The *Decline and Fall of the Catholic Church in America*. Manchester, NH: Sophia Institute Press, 2003.

Crotty, Francis. *Implementation of Ignatian Education in the Home*. Napa, CA: Kolbe Press, 1995.

Cubanski, Eileen. "NAPC*IS: The hope and promise of Catholic Education." *Catholic Educator*, 2 (Fall, 2007): 13–16.

Cubanski, Eileen. "The Teacher: The Heart of Catholic Education." *Catholic Educator*, 4 (Winter, 2009): 10–12.

Guernsey, Dan and Barott, James. "Conflict in Independent Catholic Schools." *Catholic Education: A Journal of Inquiry and Practice*, 11, 4 (June 2008): 485–502.

NAPCIS. *Relationship Between Private Catholic and Independent Schools and the Local Ordinary*. A NAPCIS Position Paper. (n.d.). Available at http://www.napcis.org/resources.html

Notre Dame Task Force on Catholic Education. *Making God Known, Loved, and Served The Future of Catholic Primary and Secondary Schools in the United States*. Notre Dame, IN: University of Notre Dame, 2006.

Pattison, Mark. "Catholic education is in 'mission confusion,' says longtime educator." *Catholic News Service* (May 10, 2010).

Pius XI. *Divini Illius Magistri*. 1929. In *Five Great Encyclicals*, 36–75. New York: The Paulist Press, 1939.

Schmiesing, Kevin. "Integrating Faith and Academics: A Report on the Catholic High School Honor Roll's Academic Component." *Catholic Educator*, 1 (Spring 2007): 16–17.

Shimabukuro, Gini. *A Call to Reflection: A Teacher's Guide to Catholic Identity for the 21st century.* Washington: National Catholic Education Association, 1998.

Spencer, Robert. "Desert Blossoms." *Sursum Corda* (Spring, 1996).

Steinfels, Peter. *A People Adrift: The Crisis of the Roman Catholic Church in America.* New York: Simon & Schuster, 2003.

Sullivan, James A. "Catholics United for the Faith: Dissent and the Llaity." In *Being Right Conservative Catholics in America*, edited by Mary Jo Weaver & R. Scott Appleby, 107–37. Bloomington: Indiana University Press, 1999.

Varacalli, James A. *The Catholic Experience in America.* Westport: Greenwood, 2005.

Varacalli, James A. "The Necessity of the Catholic School in America in a Time of Cultural Crisis: propositions and proposals." *Catholic Social Science Review* 15 (2010): 299–310.

Watzke, John L. "Alternative Teacher Education and Professional Preparedness: A Study of Parochial and Public Schools Contexts." *Catholic Education: A Journal of Inquiry and Practice*, 8, 4 (June 2005): 463–92.

Watzke, John L. Teachers for Whom? A Study of Teacher Education Practices in Catholic Higher Education. *Catholic Education: A Journal of Inquiry & Practice*, 6, 2 (December 2002): 138–65.

Weinig, Kenneth M. "Teacher Preparation in Catholic Colleges." *New Oxford Review* (April, 2007): 29–34.

Zehnder, Christopher. "Authentic Catholic Schools." *Los Angeles Lay Catholic Mission* (January, 1999).

37

History of the National Catholic Educational Association

Karen M. Ristau

COMING TOGETHER

A wish that students coming to the seminary at The Catholic University of America (CUA) were better and more uniformly prepared led eventually to what was to become the National Catholic Educational Association (NCEA). In 1898, Father Thomas J. Conaty, rector at CUA, organized the Educational Conference of Seminary Faculties. Fifteen seminary presidents responded favorably to Conaty's invitation and voted to establish a formal organization. "They were not impressed, however, with Conaty's appeal that they affiliate with Catholic University and focus their programs toward preparing students to meet the University's requirements" (Plough 1967, 66).

Broadening his vision to establish a national organization that would include Catholic education at all levels, Conaty next called together Catholic college leaders. Fifty-three colleges were represented at an April 1899 meeting. In his opening address, Conaty announced his purpose. Conaty told his audience he hoped for "the permanent establishment of an association of colleges, with annual meetings, in which college conditions shall be thoroughly questioned and answered" (Plough 1967, 163). Aware of the seminary rectors' resistance to affiliating with Catholic University, Conaty took the approach of voluntary association—a much more palatable idea, which would prove successful.

The Parish School Conference evolved from a request Conaty made to bishops to send a representative of the parish schools to meet with the newly formed Association of Catholic Colleges in July of 1902. When this group of parish-level educators decided to organize permanently, it was time to make Conaty's hope for a national association a reality. His plan for a unified system, however, would never be fully realized.

The formal beginning of what was originally named the Catholic Educational Association (the name was formally changed to the National Catholic Educational Association in 1927) took place in St. Louis in the summer of 1904. It was at this meeting that three organizations agreed to become three departments of one Association with the stated mission

To advance the general interests of Catholic education, to encourage the spirit of co-operation and mutual helpfulness among Catholic educators, to promote by study, conferences and discussion, the thoroughness of Catholic educational work in the United States.

NCEA Constitution, 1904

Father Francis Howard, at that time the chair of the Columbus Ohio Diocesan School Board, became first the association's secretary and soon after the executive secretary. Thomas J. Conaty in the meantime had been appointed as bishop of Monterey-Los Angeles. Distance and new duties prevented his further activity with the new association.

GROWTH: CHANGES AND ADDITIONS

Other needs of the Catholic educational community would lead to the addition of other departments to the original three founding departments of the NCEA and provide insight into the historical growth of the association. These groups remain in some configuration or another to the present time.

Secondary Department

In the beginning, Father Francis Howard was determined to keep all the departments together. He was opposed to new departments and strove to give all segments equal representation in planning and in difficult and often contentious conversations about standard curriculum. Nonetheless, 25 years after the founding of the NCEA, the secondary department became its own unit in 1929. The High School department, as it was known then, had previously been part of the Colleges Department. This move coincided with the trend to separate secondary education from earlier definitions of "colleges," which often had included secondary curriculum and secondary-level students.

Superintendents

In the nineteenth century, Catholic educators asked, in the light of the professionalization of public education, how they might help their schools measure up. The answer came with the appointment of diocesan superintendents, which was the beginning of centralization. At the Catholic Educational Association's second annual meeting, in 1905, Reverend Edmund F. Gibbons, the supervisor of schools in Buffalo, New York, "urged all U.S. Bishops to appoint school superintendents, both to foster 'progress' in parochial schools and to represent diocesan interests in them" (Sprows Cummings 2009, 109). This did not happen quickly. Even though in 1930 about 40 percent of dioceses did not have superintendents, the executive board of the NCEA granted departmental status to school superintendents—a department that would be renamed the Chief Administrators of Catholic Education (CACE). Today, CACE holds an annual meeting that brings superintendents together for professional development and discussion of current issues.

A group entitled Catholic Higher Education Serving Catholic Schools (CHESCS) has become a subset of the CACE department. The members are faculty from a variety of Catholic Colleges and Universities that offer degree and certificate programs for teachers and administrators. This group was originally called the Association of Catholic Leadership Programs and was first organized in 1985. The reorganized and expanded group meets at the annual CACE meeting and at the national convention.

Elementary Department

With the separation of the secondary schools from the college members (1929), eventually the Parish School Department would be composed almost entirely of elementary schools. To describe more clearly the work of that department, it was renamed the Elementary Department in 1942. The elementary department has the largest number of members in the association.

Religious Education

At the superintendents' 1969 meeting in Atlanta, noting that much had changed in the way religion was being taught, a resolution was passed urging the formation of

> a department of religious education in every diocese which will provide staff and/or consultative resources to the office of the Superintendent of education.
>
> Augustein, Kauffman, Wister 2004, 114

A meeting to follow through on this resolution was held in early summer following the Atlanta meeting. A committee of people, composed mostly of associate superintendents, gathered in Metarie, Louisiana, and reiterated the call for diocesan religious education departments to be established and expressed the need to have direction from NCEA. Father Alfred McBride was appointed to this position by Msgr. John F. Meyers who then served as the executive director of the superintendents' department. The department first called the National Forum for Religious Education would eventually be named the NCEA Department of Religious Education. The department originally served the needs of religious educators in parish-based programs, schools and adult education programs.

The first work of the new department was to help religious educators move beyond the long-standing rote memorization of the Baltimore Catechism to the new ideas presented after Vatican II. Committees and conferences organized by this department produced a variety of documents to address mutual concerns. Self-evaluation criteria for programs and for the qualities and competencies of all religion teachers were among the early publications of the Department of Religious Education. This department began offering religious education assessment that integrated faith knowledge and behaviors, attitudes and practices, for students in the late 1970s. Assessments for adults became available in 2001. The National Association of Parish Catechetical Directors is a subset of this department.

Departments of Boards and Councils

Historical records indicate the existence of Catholic boards of education as early as the mid 1880s. In 1852, Bishop John Neuman established a central board in Philadelphia made up of both clergy and lay delegates. In 1888, the Archdiocese of New York also had an archdiocesan board (Augustein 2004, 325). The time of significant growth followed the call of Vatican II for co-responsibility and subsidiarity in 1968. Bishops sought greater involvement of lay persons, religious congregation leaders, and other clergy in the decision making processes.

> The development of Catholic education boards, commissions, and councils was seen as one way for members of the local community to take a significant role in the governance of Catholic education. More importantly, involvement of more people in the community would

build greater support for the school's mission that ultimately would enhance the quality of education and stability of the schools they served.

Haney 2004, 80

At the same time, NCEA began to advocate for the involvement of parents and other stakeholders in the policy/advisory governance of Catholic schools. Msgr. O'Neill D'Amour, a strong advocate of boards of jurisdiction, is considered the father of the Catholic School Board movement in the United States. Msgr. D'Amour, from the diocese of Marquette, Michigan, eventually served as a special assistant for boards and was primarily responsible for the addition of a department that would provide direct services to those establishing boards of education with differing kinds of influence. In1974, a Department of Boards of Education and Commission for Parent Organizations was formed.

After the demise of the Parents Organization (1989), members of diocesan and local boards were served by a commission of NCEA. The group was burdened with the title the "National Association of Boards, Commissions, and Councils of Catholic Education," which in fact named the types of grouping that existed in parishes, as some bishops and/or pastors objected to the title 'board' because it implied responsibility for policy.

In 2006, the association voted to change the name of the commission back to part of its original name, the Department of Boards and Councils. At the present time, governance of Catholic schools has become an important issue. School boards, advisory boards, and school committees are taking more responsibility for the direction of schools, and the prediction that boards would enhance the stability of the schools and enhance the quality of the school has been proved true.

Transitory sections

Over the years, the association has included other departments to serve the needs of members. Some of those mentioned have proved constant need; others served temporary needs, and have been disbanded or have been absorbed by other departments. Some of these—Newman Club chaplains, the adult education commission, teacher education, special education—have come and gone or are merged with existing departments.

An effort, however, that proved to be of lasting and critical importance to the improvement and professionalization of Catholic education was the movement encouraged and included in NCEA during the 1950–60s. Spurred by a talk given by Sr. Madeleva Wolff C. S. C. at the 1949 national convention, the Sister Formation Conference came to NCEA in 1957. Led by Sr. Emil Penet, I. H. M., the movement's goal was to have every teaching sister in possession of a bachelor's degree as a minimum standard for teaching in Catholic schools and other works in which religious women engaged. Not without difficulty and not without its detractors, the sisters took charge of their own formation through the efforts of this conference (Glinsky 2006, 360–76).

STRUCTURAL AND GEOGRAPHIC CHANGES

A challenge to NCEA came in the form of its relation to what eventually became the United States Conference of Catholic Bishops. When what was originally called the National Catholic War Council, established to provide support to military personnel in

World War I, became the National Catholic Welfare Council (NCWC) in 1919, it was to coordinate the activities of all Catholic activities and included education. Secretary General Howard opposed the plan to incorporate the Catholic Educational Association into the NCWC. Early relationships were problematic, especially since the NCEA was a totally voluntary association and Howard wished to keep it free from domination by the U.S. Bishops while maintaining good working relationships with them. However, from 1928 under Monsignor George Johnson through the presidency of Monsignor Hochwalt (1966), both Johnson and Hochwalt served as the Director of the Department of Education of the NCWC while serving as NCEA's Executive Secretary (Augustein 2008, 11–18). Timothy Walch explains how the two entities came to understand each other:

> Just as the NCEA had become the voice of Catholic teachers and educators, so did the Education Department of the National Catholic Welfare Conference become the voice of the American bishops on education.
>
> Walch 2003, 111

Traditionally, the National Catholic Educational Association asks a bishop to chair its board of directors. The bishop is chosen by the association board itself and unlike other ministerial associations serving the church does not have an episcopal moderator—that is a bishop assigned to it by the bishops' conference. In this way, the association keeps the original spirit of voluntary association and cooperation with church hierarchy without control by them.

Implications of location

St. Louis, Missouri is given credit for being the birthplace of the NCEA, but the first headquarters were housed in Columbus, Ohio, the home of its secretary general, Father Francis Howard. The association headquarters moved to Washington, D.C., in 1929 in order to be near other secular educational associations and federal government agencies.

The association moved several times in the District of Columbia. The 1960s brought an unexpected influence on the structure of the association when it was housed at One Dupont Circle in the American Council of Education building. During that time, the association staff grew in size and found itself in cramped quarters; at the same time the tenants of the building decided that the entire space should be occupied only by associations that addressed the interests and concerns of higher education. It was time to relocate.

This decision forced a physical division of the association and brought a natural distance between the NCEA and the Department of Colleges and Universities. A more distinct separation came about when federal funds became available to church-related colleges that appeared less sectarian and which were governed by boards that included a good number of lay persons. Since elementary and secondary schools were considered more sectarian, it seemed wiser for the department, renamed the Association of Catholic Colleges and Universities (ACCU) in 1989, to become more independent. This organizational separation began slowly, and finally in 1999–2000, the ACCU was separately incorporated and established as an affiliate member of NCEA. The remaining departments of NCEA, including the seminary department, moved to a building in Georgetown. The seminary department served collegiate and graduate-level seminaries, and the diminishing number of high school seminaries was obviously sectarian and did not fit well with the occupants of One Dupont Circle. The seminary department remains housed with the other departments of the association to this day.

The problems of building ownership coupled with the high costs of working and maintenance in the Georgetown area of Washington, D.C., prompted a move to Arlington, Virginia in the winter of 2009. Funds from the sale were used to establish NCEA's first endowment.

SERVICES AND SYMPOSIA

Throughout its history, NCEA used the original mission devised by Father Thomas J. Conaty to guide its activities. To "encourage the spirit of cooperation and mutual helpfulness," NCEA established regular conferences to serve the needs of members and began a yearly national convention in July of 1904. (The only years without a national gathering were the World War II years of 1940 and 1942.) The themes and titles of the national convention provide insight into the concerns of all those involved in the educational ministries of the Church over the past 100-some years. A sampling of these issues—relationship with government, human rights, role of parents, church and state, ecumenism, global dimensions, finance, excellence in curriculum, social justice teachings, advancement and development, Catholic identity, progress and technology—provides an educational history in itself. (Horrigan 1978, 31–32).

Alongside the national conventions, a number of national symposia were organized to address, in a more scholarly and thoughtful way, the critical issues of Catholic education. The first symposium was held in 1967, followed by another in 1976. The 1967 gathering addressed the growing number of problems—scarcity of teaching Sisters, rising costs, increased tuition, just and competitive salaries—which were thought to be contributing to the decline in parish school enrollment. C. Albert Koob, president of NCEA (the name had been changed from executive director), hoping that a conference would address "restructuring Catholic education to bring it more in line with the contemporary needs of Church and society" (Walch 2003, 111), brought 120 Catholic educational experts together in Washington, DC to make suggestions for the future. Although many positive recommendations were made, the hoped-for common solution to pressing problems was not achieved. A call for more research data on schools did lead to the establishment of the NCEA Data Bank on Catholic education in 1969.

This symposium did however define a new model of service to members. The symposium served as a model for regional meetings and workshops that took NCEA into the field for the first time since the 1930s. Koob felt this in itself would help to relieve the crisis of confidence many people experienced in the 1960s.

The 1980s encouraged a new group of thinkers and writers who called themselves "futurists." Futurists spoke about a new globalism, the beginning of new communication systems, attention to the preservation of natural resources, changing demographics with the introduction of new immigrant groups into American society, and different ways to consider organizations, especially in more collaborative models. Representatives from 22 Catholic organizations were called together by NCEA and the United States Conference of Catholic Bishops (USCCB) to engage in the Catholic Educational Futures Project. The goals of the symposium, held at the University of Dayton in May 1988, were as follows:

Increased understanding between and among national organizations about their ministries and missions

Agreement on the ingredients for a common vision statement for Catholic education in the U.S.
Consensus of a broad agenda for the future of Catholic education
Development of specific action plans for each of the sponsoring organizations
Determination of a date to reconvene within two to four years to reflect on the progress of the
   action plans (Grant and Hunt 1992, 238).

While the discussions focused on similarities and differences between the various organizations, the collaboration between the participants did not live up to the hopes of the plan-
ners. Common directional statements were supported by the group but the plan to
reconvene and review progress in the following years never materialized.

The National Congress on Catholic Schools for the 21st Century, a gathering sponsored
exclusively by NCEA, was held in part as a reaction to the Futures Project, which invited a
wide variety of church ministries and consequently diluted concerns held by Catholic
School people. The national congress, convened in November of 1991, was "to revitalize
and renew the climate of opinion and commitment to the future of Catholic Schooling
in the United States."

The main goals were to

Communicate the story of academic and religious effectiveness of Catholic schools to a national
   audience that includes the whole Catholic community, as well as the broader social and political
   community.
Celebrate the success of Catholic schools in the United States and broaden support for the
   continuation and expansion of Catholic schooling in the culture.
Convene an assembly of key leaders in Catholic schooling as well as appropriate representatives of
   researchers, business and public officials in order to create strategies for the future of the schools.

The commissioned papers for this meeting again reflect the critical issues which
NCEA hoped to help Catholic educators resolve. The papers—Catholic Identity of
Catholic Schools; Leadership of and on behalf of Catholic schools; The Catholic Schools
and Society; Catholic Schools Governance and Finance; and Political Action, Public
Policy and Catholic Schools addressed very familiar themes (Grant and Hunt, 1992,
243–45).

It was noted earlier that the national symposium held in 1967 moved NCEA to conduct
regional meetings and to serve members in the field. This did in fact change one of the
ways the association did business. Executive staff began to spend much of their time traveling to meet with, consult, and advise members. NCEA provides service to members in
the areas of advancement, board development and governance, financial planning, spiritual
retreats, programs on Catholic identity, and strategic planning.

Regional meetings, sponsored by individual departments, provide updated information
on programs and give members a particular time to come together beyond the national
convention. The various regions, which match the episcopal regions designated by the
Bishops Conference, host the meetings. Regional meetings also provide insight from members to the association staff regarding concerns and issues members were experiencing in
the field.

Association staff also serves members in the field through a series of small conferences
and workshops. For example, programs were delivered to meet the needs of principals,
to teach private school law to practitioners, and to help those working with students with
special needs.

NCEA AT 100 YEARS

In 2004, NCEA marked its century of service to Catholic education with a year-long celebration and recommitment embodied in the centennial theme Faithful Past—Faith-filled Future. A series of events provided NCEA members and friends with opportunities to commemorate and celebrate the rich heritage of Catholic education rooted in the contributions of the religious orders that founded the institutions and the lay leadership that has been entrusted with preserving the legacy.

A national conversation about the contributions of Catholic education to American society was begun with the publication of *One Hundred Years of Catholic Education: Historical Essays in Honor of the Centennial of the National Catholic Educational Association.* The work examined the historical, political, and social contexts that influenced the evolution of Catholic education in the United States and shaped NCEA's mission and priorities.

The Association commissioned the film *The Arms of God*, which appeared on several PBS stations nationwide. The film examined the historical roots of Catholic education and contemporary challenges and showcased the outstanding efforts of three leaders whose efforts to provide quality educational opportunities to under-served populations provided hope for a faith-filled future of Catholic education. In addition, as a centennial gift, NCEA was given the rights to reprint Timothy Walch's *Parish School: American Catholic Parochial Education from Colonial Times to the Present.*

While there was much to celebrate, the centennial was not about self-congratulation. The ultimate goal was to build on the past to create a broadly shared vision for all aspects of Catholic education so as to ensure that Catholic education and catechesis will be authentic, excellent, and accessible for all in the twenty-first century. During the centennial year, more than 100 regional and diocesan meetings convened throughout the country to provide input for the strategic planning process, and a random selection of NCEA members participated in a survey soliciting information about their experiences and expectations as Catholic educators. From these collaborations emerged the context in which the vision was shaped around the themes of Catholic *identity* of programs and institutions, *leadership* of schools and parish programs, and *engagement* with the civil society.

In January 2004, more than 250 delegates gathered in Washington, D.C., for a three-day *NCEA National Symposium on the Future of Catholic Education.* For the work of the symposium, six papers were commissioned to explore the themes (identity, leadership, engagement) and serve as catalysts for conversation. Keynote speakers and panel presentations provided the context for working sessions that developed strategic directions for the future of Catholic education in the multifaceted dimensions of ministry represented by NCEA's constituents. Utilizing a process that included table discussions among mixed groups representing various ministries and geographic areas, the delegates forged a consensus about a vision of Catholic education and developed a list of fundamental beliefs and strategies for each of the themes. The resulting *Strategic Vision for the Future of Catholic Education in the United States* committed NCEA to pursue an agenda that addressed the content of the three themes in light of the two pressing issues identified by the symposium: (1) the financial challenges facing Catholic elementary and secondary schools and the need for aggressive advocacy within the Church and civic communities to ensure that Catholic schools remain affordable and accessible and (2) the need for greater resources to promote effective catechesis with quality parish religious education programs for youth and adults.

Following the publication of the vision statement, NCEA developed its own strategic plan and invited diocesan, school, and parish religious education leaders to *Continue the Conversation* through a new diocesan process of strategic planning based on the vision statement to foster quality Catholic education at the local parish, school, and diocese levels.

During the January symposium, all of the participants were invited to a meeting with then-President George W. Bush at the White House. The president met with the NCEA board of directors prior to the general session with all delegates where the president congratulated and thanked the association for its 100 years of service to students and to the nation, offering high praise for Catholic education and his support of parental-choice initiatives. The symposium and the centennial year concluded with an official public event, the celebratory gala banquet, attended by Catholic educators, bishops, sponsors, friends of Catholic education, and national and local civic officials (McDonald 2010).

CONCLUSION

At the time of this writing, NCEA's activities and programs continue to be guided by the centennial strategic plan. However, knowledge of the history of the association, its growth, and its membership services reveals that many of the issues are not new. Catholic education continues to be faced with the challenges of finances, diversity, leadership, current pedagogical methods, and Catholic identity. The need of educators and catechists in the field informs NCEA activities, as does the original mission statement, with its emphasis on "mutual helpfulness." Even though the mission has been restated, suggesting that the association brings leadership, direction, and service to members, Father Thomas Conaty's original ideas of a volunteer association to include all persons involved in the educational ministries of the church continues to hold value.

REFERENCES AND FURTHER READING

Augustein, J. *Leaders in Times of Trails and Eras of Expansion.* Washington, DC. National Catholic Educational Association, 2008, 11–18.

Augustein, J. In *Catholic Schools in the United States: An Encyclopedia,* edited by Thomas Hunt, Ellis Joseph, and Ronald Nuzzi, 325. Westport, CT: Greenwood Press, 2004, 325.

Augustein, J., Kauffman, C., Wester, R. *One Hundred Years of Catholic Education.* Washington, D.C.: National Catholic Educational Association, 2004.

Glinsky, J. "Sister Mary Emil Penet, I. H. M.: Founder of the Sister Formation Conference," *Catholic Education A Journal of Inquiry and Practice,* 9, 3 (2006): 360–76.

Grant, M. and T. Hunt. *Catholic Schools in the United States.* New York. Garland Press, 1992.

Haney, R. in *Catholic Schools in the United States An Encyclopedia,* edited by Thomas Hunt, Ellis Joseph, and Ronald Nuzzi, 80. Westport, CT.: Greenwood Press, 2004.

Horrigan, D. *The Shaping of NCEA.* Washington, D.C.: National Catholic Educational Association, 1978.

Plough, J. *Catholic Colleges and the Catholic Educational Association: The Foundation and Early Years of the CEA 1899–1919.* PhD Diss., University of Notre Dame. 1967.

Sprows Cummings, K. *New Women of the Old Faith.* Chapel Hill: University of North Carolina Press, 2009.

Walch, T. *Parish School: American Catholic Education from Eolonial Times to the Present.* Washington, D.C.: National Catholic Educational Association, 2003.

38

Catholic Bishops' Conferences in the United States

John J. White

The United States Conference of Catholic Bishops (USCCB) is the national deliberative conference of the Roman Catholic episcopate in the United States. The USCCB is composed of all of the active and retired bishops and archbishops. While there has been a national bishops' conference of one form or another in the United States since 1919, the USCCB has existed in its current state since 2001, when two groups, the National Conference of Catholic Bishops and United States Catholic Conference were reorganized into one organization. It is a registered non-profit corporation. The USCCB has an internal pastoral function, while externally it functions to protect and to serve the Church's interests in the public sphere. The Conference consists of 16 standing committees composed exclusively of bishops; these committees are served by departments, secretariats, and offices that carry out the work of the committees. The USCCB has a staff of over 350 priests, religious, and laypersons, and is headquartered in Washington, D.C., adjacent to The Catholic University of America.

SECRETARIAT OF CATHOLIC EDUCATION

The Secretariat of Catholic Education is responsible for supporting the work of the bishops in evangelization and faith formation. It also encourages the implementation of Church documents on education coming from the Vatican or from the USCCB. Internally, the secretariat's function in K–12 education is to help sustain Catholic schools, strengthen Catholic identity, and collaborate with the Committee on Evangelization and Catechesis on issues pertaining to evangelizing and catechizing through K–12 schools. Externally, the secretariat acts as a Catholic educational lobbying group promoting advocacy on public policy issues that affect Catholic educational institutions. It also seeks to maximize the participation of students and teachers in Catholic schools in federally funded education programs.

The secretariat works through the Committee on Catholic Education, which is currently composed of eight member bishops, one consultant bishop, and eight lay and religious professionals drawn from higher education and from diocesan school systems. The Committee has a permanent staff of four. At the K–12 level the Committee works closely with the

National Catholic Educational Association (NCEA) in its work. The president of the NCEA serves on the Committee, and directives and pastoral documents that come from the bishops generally reflect the interests of the NCEA.

BEGINNINGS: THE NCWC

The bishops met often but irregularly in synods or in plenary councils throughout the organizing or "blueprint phase" in the development of the Church in the United States in the nineteenth century. Education was a major topic at these meetings, as over one-fourth of the legislation that emerged from them focused on Catholic schools (Dolan 1985, 271). The first national episcopal organization in the United States was the National Catholic War Council, founded in 1917 in order to organize Catholic efforts to assist with national mobilization during World War I, primarily in terms of collecting funds for the care of Catholic servicemen, but also to represent Catholic interests at the federal level (Slawson 2005, 6). At the conclusion of the war, Pope Benedict XV urged bishops around the world to work together to help realize the social reforms in the encyclical *Rerum Novarum* of Pope Leo XIII. Meanwhile, the United States saw the rise of a nativist, anti-immigrant and anti-Catholic movement in the post-war years. In 1919, the bishops created the National Catholic Welfare Council (changed to National Catholic Welfare Conference in 1922) out of the earlier wartime council. The intended permanence of this organization caused some bishops to oppose the NCWC, including William Cardinal O'Connell of Boston, who saw a national organization threatening local Episcopal authority (McKeown 1989, 61). Additionally, the Catholic Education Association (CEA), the predecessor to the NCEA, was concerned that the new bishops' organization, with its department of education, would eclipse the authority and usurp the functions of the CEA. To allay this concern an interlocking directorate between the CEA and the NCWC was created, which is still reflected in the organization of the USCCB's Secretariat for Catholic Education (Slawson 2005, 49).

Education was to present the NCWC with its first test. Catholic schools were seen by nativists as a foreign, divisive element in American life, and by 1922 there were several states, including Michigan and Oregon, that had organized movements seeking passage of compulsory public school laws. Oregon passed such a law in 1922, and a year later the NCWC selected a religious community that operated schools in Oregon and contested the law in their name (Shelley 1989, 441–42). In the case of *Pierce v. Society of Sisters of the Holy Names of Jesus and Mary* the U.S. Supreme Court determined that the traditional American understanding of the term *liberty* prevented the state from forcing students to accept instruction only from public schools, stating that this responsibility belonged to the child's parents or guardians, and that the ability to make such a choice was a "liberty" protected by the Fourteenth Amendment (Shelley, 454–55). This case is often cited as providing permanent protection for Catholic and other private schools.

Over the next decade the NCWC continued to seek protection for Catholic schools, particularly from perceived threats posed by the National Education Association and their allies in Congress who sought to create a Department of Education at the federal cabinet level that would eliminate local control and might ultimately lead to the "Prussianization" of American schooling. The NCWC devoted most of its efforts between the end of World War I and 1932 to resisting the creation of a Department of Education. They did so successfully, but their victory also had the effect of keeping anti-Catholicism alive among some influential sectors of American society (Slawson 247). In the years after World War II the NCWC's major external function was in seeking to increase possibilities for federal aid to parochial schools (Reese 1992, 78).

THE NCCB AND THE USCC

The years immediately after the Second Vatican Council saw changes to the national episcopal body as the Vatican called on the bishops of each country to form national conferences. As a result, in 1966 the American bishops created the National Council of Catholic Bishops (NCCB) and its secular arm, the United States Catholic Conference (USCC). The NCCB directed its attention toward the internal concerns of the Church, while the USCC performed many of the same functions as any other Washington special-interest lobbying group as it sought to protect and forward the position of the Church in the United States.

The years after the council saw a wholesale shift in how Catholic schools were staffed as many of the religious and priests who served in schools left religious life and were replaced by lay men and women. Catholic schools experienced a "near death experience" in terms of staffing, finance, and identity as they shifted from religious to lay control. The old system of school governance, staffing, and administration was disrupted without sufficient thought being given to its replacement (Steinfels 2003, 203–4).

According to Joseph Varacalli, progressives came to dominate the NCCB soon after it was founded (2005, 164–65, 71). The dominance of these progressive bishops in the NCCB meant that there was a tendency toward acceptance of a secular understanding of the ends of education among the bishops. While some individual bishops and their dioceses struggled with the problems of changes in staffing and increasing costs the NCCB did little collectively to address the crisis, and there was no sustained national effort on the part of the bishops to address the issues that these changes raised. Varacalli maintains that the anomie brought about by the combination of the exaggerated forces of protest and change characteristic of the sixties, combined with confusion over the significance of the Council, led to a significant weakening of the bishops' commitment to a "self-consciously specific form of Catholic education" and a "secularization from within" (2005, 164), while Jay Dolan points out how many Catholics began to question the value of educating children in separate, denominational schools (Dolan 1985, 442).

Nowhere is this Catholic self-doubt more succinctly captured than in Mary Perkins Ryan's *Are Parochial Schools the Answer? Catholic Education in Light of the Council* (Ryan 1964). This book was foremost a sociological critique of the ethos of separatism that Catholic schools fostered and which Ryan earmarked as inconsistent with the new and open spirit of the Second Vatican Council (Heekin 2008, 204). She also foresaw the coming of a financial crisis for parochial schools, while at the same time she questioned whether devoting so much of the Church's intellectual capital to maintaining a separate school system was desirable, particularly in light of her belief that the Church needed to direct its catechesis toward all Catholics, and not just toward the young (Ryan 1964, 7, 108).

THE NCCB ADDRESSES CHANGE AFTER THE COUNCIL

Although the bishops never formally endorsed Mary Perkins Ryan's work, her influence was felt in many areas of Catholic education and catechesis. In 1967 the NCCB issued a statement entitled "Catholic Schools Are Indispensable." Without venturing any predictions as to the form that changes to schools would take, they wrote that the current "trials and troubles" surrounding Catholic schools "will be seen for what they really are, steps toward a new era for Catholic education" (NCCB 1968, 25–27). They were more specific in the 1972 pastoral *To Teach as Jesus Did. A Pastoral Message on Catholic Education*, which was the NCCB's first major statement on education. *To Teach as Jesus Did* reflects the influence that Ryan's work had on the thinking of the episcopate. Despite affirming that parochial schools are "the most effective means available to the Church for the education of children and young people" the document does little to address the issues that were threatening to destroy the parochial school system in any concrete fashion. Instead, the bishops address the concern that the Church was devoting too many of its catechetical resources to educating children by stressing their support for Catholic education in its entirety. Rather than concentrating on parochial schools, the bishops expanded their efforts to include the entire Catholic community, focusing on adult catechesis and college-level campus ministry as well as with the education of the very young in parochial schools (NCCB 1972, 118). Only 14 of the 155 paragraphs in *To Teach as Jesus Did* deal with the crisis in Catholic schools, and while the bishops reaffirm their commitment to Catholic schools, and the bishops admit to there being a "crisis" in Catholic schools, there is no mention of any connection between the change in staffing and increased costs or the need for formation for lay teachers. Instead, the bishops recognize that there is a financial crisis but they claim that its main cause is the failure of the U.S. Supreme Court to interpret the First and Fourteenth Amendments in a manner favorable to private schools. Without concrete steps being taken to address the crisis, some writers have interpreted the bishops' collective decision not to address the crisis directly as evidence that they decided to allow the market to determine the future of Catholic elementary and secondary education (Carlin 2003, 56–57; Varacalli 2005, 161–63).

The shift away from parochial education to a cradle-to-grave form of catechesis was evident in the *National Catechetical Directory: Sharing the Light of Faith* (1979), which also treated the Christian education of all age groups equally. Instead of addressing themselves to Catholic schools, which were at that time in crisis, the bishops' statements and pastorals from the seventies and beyond support an understanding of "Catholic education" as an inclusive term that refers to Catholic faith and education in a variety of settings and not as a term applied exclusively to Catholic schools (Pollard 1996, 103–11).

To Teach as Jesus Did and the *National Catechetical Directory* were each only issued after the bishops solicited feedback from the NCEA and other interested parties within the Church by circulating drafts of each document for consultation and comment. This inclusivity established a new precedent in Church governance, and it has since become the bishops' standard method of operation. The *National Catechetical Directory* took six years and three drafts to complete, with consultations on each draft held at the diocesan, regional, and national levels (Reese 1992, 125–26).

THE BISHOPS RELEASE *IN SUPPORT OF CATHOLIC ELEMENTARY AND SECONDARY SCHOOLS*

Through the 1980s and into the 1990s, Catholic schools continued to close at an alarming rate, particularly in urban areas that had been ethnic Catholic neighborhoods. As Catholics moved to suburban areas new parishes were formed, but few of these parishes sponsored schools because parents often elected to send their children to the public schools. Financial issues also still posed problems as the cost of operating schools rose each year. In 1990, the NCCB issued *In support of Catholic elementary and secondary schools*. The bishops recognized that costs of operation had risen 500 percent in the previous 20 years, while enrollments and the total number of schools declined (NCCB 1990, 265). The bishops recognized that there was a need to establish Catholic schools in suburban areas and that there were inconsistencies in school governance between dioceses, which led them to urge each diocese to examine its system of governance and to choose that which is most efficient but which also reflects the involvement of parents, teachers, and other constituencies (NCCB 1990, 266).

The bishops set four goals that they expected to meet by 1997: (1) they reasserted their commitment to Catholic schools, (2) they pledged themselves to seeing that schools would be available to all Catholic parents who chose them, (3) they promised to seek financial assistance from private and public sources for Catholic schools, and (4) they set a goal that faculty and staff salaries would reflect what the bishops had expressed about economic justice in their pastoral *Economic Justice for All* (266).

In support of Catholic elementary and secondary schools sought to establish goals that would solidify the financial standing of Catholic schools. The bishops set fundraising for Catholic schools as a priority for dioceses, pledging themselves to open a national development office by 1992 that would assist dioceses in their diocesan fundraising efforts. By 1995 they wished to see endowments established and being grown for schools in each diocese. Building upon the 1983 *Mueller v. Allen* case, the bishops also urged Catholic parents and Catholic school districts to do all in their power to seek whatever federal monies they might be entitled to receive, thereby firmly positioning the Church on the side of the growing school-choice movement (NCCB 1990, 267–68).

Principles for Educational Reform in the United States (1995)

While the NCCB was largely concerned with intra-church education, the United States Catholic Conference continued to lobby for school choice and increased access to public funds by Catholic schools. The school-choice issue was reiterated and expanded upon in the USCC Education Committee's 1995 statement entitled *Principles for Educational Reform in the United States*. Here the bishops appealed not only to Catholics but to the nation at large, presenting certain underlying principles that they believed should guide educational reform in the United States. They stated that quality education was "an inalienable right," that the nation should "make available the broadest variety of quality educational opportunities," and that no one model should predominate (USCC 1998, 753–54). The bishops stated that school choice was a fundamental right stemming from the sacred responsibility of parents to see to the education of their children. Compulsory forms of education could violate these rights "if their children are compelled to attend classes which are not in agreement with the religious beliefs of the parents." Finally, the bishops pointed out that schools play an important role in the formation of character. Public education as well as private should "provide students with opportunities for moral and spiritual formation to complement their intellectual and physical development" (USCC 1998, 756–57).

THE 2001 REORGANIZATION AND *RENEWING OUR COMMITMENT TO CATHOLIC ELEMENTARY AND SECONDARY SCHOOLS* (2005)

In July 2001, the NCCB and the USCC were reorganized as the United States Conference of Catholic Bishops. All of the departments, committees, and secretariats of the NCCB and the USCC were part of the merger, and none of their functions were altered. In the first decade of the new millennium the bishops began to challenge the entire Catholic community to assume responsibility for Catholic education. This has led to innovative funding models in some dioceses, and it has brought many Catholics from the worlds of secular public education and business into the conversation about the future of Catholic schooling. At its June 2005 meeting, the USCCB voted to approve and release *Renewing Our Commitment to Catholic Elementary and Secondary Schools in the Third Millennium*. This document, addressed to all Catholics, urges them "to continue to strive towards the goal of making . . . Catholic elementary and secondary schools available, accessible, and affordable to all Catholic parents and their children, including those who are poor and middle class" (USCCB 2005, 1). The bishops called upon "the entire Catholic community . . . to assist in addressing the critical financial questions that continue to face . . . Catholic schools" (USCCB 2005, 11).

The bishops set four specific goals in this document. The first reaffirmed their commitment to Gospel based education; in the second, they promised that Catholic schools would be available, accessible, and affordable. Third, in order to meet this second objective, the bishops pledged themselves to sponsor initiatives in both the private and public sectors to secure financial assistance for parents, the primary educators of their children, so that they might better exercise their right to choose the best schools for their children. Finally, they stated that Catholic schools would continue to be staffed by highly qualified administrators and teachers who would receive just wages and benefits, again in keeping with the sentiments expressed in the 1986 pastoral letter *Economic Justice for All* (USCCB 2005, 2).

Renewing Our Commitment took an honest look at the demographic losses that Catholic schools were suffering. After seeing a slight rise in enrollments in the 1990s, by 2005 that trend had been reversed, with a net loss of over 170,000 students. Although more than 400 new schools were opened between 1990 and 2005, closures and consolidations meant that there was a net decline of more than 850 Catholic schools during those 15 years, nearly all of which took place in urban, inner-city, and rural areas of the nation, where the non-Catholic percentages of Catholic school population were the highest. This was also where Catholic schools were having their greatest academic impact as they outperformed struggling urban public schools (USCCB 2005, 5–6). Meanwhile, schools in suburban areas, where the Catholic population was growing most quickly, had waiting lists, and new school construction was nearly nonexistent. For all Catholic schools, the bishops reported that tuition costs had more than doubled since 1990 (USCCB 2005, 5).

Renewing Our Commitment then outlined challenges for the future. The first challenge was demographic, as internal migrations and immigration were changing the face of the American Church. Next the bishops addressed the fact that 95 percent of teachers and administrators in the Catholic school system were lay persons who needed specific faith formation and professional development. Finally, the issue of finances appeared again, but here the bishops challenged the entire Church to consider new means of financing schools. The tradition of individual parishes and parents bearing the brunt of supporting the schools has been proven inadequate, they wrote, and a new way will have to be found "that will require all Catholics, including those in parishes without schools, to focus on the spirituality of stewardship" (USCCB 2005, 11). They called on Catholic educational, business, and community leaders to address the critical issues of Catholic identity, cultural diversity, finances, just wages and benefits, academic quality—especially in the area of religious education—alternative governance models, and the marketing of Catholic schools. They also called upon Catholic institutions of higher learning to address the critical need for staffing Catholic schools by ensuring that teacher preparation programs are available to those wishing to work in Catholic schools (USCCB 2005, 14).

The response to *Renewing Our Commitment* was qualitatively different than that generated by earlier statements from the bishops. Many dioceses developed long-range strategic plans in the following years, and as parishes and dioceses wrestled with closures, consolidations, and fundraising there was an increased presence and commitment from Catholic leaders in the business community. Some dioceses, like Wichita, Kansas, successfully developed alternative means of financing parochial schools by making them tuition free to all registered Catholic families. This was achieved by having all Catholic parishes assume responsibility for supporting the schools of the diocese regardless of whether that particular parish has a school attached to it (O'Keefe 2008). Higher education began to respond positively as well. The University of Notre Dame commissioned a task force to determine in what ways the university and other Catholic colleges could respond to *Renewing Our Commitment*. Notre Dame recognized that "over the past forty years, Catholic colleges and universities have frequently neglected their responsibilities to Catholic elementary and secondary schools," even recognizing that "as staffing has shifted from religious to lay in K–12 schools, a parallel process of abandonment and secularization" has taken place in teacher-education programs at Catholic colleges and universities. (Notre Dame Task Force on Catholic Education 2006, 4). Notre Dame offered a 12-point plan that included teacher-recruitment efforts to increase lay apostolic movements in service to Catholic schools, national initiatives for marketing, increased access to public funding, and a renewed effort toward Latino outreach (Notre Dame Task Force on Catholic Education 2006, 5). Other Catholic colleges and universities have either joined Notre Dame or have developed similar initiatives, while the Catholic business community has also responded generously to the bishops' call. Thus far, efforts have largely been directed at saving urban Catholic schools rather than in the development of new schools in suburban and rural areas of the country.

REFERENCES AND FURTHER READING

Carlin, David. The *Decline and Fall of the Catholic Church in America*. Manchester, NH: Sophia Institute Press, 2003.

Dolan, Jay P. *The American Catholic Experience*. Garden City, NY: Doubleday and Company, 1985.

Heekin, Ann Morrow. "Reclaiming a Lost Leader: Mary Perkins Ryan, Visionary in Modern Catholic Education." *Religious Education*, 103, 2 (March, 2008): 196–217.

McKeown, Elizabeth. *War and Welfare: American Catholics and World War I*. New York: Garland, 1988.

National Conference of Catholic Bishops (NCCB). "Catholic schools are indispensable" *Catholic School Journal*, 16, 1 (1968): 25–27.

National Conference of Catholic Bishops (NCCB). *Economic Justice for All: Catholic Social Teaching and the U.S Economy*. Washington, DC: Author. 1986.

National Conference of Catholic Bishops (NCCB). "In Support of Catholic Elementary and Secondary Schools" in *Pastoral Letters and Statements of the U.S. Catholic Bishops, Vol. VI: 1989–1997*. Washington, DC: Author, 1998, 263–69.

National Conference of Catholic Bishops (NCCB). *Sharing the Light of Faith. National Catechetical Directory for Catholics of the United States*. Washington, DC: United States Catholic Conference, 1979.

National Conference of Catholic Bishops (NCCB). *To Teach as Jesus Did: A Pastoral Message on Catholic Education*. Washington, DC: United States Catholic Conference, 1972.

Notre Dame Task Force on Catholic Education. *Making God Known, Loved, and Served: The Future of Catholic Primary and Secondary Schools in the United States.* Notre Dame, IN: University of Notre Dame, 2006.

O'Keefe, Brian. "Wichita: Making Catholic Schools Affordable Again." In *Who Will Save America's Urban Catholic Schools?* edited by S. Hamilton, 22–23. Washington DC: Thomas B. Fordham Foundation, 2008, 22–33.

Pollard, J. E. "Why We Do What We Do. A reflection on Catholic Education and Catholic Schools." *The Living Light*, 25, 2 (1989): 103–11.

Reese, Thomas J. *A Flock of Shepherds: The National Conference of Catholic Bishops.* Kansas City: Sheed & Ward, 1992.

Ryan, Mary Perkins. *Are Parochial Schools the Answer? Catholic Education in the Light of the Council.* New York: Guild Press, 1964.

Shelley, Thomas J. "The Oregon School Case and the National Catholic Welfare Conference." *The Catholic Historical Review*, 75, 3 (July, 1989): 439–57.

Slawson, Douglas J. *The Department of Education Battle, 1918–1932: Public Schools, Catholic Schools, and the Social Order.* Notre Dame, IN: University of Notre Dame Press, 2005.

Steinfels, Peter. *A People Adrift: The Crisis of the Roman Catholic Church in America.* New York: Simon & Schuster, 2003.

United States Catholic Conference (USCC). "Principles for Educational Reform in the United States." In *Pastoral Letters and Statements of the U.S. Catholic Bishops, Vol. VI: 1989–1997*, 752–58. Washington, DC: Author, 1998.

United States Conference of Catholic Bishops (USCCB). *Renewing Our Commitment to Catholic Elementary and Secondary Schools in the Third Millennium.* Washington, DC: Author, 2005.

Varacalli, James A. *The Catholic Experience in America.* Westport, CT: Greenwood, 2005.

39

University Consortium for Catholic Education

Susan M. Ferguson and Regina A. Lloyd

This chapter presents a brief history of the preparation of teachers serving in Catholic schools in the United States, then discusses the origins of the University Consortium for Catholic Education (UCCE), its leaders, its major supporters, major obstacles it has faced, its successes and problems, and its future. The UCCE is a collaboration between Catholic colleges and universities, (arch)dioceses, Catholic schools, donors and grantors, and new Catholic educators and their students.

According to Vatican Council II, teachers in Catholic schools should be carefully prepared in both secular and religious knowledge so that a suitable education consisting of truth and love is developed. Students should be afforded intellectual training in order to be successful in professional life, but they should also be afforded the opportunity to develop Christian values. "Between pupils of different talents and backgrounds it [the school] promotes friendly relations and fosters a spirit of mutual understanding; and it establishes as it were a center whose work and progress must be shared together by families, teachers, associations of various types that foster cultural, civic, and religious life, as well as by civil society and the entire human community" (Vatican Council II 1965, §5). The Second Vatican Council called upon Catholic school educators to work closely with families to deepen Catholic identity among students.

HISTORY OF TEACHER PREPARATION

Catholic schools during Colonial times functioned mainly to spread the Catholic faith, which was considered inferior by the majority of religious leaders in the newly settled land. The Catholic population was small, and into the early nineteenth century Catholics were an insignificant and powerless minority. In 1790, Catholics numbered around 35,000 in a population of over 4 million people (Buetow 1985, 13). Between the years of 1820 and 1850, a wave of over 5 million immigrants, mostly Irish and German, made its way from European countries to the United States (Walch 2003, 24). Many immigrant children were educated in public schools that had a distinct Protestant, anti-Catholic climate. Catholic bishops viewed the establishment of Catholic schools as vital to protecting the faith of the young, and by order of the bishops of the Third Plenary Council of Baltimore in 1884, a Catholic school was to be established at every parish in the United

States (Smith 2007, 323). Not all Catholic children attended parochial schools, however, and enrollment was small in comparison to their total population. For many families, Catholic school was an expense that could not be absorbed. Others preferred the public school option, and some simply did not recognize the need to send their children to school.

The increased number of Catholic schools translated into the demand for teachers to educate those who would attend. Vowed women religious made the greatest sacrifices in order to fulfill the mission of serving God by teaching His people. Their prayer life and community living centered on service to students, the school, and ultimately to God. Training for service in the schools focused on building students' spiritual foundation, character formation, and general intellectual development rather than formal training in academics and the ways of the classroom. Sister-teachers spent a very short amount of time in the Mother House before they were sent into the schools; thus, novice teachers learned the ways of the classroom while on the job, mentored by veteran teachers. This craft system of sister-teacher training was the predominant form of training and lasted until the 1930s and 1940s when a teacher certification movement required by state legislatures emerged. (Walch 2003, 137).

Catholic colleges and universities had long trained vowed religious to educate students of Catholic schools, yet many programs needed to offer more and better training. According to Timothy Walch's book, *Parish School*, Catholic University of America (CUA) became a focal point of improved teacher training early on. In 1902, CUA Professor Edward Pace established the Institute of Pedagogy in New York City to provide training to Catholic school teachers with the belief that pedagogical formation is one of the best means of improving educational custom (Walch 2003, 138). Success of the program was evident and Pace was able to convince the president of CUA to open a department of education on the main campus. Similar movements ensued elsewhere in the country as a result.

The call to design better teacher-preparation programs was similarly met by the University of Notre Dame in 1918. A summer institute devoted to the task of preparing women religious for service in Catholic schools formed many dedicated teachers over the years. Unfortunately, the University's Department of Education was closed in the early 1970s, at which time the program was halted.

In 1850 the Marianists (Society of Mary) founded St. Mary's Institute in Dayton, Ohio. St. Mary's Institute, which later became known as the University of Dayton, had a rich tradition of training the Marianists and other communities of vowed religious to teach in Catholic schools. The practice continued in earnest until about 1998. Presently, the School of Education and Allied Professions remains committed to preparing teachers for this very important role; however, those now being trained are most often members of the lay community.

While colleges and universities around the country trained vowed religious to teach the youth, the latter part of the twentieth century realized a shift to a greater number of lay teachers in Catholic schools. A decreasing number of priests and religious dedicated to teaching, both women and men, was the primary reason for the shift. Pay was nominal, work was demanding, and the call for more to join the order was never-ending. According to material presented by Dean Shane P. Martin, Ph.D., at the 7th Annual Dean's Convocation at Loyola Marymount University in November 2010, religious staff at U.S. Catholic schools peaked in the 1960s at close to 130,000. Today, that number has dramatically decreased to approximately 5,749. Conversely, lay staff has increased from nearly 10,000 in the 1950s to approximately 148,567 today (Martin 2010).

ALTERNATIVE TEACHER-PREPARATION PROGRAMS

The Church believes it imperative to train educators ingrained with an authentic Catholic identity since it is vital for those who work in the schools to have a solid spiritual formation. The Second Vatican Council called upon the faithful "to assist to their utmost in finding suitable methods of education and programs of study and in forming teachers who can give youth a true education" (Vatican Council II 1965, §6). Institutions of higher education around the country worked to design alternative teacher preparation programs that would promote service to parochial schools.

In 1994, Notre Dame introduced the first teacher-preparation program of its kind, the Alliance for Catholic Education (ACE). Founded by Rev. Timothy R. Scully, C.S.C., and Rev. Sean D. McGraw, C.S.C., ACE was created as a graduate-level teaching service program to prepare highly motivated new teachers with an intensive two-year service experience encompassing professional preparation, community life, and spiritual growth. It was designed to provide a constant pipeline of qualified teachers to under-resourced Catholic schools in regions with the greatest need (DiMaria 2004, 24). Given that Notre Dame's Department of Education remained closed at the inception of ACE, initial participants received a master of education degree through an academic program administered by faculty from the University of Portland. With notable success, the ACE program expanded and gained national recognition. By 1998, the academic administration of the program was housed at the newly created Institute for Educational Initiatives at Notre Dame and chose to continue the program without the aid of Portland. As a result, ACE teachers earned a master of education degree from the University of Notre Dame. Pacific Alliance for Catholic Education (PACE) became the name of the program that continued at the University of Portland.

By 1999, ACE was afforded the opportunity to expand its program beyond 90 teachers per cohort. Rather than compromise the personal, professional, and pastoral-attention characteristics of the program, it decided instead to replicate its model at other colleges and universities. In 2000, at the invitation of the University of Notre Dame, representatives of Catholic colleges and universities with an interest in preparing teachers for service in Catholic schools met in South Bend, Indiana. Notre Dame was available for consultation and also offered credence to the fact that there was indeed a need for such teacher-training programs, which strengthened the initiative and made it easier to sell to the stakeholders (D. Murphy, personal communication, December 6, 2010).

One year after the initial meeting, Notre Dame had secured necessary grant funds to offer support to those institutions interested in beginning a teacher-training program similar to ACE. The grant funds were also available to institutions interested in strengthening their already-established graduate-level teacher-training programs, such as the University of Dayton's Lalanne program. Additional funding was contributed by Notre Dame, and participating universities designated large sums of money to initiate and sustain their own programs.

A partnership of university programs had begun and additional programs were soon developed. By 2001, a total of nine programs had been launched. In addition to ACE, PACE, and Lalanne, these consisted of EPICS at Seton Hall University; LEAPs at

Valparaiso University; Operation TEACH at the College of Notre Dame, Baltimore; PACT at Providence College; PLACE Corps at Loyola Marymount University; and UCTC at Boston College (Davies and Kennedy 2009, 251).

BIRTH OF UCCE

Initially, many programs were financially, strategically, and technically dependent on Notre Dame, but once they were off the ground their dependence began to subside. The insight from Notre Dame provided information on how the ACE program functioned; subsequently, these ideas evolved in different ways and each program developed its own distinct identity. Program administrators felt the need to be self-directed and to organize in a more formal structure, and some realized that there were different means for support in sustaining their programs. Joined by the Urban Catholic Teacher Corps (UCTC) of Boston College, founded in 1995 and operating independently by 1997, program directors began to formally meet on a semi-annual basis in the fall of 2001. Their purpose for meeting was to exchange information and best practices as well as to offer mutual support. The organization accepted the name University Consortium for Catholic Education (UCCE) in 2004 after many meetings at Notre Dame, and in spring 2005, the founding institutions approved UCCE by-laws. The UCCE had become a formalized organization that would bring about collaboration between Catholic colleges and universities, (arch)dioceses, and K–12 Catholic schools. Its mission: to support primarily Catholic colleges and universities as they design and implement graduate-level teaching service programs for the purpose of service to K–12 Catholic and parochial schools in the United States (UCCE Website, accessed October 22, 2010).

The UCCE elects a chair and co-chair who each serve a two-year term. Each January there is a directors' meeting, and each summer there is a conference, which is held at a UCCE program host university. All directors are expected to attend the January meeting as well as the summer conference, and all are encouraged to take at least two participants of their program to the summer conference, preferably a first-year and a second-year teacher (J. Mergler, personal communication, January 18, 2011). The summer conference has developed into a well-organized gathering that provides discussion of issues of common concern, opportunities to share experiences, exploration of further joint initiatives, a welcome for new programs into the organization, strategies to become a growing presence, and attempts to expose participants to the bigger movement that is the UCCE. Conference participants are exposed to professional and spiritual growth opportunities that they are able to take home to their own living communities, share with their own programs, and implement in their placement K–12 schools.

UCCE TODAY

The UCCE is a successful, flourishing model of educator formation focused on continual improvement of Catholic school teacher training because its members believe that the Catholic school is at the heart of the Church (Congregation for Catholic Education 1977, §9). While non-Catholics are not excluded from these programs, all participants must possess an appreciation for and be supportive of Catholic education. The various UCCE programs recruit those who are devoted to teaching and ministry and demonstrate leadership of the Catholic faith in general. Each program operates on a foundation of three pillars: community, education/professional development, and spirituality. Together, these three pillars work in harmony to form spiritual teachers who convey the Catholic faith through their professional and personal lives.

As sister-teachers witnessed the Catholic faith by living in community during the 1800s and 1900s, so do teachers of all UCCE programs commit to simple living in intentional Christian communities. This way, they are afforded the opportunity to share household responsibilities, support each other, and share their faith and spiritual lives. Faith-sharing meetings allow participants to discuss witness to their faith and service on a regular basis. Additionally, simple living in intentional communities offers solidarity with students and families they serve in under-resourced schools, allowing them to relate on a more personal level. Some program alumni who appreciate the benefits of living in community, especially the fostering of personal and spiritual growth, have chosen to live in a community arrangement after completing their programs.

UCCE teachers complete graduate coursework at their respective universities in addition to their two-year commitment to teach in an under-resourced Catholic school. Each program consists of required courses directed toward teaching specifically in Catholic schools. Classes may be offered during summer months, during the academic year, or both depending on the program. Several programs offer online classes while others prefer the traditional classroom setting, and some offer a combination. Every program offers an accredited graduate degree in education as well as a valuable teaching experience.

Through UCCE programs, over 400 teachers are placed in under-resourced Catholic schools every year supporting the outreach of Catholic higher education to K–12 schools and forming young men and women to be leaders and lifelong advocates of Catholic education (UCCE website, accessed October 9, 2010). Because these programs nurture leadership qualities, many graduates of the initial two-year program continue their education to receive additional degrees in education and assume administrative roles.

The UCCE encourages and supports alumni of the program who are committed to the effort of sustaining Catholic education beyond their initial two years of service. Since the establishment of ACE, over 2,220 teachers formed through the UCCE model have graduated from host universities (Davies and Kennedy 2009, 253). The majority of those who have continued teaching one year later remain in Catholic schools, though not all in their placement schools. Others have desired to explore religious life after graduation—an indication that the formation element of the UCCE can be quite powerful. Other program graduates have pursued alternative careers with the intent of achieving alternate personal or professional goals, and have been able to advocate for Catholic education through their service to a variety of sectors of public life. Finally, some graduates have continued teaching, but in non-Catholic schools.

Current membership in the UCCE has grown to 15 programs in 53 dioceses throughout the United States (UCCE website, accessed October 9, 2010). The two most recent programs to join are GRACE at the University of St. Thomas, Houston, and the Remick Fellowship Program at St. Mary's University of Minnesota, both of which joined in 2007. A brand new program created at St. Joseph's University of Philadelphia will become a member of the consortium in the summer of 2011 (J. Mergler, personal communication, January 10, 2011). Other programs established since 2001 and now members of the UCCE are: LANCE at Christian Brothers University; LU-CHOICE at Loyola University of Chicago; LUMEN at the University of Great Falls; and Magis Catholic Teacher Corps at Creighton University (Davies and Kennedy 2009, 251).

The power and potential of collaboration among Catholic universities and dioceses in support of one another is monumental. While each teacher service program in the UCCE has subtle differences, each has impacted participants with positive lasting effects that simply cannot be measured.

In an effort to be affiliated with other faith-based programs, the UCCE is a member of the Catholic Volunteer Network. This relationship provides a forum for sharing ideas and fosters support among those devoted to fulfilling God's mission of helping one another. It also provides a means of exposing more people to the work of the UCCE, with the hope of recruiting strong candidates for participation in one of the many college or university programs.

As a result of the significant work performed by the UCCE since its inception, the National Catholic Educational Association (NCEA) awarded the UCCE the C. Albert Koob Award in 2006. This award honors a distinguished individual or organization that has made an extraordinary contribution to Catholic education on a regional and national level (Davies and Kennedy 2009, 25).

UCCE FUTURE

It is anticipated that there will be even greater collaboration among programs participating in the UCCE for purposes of research, teacher and administrator preparation, and entrepreneurial outreach programs. It is also anticipated that success of the UCCE will attract additional members and launch new programs as it continues to serve an increasing number of (arch)dioceses across the country.

While the UCCE is poised for growth, the hope and potential for growth are limited by funding. Initial grants for start-up have been expended, and all programs are self-supporting since the UCCE does not have any money collectively to offer. Funds from partner schools, private donations, and support from their own universities are main sources of money that sustain each program. A few programs are fortunate to have endowments. There is always a need for additional financial support, which assists with expenses such as travel to conferences, hiring of additional staff to provide administrative assistance, and sustaining alumni so they can continue to serve God through teaching.

Beyond finances, there is a very real concern about locating sufficient teaching positions for prospective participants. Consolidation and closing of Catholic schools has eliminated positions that may have otherwise been offered to those who would like to enroll in a UCCE program. The changing ways in which people spend their money, coupled with the continually increasing cost of a Catholic education, have resulted in a growing number of families unable or unwilling to pay (D. Murphy, personal communication, December 6, 2010). In 1960, nearly 5.5 million students were enrolled in Catholic schools throughout the country. Today, that number is closer to 2.1 million students (convocation, Loyola Marymount University, Los Angeles, CA, November 8, 2010). With Catholic school teachers working longer in order to retire more comfortably, even fewer positions are available for potential program participants. It can be a real challenge to locate a sufficient number of placement opportunities to meet demand.

CONCLUSION

Catholic schools play an enormous role in the evangelization of the United States while providing students intellectual training and the opportunity to develop Christian values.

With the ability to create such an impact, it is the responsibility of all Catholic faithful to do their part to ensure that Catholic schools maintain an active presence throughout the country. An ever-increasing dependence on laity to teach in Catholic schools has led to the creation of teacher-training programs designed specifically for those devoted to the call. The collaborative nature of the UCCE has been a driving force behind uniting these university programs with each other, with (arch)dioceses, and with K–12 schools in which they serve for the purpose of discussing common concerns, sharing experiences, and strategizing ways to become a growing presence in the country. The interdependence of professional development, community, and spirituality—the three pillars on which all UCCE programs are built—instills teachers with a greater sense of their vocation and empowers them to make a positive and lasting impact through their teaching according to God's will.

REFERENCES AND FURTHER READING

Buetow, Harold A. *A History of United States Catholic Schooling*. Washington, DC: National Catholic Educational Association, 1985.

Congregation for Catholic Education. *The Catholic School* (1977). http://www.vatican.va/roman_curia/congregations/ccatheduc/documents/rc_con_ccatheduc_doc_19770319_catholic-school_en.html (accessed November 10, 2010).

Davies, Molly, and Karen Kennedy. "Called to Collaboration: The University Consortium for Catholic Education." *Catholic Education: A Journal of Inquiry & Practice* 13 (2009): 248–75.

DiMaria, Frank. "University Programs Provide Teachers for Under-Resourced Catholic Schools: ACE Partnership Consortium Creates Constant Supply of Teachers." *Momentum* 35 (2004): 24–26.

Martin, Shane P., Ph.D. "LMU Center for Catholic Education and the Future of Los Angeles Catholic Schools." Presentation at the School of Education Annual Dean's Convocation at Loyola Marymount University, Los Angeles, CA, November 2010.

Mergler, J. Personal communication, January 18, 2011.

Murphy, D. Personal communication, December 6, 2010.

Smith, Paige A. "The University Consortium for Catholic Education (UCCE): A Response to Sustain and Strengthen Catholic Education." *Catholic Education: A Journal of Inquiry and Practice* 10 (2007): 321–42.

"University Consortium for Catholic Education." http://www.ucceconnect.com (accessed October 22, 2010)

Vatican Council II. *Declaration on Christian Education*. Boston, MA: St. Paul Editions, 1965.

Walch, Timothy. *Parish School: American Catholic Parochial Education From Colonial Times to the Present*. Washington, DC: The National Catholic Education Association, 2003.

Part IV

ISLAMIC SCHOOLS

40

Islamic Schools

Karen E. Keyworth

The growth of private full-time K–12 Islamic schools in the United States is a story of two distinct groups, the Sister Clara Muhammad schools (SCMS) and the immigrant community-based schools (ICSs), that began and developed very differently but are growing more similar over time. Furthermore, both groups grew their schools out of a desire common to most religious private schools—to provide a holistic, identity-shaping educational experience in which the child's spiritual education reflects the religious beliefs and values of the parents.

There are 235 to 240 full-time Islamic schools in the United States, serving between 26,000 and 35,000 students. Predominately preK–8 with an average of 121 students or fewer, they are located primarily in urban/suburban areas. Close to half of them are completely independent of a mosque or other entity, and 85 percent were founded after the mid-1990s, with most SCMSs founded significantly earlier. Over two-thirds are expanding or constructing their school building (Keyworth 2009, 7–13). All teach Qur'an memorization and understanding, and many offer in-depth Arabic-language instruction. They are seeking accreditation, concerned about increasing professional development, and constantly looking for ways to increase revenues. Their students are given standardized tests and participate in community service, interfaith dialogue, and typical after school activities such as sports, Girl/Boy Scouts, and tutoring. In general, Islamic schools are fairly typical of the average religious private school in the United States.

THE SISTER CLARA MUHAMMAD SCHOOLS

The development of the SCMSs closely follows that of the Nation of Islam (NOI). Begun as a homeschooling effort in Detroit in 1932 by Sister Clara Muhammad, wife of NOI leader Elijah Muhammad, the schools were initially named "University of Islam" to emphasize the universal and advanced nature of the curriculum, although they were elementary and secondary schools (Rashid and Zakiyyah Muhammad 1992, 178). American schools at the time were segregated and openly racist, and the University of Islam/SCMSs offered African American children a chance to form nascent identities, shielded from the stunting, contorting forces of racism. As Muhammad asserted: "Our children should be trained in our own schools, not dropped into the schools of the enemy where they are taught that whites have been and forever will be world rulers" (Muhammad 2009, 171). These were the first, and for 30 years the only, schools in which all aspects of teaching/learning were imbued with a sense of the naturalness of the Black people's world-wide and historical contributions.

Reflecting the organizational structure of their NOI "parent," these schools were fairly centralized in their curriculum, administration, and development. The 1940s, 1950s, and early 1960s saw their fledgling growth as the NOI established itself in major metro-politan areas. The schools were integral to that development, part of a centralized protocol whereby a new community's initial steps were to establish a temple [mosque] *and* a school. This was not the pattern immigrant-based schools would follow in the 1980s and 1990s.

As the University of Islam/SCMSs grew, so, however, did their exposure to mainstream Islam and the inherent conflict that arose around two core beliefs: the oneness of God and the priority of race. The NOI believes that, "Allah (God) appeared in the person of Master W. Fard Muhammad, July, 1930, the long awaited 'Messiah' of the Christians, and the 'Mahdi' of the Muslims" (Muhammad 2009, 164). Mainstream Islam, on the other hand, teaches the oneness of God (no forms incarnate) and the Abrahamic line of prophets that ends with the Prophet Mohammed. Furthermore, NOI believes in the superiority of Blacks over "white devils," a doctrine that is in direct opposition to the Qur'an; 49:13 (A. Z. Hammad's translation) says, "O humankind! Indeed, We have created all of you from a single male and female. Moreover, We have made you peoples and tribes, so that you may come to know one another. And, indeed, the noblest of you, in the sight of God, is the most God-fearing of you." These doctrinal differences would eventually bring the University of Islam/SCMSs to a crisis.

Despite the turmoil of Malcolm X leaving the NOI for mainstream Islam, the mid-1960s were a time of growth for the University of Islam/SCMSs. Then, in 1975, Elijah Muhammad died and left his son, W. D. Mohammed, to lead the NOI. Unlike his father, W. D. Mohammed, was versed in multiple interpretations of Islam and over time had come to the conclusion that the NOI was espousing beliefs contradictory to Islam. Consequently, he began a stunning transition of the NOI to mainstream Islamic beliefs that impacted the SCMSs profoundly.

As W. D. Mohammed aligned foundational beliefs with Islam, restructured the University of Islam curriculum and organization, and renamed the schools in honor of his mother, Sr. Clara Muhammad, the restructuring created enormous organizational stress. Many schools grew stronger and independent, but some grew weak. Overall, the number of schools decreased from 41 in 1975 to 38 schools in 1992 (Rashid and Muhammad 1992, 183) to 23 by 2008 (Keyworth 2008, 1). The strongest of these remaining schools, however, are vibrant, energetic, and growing, having built independent support bases and proven to be essential community assets. In the words of one school, "Building a community in schools that began under the 'old' Nation of Islam leadership is a challenge with multiple dimensions. Demographic, philosophical, ideological, organizational, economic and other social issues are reflected in the complete change in ori-entation from a Black Nationalist organizational structure and social ethic to a global, multi-ethnic, multi-linguistic, multi-cultural, universal Islamic philosophy. This transforma-tion in educational philosophy and community life led for the last 30 years by Imam W. D. Mohammed has now emerged as a significant model for education, community transforma-tion and universal human acceptance" (Clara Muhammad Schools, at www.claramu hammadschools.org).

THE IMMIGRANT COMMUNITY-BASED SCHOOLS

Part of the stimulus for the mid-1970s cataclysmic change in the SCMSs was the increased exposure to mainstream Islam, amplified by the growing number of Muslim immigrants. These immigrants were initially intrigued by the NOI but eventually affronted by its controversial doctrines. It is unknown to what extent issues of race might have impacted that reaction. Meanwhile, the NOI felt equally affronted by the immigrants' unquestioning embrace of that same racist system against which the NOI was struggling. These fundamental differences created a mutual mistrust and turning away that both communities are only just now beginning to address.

Similar to the SCMSs, the immigrant community-based schools (ICSs) sought to create a learning environment rich with Islam, Arabic language, the Qur'an, and strong moral values. But the similarities ended there, as the immigrants identified more with the dominant white society than with minorities, despite immigrants' oftentimes distinctive appearances. The first ICSs began in the late 1970s in the New York/New Jersey area. Surprisingly, these schools struggled from weak community support created by the complex attitudes that many immigrants held toward the West. The desire to integrate into their new country meant parents valued their children learning English as a native language, excelling in prestigious schools and universities, obtaining well-paying employment, and achieving the American dream—things they felt could not be accomplished in private Islamic schools. Attitudes held by immigrants from post-colonial societies in which Islamic schooling had been maligned by the colonial powers favored a Western education. Unlike in the SCMSs, where children's identity was paramount, personal concerns of children's identity issues were little understood by either immigrants or the larger American society, and integration came at a price as children struggled to sort out their identities, finding little help in public schools not designed to address this issue. Although they did not wish to put their children in Islamic schools, immigrant parents did wish for their children to learn Islam, recite the Qur'an, and "be Muslim," and they felt that this could be accomplished by establishing weekend or "Sunday" schools at local mosques. Consequently, and unlike the NOI, immigrant communities focused first on building mosques and then schools.

Throughout the 1980s, however, a growing awareness by immigrants of the problems their children faced in public schools, coupled with an increasing financial ability, led to a phenomenal growth of ICSs (excluding SCMSs) in the 1990s from 50 schools in 1987 (Ismail 1989, 79) to about 208 in 2008 (Keyworth 2009, 25). Given the challenges by media and general need for Americans to understand more about Islam and Muslims in the United States post 9/11, it is important at this juncture to address the question/assertions of overseas influence on the schools and the resulting fear that Islamic schools might produce violent extremists. In fact, all known American Muslim extremists have come out of public schools and not Islamic schools. Fears exist despite this fact and fuel a widely held notion that mosques control the schools and overseas entities control the mosques. While it is beyond the scope of this work to evaluate the impact of overseas entities on mosques, important data exists that evaluates the impact of mosques on Islamic schools. First, data shows that in only 21 percent of schools, governance is mosque-based. The remaining 79 percent of schools govern as follows: 29 percent govern autonomous of their local mosque; 5 percent govern autonomous of their non-mosque organization; and 45 percent govern themselves totally independent of any other organization (Keyworth 2009, 32–33). Second, the job of being a school principal in an American Islamic school is extremely

complex, requiring highly specialized skills (discussed below) that would have been difficult, if not impossible, for overseas groups to impact. Third, in November of 2002, the
Islamic Schools League of America (ISLA), a national organization for full-time Islamic
schools, stopped forwarding resumes to its listserve (the IECN) from overseas educators
who were searching for employment in the United States. This was brought about by a
complete lack of interest on the part of the IECN membership of Islamic school educators
and administrators, who indicated they preferred to hire from within the United States,
primarily because overseas educators were not trained to teach in a way that American-
Muslim students and Islamic schools expected and did not understand well the social
milieu in which the students lived. There is no support for the suspicion that Islamic
schools ever were or are today run or significantly influenced by overseas organizations.
In fact, the data points to quite the opposite—a community of schools that is independent
and responsive to the needs of its American-Muslim students.

During the heyday of the 1990s when the bulk of Islamic schools were founded, similar
dynamics existed in Muslim communities across the United States that impacted the
future development of the schools. Given the fact that a school is often involved with
neighborhoods and school districts, the founding boards of these schools—mostly
immigrant males—realized they needed someone who was well educated, spoke English
as a native language, and could move fluidly between the immigrant and local communities. Since very few first-generation children of immigrants were old enough to have
achieved the necessary education or experience, the logical choice was the American-
Muslim convert. Subsequently, converts—particularly women—carried out much of the
founding administrative and faculty work of ICSs in numbers far greater than their occur-
rence in the American-Muslim population would warrant, carving out positions of leadership and shaping the core and direction of American Islamic education. This has been
observed elsewhere, "In some countries, as Roggero notes is the case in Italy, new converts
to Islam are playing especially important leadership roles. Because of their knowledge of
the language and culture, their generally high levels of education, and their enthusiasm
for the new religion of choice, they are active in helping Muslim communities adapt to life
in the West and reinterpret Islam to be relevant for the time and place. They also serve as
intermediaries between government agencies and Muslim communities" (Haddad 2002, 12).
The specific impact of this small group on American Islamic schools has never been
studied, but given their common experiences and dominance in the schools, the
American-Muslim convert cannot help but have been influential in ways unique to
their group.

Problematically, most immigrant-dominated school boards and communities were not
generally familiar with the American cultural behaviors and expectations governing professional relationships, nor were they used to women in leadership positions. Although the
vast majority of schools work out their issues and learn from their mistakes, the problem
is real, and for one school in California it reached the courts: "A Superior Court jury has
ordered the Islamic Society of Orange County and two of its officials to pay the former
principal of its elementary school nearly $800,000, agreeing that they discriminated against
her when she was fired two years ago. . . . the main thrust of the case was gender bias
because [she] had challenged her male superiors" (Gottlieb 2005). While female educators
struggled against strong gender bias held by immigrant leaders, male educators, both
immigrant and non-immigrant, suffered too from problematic attitudes on the part of
boards regarding professional relationships wherein a rigid hierarchy of status and prestige

encouraged a disregard for those in positions perceived as "inferior." This poisoned the atmosphere of more than one school and led to educator burnout and turnover.

School boards, however, have worked and continue to work to develop more professional attitudes and behaviors in an effort to retain their principals and faculty. Although they have made excellent progress, ICSs today continue to address this slowly improving yet problematic dynamic. On-going professional development is important to maintain these recent changes, and it is hoped that as the relatively young population of American-Muslims matures and takes on leadership roles, attitudes brought from overseas will cease to hold as much sway as in the past. Schools need to be aware that as new immigrants arrive, efforts must be made to transfer institutional knowledge so that these hard-won lessons can continue to provide a source of stability and growth for the schools.

As a result of the challenges schools have faced and the talent they possess, Islamic schools are growing and expanding. Based on data, we can now articulate a profile of the "typical" full-time Islamic school: average sized for a parochial school—100 students or fewer; young—six years or younger; growing; professionally oriented; and independently governed (Keyworth 2009, 33).

CURRENT ISSUES AND DYNAMICS

Curriculum is one of the most foundational yet often vexing issues with which schools grapple, and Islamic schools are no different. For numerous reasons such as geographical distance, connectedness to local public school curricula, the heterogeneity of the Muslim community, and more, there is no national curriculum for Islamic schools today, nor is there likely to be one in the future. When a school is founded, it typically uses the most prestigious local public school's curriculum and then adds Islamic Studies, Qur'an Recitation, and Arabic-language courses. As the school matures, it tends to adjust its curriculum, focusing first on Islamic Studies and the search for textbooks and materials that support the desired curriculum and meet the needs of American-Muslim students. During this curriculum review, most schools will explore the challenge of integrating Islam across the curriculum. Without exception, Muslim educators prefer to integrate Islam across the curriculum. Equally without exception, they find this a very difficult task that few can take on. According to Freda Shamma:

> Curriculum writers usually take one of two approaches. The older approach . . . is to attempt to put all Islamic knowledge/thinking into one Islamic Studies class, while the remainder of the curriculum remains secular. The second approach is to attempt to rewrite the curriculum of every subject so that Islamic knowledge/thinking is integrated into every subject. The limited curriculum approach is both more traditional and, for the time being, more practical than the integrated curriculum approach. Advocates of this curriculum approach point out that Islamic schools have to have curricula and textbooks NOW, and the integrated curriculum is years away from having any such thing (lessons, not texts, are currently being developed). In order to have something to teach, it is more practical to aim at developing a curriculum for one subject, Islamic Studies, and assume that Muslim teachers in the other subjects will do a reasonably good job of Islamizing the secular curriculum.
>
> The Islamic Schools League of America, at www.theisla.org

The challenge to educators is not to create the one perfect curriculum that meets the needs of the greatly heterogeneous Muslim community, because that cannot be done.

The challenge is to create several curricula that will form the foundation of an excellent Islamic education for American-Muslim children and to develop textbooks, lessons, and materials that will support these curricula. These efforts by American-Muslim educators have not gone unnoticed, attracting the attention of Muslim educators from around the world as some of the most dynamic and innovative in Islamic education today.

Textbooks and support materials are equally important because they support the curriculum a school chooses. Since most Islamic schools use a local or state curriculum, they also use the textbooks that the local schools use to support that curriculum, thereby answering most of the questions of what is being taught in Islamic schools. These texts, however, do not address the religious aspect of curricula. When Islamic schools first started, most Islamic studies textbooks were either designed for weekend or "Sunday" schools or imported from overseas. While these were valiant efforts, neither choice met the needs of the schools: overseas texts employed fairly poor teaching techniques and were unsuited to the American milieu, while weekend school texts were beginning essentially from scratch and needed time to overcome publication start-up problems. Over the last two decades, however, textbook writers have made significant headway. Today almost all Islamic schools use religious texts from the several American-Muslim publishing companies that provide a growing choice of well-written, colorful, well-constructed textbooks with attractive artwork and the religious content the schools need.

A surprising challenge that most ICSs face is how to convince their communities to choose private Islamic education as an alternative to public school. As two authorities point out: "The reasons are not yet clear, but the numbers speak for themselves: only 32,000 children—about 3.8% of school aged Muslim children—attend full time Islamic schools in the U.S. This is significantly lower when compared with the general U.S. population, of which 11% of school-aged children attend private schools. Using the *smallest* population estimate of 2.35 million Muslims, Islamic schools *ought* to have 93,500 students" (Keyworth and Ahmed 2009, 37). Muslim educators indicate that parents are hesitant to enroll their children for several reasons: private tuition is a financial burden, children might become isolated from the larger American community, and children might become "too conservative." These attitudes are similar to those in a study on Jewish private schools, which found three significant attitudes impacted parents' decisions: The aspirations for one child's Jewish development—i.e., the extent to which parents hoped their children would develop a strong Jewish identity; the perception of day schools as effective instruments of Jewish education; and the perception that day schools "ghettoize" their children and the concomitant fear that children enrolled in day schools do not learn how to relate to non-Jews and that they turn out "too religious" (Wertheimer 2005, 17).

With the exception of financial worries, for parents of children in Islamic schools, some of what others perceive as *concerns*, they perceive as *desires*. The wish to provide a "safe haven" from social ills such as drugs, alcohol, and premarital sex is a main drive to choose an Islamic school, but that "safe haven" is frequently interpreted as isolation by other parents. From the perspective of Muslim educators, neither "safe havens" nor isolation captures the reality of the schools. Islamic schools, like most private schools, involve students in life beyond the school walls. Because contributing to the community through social justice and helping the poor is a core teaching of Islam, Islamic schools from elementary to high school are involved in a wide range of community activities such as soup kitchens, Scouting, interfaith activities, and more. These activities need to be brought more to the attention of the Muslim community so prospective parents may decide based on fact and not stereotype.

Regarding some parents' worry of their children becoming "too" religious, there is research to show that the more people understand their religion, the less likely they are to engage in extreme behavior. According to a study that compared the beliefs and views of Pakistani Muslims chosen through a random government lottery to attend the Hajj with those who were not chosen to attend, those who attended the Hajj returned with stronger notions of equality and harmony, "Although the Hajj may help forge a common Islamic identity, there is no evidence that this is defined in opposition to non-Muslims. On the contrary, the notions of equality and harmony appear to extend to adherents of other religions as well. These results contrast sharply with the view that increased Islamic orthodoxy goes hand in hand with extremism" (Clingingsmith, Khwaja, and Kremer 2008, 1135). An Islamic school is filled with faculty who, although conservative in its outlook, is well versed in the teachings of Islam and provides a strong refutation of extremist beliefs. Such information could offer some reassurance to parents that Islamic schools might have a similar effect.

Another reason Muslim parents might shy away from Islamic schools is the perceived quality of education—a bit of a Catch-22 conundrum. As schools go, most Islamic schools are young, having been established in the 1990s. Young schools must build and strengthen themselves over time. However, during that strengthening phase, the schools might not provide as good an education as the local public schools. Therefore, they are quite rightly perceived as sub-par. Being perceived as sub-par, however, restricts their ability to attract students and tuition money, further restricting their ability to improve and in turn calcifying negative perceptions. Once a school has made significant improvement in the quality of education it delivers, it must overcome those calcified attitudes, and that consumes scarce resources. Nevertheless, Islamic schools are finding effective ways to address the misperceptions in their own Muslim communities about the quality of education they offer by using savvier public relations techniques that stress their low student-to-teacher ratio, higher test scores, and acceptance of their graduates to prominent universities.

Another challenge is the dynamics of demographics. The Muslim population in the United States is fairly young, with only 5 percent of Muslims over the age 65. This impacts the "wisdom reservoir" for Muslim educators. Societies often take for granted or perhaps do not notice the institutionalized knowledge and wisdom available from those who have blazed trails before them, but when that group of elders has just begun to grow in a community, one feels the struggle. If a Catholic school principal needs advice or help, he or she can turn to a number of working or retired Catholic principals for guidance. If a Catholic school has an emergency need for a principal or teacher, there are a number of retired or semi-retired Catholics with the necessary credentials and experience to quickly step in and help the school. When problems arise, there are experienced Catholic arbitrators who know the issues and the schools well and do not require a crash course on Catholic beliefs in order to understand the nuances that an experienced person inside the Catholic schools has learned over a career. For an Islamic school, that is not usually the case. Most of the people who founded the Islamic schools are still fully engaged in work, many at the peak of their professional careers, and rarely have the time to help. As the Muslim community ages, these demographics will balance themselves naturally, but in the meantime, not having this reservoir of wisdom challenges Muslim educators and makes the role of a created community more critical.

THE WAY FORWARD

Today the challenges faced by the SCMSs and the ICSs—growth and improvement—are far more similar than different and result from an increasing demand for Islamic education. The schools are finding solutions to their challenges in interesting ways. For example, to lessen the enormous expense of a high school, some are partnering with community colleges and offering dual enrollment—students can graduate high school with two years of college already completed. Some Islamic schools are also Montessori schools, an important factor for many parents. A few are taking advantage of their private status to create schools that break the public schooling mold, focusing on individualized instruction, self-directed and experiential learning, non-grade learner groupings, and progressive forms of curriculum design more in line with the American private school tradition.

Gradually the ICSs and the SCMSs are realizing that in their search for the spiritual core of their Islamic curricula there is much to learn from each other. The SCMSs have spent the better part of a century refining their efforts to build a positive Muslim identity strong enough to withstand a sometimes destructive dominant society. Muslim children, post 9-11, need to possess a strong and positive sense of self as the schools reach out to the larger community. Equally, the ICSs are skilled at presenting clear Islamic doctrine, sharply focused on core teachings. If combined, the strong identity and spiritual clarity would better equip American-Muslim children to contribute to and enrich American society.

ISSUES MUSLIM EDUCATORS ARE EXAMINING AND EXPLORING IN THEIR SCHOOLS

Muslim educators are working with determination and passion to improve the quality of education they offer to students. That work tends to be somewhat isolated because the schools are not in close proximity to one another geographically. However, the Islamic Schools League of America (ISLA), an online organization that connects and networks full-time Islamic schools, has operated a listserv and website for over a decade that has helped create a robust online community of Muslim educators. The listserv provides a critical platform for encouragement, exploration of new ideas, collegial assistance, in-depth discussions, employment opportunities, and the development of a shared Islamic educational philosophy that is uniquely American. Another critical support for Muslim educators is the annual Education Forum sponsored by the Islamic Society of North America (ISNA) and the Council of Islamic Schools in North America (CISNA). This forum is the only opportunity for Muslim educators to gather in one physical space and share their issues face to face. The types of issues discussed online and at the forum are generally as follows:

- Professional development, credentialing, and certifications;
- Curricula: integrating Islam into the curriculum; character education, values-based education, standards for Islamic studies and Arabic curriculum and instruction;
- Identity;
- Challenges of developing and sustaining a shared vision, mission, and goals of all stakeholders;
- Middle/high school academic, psycho-social, and emotional preparation to leave the Islamic school and enter public schools;
- Politics of the school;
- Muslim or non-Muslim teachers;

- Modest dress for students and faculty—defining what this means and implementing it;
- Lack of space; and
- Language barriers—immigrant students, teachers, administrators, and parents.

Islamic schooling in the United States is a story born of necessity and nurtured by determination. There is every reason to believe the schools will continue to grow as they learn from their mistakes, come together as a nationwide community, and reap the benefits of their students' accomplishments. Islamic schools are an American success story.

REFERENCES AND FURTHER READING

Clara Muhammad Schools, "Welcome to SCMS! Clara Muhammad Schools," http://www.claramu hammadschools.org/welcome-to-scms.html (cited February 3, 2011).

Clingingsmith, David, Asim Ijaz Khwaja, and Michael Kremer. Estimating the Impact of the Hajj: Religion and Tolerance in Islam's Global Gathering. *SSRN eLibrary* (April). http://papers.ssrn.com/sol3/papers.cfm?abstract_id=1124213 (accessed February 3, 2011).

Gottlieb, Jeff. "Fired Principal Awarded $788,000." *Los Angeles Times*, September 13, 2005. http://articles.latimes.com/2005/sep/13/local/me-islamic13 (accessed February 3, 2011).

Haddad, Yvonne Yazbeck. *Muslims in the West: From Sojourners to Citizens*. New York: Oxford University Press, 2002.

Imam, Seema. "Islamic Schools in America: The Way Ahead." *Al Jumuah Magazine*, (January 2007): 24–34.

Islamic Schools League of America (ISLA), at www.theisla.org.

Ismail, Sha'ban M. *In-Depth Study of Full-Time Islamic Schools in North America: Results and Data Analysis*. Plainfield, IN: Islamic Society of North America, 1989.

ISNA-CISNA Education Forum, Islamic Society of North America & Council of Islamic Schools in North America. http://www.isna.net/Conferences/pages/Education-Forum.aspx.

Keyworth, Karen. "Fast Facts About Islamic Schools in the U.S. Islamic Schools League of America." http://www.theisla.org/staticpages/index.php/PublicationsArticlesPapers (accessed February 3, 2011).

Keyworth, Karen. "Islamic Schools of America: Data-Based Profile." In *Educating the Muslims of America*, edited by Yvonne Yazbeck Haddad, Farid Senzai, and Jane I. Smith, 21–37. New York: Oxford University Press, 2009.

Keyworth, Karen, and Kathy Ahmed. "Islamic Schools: Coming of Age." *Islamic Horizons* 38 (March/April 2009): 32–43.

Muhammad, Elijah. *Message To The Blackman In America*. Phoenix, AZ: Secretarius MEMPS Publications, 2009.

Nation of Islam—Settlement No. 1, "AsSalaam Alaikum - Welcome to Nation of Islam - Settlement No. 1." http://www.seventhfam.com/ (accessed February 3, 2011).

Rashid, Hakim M., and Zakiyyah Muhammad. "The Sister Clara Muhammad Schools: Pioneers in the Development of Islamic Education in America." *Journal of Negro Education* 61 (1992): 178–85.

Shamma, Freda. "The Status of Islamic Curricula—an Overview." http://www.theisla.org/staticpages/index.php/CurriculumTarbiyah (accessed February 3, 2011).

Tauhidi, Dawud. "The Tarbiyah Project: An Overview." http://www.theisla.org/staticpages/index.php/TarbiyahProject (accessed February 3, 2011).

Wertheimer, Jack, "Linking the Silos: How to Accelerate the Momentum in Jewish Education Today." *Avi Chai Foundation, December 2005*. http://www.avi-chai.org/Static/Binaries/Publications/Linking%20The%20Silos_0.pdf (accessed February 3, 2011).

41

Islamic Schools League of America

Karen E. Keyworth

The idea for the Islamic Schools League of America (the ISLA) was conceived during a telephone conversation between Judith Amri, parent of children in an Islamic school, and Karen Keyworth, founding principal of an Islamic school. Both Amri and Keyworth felt there was a need for an organization that would help the schools organize themselves both internally and externally so they could provide a higher quality educational experience for students.

Our Vision: *The Islamic Schools League of America envisions and works towards the day when Islamic schools will be the preferred centers for learning and leadership that nurture and encourage America's youth to develop their innate creativity and inquisitive nature in the pursuance of academic excellence while anchoring their hearts and souls in a moral framework of a God-centered life.* (Cite as Islamic Schools League of America, at www.theisla.org)

After determining there were no other groups actively providing a national platform for the full-time schools, Amri and Keyworth became the primary founders of the ISLA. Amri (with assistance from Ali Al-Shwaikhat and Ahmed Al-Wazir) incorporated the organization in 1998 in the state of Virginia. The ISLA is a virtual organization with 501(c)(3) status that is dedicated to facilitating the work of full-time K-12 Islamic schools and Muslim educators. The ISLA is not, as is commonly mistakenly believed, a school. Today, the ISLA has an active board and is making the transition from a start-up organization to an established institution.

THE ISLA'S WORK

The ISLA began its work with two main projects—first, creating a virtual community for educators in the schools and second, establishing and maintaining an accurate and current list of the full time K-12 Islamic schools in the United States and Canada. Because the ISLA was run by volunteers, these two projects would consume most of the ISLA's limited resources for the first five years.

Creating an Online Community

The virtual community grew out of the need to connect Muslim educators across wide geographical regions from New York to Los Angeles. The largest concentration of full-time Islamic schools is in the New York and New Jersey area and constitutes only

17.5 percent of all schools (Keyworth and Ahmed 2009, 37). The remaining schools are spread far and wide across cities and states, many being the only Islamic school in their city. Thus, ISLA took full advantage of the growing Internet and formed a listserv called the Islamic Educators Communication Network (IECN), which was and remains the ISLA's primary platform for its virtual community. Beginning with 30 members in 1998, today it connects approximately 450 Islamic school educators across the United States and Canada.

The IECN was carefully crafted to provide a dynamic and safe place for Muslim educators to connect, learn, share, and grow. First, the list is "closed," requiring prospective members to indicate their affiliation with either a U.S. or Canadian full-time Islamic school or be a university student (planning a future in Islamic education) to be admitted. Second, the list is not moderated. Both these protocols were put in place for very important reasons that, in retrospect, have proven wise. In the late 1990s, most immigrant Muslim communities reflected the culture of their dominant immigrant group, which was often further influenced by a highly conservative trend influenced by the Salafi movement (Lee 2006). Islamic schools, however, demanded talents that brought together people from various backgrounds, some conservative and some not. This situation resulted in strongly conformist religious people who were *outside* the field of education attempting to impose the most restrictive interpretation of Islam on the budding Muslim education community that was far more open-minded than might have been assumed. This imposition from outside the education community threatened to stifle the growth of an independent and "home-grown" Islamic education milieu in the United States. The ISLA founders knew that to ensure the development of a grassroots American Islamic education community with its own unique philosophy and authentic "voice," such stifling elements would have to be kept at arm's length while those working directly in education would be given an open forum to connect with one another, solve problems, and share ideas and resources. To accomplish this, membership in the IECN listserv was, and still is, strictly controlled, requiring applicants to fill out a form that is then vetted by the ISLA. Furthermore, limiting the size and composition of the listserv to only educators, board members, and activist parents/community members in the schools and then allowing that group to impact one another without restraint accelerated development of the online community.

The second protocol of having no moderator to monitor postings also contributed to the establishment of an authentic, bottom-up development of a shared American Islamic educational philosophy. The goal in leaving posting as uncontrolled as possible was to allow educators to say what they wished without reservation, beyond being polite and sticking to the topic. Whether a member expressed a highly conservative or liberal point of view, that post would be received with respect and tolerance. The critical objective was that the online community be able to establish an authentic voice, regardless of what that voice said. The new element that began to impact these discussions—and what had been missing from many religious listservs—was the introduction of critical thinking. Many religious listservs reflected the general behavior of the Muslim community, which was to defer fairly quickly to the most conservative religious interpretation or *fatwa* (a religious opinion or decree issued by a recognized Islamic scholar or authority). Because the IECN membership was a mix of liberal and conservative, immigrant and U.S. born, male and female, and an unusual number of "trailblazer" personalities willing to speak their minds, the listserv reflected a strong respect for critical thinking and a willingness on the part of members to hold other members accountable for statements made online.

On other listservs in the late 1990s when the IECN was established, one would commonly read statements reflecting dogmatic thinking similar to the following: "According to Imam XXX, it's *haram* [forbidden] to have boys and girls sit together. Therefore, you cannot do that." It quickly became clear, however, that such statements were neither influencing nor swaying opinions and were, in fact, being discounted. This was partly because educators had real problems such as limited budgets and classroom space that could not be solved by a slavish adherence to *fatwas* formulated in other countries with other realities. In a recent discussion about school libraries and whether books such as *Harry Potter* promoted witchcraft and should be included, one IECN member wrote, " . . . nice to hear extended opinions without resorting to black and white statements of haram-ness" (IECN Jan 2011).

Muslim educators in Islamic schools understood well the realities of running an Islamic school in the United States, while others outside the field simply did not know about them. Because the IECN kept out those who did not know the realities (but who would have tried to impose their views) and allowed only those who could prove a strong connection to an American (or Canadian) full-time Islamic school, the listserv offered (and still offers) a place where real solutions to real problems could be constructed within an Islamic framework bounded by critical thinking. The result has been that over the past 13 years, a vibrant and independent professional community of Muslim educators has developed. The unfettered discussions in which ideas could be fully and critically explored have facilitated the development of an online Muslim education community and shared philosophy that is wholly Islamic, while uniquely American.

Counting the Schools

The ISLA's second main project was to establish an accurate and current list of the full-time K–12 Islamic schools in the United States, and this was completed when the bulk of the schools were verified in 2004. Since then, the list has been maintained by actively seeking out and adding new schools, culling out closed schools, and updating information as it changes. While this seems fairly straightforward, the initial work took several years to complete and proved a daunting task. The ISLA now has the most accurate and complete listing of full-time Islamic schools ever compiled, establishing that as of 2006 there were 235 full-time Islamic schools in the U.S., serving approximately 32,000 students (Keyworth 2009, 28). Although not anticipated initially, this one accomplishment has become an important springboard for further research critical to Islamic education in the United States.

Ongoing Service to the Schools

The ISLA serves the schools through a variety of services and projects, some of which are articulated here. In 2002, the ISLA launched its website, www.4islamicschools.org. In 2011, as part of an ongoing effort to grow the organization and a specific effort to improve name recognition, the ISLA changed its domain name to www.theisla.org. A critical change with the new website was the introduction of data collection on-site. Making data collection more automated allows the ISLA to do more work with fewer resources while still benefitting scholarly research. The website is designed to serve the schools by offering a wide range of resources such as job openings, current research, research archives, shared school forms, best practices in both school management and instructional resources, school achievements, grant information, reviewed reading lists for students, and more. In 2006, the ISLA partnered with National-Louis University to hold its first Leadership Conference, focused on school accreditation. The following year, the ISLA partnered with

Georgetown University and the Graduate School of Islamic and Social Sciences to hold Leadership Conference 2007, which explored Islamic spiritual curricula and discussed criteria for determining what serves the children's spiritual education needs. In 2008, the ISLA began a considerable research undertaking of a multi-year, in-depth, qualitative, and quantitative study of the schools that continues today.

DYNAMICS, CHALLENGES, AND OPPORTUNITIES

Belonging

Most people assume that being female in a Muslim immigrant community would present a problem when establishing an organization—and they would be right . . . and wrong. On a local level where people meet face to face, being a female has presented barriers to organizing. On the Internet, however, those barriers are removed, and the ISLA was welcomed into the online community.

Starting an organization is difficult from every angle. Therefore, it is complicated to tease apart the strands of difficulty—start-up, gender, scope of mission, and finances. When the ISLA first began, more men in leadership positions offered encouragement and a hand-up than those who did not. The problem was more an issue of networking. In the ISLA's experience, if one could connect to the leadership on a personal/professional level, demonstrate the organization's worth, and show an ability to grow, the leadership would accept the new organization. A major problem was connecting to the leadership because of geographical distance. Once physically in a room with the leaders of the major organizations, the ISLA founders found an interested audience.

That said, while men in other start-up organizations could move seamlessly into private spaces with male leaders, the ISLA founders could not. Because the Muslim community is so small, personal relationships are important, and the barriers to establishing those relationships likely had a negative effect on the ISLA's development. On the positive side, being on the fringe helped the ISLA avoid becoming distracted with fruitless organizational politics and, instead, focus on serving the community of educators in a concrete way. By being highly focused, the ISLA progressed quickly. Although it is impossible to prove either way, gender barriers likely did *not* enter into the ISLA's struggle in a meaningful way at the national/macro level. At the same time, both founders were experienced professionals who had been in the American workplace for many years, and they projected confidence and abilities that others found reassuring. Perhaps being outgoing and assertive women helped overcome barriers that other women found difficult to push through.

At the micro/personal level, however, there were many conditions that pushed the ISLA toward establishing itself as a virtual/online organization: cost of an office, increasing use of the Internet, geographically dispersed locations of the schools, and the limited ability of women in the Muslim community to organize and use community space. At that time, it was a rare exception for a mosque in the United States to have women decision makers or even token women on their boards. This was true, although to a lesser extent, for Muslim organizations. Weighing this barrier against the unlimited freedom the Internet offered made being a virtual organization an attractive choice.

Funding

Perhaps the most difficult problem the ISLA has faced and continues to face is funding. When the ISLA first formed, it tackled the same funding problems as other start-up organizations, but it also dealt with an additional funding barrier of being a minority. For example, everyone, including Muslims, will potentially donate to causes such as cancer research, but few if any *non*-Muslims consider donating to Islamic organizations and causes. Therefore, as a minority nonprofit, the ISLA was already drawing from a highly restricted pool of potential donors. The Muslim population of approximately three to four million (estimates range from two to seven million) constitutes less than 2 percent of the U.S. population. In addition, although money from overseas donors was also a viable option at the time, the ISLA did not seek or obtain such donations.

Following the tragedy of 9/11, the ISLA's ability to raise funds was further restricted, " . . . in an atmosphere of fear perpetuated by United States' government policies, the League [ISLA] is effectively cut off from their sources of funding. The [ISLA] is afraid to raise funds from overseas, Muslims in America are afraid to donate to the [ISLA], and also non-Muslim organizations in America are afraid to donate and/or partner with the [ISLA]" (Al-Kabour 2007, 5). Muslims, in response to the increasing rise of "Islamophobia" and concurrent challenges to prove their "American-ness," are donating their money to non-Muslim organizations and causes, forever removing that funding from the Muslim organizations. The ISLA's ability to support itself financially has become and remains extremely difficult.

CONCLUSION

The ISLA continues to support Islamic education by working collaboratively with Muslim organizations, the U.S. Department of Education (data collection), universities, researchers, and other groups relevant to private education such as AdvancEd. Islamic schools in America are ideally situated to strengthen the American Muslim community's own blend of intellect, modernity, and Islam as reflective of the reality in which Muslims live in the United States; the ISLA intends to facilitate that, always keeping Islam as its spiritual and moral compass and servant-leadership as its philosophy.

REFERENCES AND FURTHER READING

Aamir Rehman. "The Human Capital Deficit in the Islamic Non-Profit Sector. Institute for Social Policy and Understanding," April 1, 2004. http://www.ispu.org/detailed_publication.php?type=reports&id=379.

Al-Kabour, Sarah. 2007. "Funding Issues Faced by a Muslim Nonprofit in Post–9/11 America. May 2." http://www.theisla.org/staticpages/index.php/PublicationsArticlesPapers.

Council of Islamic Schools in North America. CISNA. http://cisnaonline.org/.

Haddad, Yvonne Yazbeck. 2002. Muslims in the West: From Sojourners to Citizens. Oxford University Press, USA, April 11.

Islamic Schools League of America. ISLA. http://www.theisla.org/.

Islamic Society of North America. ISNA. http://www.isna.net/home.aspx.

Keyworth, Karen. 2009. Islamic Schools of America: Data-Based Profiles. In Educating the Muslims of America, ed. Yvonne Yazbeck Haddad, Farid Senzai, and Jane I. Smith, 21–37. Oxford University Press, USA, February 26.

Keyworth, Kare, and Kathy Ahmed. "Islamic Schools: Coming of Age." Islamic Horizons 38 (March/April 2009): 32–43.

Lee, Umar. "Rise and Fall of The Salafi Movement (Complete)." Umar Lee. January, 2007 http://www.umarlee.com/rise-fall.html.

U.S. Department of State. Muslims in America—A Statistical Portrait. http://www.america.gov/st/peopleplace, 2007. english/2008/December/20081222090246jmnamdeirf0.4547083.html.

Part V

ORTHODOX SCHOOLS

42

Greek Orthodox Schools

Effie N. Christie

GREEK IMMIGRANTS IN THE UNITED STATES

The first Greek language school was established in the United States in St. Augustine, Florida, in 1777. It was not until 1864, however, that the first Greek Orthodox Church was founded in New Orleans, Louisiana. The Greek Orthodox Archdiocese of North and South America incorporated the Greek Orthodox Church in 1922, establishing the ecclesiastical life of the Greek community as an organization in the Americas (Garcia and Fishman 1997).

In order to better understand the development of Greek language schools in the United States, the story of immigration should be overviewed briefly. Restrictions to immigration through the Johnson-Reed Act of 1924 had an impact on immigrants' desires to acquire citizenship. By 1940, the American-born Greek became the majority of Greeks in the United States and eventually many of the makeshift structures used for church services and Greek schools saw permanency in new buildings. After abandoning the quota system through the Immigration Act of 1965, non-quota Greeks came as displaced persons, close relatives of Greek American citizens, or with student visas. A total of 673,360 Greeks immigrated to the United States from 1820 to 1982 (Garcia and Fishman 1997).

THE RISE OF THE GREEK LANGUAGE SCHOOL

Central to the life of the Greek family was the church and the Greek language. Whenever a group of immigrants settled in an area, they quickly organized to found a church, which was usually followed by a school. A full-time day parochial school and an afternoon school were the two forms of Greek-organized education that evolved from the flow of immigration to America. The day schools reached a small number of Greek youth, unlike the afternoon schools, which had a greater impact for several reasons. For the most part, afternoon school activities were held on the church premises and at local public schools. In Greek schools' early years, books and materials had an orientation towards children who spoke Greek. In today's Greek afternoon schools, the effort has more recently been to introduce students who want to learn Greek as a second language, though they may not hear it at home. Children attend the afternoon school after spending the day at the public school. Each church priest sets the schedule and hours of instruction depending often on the size of the parish and the available resources. Presently there are 340 afternoon schools in the United States with an enrollment of 30,000 students.

THE DAY SCHOOLS

The early Greek immigrants established the parochial or day school patterned after the primary school in Greece. The teachers in these schools were priests or teachers brought to the United States from Greece who used textbooks published in Greece as the base for instructing the students. The objective was to educate children in the mother tongue for an eventual return to the homeland. In 1968 the Bilingual Education Act allowed public schools to provide a bilingual program when sufficient numbers of non-English speaking children were registered at a school. This resulted in large numbers of Greek-speaking children leaving the parochial schools. Teachers also left the parochial schools to teach in these programs with better salaries and benefits. While the public school bilingual program stressed both English and Greek, thus meeting the needs of children who would ultimately remain in the United States, the parochial schools were not structured to offer a curriculum in both languages. The Greek parochial schools today have incorporated both Greek and English in the curriculum with teaching staff that have fluency in both languages; however, the Greek Orthodox Archdiocese still emphasizes Greek language literacy. According to the Greek Orthodox Archdiocese of America's website, 26 day or parochial schools currently operate in the United States, with 11 located in New York. Others are located in Illinois, California, Massachusetts, Texas, Florida, Georgia, Maryland, Arizona, Alabama, Pennsylvania, Tennessee, and Utah. The enrollments listed in the 2010 Yearbook range from 32 students in Phoenix, Arizona, to 678 in Houston, Texas. There are also four pre-school or day-care centers in Georgia, Illinois, and New York. The total enrollment figure is 4,305 students in the day or parochial schools in the United States. The curriculum varies from school to school and does not appear to be standardized. The School of the Transfiguration in Corona, New York lists grade levels from pre-kindergarten to the ninth grade. St. Demetrios Greek-American School in Astoria, New York, lists grade levels from pre-kindergarten to the twelfth grade. The schools offer curricula that are state approved, and teach Greek as a second language as part of the curriculum. At the Cathedral School in New York City, for instance, the curriculum includes the study of both modern and ancient Greek. The students at this school also study French in grades five through eight. The day schools operate under the umbrella of the Greek Orthodox Archdiocese.

DEPARTMENT OF SUNDAY SCHOOLS

In addition to the day schools and afternoon schools, a third school, the catechetic or Sunday school emerged, which was also connected to the Greek Church. Each Greek Orthodox Church usually operated a Sunday school program for catechetic teachings intended to pass on the principles of the Greek Orthodox faith. Most of the materials were written and presented in the Greek language. Today's curriculum is taught both in English and Greek due to the fact that an increasing number of the children came from mixed marriages where the Greek language is not spoken in the home. This development did not come without controversy. The Greek Orthodox Church and the Greek language were considered an integral part of each other forming an uncompromising philosophy upon which the education of the youth in the Greek language became a priority for the Greek family.

The Sunday school was a U.S. phenomenon for the Greek Church, since the schools in Greece also had the responsibility for religious teachings. With few exceptions, both the afternoon schools and the Sunday schools established in local parishes had the responsibility to provide religious instruction and teach the Greek language and customs of the old country (Fitzgerald 1995). The Department of Sunday Schools, established in 1932, was a realization that the Old World system of the connection of the religious teachings to the Greek language as a curriculum standard could not be maintained in the American structure. In 1950, the Tenth Clergy-Laity Congress of the Greek Orthodox Archdiocese formally announced the adoption of English for the parish Sunday school. The 1970 Laity-Clergy Congress debated the use of the vernacular in both church services and Sunday school instruction. Archbishop Iakovos led the majority of the delegates to affirm the use of Spanish, Portuguese, French, or English as needed in both the church services and the Sunday Schools. With the transition to English in church services and in Sunday schools, the afternoon and Saturday schools then became the backbone of Greek language instruction in America.

HOLY CROSS GREEK ORTHODOX SCHOOL OF THEOLOGY

One cannot leave the discussion of Greek schools in America without examining the Holy Cross Greek Orthodox School of Theology which opened its doors with fourteen students in 1937 as Holy Cross Greek Archdiocese Theological Institute at Pomfret Center, Connecticut. Holy Cross became a professional five-year college and seminary only after World War II brought to an end the idea that the institute would only serve as a preparatory seminary with students completing their theological education in Greece or in the Ecumenical Patriarchate (Constantelos 2005, 217). In 1944, St. Basil's Teacher's College was established to train Greek-language school teachers and bilingual secretaries. In 1946, the move to Brookline, Massachusetts, established Holy Cross as a significant achievement for the church. In the 1970s, St. Basil's Academy merged with Hellenic College. Holy Cross today offers several programs and degrees as a graduate College and Hellenic College offers undergraduate programs.

REFERENCES AND FURTHER READING

Constantelos, Demetrios J. *Understanding the Greek Orthodox Church*, 4th ed. Brookline MA: Hellenic University Press, 2005.

Fenton, Helke, and Melisa Hecker, eds. *The Greeks in America 1528–1977*. Dobbs Ferry, NY: Oceana Publications, 1978.

Fitzgerald, Thomas E. *The Orthodox Church*. Westport, CT: Praeger Publishers, 1995.

Garcia, Ofelia, and Joshua A. Fishman, eds. *Multilingual Apple: Languages in New York City*. New York: Mouton de Gruyter, 2002.

Greek Orthodox Archdiocese of America. *2010 Yearbook*. Ronkonkoma, NY: Ocean Printing 2010.

Greek Orthodox Archdiocese of North and South America. Department of Greek Education, at http:// www.goarch.org/archdiocese/departments/greekeducation/archdiocesanschools.

Greene, Meg. *The Greek Americans*. Farmington Hills, MI: Lucent Books, 2003.

Koken, Paul, Theodore Constant, and Serephim G. Canoulas. *A History of the Greeks in the Americas 1453–1938*. Livonia, MI: First Page Publications, 2004.

Vrame, Anton C., ed. *The Orthodox Parish in America: Faithfulness to the Past and Responsibility for the Future*. Brookline, MA: Holy Cross Orthodox Press, 2003.

Ware, Timothy. *The Orthodox Church*. London: Penguin Books, Ltd., 1997.

Part VI

ISSUES IN FAITH-BASED SCHOOLING

43

Faith-Based Charter Schools and Public Policy

Janet Mulvey and Arthur Maloney

This chapter traces the complex issues of education and religion and nonsectarian schools versus schools of faith, operated by a wide range of religious groups. This process of religious education occurred historically in four major phases: (1) the early U.S. historical period between Colonial America and the 1840s saw religion and education as one effort; (2) the middle period, starting in the 1830s with leaders like Horace Mann and Henry Barnard, saw the creation of the so-called common school, which was public but Protestant; (3) Catholics who arrived from Europe created a separate parish school system with private funding; and (4) the current voucher and charter school movements have created a blur between church-state and public-private funding, as the United States struggles to determine the difference between "supporting" and "establishing" public religious institutions.

COLONIAL AMERICA AND EDUCATION

Faith-based schooling in the United States is historically based. In Colonial times, although schools were not claimed as religious institutions, the influence of the Protestant society played a leading role in establishing the curriculum and standards of the time. Based on the King James Bible, lessons and teachings formed the schema of Puritan theology. Newsom explains:

> . . . ministers played the leading roles on local school committees, and instruction was permeated with the themes and content of Puritan theology. In other colonies, the theology of the dominant forms of local Protestantism profoundly shaped teaching aims and methods.
>
> Newsom 2002, 66–67

Thus, forerunners to Horace Mann's Common School established in the 1830s were religiously based institutions where textbooks such as the *New England Primer* had children reciting the ABCs based on teachings and/or familiarity with the Bible. As the Academic American Society explained:

Every school child, whether Puritan or not, was explicitly reminded by these primers of the sacred quality of language, which Christians had long regarded as a divine gift, as well as of their own sinful nature: "A: In Adam's Fall, We Sinn'd All." School children in reading classes also recited the Lord's Prayer and memorized scripture. Online@ . . .www.academicamerican .com/colonial. . .puritannewengland.html.

In addition, teachers were often sponsored and recommended by religious organizations who had vetted teachers' sense of loyalty and dedication to the religious beliefs and behaviors of the Protestant faith.

MIDDLE PERIOD: ESTABLISHING AND FUNDING THE COMMON SCHOOL

Mann's purpose in establishing the "common school" was to foster the principles of democracy through free state-funded institutions. Mann asserted that private schools were detrimental to a democratic society and advocated for all children to attend schools that were funded by the state. These schools allowed all who were unable to pay for education to attend a school, and the landscape of funding was changed from the "earlier practice of distributing tax dollars to schools under private control . . . non-public schools were increasingly cast as un-American and divisive" (p. np) Online @ http://education.state university.com/pages/2339/Protestant-School-Systems.html.

The common school, however, remained distinctly religious. The Protestant foundation, more inclusive of all the Protestant sects, caused little controversy until religious diversity began to characterize the American landscape. However, Catholics challenged the premise that all children must attend public schools, when Governor Walter Pierce of Oregon successfully received support on a state-wide referendum that required all children to attend only public schools. Catholics, through the Society of Sisters of the Holy Names of Jesus and Mary, joined forces with an independent school, the Hill Military Academy, and challenged the laws under the Fourteenth Amendment in *Pierce v. Society of Sisters* (1925). The Oregon law compelling attendance at public schools was ruled unconstitutional. The Society of Sisters charged that parents had the right to choose the type of education for their children. The U.S. Supreme Court affirmed "the right of private schools to exist and the right of parents to 'direct the upbringing and education' of their children" (*Pierce v. Society of Sisters* 268 U.S. 510 [1925]).

Protestant faith-based schools continued to enjoy stable enrollments through the 1930s, until the practices of the faith-based schools began to resemble the public school model. Enrollments declined steadily for the Protestant schools but grew significantly in Catholic domains through the mid-1960s. In the nineteenth century, Catholic bishops ordered each parish to build a school to house the increasing numbers of Catholic immigrants from Europe. By 1965, the church's network of parochial schools numbered more than 12,000 schools in the United States, enrolling some 5.6 million pupils (Vitello and Hu, *New York Times* January 18, 2009 A1, 14–15).

The number of Catholics once attending its parochial-run schools was about 50 percent of the total Catholic student population in the mid-960s. A number of middle class and more affluent parents were able to offset the tuition assistance for those less able to pay but who desired education in the Catholic school environment. Today, enrollment estimates in the Catholic schools number approximately 15 percent of the Catholic student population, a drastic drop to about 7,400 Catholic schools with 2.2 million students.

Included in the 15 percent attending Catholic schools are a rising number of less-affluent immigrants and poor working-class families, not able to afford increasing tuition rates that are needed to fund these schools (Mulvey, Maloney and Cooper 2010, 25).

The most recent example of the decline was reported in the *New York Times*, on September 21, 2010, when Archbishop Timothy Dolan announced that he plans to close at least 30 more elementary schools within the New York Archdiocese. The affected 56,000 students displaced from these Catholic parish schools students will overcrowd the already underfunded, overloaded public school system, causing concern on both sides of the issue. Parents who want their children to attend a Catholic or faith-based school and those who administrate the public school system in New York are seeking an alternative to solve the problem (Vitello, *New York Times* September 21, 2010 A1).

BLURRING PERIOD: PUBLIC, PRIVATE, AND RELIGIOUS SCHOOLS COME TOGETHER

Today, enrollments in private tuition faith-based schools have declined while frustration with a failing public school system is increasing. Charter Schools both public and faith-based have become an alternative to the public school system and are growing in numbers, size, and diversity. The charter movement, begun in 1991 in Minnesota, had as its intent reform linked to basic values in learning, opportunity for those unable to afford private institutions, and parental choice.

As some public schools began to suffer from lack of funding, inexperienced teachers, and failing scores, the lure of the charter school became even more appealing. Supported by national, state, and local governments, the movement has had and continues to enjoy support from public and private organizations, including those institutions affiliated with religious teachings and interests.

Implications of the increasing number of charter schools with religious overtones resound both positively and negatively with the American public. Cases opposing faith-based charter schools, brought before the courts, have resulted in a diversity of opinion, and lines that seemed clear in separating church and state have now become blurred. There are those who argue that

> Faith has always been an important part of education in the United States, from the earliest days of the colonies and the starting of the nation, whether it is a belief in God and formalized religion or a sense of national pride and "In god We Trust"—a hope that God will protect our nation and its people—or even a faith in humanity, often called humanism, that gives ethical lessons to students in a traditional, but non-sectarian context.
>
> Cooper 2007, 24

The tension between secular education and the values and religious beliefs stressed in sectarian education is one of the strains placed on conversion from private-religious to Charter status.

CASE 1: CATHOLIC TO CHARTER

Catholic schools across the landscape are facing a particular crisis, as the recent closing of 30 Catholic elementary schools in the New York Archdiocese indicates. Financial difficulties, clergy scandal, and decreasing enrollments nationwide have decreased their attractiveness and influence in even the Catholic communities. Choice for alternative schooling, charter and magnet are now competing with religiously affiliated schools that receive funding once designated for public schools.

Although Catholic schools have outperformed their public counterparts, some parents are looking for an alternative to tuition-based schooling, and charter schools offer that alternative. Catholic leadership, lay and clergy, are seeking ways to save their schools without compromising the qualities that make Catholic schooling unique. Some have begun the transition to charter school status hoping to salvage the message of moral integrity, faith, and character while maintaining the staff and locations now in jeopardy of closing.

The conversion to charter school status requires that a school board have directors to take responsibility for the school's activities and operation. Ultimately the school's board cannot have an affiliation with Catholic parishes, formerly responsible for allocating funds and driving curriculum. Enrollment in charter schools mandates that children be accepted regardless of ethnicity or faith and selected through a lottery system.

Examples of Conversions

Trinidad Campus of Center City Public Charter Schools offers an example of a Catholic school conversion to charter school status. Students at Trinidad, located in Washington, D.C., line up every morning, dressed in plaid uniforms or navy slacks, and recite the mission of the school. While the Lord's Prayer has been eliminated, students promise to "pursue excellence in character, conduct and scholarship." Students enter the same classrooms, have the same teachers, and can go to the same nuns for advice. Religious artifacts have been removed from classrooms, but the cross over the entrance of the school remains intact.

The Archdiocese in Miami was the first to adopt the charter school movement as a possibility of retaining use of their buildings and maintaining some influence of the Catholic school ethos with after-school activities, including religious education. Eight Catholic schools closed their doors in the spring of 2009 and re-opened those same doors, in the fall, as charter schools. Leasing these buildings to charter schools, the parishes are now able to derive revenue to assist in their financial challenges.

Parents of the former Catholic schools are upset by the closings but mollified by the fact that the schools do not have to be influenced by and can operate outside the local public school boards. The revenue from the leasing agreements allows the parishes to remain open and conduct after-school religion education classes in the same buildings. Brother Richard Di Maria states, "They're not Catholic schools, but Pastors in many cases will develop after-school programs in religion education, and due to the present state of the economy, many parents are choosing to remain in familiar places and attend the charter school" (Mulvey, Maloney and Cooper 2010, 30).

Dioceses in Brooklyn, Miami, and Washington, D.C., continue to grow in conversions from Catholic to charter. Families affected by this practice have expressed mixed feelings about the movement: some are happy that the schools remain open with increased resources and more opportunity, while others are concerned that religious education has been compromised or eliminated, changing the purpose of Catholic schooling.

CASE 2: PROTESTANT CHRISTIAN TO CHARTER

Protestants, who continue to be the most dominant religious group dating from the colonial period to the present, are struggling to remain an energetic and influential cultural force in the United States. The increasing diversity of religious beliefs threatens this dominance. Not unlike the Catholic schools, the Protestant schools are experiencing the same financial challenges with decreasing enrollments and fewer resources to maintain private schooling.

Similar to Catholic schools, the Christian Day Schools and other private Protestant educational establishments are struggling with economic pressures and are searching for ways to keep Christian values in their schools and provide affordability to their followers. The questions that face twenty-first century Christians, according to the *Protestant School Systems* are (1) How will they remain affordable to their middle-class clientele and support poorer families? (2) How religiously pluralistic can schools rooted in particular theological traditions become before they lose their identity? (3) How will Protestant schools respond to the availability of tax dollars for private education expenses?

The struggle to maintain an influential voice in American culture is necessitating a change in the structure and delivery of Christian education in private institutions. The charter school movement and the U.S. Supreme Court decision (2002) that ruled in favor of vouchers for parents' school choice in Cleveland have contributed to their claim. Vouchers receive support in some states and have encouraged religious programs in tax-supported schools. Other states such as Florida have declared the voucher program unconstitutional, contending they create tension and lack of clarity in the separation of church and state.

One of the biggest concerns expressed is the curriculum and textbooks that seem to undermine tolerance and acceptance of the diversity evident in the United States. In a report by Francis Patterson, who found, after examination of a series of textbooks published by large fundamentalist groups and adopted by Christian schools, a disturbing trend: "the books frequently resemble partisan, political literature more than do the traditional textbooks used in public schools" (Patterson 2001, 24).

Other Examples of Conversions

The Palmetto Christian School, in Florida, has decided to convert to charter school status. Housed in a building that has direct access to its church, this K-8 school will rename itself the Palmetto Charter School and receive state funding for its operation. Following the example of the Archdiocese of Miami, the Palmetto School will close its site due to insufficient funding, but will re-open receiving tax support. The school seeks to maintain much of the status quo of a Christian school, keeping the same staff, the same site, permission to hold assemblies and events at the church, and hiring the same principal.

State funding will pay approximately $5,750 per pupil, and with the estimated increase in enrollment the school should realize $1.71 million, of which $30,000 will be paid to the church for leasing. The concern lies in the fact that the board governing the new charter school includes the former principal of Palmetto Christian School and the pastor of the church, a violation of intent for charter school boards.

Further investigation of Palmetto Charter School reveals the following: (1) in the cafeteria of the school are crosses with the motto "Training children to become champions for Jesus," (2) the science laboratory contains textbooks that promote intelligent design over evolution (e.g., *What Darwin Didn't Know*), and (3) former administrators constitute the governing board. When questioned about these findings, Principal Bustle responded that state standards would be followed and religion would play no part in the curriculum.

Barry Lynn, executive director of the Washington-based advocacy group Americans United for Separation of Church and State questions whether school stakeholders are eluding the law. "This is problematic particularly if you have the same personnel as when it was a private religious school. One wonders if the people running the school will treat it as purely secular, purely public institution" (Lynn 2009, 7).

Idaho began its Nampa Charter School, Nappa Valley Academy, in 2009. The first sixth-graders began the year with an emphasis on Latin, while the 9th graders began their introduction to Western civilization with the Bible as the main textbook. When questioned about this practice, the headmaster of the school confirmed that the Bible would also be used to study literary and historic value. Nampa Charter School is located on 17 acres across from the New Heart Fellowship Church and shares office space with the church.

Nampa Valley Academy is reported to be one of the largest charter schools in Idaho, attracting new students from kindergarten through ninth grade. Many parents in the area have complained to the state that the school seems to be founded on and teaching Christian doctrine. Isaac Moffet, founder of the school, denies the complaints from parents but also disagrees with the present-day philosophies of public education. He sharply criticizes the works of renowned educators John Dewey, Jean Piaget, and Howard Gardner, categorizing them as "secular progressives and atheists," bemoaning their influence on present-day education. Perhaps most telling is Moffet's claim that "classical education (at the Academy) has given the student freedom to serve God in whatever capacity He has willed. A student's education will teach him to form an informed biblical opinion" (Hoffman, Nathaniel, *Charter school walks church state line*, July 8, 2009, 97).

Courts at the state and national level have been inconsistent in adjudicating cases in favor or not of vouchers and charter schools biased in favor of one God or another. The result has begun to obscure the purpose of public schooling. The use of textbooks and curriculum that influence religious thinking promotes a more stratified society, politically and religiously undermining the democratic process of tolerance and unity.

CASE 3: HEBREW CULTURAL CHARTER SCHOOLS

Like other religious groups, a significant element of Jewish organizations has taken advantage of the unique opportunities that have accompanied the national infatuation with the charter school movement, believing it to be an example of transformational reform. Seizing upon this window of opportunity for all religious groups, Jewish entrepreneurs have taken advantage of three factors that have undoubtedly caused the erosion of the wall of separation and a blurring of the lines for government agencies swept up in the hysteria for anything charter. The factors include:

- Signals from the Supreme Court regarding a relaxation of guidelines with government involvement in religion.
- The changing political climate and acceptance of the charter school movement nationally as having a major impact on the change process. In effect, anything charter is better than what is.
- The dramatic downturn in the national economy seriously affecting the viability of religious Jewish day schools, and concern among influential Jewish leaders that assimilation and intermarriage have seriously undermined the future of the Jewish tradition in America.

Kiryas Joel

What was only 10 years ago viewed as excessive entanglement with religious institutions has now become acceptable under the banner of cultural academies, which, while removing the symbols of religious affiliation, have maintained strong ties to religious purposes formerly served by private academies. A case in point, which provides insight into the changing landscape of church-state relations, can be found in the examination of the Kiryas Joel School District in New York State.

The ultimate survival and continued existence of Kiryas Joel, a publicly funded Jewish theocratic enclave in upstate New York, has provided the groundwork for a series of judicial openings for the comprehensive reconsideration of church–state relations. While not specifically related to the charter school movement, the Supreme Court case in 1994 (*Board of Education of Kiryas Joel Village School District v. Grumet*) and the subsequent state proceedings that ultimately upheld the existence of Kiryas Joel are key decisions in explaining a national wave of religious organizations seeking public funds in establishing culturally based charter academies (Mulvey et al. 2010, 109).

In an otherwise fractured decision, with many justices expressing differing opinions, the common theme that emerged among the centrists on the court was for a reconsideration of Supreme Court precedents that seemed to require "hostility toward religions, religious ideas, religious people or religious schools" (Ball 1994,12). This case demonstrates how these arguably religious organizations successfully recast their schools for public funding around values, culture, language, or the so-called neutral evaluation of classical religious texts. Kiryas Joel and its subsequent progeny in the charter school movement have signaled a new direction in thinking about religion in public education that has contributed to an even greater blurring of the lines between church and state (Mulvey et al. 2010, 114).

> As Hillman points out, "Over the past three decades, the Supreme Court's Establishment Clause jurisprudence has mirrored the shift in public opinion by becoming more accommodating of relationships between religious groups and public entities. Two components of this trend have facilitated the creation of religious charter schools. First, the Supreme Court has allowed states increasing flexibility to direct funding to schools run by religious groups. Second, it has reduced the importance of the "entanglement" prong in First Amendment jurisprudence. Because the supervision of religious groups by chartering agencies raises potential entanglement concerns, this change has made it easier for the two to work together."
>
> Hillman, 2008, 574

Ben Gamla

Perhaps the first major effort to test the religious boundaries and public funding took place in south Florida in the form of the Ben Gamla Hebrew Charter School, the nation's first Hebrew-language charter school. "With consistent claims of cultural celebration around the study of modern Hebrew and strong denials of religious affiliation, the mission and program of Ben Gamla and its supporting foundation are nonetheless building Jewish identity and tradition in the face of increasing American assimilation" (Mulvey et. al. 2010, 39). Jewish leaders behind the movement of Hebrew charters around the country acknowledge unequivocally that their chief interest is not merely the development of Hebrew speakers, but the promotion of a Jewish identity amid the fears of assimilation (Tobin 2009).

Despite many challenges from local editorial boards, the American Civil Liberties Union (ACLU), Americans United for the Separation of Church and State, the Broward County School District, and the local Jewish community, the Ben Gamla Foundation, led by former Congressman Peter Deutsch, revised, retracted, and reconsidered controversial and offending elements of their program. For example, the Hebrew curriculum was resubmitted on four different occasions over several months before ultimately being approved by the County School Board (*Miami Herald*, August 30, 2007).

Regardless of the concerns around religious affiliation and religious symbols, there is a consistent theme that the purpose of the school is to create a structure of Jewish identity and the preservation of a rich cultural affiliation. There is significant disagreement in the Jewish community itself regarding the notion that Hebrew cultural charter schools can avoid breaching the now delicate lines and uncertain balance between church and state.

As Harvard Law School constitutional scholar Noah Feldman points out, "What, after all, is the point of a Jewish cultural school if not to bring the students to an appreciation and acceptance of Jewish values? And what are those values if not the outgrowth of Judaism's millenniums of religious faith and practice?" (Feldman 2007, 13).

The charter school experiment brings together many potentially volatile elements: millions of Jewish philanthropic dollars, billions of taxpayer dollars, racial politics, and vastly different interpretations of both constitutional law and the competing strains of universalism and particularism within Jewish tradition' (Wiener 2010, 1–5).

In addition to Peter Deutsch and the Ben Gamla Foundation, another major movement in Jewish charter education can be found in the work of Michael Steinhardt and his foundation, based in New York. Steinhardt is seeking to create 20 additional Hebrew charter schools starting up by 2015 as a way to strengthen Jewish identity without the expense of private Jewish day schools (Weiner 2010).

The Hebrew Language Academy

Steinhardt began his promise by opening the Hebrew Language Academy (HLA) in September 2009 in Brooklyn, New York. While Steinhardt has taken note of Ben Gamla's efforts in South Florida, he and his foundation have chosen a different philosophy of Jewish cultural charter school organization and mission. Although they share the vision of preserving Jewish cultural identity, they differ in the extent to which the attraction of a diverse element to the school is emphasized. Steinhardt envisions a school that, while attracting members of the Jewish community, also includes multicultural and ethnic members of the surrounding community.

Peter Deutsch disagrees, telling *The Jewish Week* that "he thinks the [Steinhardt's] HLA approach is 'misguided'." Indeed, says Deutsch, whose official role with Ben Gamla is as pro bono attorney, "Very few Jews are going to put together the amount of time, money and effort to build a school where the majority of kids are not Jewish. It doesn't deal with the fundamental challenge of the American Jewish community, that you don't have kids getting a Jewish education" (Wiener 2010, 3–5).

Deutsch said, "If you really want to change the Jewish community, what's so great about a gentile speaking Hebrew? It's amazing, but not important from a Jewish communal perspective." In contrast, he said, Ben Gamla from a Jewish perspective is "off-the-charts amazing. It's changing lives. It works. It's a model that really can change the Jewish community in America" (Wiener 2010, 3–5).

Despite their differences, close scrutiny of both schools would reveal, not unexpectedly, a decidedly white, Jewish population that in no way manages to achieve a reflection of the surrounding communities. Specifically, Singer recently pointed out in the *Huffington Post* that, "While 15% of the students in New York City are white, white children make up two-thirds of the students attending the (HLA) school. This is essentially a private religious school for white Jewish families financed with government money. The parents have made this very clear, explaining in a *New York Times* article that if it were not the Hebrew Language Academy they would be paying $20,000 a year to send their children to private religious schools. Additionally, the curriculum is chauvinistically pro-Israel. There are Israeli flags all over the building and children sing songs about Israeli pioneers who built homes on empty land, the area's Arab population conveniently ignored" (Singer 2010, 1).

Daniel Treiman, a writer for the *Jewish Daily Forward*, expresses a widespread belief among many in the Jewish community by asking the question: " . . . what if government-funded charter schools devoted to reinforcing the pride—and prejudices—of particular ethnic groups became the norm? It's difficult to see how this would lead to a more cohesive, tolerant America. And that's why it's hard to imagine this model would ultimately be good for America's Jews" (Treiman 2007, 1).

Hillman observes that charter schools " . . . have a greater warrant than traditional public schools to maintain a particular normative mission in support of their constituency. The traditional contest of values that takes place in the electoral process and at school board meetings gets partially replaced by giving students a choice of schools, each with a distinct normative identity" (Hillman 2008, 573).

But what actually constitutes that normative identity? How does the current movement among Jewish and all religiously oriented charters avoid the disorder of social fragmentation, the lack of accountability, and the monitoring of the re-aligned wall of separation?

If charter schools were supposed to serve as educational alternatives to the public schools—using specialized, creative teaching methods, the public's appetite for anything charter has severely minimized the original constructs for progressive educational alternatives. Nowhere is this more in evidence than in religious/cultural charter schools where traditional formats, selectively screened populations, and school uniforms have strangely returned us to the romantic notions of 1950s parochial education. Further, the predicted "Balkanization effect" has seemingly come to pass, as we have seen in this selection. In expressing concern about the already deepening divisions in our society among various groups, Kozol asks, "[H]ow much more fragile might relationships between such groups become if we permit ourselves to concretize and deepen these divisions by the spawning of a multitude of ideologically, religiously, or ethnically established schools, supported by taxpayers?" (Kozol 2007, 143).

CASE 4: MINNESOTA: ISLAMIC CHARTER SCHOOL

Similar to the Catholic and Christian charter school debate is the advancement of charter schools promoting Islam. Minnesota, the first state to pass charter laws in 1991, is hosting Muslim associations who have opened and are supporting Tarek ibn Ziyad Academies (TiZA) on two campuses. The concern lies with the operation, placement, and studies within the academies.

The original intent of Minnesota's charter law was to give teachers, not parents, more control over curriculum and with fewer restrictions. Charter schools created under Minnesota state law must find a sponsor to apply to a school board and if denied apply to the Commissioner of Education. Once the law was passed and application made, the state approved the Ziyad Academy in 2003.

The ACLU, alleging that TiZA violates the Establishment Clause of the First Amendment of the United States Constitution, as well as the Establishment Clause of the Minnesota Constitution, has filed several law cases. The basis of the lawsuits asserts that TiZA is aligned with the Islamic religion in 17 specific ways. For our purposes, we will examine four areas where lines have been crossed between secular and religious education.

1. Entanglement with the Muslim American society of Minnesota, which asserts according to Maeglin " . . . a local affiliate of the Muslim American Society states as its goal . . . " " 'shall be to attain the pleasure of Allah (God)' and to present the message of Islam to Muslims and non-Muslims" (Maeglin 2010, 63).
2. Entangling Housing Arrangements, including the association of the schools' physical locations within religious establishments. TiZA leases space from buildings owned and supported by Muslims, who gain financially from the rent.
3. Dress Code and Language Requirement is reported in the *Minnesota Monthly* (2007) as TiZA "advances, endorses, and prefers Muslim clothing, particularly for the girls who wear skirts that extend below the knee . . . head scarves are voluntary but all girls wear them . . . the school has a central carpeted prayer space, and vaguely religious-sounding language is used" (Featherly 2007, 1–3).
4. Prayer in School has been claimed in the court case against TiZA. Minnesota Public Radio has reported that "the school illegally promotes religion by . . . holding prayer during class time . . . and that lost class time is never made up" (Nelson and Baier, MPR, "School Accused of Promoting Islam Countersue ACLU," July 29, 2009).

The claims against TiZA by the ACLU include violations of the Establishment Clause of the First Amendment to the United States Constitution and the Minnesota State Constitution. In addition, the lawsuit claims a violation of the Minnesota charter school law: the location of the schools, an improper leasing agreement with a sectarian body, and lack of proper certification of teachers within the school. The courts have dismissed the allegations and it remains to be seen if the state regulatory bodies will pursue the case. The final determination leaves us in an indeterminate state: the court dismissed the ACLU, stating it has no standing in the case, but did not adjudicate in favor of TiZA. What occurs in the future remains to be seen.

SUMMARY

Charter schools continue to be an alternative to both private and public education. They have become prominent in the political and social landscape of the country. President Obama and U.S. Secretary of Education Arne Duncan promote charters as a hope for excellence and competition among schools. Concerned over the ranking of the United States worldwide in both reading and math, charters have promised a more successful outcome and are increasing in numbers across the nation. Charter schools publicly funded and without all the restrictions of a public school have brought choice and innovation for students and communities.

Faith-based schooling has its history in the development of education in the United States. Common (public) schools became the first tuition-free schools focused on educating all children, and those who chose to send their children to private or religious institutions paid tuition. Financial hardships and declining enrollments have forced many religious schools to close. The charter school movement, intended for parental choice to escape failing public schools, has opened the doors for publicly funded faith-based education.

Religious organizations, in their struggle to survive, have embraced the charter movement as a way to retain some control over their flocks and to remain financially solvent. They symbolize a choice for parents, a competitive force for public schools, and a lifeline for financial solvency and influence within the religious communities. Catholic, Protestant, Jewish, and Muslim communities have all entered the charter school movement and are all receiving tax dollars while incorporating religious tones to their curricula.

Establishment of faith-based charter schools has raised public concern over the blurring of lines separating church and state. The courts have become active in hearing each case as they are brought for hearing. At issue is the interpretation of the U.S. Constitution's First Amendment, which states two interpretable requirements: that the government should neither prohibit religious practices nor establish them (i.e., create a state religion). According to Thomas Jefferson, "a wall of separation" was created between church and state, protecting the right of groups to create their own devotional practices without government interference.

State courts and the Supreme Court of the United States have become increasingly involved in adjudicating cases brought forth to challenge the Establishment and Free Exercise clauses of the Constitution. In each case, thus far, the decisions seem to be in favor of special groups, whether they are religious, ethnic, or cultural. The increasing diversity of society in the public and private domains has resulted in the courts allowing vouchers, aid for special education, tax credits, and other expense benefits for non-public education programs. In the words of James C. Carper:

> Often the future is merely the past in different garb. If the aforementioned trends continue, perhaps the education landscape will resemble that of the Colonial era, with a variety of educational institutions sharing equally in public resources and contributing in different ways to the accomplishment of public purposes. Education of the public rather than public education might become the primary concern of the state. The winds of change continue to blow.
>
> Carper 2001, 110

REFERENCES AND FURTHER READING

Academic American Society . . .www.academicamerican.com/colonial. . .puritannewengland.html.

Ball, William. "The Church-State Game: A Symposium on Kiryas Joel." In *Blurring the Lines: Charter, Public and Private Schools Coming Together*, edited by Janet Mulvey, Bruce S. Cooper, and Arthur T. Maloney. Charlotte: Information Age Publishing, 2010.

Board of Education of Kiryas Joel Village School District v. Grumet, 512 U.S. 687, (1994).

Bustle, Brian. Palmetto Christian to Become Public School. Herald Tribune. (Retrieved from www.heraldtribune.com/article/20091102). A1.

Carper, James. C. "The Changing Landscape of U. S. Education". *Kappa Delta Pi Record* 37, 3 (2004): 106–10.

Cooper, Bruce, S. Foreword. In *Religious Charter Schools: Legalities and Practicalities*, edited by L. Weinberg. Charlotte, N.C.: Information Age Publishing, 2007.

Cooper, Bruce, S. "Public, Private School Convergence Present Policy Opportunity." *School Reform News*. The Heartland Institute, October 10, 2010.

DiMaria, Richard. " Archbishop Conversations." www.miamiarchdiocese.org (2009).

Dolan, Archbishop Timothy. "Archbishop Wants to Prune Catholic Schools." In: Vitello, Paul *New York Times* September 21, 2010.

Featherly, Kevin. "Brothers' Keeper." Minnesota Monthly. (Retrieved from http://www.minnesota -monthly.com) March 2007, 1–3.

Feldman, Noah. "The Way We Live Now, Universal Faith." *The New York Times Magazine* (August 26, 2009), 13. http://www.nytimes.com/2007/08/26magazine/26wwlnledt.html?pagewanted=2 &_r=1&ref=magazine.

Hillman, Benjamin Siracusa. "Is There a Place for Religious Charter Schools?" *Yale Law Journal* 118:554. http://www.yalelawjournal.org/images/pdfs/753.pdf.

Hoffman, Nathaniel. Charter School Walks Church, State Line: Classical Academy Plans to Teach Conservative Worldview, Bible. *Boise Weekly*, 2009. Retrieved from http//www.boiseweekly.com/boise/classical-class/Content?oid=1098884.

Kozol, Jonathan. *Letters to a Young Teacher*, New York: Crown Publishers, 2007.

Lynn, Barry. *First Freedom First: A Citizen's Guide to Protecting Religious Liberty and the Separation of Church and State*. Boston: Beacon Press, 2009.

Maeglin, Thomas. "Minnesota Islamic Charter School Blurs the Line." In *Blurring the lines: Charter, Public and Private Schools Coming Together*, edited by Janet Mulvey, Cooper, Bruce and Maloney, Arthur. Charlotte: Information Age Publishing, 2010.

Mulvey, Janet, Bruce S. Cooper and Arthur T. Maloney. *Blurring the Lines: Charter, Public and Private Schools Coming Together*. Charlotte: Information Age Publishing, 2010.

Nelson, Tim and Elizabeth Baier, "School Accused of Promoting Islam Countersue ACLU." *Minnesota Public Radio* July 29, 2009.

Newsom, Michael. "Common School Religion: Judicial Narratives in a Protestant Empire." *Interdisciplinary Law Journal*, Vol. II: 219, 2002.

Patterson, Francis *With God on Their Side*. 2001. http://www.rethinkingschools.org/specialreports.

Pierce v Society of the Sisters of the Holy Names of Jesus and Mary, 268 U.S. 510 (1925).

Protestant School Systems—colonial and Nineteenth Century Protestant Schooling, Early Twentieth-Century Protestant School. Retrieved from http://education.stateuniversity.com/pages2339/Protestant-School-System.htm#ixzzIF5JC53ks (September 10, 2010).

Sharpen Line Between Church and State. Our Opinion: Privately Run Charter Schools Need More Scrutiny. *Miami Herald*. August 30, 2007. 26A. Retrieved from Miami Herald Archives, newslibrary@newsbank.com.

Singer, Alan. "Charter Schools Don't Do Miracles." *Huffington Post*, June 30, 2010. http://www.huffingtonpost.com/alan-singer/charter-schools-dont-do-m_b_627600.html.

Tobin, Jonathan. "A Charter for Failure." *Jewidh Daily Forward*, February 13, 2009. http://www.forward.com/articles/15099 (accessed September 12, 2010).

Treiman, Daniel. "The Charter School Temptation". *Jewish Daily Forward*, August 27, 2010. http://www.forward.com/articles12022 (accessed August 27, 2010).

Vitello, Paul. "New York Archbishop Wants to Close Catholic Schools." *New York Times*. September 21, 2010.

Vitello, Paul, and Hu, Winnie. "For Catholic Schools Crisis and Catharsis." *New York Times*, January 18, 2009 A1, 14–15.

Wiener, Julie. Fresh Debate Over New National Charter School Movement. *The Jewish Week*. February 3, 2010, 1. http://www.thejewishweek.com/news/new_york/fresh_debate_over_new_national_charter_school_movement (accessed August 28, 2010).

44

State and Federal Regulation
of Faith-Based Schools

Ralph Mawdsley

Faith-based schools have codes of conduct for students and employees that are governed by religious beliefs. Since these schools are most generally known as religious schools, or, more broadly, as non-public schools, those terms will be the ones most frequently used in this chapter.

RELIGIOUS SCHOOLS AND PARENTS' CONSTITUTIONAL RIGHTS

The authority of states to regulate education is implied in the Tenth Amendment of the U.S. Constitution and was reinforced in *Pierce v. Society of Sisters* where the Supreme Court observed that

> No question is raised concerning the power of the state reasonably to regulate all schools, to inspect, supervise and examine them, their teachers and pupils to require that all children of proper age attend some school, that teachers shall be of good moral character and patriotic disposition, that certain studies plainly essential to good citizenship must be taught, and that nothing be taught which is manifestly inimical to the public welfare.
>
> Pierce 1925, 534

The Supreme Court in *Pierce* determined that a state's legislative act requiring all students to attend public schools violated a parent's right under the liberty clause of the Fourteenth Amendment to direct the education of their children. However, the seeds of future conflict were contained in the Court's decision. As reflected in the quotation above, states still retained considerable regulatory authority over nonpublic schools. Thus, while the *Pierce* Court held that a state could not legislate nonpublic schools out of existence, it left for a future date the determination as to whether states might accomplish the same goal through extensive regulations. In *Pierce*, with the only limitation on state regulatory authority being the reasonableness of the regulations, the Court, in a sense, invited an opportunity in the future to test the stretchable limits of the elastic concept of reasonableness.

Forty-seven years after *Pierce*, in *Wisconsin v. Yoder*, the Supreme Court revisited the subject of state control over nonpublic education. However, this time the issue was the regulatory authority of the State of Wisconsin to impose its compulsory attendance statute on Amish children whose parents refused to permit them to attend high school once they had completed the eight years of an Amish school. Thus, at issue were the two to three years between completion of eighth grade (ages 13 or 14) and the compulsory attendance age of 16. Three Amish parents were convicted of truancy for refusing to permit their children to attend the public high school and each was fined $5.

In presenting their case, the Amish parents had the advantage of the Free Exercise Clause in the First Amendment, which had not been made applicable to the states at the time of *Pierce*. The parents in *Pierce* had presented their claim under the liberty clause of the Fourteenth Amendment, and it was under this clause that the Court declared that parents had a protectable constitutional right "to direct the upbringing and education of children" (Pierce 1925, 534). In addition to relying on this liberty clause protection, the *Yoder* Court created a free exercise clause tripartite test to assess whether state action impermissibly infringed upon religious beliefs:

1. whether an activity objected to by the state is rooted in legitimate and sincerely held religious beliefs;
2. whether a party's religious beliefs have been burdened by the state's action and the extent of or impact on their religious activity;
3. whether the state has a compelling interest justifying its action and the burden imposed on the party's religious activity.

In affirming the Supreme Court of Wisconsin's reversal of the Amish parents' truancy convictions, the U.S. Supreme Court found that the Amish 300-year tradition as an identifiable religious sect following their religious beliefs that limited contact with the secular world, with a history of its members being successful and self-reliant members of society, was threatened by the state's compulsory attendance statute. Indeed, as the Court observed, the vocational opportunities on the Amish farms, afforded to young people who had completed eighth grade, were not only a satisfactory alternative to the additional two to three years of high school, they also preserved the integrity of the Amish religious community by diminishing the likelihood that children would be attracted away once they enrolled in a public high school (*Wisconsin v. Yoder* 1972, 203).

Yoder represented the high-water mark of the Free Exercise Clause. Eighteen years later in *Employment Division v. Smith*, the U.S. Supreme Court dealt the Free Exercise Clause, as a defense to government regulation, a near-fatal blow. The Court determined that the Free Exercise Clause would no longer be a defense to "a neutral, generally applicable regulatory law" (Employment Division 1990, 880). The impact upon litigation involving the use of the Free Exercise Clause as a defense to government laws and regulations was immediate and dramatic. Although the Court later carved out an exception to *Employment Division* in *Church of the Lukumi Babalu Aye, Inc. v. City of Hialea*, where government actions that are hostile to a particular religion still constitute violations of free exercise, the harm had been done. Thus, when the Supreme Court was called upon to decide, in *Locke v. Davey*, whether a State of Washington regulation prohibiting the use of state scholarship funds for a person majoring in theology violated the free exercise clause, it refused to find a free exercise violation even though the regulation was not, as Justice

Scalia observed in his dissent, neutral toward religion. In relying on what it referred to as "the play in the joints" between the free exercise and establishment clauses, the *Davey* Court left states with wide discretion under their own constitutions to regulate religious matters without violating the federal Constitution's free exercise clause.

The liberty clause's right of parents to direct the education of their children still maintains some viability against arbitrary state action. Thus, in *Barrow v. Greenville Independent School District*, the Fifth Circuit Court of Appeals held that when a teacher was denied an assistant principal position by the superintendent because she enrolled her children in a private school, she had a claim against the superintendent for violation of her right to educate her children in a private school. Similarly, in *Barrett v. Steubenville City Schools*, the Sixth Circuit Court of Appeals held that an elementary teacher who was repeatedly denied a teaching position by the school district superintendent because the teacher's child attended a religious school was entitled to a trial as to whether his liberty clause child-rearing right had been violated. Both courts found the law so well established regarding parent choice of the venue for their children's education that the superintendents were denied qualified immunity for their actions in denying the positions.

STATE REGULATION OF RELIGIOUS SCHOOLS

The Supreme Court's decision in *Yoder* energized many religious schools in the 1970s and 1980s (many of them new schools) to challenge the efforts of state departments of education and local school districts to impose upon them the same statutes and regulations used for public schools. Generally, the success of these challenges varied among the states and frequently devolved into a discussion of reasonableness of the regulations or whether the *Yoder* compelling-interest test had to be applied to schools of religious groups that did not look or function like the Amish.

Even before *Employment Division v. Smith*'s evisceration of the free exercise clause, one can argue that courts had undercut the *Yoder* test by replacing the compelling interest test with a bland reasonableness test. Judicial confusion in infusing a discussion of "reasonableness" into the *Yoder* compelling interest redefined the nature of compelling interests. The *Yoder* Court viewed compelling interests from the perspective of the final product or outcome, in that case whether the Amish children after only eight years of formal education were prepared adequately "to participate effectively and intelligently in our open political system . . . [and] to be self-reliant and self-sufficient participants in society" (Yoder 1972, 221). As the Court observed, the record supported that Amish members were "productive and very law-abiding members of society" (Yoder 1972, 222). The inference from the *Yoder* reasoning was that alternative methods can achieve the state's outcomes without necessarily requiring "a hydraulic insistence on conformity to majoritarian standards" (Yoder 1972, 217).

What the *Yoder* Court applied to the State of Wisconsin's effort to impose its compulsory attendance law on the Amish was a least-restrictive means test, without using that precise terminology. In a series of three unemployment compensation cases beginning in 1963 with *Sherbert v. Verner*, the Supreme Court, in reversing denial of unemployment compensation benefits to workers discharged for refusing to perform work in violation of religious beliefs, reasoned that it "would plainly be incumbent upon the state to demonstrate that no alternative forms of regulation would combat [the abuses associated with accommodating religious beliefs] without infringing First Amendment rights" (Sherbert 1963, 407). The notion that the state had a duty to demonstrate in free exercise cases that no reasonable alternatives existed before pursuing a course of action contrary to a person's religious beliefs existed prior to *Yoder*, and, in fact, was reflected in *Yoder*.

The Supreme Court, in *Employment Division v. Smith* (another unemployment compensation case), did not reverse the *Sherbert* line of cases but did limit their effect only to unemployment compensation cases. However, this post-*Employment Division* limitation does not explain the reluctance of courts prior to *Employment Division* to apply the test to state regulation of religious nonpublic schools. In determining whether alternatives existed to the application of public school teacher-certification requirements to nonpublic schools, courts prior to *Employment Division* clearly did not apply the least-restrictive means test with the same vigor as the Supreme Court had applied the test to employee religious beliefs in the unemployment compensation cases.

Occasionally though, courts displayed flashes of enlightenment in distinguishing between methods and outcomes. In *People v. DeJonge*, the Supreme Court of Michigan, in holding that application of the state's teache- certification requirement to homeschooling violated parents' free exercise rights, distinguished between the state's interest in education and the state's enforcement of teacher certification as a necessary means to achieve that end.

> The state has focused upon the incorrect governmental interest. The state's interest is not ensuring that the goals of compulsory education are met, because the state does not contest that the DeJonges are succeeding at fulfilling such aims. Rather, the state's interest is simply the certification requirement of the private school act, not the general objectives of compulsory attendance. The interest the state pursues is the manner of education, not its goals.
>
> People 1993, 137

In general, state and lower federal courts interpreted and applied the Supreme Court's constitutional guidelines with varying degrees of understanding and consistency, and the result became a crazy quilt of case law. Court decisions failed to agree regarding compliance of nonpublic schools with state approval, curriculum, and teacher certification requirements. In *State v. Olin*, a state compulsory attendance requirement—that students attend a school with a certified teacher—was unreasonable as applied to a non-Amish child in an Amish school, whereas in *Fellowship Baptist Church v. Benton*, a state statute exempting Amish schools from teacher-certification requirements did not apply to a Baptist school. In *Bangor Baptist Church v. State of Maine*, the Department of Education did not have express statutory authority under the compulsory attendance statute to impose direct sanctions against unapproved private schools, whereas in *State v. Faith Baptist Church of Louisville*, the enforcement of compulsory attendance statutes included authority to enjoin operation of the school and to incarcerate the pastor.

Case law regarding compliance with state curricular requirements presented the same differing results. In *State of Ohio v. Whisner*, state curriculum requirements regulating not only the courses to be offered but also the amount of instructional time to be allocated to the subjects offered were held unreasonable, whereas in *State v. Shaver*, state department of education regulations specifying the courses to be offered were held to be reasonable. In *Kentucky State Board v. Rudasill*, a Kentucky constitutional provision providing that no man shall "be compelled to send his child to any school to which he may be conscientiously opposed" prohibited Kentucky from requiring that any teacher in a nonpublic school be certificated and prohibited the state's determination of basic texts to be used in private or parochial schools. However, in *Care and Protection of Charles*, a statutory provision whereby a Massachusetts school committee could not withhold such approval to operate a nonpublic school on account of religious teaching, did not exempt home-instruction parents from the obligation to furnish outlined curriculum, materials to be used, and qualifications of instructors.

The confrontation between the state and religious schools diminished beginning in the late 1980s as state legislatures intervened and enacted laws freeing nonpublic schools from many of the more onerous state requirements. However, state cases still arise, as in *Valley Christian School v. Montana Public High School Association*, upholding the authority of a state board of education to require teachers in religious schools to satisfy state certification requirements. Generally though, legal issues have moved on to other contentious areas, especially those related to participation of religious schools in state athletic associations.

RELIGIOUS SCHOOLS AND STATE ATHLETIC ASSOCIATIONS

In *Denis J. O'Connell High School v. Virginia High School League*, the Fourth Circuit Court of Appeals reversed a district court injunction ordering a state athletic association to accept the application of a religious school. The court of appeals found the athletic association classification limited to public schools and excluding private schools to be a rational one under the equal protection clause because of the lack of specifically designed private school recruiting areas and the difficulties created in enforcing the transfer rule. In effect, the court endorsed the notion that because religious schools are perceived as the most likely source of violations of the transfer rule, they need to be eliminated entirely from even the possibility of becoming a problem by not permitting them to become members of the association. The reasoning of *Denis J. O'Connell High School* was followed by the Third Circuit in *Valencia v. Blue Hen Conference*, where the court of appeals upheld a federal district court decision that an athletic conference's refusal to permit a religious school to join did not violate the equal protection clause or impermissibly burden the free exercise rights of the school because the public high school association's exclusion of nonpublic (including religious) schools was supported by legitimate interests in preventing athletic recruiting and maintaining a competitive balance among schools within the association. Sometimes, litigation can have the salutary effect of causing change. A Texas federal district court, in *Jesuit College Preparatory School v. Judy*, reached a similar result to the Fourth Circuit decision in *Denis J. O'Connell High School*, but the case had a positive result in that the Texas University Interscholastic League changed its rules to permit the religious school to participate.

Once religious schools are permitted to be members of state athletic or activities associations, they are entitled to the same constitutional fairness in interpreting association rules as are public school members. In *Brentwood Academy v. Tennessee School Athletic Association*, a case that twice appeared before the U.S. Supreme Court, the Court held in the first appearance that a state athletic association was a state actor and could be sued by a religious school penalized for allegedly violating the association's "undue influence" rule. However, in the second appearance six years later, the Court reversed a damages award for the religious school, holding that the association's enforcement of its anti-recruiting rule did not violate the school's First Amendment rights.

Membership in an athletic association means that private schools are governed by the same rules that apply to public schools. In *Rottman v. Pennsylvania Interscholastic Athletic Association*, the coach of a Catholic high school girls' basketball team, suspended for one year for recruiting violations, lost her claim that the anti-recruiting rule was an unconstitutional violation of free speech. The association had determined that the coach's repeated attention to an eighth-grade player was intended to influence her to attend the Catholic high school. The court rejected the coach's free speech claim, finding that contacts with a player are not matters of public concern, and even if they were, the association had an overriding interest in "promoting academics over athletics, protecting students from exploitation, and maintaining competitive equity" (Rottman 2004, 931).

HOME INSTRUCTION

No one seems to have an accurate number of the homeschooled students in the United States, but one estimate places the number between 1.7 and 2.2 million children (Ray 2004, 1). For a sense of perspective, "more children are educated at home than are educated in the public schools of Wyoming, Vermont, Delaware, North Dakota, Alaska, South Dakota, Rhode Island, Montana and Hawaii-combined. In fact, the total number of children educated in home schools outnumbers the aggregate of children educated in the public schools of forty-one individual states" (Colwell and Schwartz 2003, 381). What is clear is that the overwhelming reason for most parents in choosing to home school their children is grounded in religious faith.

All 50 states recognize that while home schools are classified as schools for purposes of fulfilling compulsory attendance requirements, they differ widely in the amount of regulation. A survey compiled of all 50 states plus the District of Columbia (collectively referred to as "states") reveals the wide disparities among states, although some common themes occur. In addition to reporting the full result of their survey, the authors provided the following information in a useful summary:

1. Thirty-four states have statutes and/or administrative regulations directly addressing home schools;
2. Forty-two states require notification by those providing home instruction, with 33 requiring notification to local officials, 7 to state officials, and 1 to either local or state officials;
3. Forty-five states specify home schools to operate a specific number of days and/or hours each year;
4. Forty-four states set curriculum requirements;
5. Twenty-one states do not have specific qualifications for parents or non-parents as instructors; on the other hand, two states (Alabama and Michigan) require all instructors, including parents, to be certificated, but beyond these two states, qualifications vary widely as to diplomas, degrees, or certifications required for instructional purposes (Colwell and Schwartz 2003, 392–95).

Obviously, those desirous of homeschooling their children need to determine the statutory requirements in their state before undertaking the venture. The penalty for noncompliance with a state's compulsory attendance generally is a truancy charge.

Historically, state response to homeschooling has not been particularly sympathetic or understanding. In addition to a significant judicial record of truancy convictions for parents who chose homeschooling despite not meeting state requirements (State v. Patzer 1986), courts have upheld a wide range of regulatory methods affecting home schools (*Goulart* 2003, *Battles* 1995).

FEDERAL STATUTES AND RELIGIOUS SCHOOLS

The most prominent litigated areas involving religious schools involve federal nondiscrimination statutes. These federal statutes generally have state counterparts that tend to follow federal statutes, although many states also have categories such as marital status and sexual orientation not expressly recognized at the federal level. Nonetheless, whether or not state claims are brought against religious schools, virtually all cases involve alleged violations of federal statutes. The judiciary's interpretation of these statutes as applied to religious schools can have a profound effect on the operation of religious schools.

Federal nondiscrimination statutes are divided into two broad groups: those that prohibit discrimination in employment and those that prohibit discrimination in educational institutions receiving federal assistance. The employment statutes include Title VII of the Civil Rights Act of 1964, which prohibits discrimination on the basis of race, color, religion, sex, and/or national origin; the Age Discrimination Act in Employment Act of 1967, which prohibits discrimination against persons 40 years of age or older; the Americans with Disabilities Act, prohibiting discrimination on the basis of disabilities in employment, by state and local governments, and in public accommodations; and the Family and Medical Leave Act, which accords employees the right to extended leave for personal and family medical needs and illnesses. A less litigated federal statute is the Uniform Services Employment and Reemployment Act (USERRA), which prohibits discrimination because of membership, application for membership, performance of service, application for service, or obligation of a person in the uniformed services.

Statutes requiring the reception of federal assistance before they apply to faith-based schools include the Rehabilitation Act of 1973, which prohibits discrimination on the basis of disabilities; Title IX of the Educational Amendments of 1972, which prohibits gender discrimination; the Equal Pay Act of 1963, which prohibits gender-based wage discrimination; and Title VI of the Civil Rights Act, which prohibits discrimination on the basis of race, color, or national origin. Application of these federal statutes and their regulations have had a profound effect on faith-based schools.

Remedies for discrimination can also be pursued under two other federal statutes that can apply to both employment and non-employment situations. Section 1981 of the Civil Rights Act prohibits discrimination on the basis of national origin and race in the making of contracts. Section 1983 of the Civil Rights Act, which contains no discriminatory categories of its own, is a vehicle for seeking damages for violations of federal constitutional and statutory rights. However, section 1983 generally does not apply to religious schools because they lack sufficient contacts with government to qualify as state actors (Rendall-Baker 1982).

FUNDAMENTAL PUBLIC POLICY AND RELIGIOUS SCHOOLS

The U.S. Supreme Court, in *Bob Jones University v. U.S.*, introduced the concept of fundamental public policy to education law. In that case, the Court upheld the IRS's revocation of the tax-exempt status for a fundamentalist Christian university that, at that time, had racially discriminatory rules grounded in its interpretation of the Bible prohibiting interracial dating and marriage.

Although the University has since changed its policies and regained its tax-exempt status, the Court's decision galvanized the attention of religious schools at a time when they were locked in conflict as to whether states and local school districts had Yoder compelling interests in regulating religious education. Bob Jones University added yet another layer of government control over religious schools, in this case, what the Court referred to as "fundamental public policy" (Bob Jones University 1983, 596). Although the government interest advanced in *Bob Jones University*, "eradicating racial discrimination in education" (Bob Jones University 1983, 604) was different qualitatively from the teacher-certification statutes used to measure the quality of religious school instruction, the lingering question after *Bob Jones University* was whether the Court's decision might become the vehicle to elevate other (or all) compelling interests into fundamental public policies. To date, however, no other government interest has been so elevated, although courts have come tantalizing close with gender and sexual-orientation discrimination.

In *United States v. Commonwealth of Virginia*, the Supreme Court used an intermediate equal protection standard, "exceedingly persuasive justification" (United States 1996, 531), to strike down Virginia Military Institute's exclusion of women. However, the Court stopped short of equating gender-based discrimination with the race-based discrimination in *Bob Jones University*, and in any case, the decision had no direct impact on faith-based schools since it was decided under the equal protection clause of the Fourteenth Amendment.

Nonetheless, the Virginia Military Institute's case raised the visibility of gender issues that can arise in religious schools, because female pregnant out-of-wedlock students and teachers are subject to discipline for being in conflict with their schools' religious values. In *Vigars v. Valley Christian Center of Dublin, California*, a federal district court determined that the dismissal of a teacher for out-of -wedlock pregnancy was not permitted under Title VII, although the school had a protected First Amendment right to discharge the teacher for adultery. Thus, while the school had a First Amendment defense based on a religious belief of a "dislike of pregnancy outside of marriage," this had to be balanced at trial against the discrimination claim that "only women can ever be fired for being pregnant without benefit of marriage" (Vigars 1992, 808). Similarly, in *Cline v. Catholic Diocese of Toledo*, the Sixth Circuit Court of Appeals ruled that, although the diocese had a premarital sex policy and stated a nondiscriminatory reason under Title VII for nonrenewing a teacher pregnant out-of-wedlock, the teacher still was entitled to go to trial as to whether the contract nonrenewal "constituted discrimination based on her pregnancy as opposed to a gender-neutral enforcement of the school's premarital sex policy" (Cline 2000, 658).

However, in a case decided under a state marital-status discrimination statute, the Supreme Court of Montana, in *Parker-Bigaback v. St. Labre School*, determined that a Catholic school's termination of a female counselor's contract for living with a man without being married did not violate the statute because this case was not about discrimination but about "the school's right to freely exercise its religion through its employment practices and an employee. . . . [and] conduct which [the teacher] agreed to avoid when she signed her employment agreement" (Parker 2000, 364). However, when religious beliefs about extra-marital sexual conduct are balanced against gender discrimination in out-of-wedlock pregnancy cases, punishment of only the pregnant female employee is not likely to be successful. In *Boyd v. Harding Academy of Memphis*, a religious school's discharge of a pregnant female teacher was upheld where the school had a practice of enforcing its prohibition of out-of-wedlock sexual misconduct against both women and men.

In the area of sexual-orientation discrimination, the District of Columbia Court of Appeals decision, in *Gay Rights Coalition v. Georgetown University*, indicates that even clearly held religious beliefs may have to accommodate changing expressions of public policy. In this case, student gay/lesbian groups brought suit against a Jesuit university under a District of Columbia ordinance prohibiting discrimination in the use of or access to facilities and services based wholly or partially on the basis of sexual orientation. Despite the university's religious belief opposing homosexuality, the court of appeals determined that the District of Columbia could protect both its interest in "the eradication of sexual orientation discrimination" (Gay Rights 1987, 33) and the university's religious beliefs if the university were required to provide facilities and services to gay/lesbian students without having to formally recognize the student group. Citing to *Bob Jones University*, the District of Columbia Circuit reasoned that "government has a compelling interest in the eradication of other forms of discrimination" and concluded that "discrimination based on sexual orientation is a grave evil that damages society as well as its immediate victims" (Gay Rights 1987, 38). Religious educational institutions that have exclusionary practices based on sexual orientation, but not grounded in religious beliefs, have little chance of prevailing when challenged under state or local anti-discrimination laws prohibiting discrimination based on sexual orientation.

The U.S. Supreme Court's 2010 decision in *Christian Legal Society Chapter of the University of California, Hastings College of the Law v. Martinez* has suggested, even though the case dealt with a public law school, that religious beliefs against homosexuality are not likely to keep gay/lesbian groups out of schools in states that prohibit sexual orientation discrimination. In *Christian Legal Society*, a majority of the Supreme Court held that a law school's nondiscrimination policy against sexual orientation discrimination could be enforced against the Christian Legal Society chapter, which had to be open to "all comers" if it wanted to participate in the law school student groups' benefits. The Court rejected the Society's free expression argument that "[t]here can be no diversity of viewpoints in a forum if groups are not permitted to form around viewpoints" (Christian Legal Society 2010, 89). However, some states exempt religious schools from sexual orientation nondiscrimination statutes where the school's objection is grounded in religious beliefs (Romeo 2005).

The Supreme Court's rationale in *Christian Legal Society* and the District of Columbia Circuit's rationale in *Gay Rights* leave in doubt how much vitality an organization's religious belief opposing homosexuality has. Once the courts permit the gay/lesbian groups access to Society meetings in *Christian Legal Society* and access to university services in *Gay Rights*, to what extent has the right of the Society or the university to practice its religious beliefs about homosexuality been diminished? If Christian Legal Society members or Georgetown University personnel preached and taught their religious beliefs that homosexuality is sinful, would such expression be actionable by gay and lesbian participants as harassment? In effect, do religious organizations, including schools, have the right to their beliefs, but not the right to practice those beliefs?

RELIGIOUS BELIEF AND PRACTICE

The distinction between faith and practice has never been an easy one to make. Over 100 years ago, in *United States v. Reynolds*, the Supreme Court, in addressing the authority of government to deal with religions, recognized a distinction between religious belief and religious practice by declaring that government could regulate the latter but not the former. The notion, though, that government can interfere with religious practices but cannot regulate or punish religious beliefs is really a false dichotomy. To suggest that the government has conferred some benefit by not probing into peoples' minds to change their beliefs, but only seeks to affect how one carries out one's beliefs, is the archetypal strawman argument. By stating government's role in context of a dichotomy—belief and practice—one is left with the illusory impression that government is not being unreasonable by only affecting one side of the equation.

What makes religion unique among protected rights is that the importance of a religious belief in a person's life will always be subjective. The centrality and criticality of religious beliefs are not susceptible to an objective test. In *Gay Rights*, despite the appeals court's assertion that "nothing can penetrate the constitutional shield protecting against official coercion to remove a religious belief or to endorse a principle opposed to that belief" (Gay Rights 1987, 25), no one in the university should have assurance that permitting the groups access to the campus would not lead eventually to the silencing of the university's religious belief regarding homosexuality. For example, could the university include its position regarding homosexuality as part of a doctrinal statement to be signed by all faculty? If so, could a faculty member be discharged for espousing views contrary to the doctrinal statement?

What courts overlook is that a statement of belief is of little effect if the religious organization cannot enforce those beliefs among those within the organization. The enforcement function that a religious organization must have to protect the verity and purity of its belief system is the very function undercut by government policies mandating uniformity of practice (or, at the very least, penalizing the refusal to conform to a uniform practice). To penalize a religious organization's practice of its belief system, however much a court may disagree with it, is to threaten the very purpose and vitality of that organization. The balance between religious belief and practice is fragile and, unless courts are vigilant, those with the most distinctive and different religious beliefs can find their beliefs gradually eroded by the irresistible press for compromise. When militancy of religious beliefs is reduced to an egalitarian common denominator, those who believe the most will have to accommodate themselves to those who believe the least.

In 1992, William Bentley Ball, the great religious liberty advocate who had argued and prevailed in *Yoder* on behalf of the Amish before the U.S. Supreme Court, observed a few years before his death that,

> [p]olitically, judges do not want to sound anti-religious and they therefore, with routine magnanimity, acknowledge the 'sincerity' of the religious claimant's beliefs—all too volubly, or all too thoughtlessly—merely setting the stage for the *Reynolds* bromide: you can believe what you like, but the law may interfere with actions based on your beliefs.
>
> Ball 1992, 812

REFERENCES AND FURTHER READING

Age Discrimination Act in Employment Act of 1967, 29 U.S.C. § 621 *et seq.*

Americans with Disabilities Act, 42 U.S.C. § 12101 *et seq.*

Ball, William Bentley, "Accountability: A View from the Trial Courtroom," *George Washington Law Review* 60 (1992): 809–17.

Bangor Baptist Church v. State of Maine, 576 F. Supp. 1299 (D. Me. 1983).

Barrett v. Steubenville City Schools, 388 F.3d 967 (6th Cir. 2004).

Barrow v. Greenville Independent School District, 332 F.3d 844 (5th Cir. 2003).

Battles v. Arundel County Bd. of Educ., 904 F. Supp. 471 (D. Md.1995), *aff'd*, 95 F.3d 41 (4th Cir. 1995).

Bob Jones University v. U.S., 461 U.S., 574 (1983).

Boyd v. Harding Academy of Memphis, 88 F.3d 410 (6th Cir. 1996).

Brentwood Academy v. Tennessee School Athletic Association, 531 U.S. 288 (2001).

Brentwood Academy v. Tennessee School Athletic Association, 551 U.S. 291 (2007).

Care and Protection of Charles, 504 N.E.2d 592 (Mass. 1987).

Christian Legal Society Chapter of the University of California, Hastings College of the Law v. Martinez, 130 S.Ct. 2971 (2010).

Church of the Lukumi Babalu Aye, Inc. v. City of Hialeah, 508 U.S. 520 (1993).

Cline v. Catholic Diocese of Toledo, 206 F.3d 651 (6th Cir. 2000).

Colwell, Brad and Brian Schwartz, "Implications for Public Schools: Legal Aspects of Home Schools," *Education Law Reporter* 173 (2003): 381–95.

Cumming, Joy and Ralph Mawdsley, "Establishment Clauses, Legislation and Private School Funding in the United States and Australia: Recent Trends," *International Journal of Law & Education* 14 (2009): 63–83.

Denis J. O'Connell High School v. Virginia High School League, 581 F.2d 81 (4th Cir. 1978)*Employment Division v. Smith*, 494 U.S. 872 (1990).

Equal Pay Act, 29 U.S.C. § 206(d) (1).

Family and Medical Leave Act, 29 U.S.C. § 2611 et *seq.*

Fellowship Baptist Church v. Benton, 815 F.2d 485 (8th Cir. 1987).

Gay Rights Coalition v. Georgetown University, 536 A.2d 1 (D.D.Cir. 1987).

Goulart v. Meadows, 345 F.3d 239 (4th Cir. 2003).

Jesuit College Preparatory School v. Judy, 231 F. Supp. 2 520 (W.D. Tex. 2002).

Kentucky State Board v. Rudasill, 589 S.W.2d 877 (Ky. 1979).

Locke v. Davey, 540 U.S. 712 (2004).

Mawdsley, Ralph. "Employment Division v. Smith Revisited: The Constriction of Free Exercise Rights Under the U.S. Constitution," *Education Law Reporter* 76 (1992): 1–16.

Mawdsley, Ralph. "Free Speech and Procedural Due Process Rights for Private Members of State Athletic Associations: The Supreme Court Speaks in *Brentwood Academy II*," *Education Law Reporter* 228 (2008): 603–26.

Mawdsley, Ralph. *Legal Problems of Religious and Private Schools* (Dayton, OH): Education Law Association, 2006.

Mawdsley, Ralph. "Tax Exempt Bond Financing for Religious Educational Institutions: What is Required Under the U.S. Constitution," *Education Law Reporter* 221(2007): 459–83.

Mirkay, Nicolas A. "Losing Our Religion: Reevaluating the Section 501(C) (3) Exemption of Religious Organizations That Discriminate," *William and Mary Bill of Rights Journal* 17 (2009): 715–64.

Parker-Bigaback v. St. Labre School, 7 P.3d 361 (Mont. 2000).

People v. DeJonge, 501 N.W.2d 127 (Mich. 1993).

Peterson v. Minidoka County Local School District, 118 F.3d 1351, *as amended*, 132 F.3d 1258 (9th Cir. 1997).

Pierce v. Society of Sisters, 268 U.S. 510, 534 (1925).

Ray, Brian D. *Worldwide Guide to Homeschooling*. Salem, OR: *National Home Education Research Institute*, 2004.

Rehabilitation Act of 1973, 29 U.S.C. § 794.

Rendell-Baker v. Kohn, 457 U.S. 830 (1982).

Romeo v. Seton Hall University, 875 A.2d 1043 (N.J. Super. App. Div. 2005).

Rottman v. Pennsylvania Interscholastic Athletic Association, 349 F. Supp. 2d 922 (W.D. Pa. 2004).

Section 1981 of the Civil Rights Act, 42 U.S.C. § 1981.

Section 1983 of the Civil Rights Act, 42 U.S.C. § 1983.

Sherbert v. Verner, 374 U.S. 398 (1963).

State v. Faith Baptist Church of Louisville, 301 N.W.2d 571 (Neb. 1981).

State v. Olin, 415 N.E.2d 279 (Ohio 1980).

State v. Patzer, 382 N.W.2d 631 (N.D. 1986).

State v. Shaver, 294 N.W.2d 883 (N.D. 1980).

State of Ohio v. Whisner, 351 N.E.2d 750 (Ohio 1976).

Title VI of the Civil Rights Act. 42 U.S.C. § 2000d.

Title VII of the Civil Rights Act of 1964. 42 U.S.C. § 2000 et *seq.*

Title IX of the Educational Amendments. 20 U.S.C. § 1681 et *seq.*

Uniform Services Employment and Reemployment Act. 38 U.S.C. § 4311.

United States v. Commonwealth of Virginia, 518 U.S. 515 (1996).

United States v. Reynolds, 98 U.S. 145 (1879).

Valencia v. Blue Hen Conference, 476 F. Supp. 809 (D. Del.1979), *aff'd without opinion*, 615 F.2d 1355 (3d Cir. 1980).

Valley Christian School v. Montana Public High School Association, 86 P.3d 554 (Mont. 2004).

Vigars v. Valley Christian Center of Dublin, California, 805 F. Supp. 802 (N.D. Cal. 1992).

Wisconsin v. Yoder, 406 U.S. 205 (1972).

45

Leading Supreme Court Decisions on Faith-Based Schools

Charles J. Russo

Insofar as religion was a major factor leading to the development of what became the United States, it should not be surprising that the Founding Fathers addressed its place when they amended the Constitution. In fact, when the Constitution was amended, and ratified by the states in 1791, the First Amendment became part of the Bill of Rights.

Pursuant to the First Amendment, "Congress shall make no law respecting an establishment of religion, or prohibiting the free exercise thereof." While the First Amendment prohibits Congress from establishing religion, in 1940 the Court applied the First Amendment to the states through the Fourteenth Amendment in *Cantwell v. Connecticut* (1940) wherein it invalidated the convictions of Jehovah's Witnesses for violating a statute against the solicitation of funds for religious, charitable, or philanthropic purposes without prior approval of public officials. Consequently, individuals now have the same protection against both the federal and state governments with regard to issues involving religion.

As important a role as religion has had in American history, the Supreme Court did not address a case involving faith-based schools and education under the First Amendment until 1947 in *Everson v. Board of Education* (*Everson*). In the interim, the Court resolved more K–12 cases on religion under the First Amendment than any other subject involving schools.

Appeals to history over the original intent of the Establishment Clause fail to provide clear answers as to the meaning of the First Amendment, stemming largely from the fact that close ties between religion and government began during the colonial period. In fact, up until the Revolutionary War, there " . . . were established churches in at least eight of the thirteen former colonies and established religions in at least four of the other five" (*Engel v. Vitale*, 1962, 428 n. 5).

Instead of examining the lengthy history of the different approaches to the Establishment Clause, suffice it to say that two major camps emerged at the Supreme Court and elsewhere in the federal judiciary: separationists and accommodationists. On the one hand are supporters of the Jeffersonian metaphor that calls for erecting a "wall of separation" between church and state, language that does not appear in the Constitution; this is the perspective most often associated with the Supreme Court over the past 50-plus years. On the other hand, accommodationists maintain that the government is not prohibited from permitting some aid or accommodating the needs of children under the so-called child benefit test or from accommodating the religious preferences of parents who send their children to public schools.

This chapter focuses on United States Supreme Court cases rather than state cases. Yet, it is important to recognize that developments at both levels often overlap. In other words, while many cases arise under state law, such as vouchers in Cleveland, Ohio (see *Zelman v. Simmons–Harris* 2002), they are often ultimately resolved on the basis of the Federal Constitution. It is thus worth noting that the Federal Constitution is more open to some forms of aid to religious schools than its state counterparts, a distinction that emerged during the latter part of the nineteenth century.

PRE-HISTORY

Prior to the emergence of its modern Establishment Clause jurisprudence in *Everson*, the Supreme Court examined two cases that significantly impacted faith-based schools and their students. In both cases, the Court relied on the Due Process Clause of the Fourteenth Amendment rather than the Establishment Clause.

Pierce v. Society of Sisters of the Holy Names of Jesus and Mary

The first, and more far-reaching, of the Supreme Court's two early cases on religion and education was *Pierce v. Society of Sisters of the Holy Names of Jesus and Mary* (*Pierce*, 1925). In *Pierce*, the leaders of a Roman Catholic school and a secular school, the Hill Military Academy, challenged a voter-approved initiative in Oregon that led to the enactment of a new compulsory attendance law. The law required all students who did not need what would today be described as special education, between the ages of 8 and 16 who had not completed the eighth grade, to attend public schools.

After a federal trial court enjoined enforcement of the statute, the Supreme Court unanimously affirmed that enforcing the law would have seriously impaired, if not destroyed, the profitability of the schools while diminishing the value of their property. Although recognizing the power of the state "reasonably to regulate all schools, to inspect, supervise, and examine them, their teachers and pupils . . . " (*Pierce* 1925, 534), the Court focused on the schools' property rights under the Fourteenth Amendment. The Court grounded its judgment on the realization that the schools sought protection from unreasonable interference with their students and the destruction of their business and property. The Court also decided that while states may oversee such important features as health, safety, and teacher qualifications relating to the operation of non-public schools, they could not do so to an extent greater than they did for public schools.

Cochran v. Louisiana State Board of Education

Cochran v. Louisiana State Board of Education (*Cochran*, 1930) involved a state law providing free textbooks for all students in the state, regardless of where they attended school. A taxpayer unsuccessfully challenged the law on the ground that it violated the Fourteenth Amendment by taking private property through taxation for a non-public purpose. As in *Pierce*, the Supreme Court resolved the dispute based on the Due Process Clause of the Fourteenth Amendment rather than the First Amendment's Establishment Clause.

In unanimously affirming the judgment of the Supreme Court of Louisiana that since the students, rather than their schools, were the beneficiaries of the law, the Court agreed that the statute had valid secular purpose. As such, the Supreme Court anticipated the child benefit test that emerged in *Everson v. Board of Education* (1947) As discussed below, while the Supreme Court has consistently upheld similar textbook provisions, as reflected in the companion chapter to this one, state courts have struck them down under their own more restrictive constitutions.

STATE AID TO FAITH-BASED SCHOOLS

Unlike its thinking with regard to prayer and religious activity in public schools, wherein the Justices have consistently forbidden such practices, the Supreme Court's Establishment Clause perspective on state aid to K–12 education, sometimes referred to as "parochiaid," evolved through three phases. During the first stage, beginning with *Everson v. Board of Education* in 1947 and ending with *Board of Education of Central School District No. 1 v. Allen*, in 1968, the Court created the Child Benefit Test, which allows selected forms of publicly funded aid on the ground that it helps children rather than their faith-based schools. The time period between *Lemon v. Kurtman* in 1971, by far the leading case on the Establishment Clause in educational settings, and *Aguilar v. Felton* in 1985, the second phase, was a low point from the perspective of supporters of the child benefit test because the Court largely refused to move beyond the limits it initiated in *Everson* and *Allen*. In *Zobrest v. Catalina Foothills School District* in 1993 the Court resurrected the child benefit test, allowing it to enter a phase that extends through the present day in which more forms of aid have been permissible.

In light of this history, the following sections examine the major Supreme Court cases involving state aid to faith-based schools and their students, essentially in the order in which they were litigated. The topic headings cover transportation, textbooks, secular services and salary supplements, aid to parents (divided into tuition reimbursements and income tax returns), reimbursements to faith-based schools (covering instructional materials and support services), and vouchers.

Transportation

As noted, *Everson v. Board of Education* (1947) was the first Supreme Court case on the merits of the Establishment Clause and education. *Everson* involved a law from New Jersey permitting local school boards to make rules and enter into contracts for student transportation. After a local board authorized reimbursement to parents for the money they spent on bus fares sending their children to Catholic schools, a taxpayer filed suit claiming that the law was unconstitutional in two respects: first, in an approach not unlike the plaintiff's unsuccessful argument in *Cochran*, he alleged that the law authorized the state to take the money of some citizens by taxation and bestow it on others for the private purpose of supporting non-public schools in contravention of the Fourteenth Amendment; second, he charged that the statute was one "respecting an establishment of religion" because it forced him to contribute to support church schools in violation of the First Amendment.

The Supreme Court rejected the plaintiff's Fourteenth Amendment claim in *Everson* in interpreting the law as having a public purpose, adding that the First Amendment did not prohibit the state from extending general benefits to all of its citizens without regard to their religious beliefs. The Court placed student transportation in the same category of other public services such as police, fire, and health protection. In what could be viewed as something of a Trojan Horse because of difficulties it would create for state aid to faith-based schools, Justice Black's majority opinion introduced the Jeffersonian metaphor into the Court's First Amendment analysis, writing that: "[t]he First Amendment has erected a wall between church and state. That wall must be kept high and impregnable. We could not approve the slightest breach" (*Everson* 1947, 18).

Following *Everson*, states must choose whether to provide publicly funded transportation to students who attend faith-based schools. As examined in the companion chapter, "State Supreme Court Decisions and Faith Based Schools," lower courts, relying on state constitutional provisions, reached mixed results on this issue.

In *Wolman v. Walter* (*Wolman*, 1977), the Supreme Court considered whether public funds could be used to provide transportation for field trips for children who attended faith-based schools in Ohio. The Court held that the practice was unconstitutional because insofar as field trips were oriented to the curriculum, they were in the category of instruction rather than that of non-ideological secular services such as transportation to and from school.

Textbooks

Relying on the First, rather than the Fourteenth, Amendment, in *Board of Education of Central School District No. 1 v. Allen* (1968), the Supreme Court essentially followed its precedent from *Cochran* in affirming the constitutionality of a statute from New York that required local school boards to loan books to children in grades 7 to 12 who attended non-public schools. The law did not mandate that the books had to be the same as those used in the public schools but did require that titles be approved by local board officials before they could be adopted. Relying largely on the child benefit test, the Court observed that the statute's purpose was not to aid religion or non-public schools and that its primary effect was to improve the quality of education for all children.

Other than for the delivery of special education services to individual students as in *Zobrest v. Catalina Foothills School District* (1993), *Allen* represented the outer limit of the child benefit test for large groups of children prior to the Supreme Court's ruling in *Agostini v. Felton* (1997) discussed below. The Justices upheld like textbook provisions in *Meek v. Pittenger* (1975) and *Wolman*, both of which are also examined in more detail below.

Secular Services and Salary Supplements

The Supreme Court's most important case involving the Establishment Clause and education was *Lemon v. Kurtzman* (1971). In *Lemon*, the Court invalidated a statute from Pennsylvania calling for the purchase of secular services and a law from Rhode Island that provided salary supplements for teachers in non-public schools. The Pennsylvania law directed the superintendent of education to purchase specified secular educational services from non-public schools. Officials directly reimbursed the non-public schools for their actual expenditures for teacher salaries, textbooks, and instructional materials. The superintendent had to approve the textbooks and materials, which were restricted to the areas of mathematics, modern foreign languages, physical science, and physical education. In Rhode Island, officials could supplement the salaries of certificated teachers of secular subjects in non-public elementary schools by directly paying them amounts not in excess of

15 percent of their current annual salaries; their salaries could not exceed the maximum paid to public school teachers. The supplements were available to teachers in non-public schools where average per pupil expenditures on secular education were less than in public schools. In addition, the teachers had to use the same materials as were used in public schools.

In striking down both laws, the Supreme Court enunciated the three-part test known as the *Lemon* test. In creating this measure, the Court added a third prong, dealing with excessive entanglement, from *Walz v. Tax Commission of New York City* (1970), which upheld New York State's practice of providing state property tax exemptions for church property that is used in worship services, to the two-part test it created in *School District of Abington Township v. Schempp* and *Murray v. Curlett* (1963), companion cases dealing with prayer and Bible reading in public schools. In *Lemon* the Court wrote that:

> Every analysis in this area must begin with consideration of the cumulative criteria developed by the Court over many years. Three such tests may be gleaned from our cases. First, the statute must have a secular legislative purpose; second, its principal or primary effect must be one that neither advances nor inhibits religion; finally, the statute must not foster "an excessive government entanglement with religion."
>
> *Lemon*, 1971, 612–13

As to entanglement and state aid to faith-based schools, the Court identified three other factors: "[W]e must examine the character and purposes of the institutions that are benefitted, the nature of the aid that the State provides, and the resulting relationship between the government and religious authority" (*Lemon* 1971, 615).

In *Lemon* the Supreme Court maintained that aid for teachers' salaries was different from secular, neutral, or non-ideological services, facilities, or materials. Reflecting on *Allen*, the Court remarked that teachers have a substantially different ideological character than books. In terms of potential for involving faith or morals in secular subjects, the Court feared that while the content of a textbook can be identified, how a teacher covers subject matter is not. The Court added that conflict can arise when teachers who work under the direction of religious officials are faced with separating religious and secular aspects of education. The Court held that the safeguards necessary to ensure that teachers avoid non-ideological perspectives give rise to impermissible entanglement. The Court contended that an ongoing history of government grants to non-public schools suggests that these programs were almost always accompanied by varying measures of control.

AIDS TO PARENTS

Tuition Reimbursement

Two months after *Lemon*, the Pennsylvania legislature enacted a statute that allowed parents whose children attended non-public schools to request tuition reimbursement. The same parent as in *Lemon* challenged the new law as having the primary effect of advancing religion. In *Sloan v. Lemon* (*Sloan*, 1973) the Supreme Court affirmed that the law impermissibly singled out a class of citizens for a special economic benefit. The Justices thought that it was plain that this was unlike the "indirect" and "incidental" benefits that flowed to religious schools from programs that aided all parents by supplying bus transportation and secular textbooks for their children. The Court commented that transportation and textbooks were carefully restricted to the purely secular side of church-affiliated schools and did not provide special aid to their students.

The Supreme Court expanded on *Sloan's* analysis in a case from New York, *Committee for Public Education and Religious Liberty v. Nyquist* (*Nyquist* 1973). The Court ruled that even though the grants went to parents rather than to school officials, this did not compel a different result. The Court explained that since parents would have used the money to pay for tuition and the law failed to separate secular from religious uses, the effect of the aid unmistakably would have provided the desired financial support for non-public schools. In so doing, the Court rejected the state's argument that parents were not simply conduits because they were free to spend the money in any manner they chose since they paid the tuition and the law merely provided for reimbursements. The Court indicated that even if the grants were offered as incentives to have parents send their children to religious schools, the law violated the Establishment Clause regardless of whether the money made its way into the coffers of the religious institutions.

Income Tax

Another section of the same New York statute in *Nyquist* aided parents via income tax benefits. Under the law, parents of children who attended non-public schools were entitled to income tax deductions as long as they did not receive tuition reimbursements under the other part of the statute. The Supreme Court invalidated this provision in pointing out that in practical terms there was little difference, for purposes of evaluating whether such aid had the effect of advancing religion, between a tax benefit and a tuition grant. The Court based its judgment on the notion that under both programs qualifying parents received the same form of encouragement and reward for sending their children to non-public schools.

In *Mueller v. Allen* (*Mueller* 1983), the Supreme Court upheld a statute from Minnesota that granted all parents state income tax deductions for the actual costs of tuition, text-books, and transportation associated with sending their children to K–12 schools. The statute afforded parents deductions of $500 for children in grades K–6 and $700 for those in grades 7 to 12. The Justices distinguished *Mueller* from *Nyquist* primarily because the tax benefit at issue was available to all parents, not only those whose children were in non-public schools, and the deduction was one among many rather than a single, favored type of taxpayer expense. In acknowledging the legislature's broad latitude to create classifications and distinctions in tax statutes, and that the state could have been considered as gaining a benefit from the scheme since it promoted an educated citizenry while reducing the costs of public education, the Court was convinced that the law satisfied all three of *Lemon's* prongs. The Court paid scant attention to the fact that since the state's public schools were essentially free, the expenses of parents whose children attended them were at most minimal and that about 96 percent of the taxpayers who benefitted had children who were enrolled in religious schools.

REIMBURSEMENTS TO FAITH-BASED SCHOOLS

On the same day that it resolved *Nyquist*, in a second case from New York, the Supreme Court applied basically the same rationale in *Levitt v. Committee for Public Education and Religious Liberty* (*Levitt* 1973). Here the Court invalidated a law allowing the state to reimburse non-public schools for expenses incurred while administering and reporting test results as well as other records. Insofar as there were no restrictions on the use of the funds, such that teacher-prepared tests on religious subject matter were seemingly reimbursable, the Court observed that the aid had the primary effect of advancing religious education because there were insufficient safeguards in place to regulate how the monies were spent.

In *Wolman v. Walter* (1977), the Supreme Court upheld a law from Ohio that allowed reimbursement for religious schools that used standardized tests and scoring services. The Justices distinguished these tests from the ones in *Levitt* because the latter were neither drafted nor scored by non-public school personnel. The Court also reasoned that the law did not authorize payments to church-sponsored schools for costs associated with administering the tests.

In *Committee for Public Education and Religious Liberty v. Regan* (1980), the Supreme Court reexamined another aspect of *Levitt* after the New York State legislature modified the law. Under its new provisions, the statute provided reimbursements to non-public schools for the actual costs of complying with state requirements for reporting on students and for administering mandatory and optional state-prepared examinations. Unlike the law in Ohio, this statute permitted the tests to be graded by personnel in the non-public schools who were, in turn, reimbursed for these services. The law also created accounting procedures to monitor reimbursements. The Court conceded that the differences between the statutes were permissible because scoring of essentially objective tests and recording their results along with attendance data offered no significant opportunity for religious indoctrination while serving secular state educational purposes. The Court concluded that the accounting method did not create excessive entanglement since the reimbursements were equal to the actual costs.

Instructional Materials

In *Meek v. Pittenger* (1975), the Supreme Court examined the legality of loans of instructional materials, including textbooks and equipment, to faith-based schools in Pennsylvania. Although the Court upheld the loan of textbooks, it struck down parts of the law on periodicals, films, recordings, and laboratory equipment as well as equipment for recording and projecting because the statute had the primary effect of advancing religion due to the predominantly religious character of participating schools. The Court feared that since the only statutory requirement imposed on the schools to qualify for the loans was that their curricula had to offer the subjects and activities mandated by the commonwealth's board of education. The Court thought that since the church-related schools were the primary beneficiaries, the massive aid to their educational function necessarily resulted in aid to their sectarian enterprises as a whole.

The Supreme Court reached similar results in *Wolman v. Walter* (1977) in upholding a statute from Ohio which specified that textbook loans were to be made to students or their parents, rather than directly to their non-public schools. The Justices struck down a provision that would have allowed loans of instructional equipment, including projectors, tape recorders, record players, maps and globes, and science kits. Echoing *Meek*, the Court invalidated the statute's authorizing the loans in light of its fear that since it would be impossible to separate the secular and sectarian functions for which these items were being used, the aid inevitably provided support for the religious roles of the schools.

In *Mitchell v. Helms* (2000), a case from Louisiana, the Supreme Court expanded the boundaries of permissible aid to faith-based schools. A plurality upheld the constitutionality of Chapter 2 of Title I, now Title VI, of the Elementary and Secondary Education Act (Chapter 2 2010), a federal law that permits the loans of instructional materials including library books, computers, television sets, tape recorders, and maps to non-public schools.

The Court relied on the fact that *Agostini v. Felton*, discussed below, modified the *Lemon* test by reviewing only its first two parts while recasting entanglement as one criterion in evaluating a statute's effect. Since the purpose part of the test was not challenged, the plurality believed it necessary only to consider Chapter 2's effect, concluding that it did not foster impermissible indoctrination because aid was allocated pursuant to neutral secular criteria that neither favored nor disfavored religion and was available to all schools based on secular, nondiscriminatory grounds. In its rationale, the plurality explicitly reversed those parts of *Meek* and *Wolman* that were inconsistent with its analysis on loans of instructional materials.

Support Services

In *Meek v. Pittenger* (1975), the Supreme Court invalidated a Pennsylvania law permitting public school personnel to provide auxiliary services on-site in faith-based schools. At the same time, the Court forbade the delivery of remedial and accelerated instructional programs, guidance counseling and testing, and services to aid children who were educationally disadvantaged. The Court asserted that it was immaterial that the students would have received remedial, rather than advanced, work since the required surveillance to ensure the absence of ideology would have given rise to excessive entanglement between church and state.

Wolman v. Walter (1977) saw the Supreme Court reach mixed results on aid. In addition to upholding the textbook loan program, the Court allowed Ohio to supply non-public schools with state-mandated tests while allowing public school employees to go on-site to perform diagnostic tests to evaluate whether students needed speech, hearing, and psychological services. The Court also allowed public funds to be spent providing therapeutic services to students from non-public schools as long as they were delivered off-site. The Court prohibited the state from loaning instructional materials and equipment to schools or from using funds to pay for field trips for students in non-public schools.

In *Zobrest v. Catalina Foothills School District* (1993) the Supreme Court entered a new phase of its Establishment Clause jurisprudence in a dispute over a school board's refusal to provide a sign-language interpreter, under the Individuals with Disabilities Education Act (2010), for a deaf student in Arizona who transferred to a Catholic high school. The Court found that an interpreter provided neutral aid to the student without offering financial benefits to his parent or school and there was no governmental participation in the instruction because the interpreter was only a conduit to effectuate the child's communications. The Court relied in part on *Witters v. Washington Department of Services for the Blind* (1986), wherein it upheld the constitutionality of extending a general vocational assistance program to a blind man who was studying to become a clergyman at a religious college. The Supreme Court of Washington subsequently interpreted its state constitution as forbidding such use of public funds and the Supreme Court refused to hear an appeal (*Witters v. State Commission for the Blind* 1989).

A year later, in *Board of Education of Kiryas Joel Village School District v. Grumet* (1994), the Supreme Court reviewed a case where the New York State legislature created a school district with the same boundaries as a religious community in an attempt to accommodate the needs of parents of children with disabilities who wished to send them to a nearby school that would have honored their religious practices. After state courts invalidated the law, the Court affirmed that the law was unconstitutional. The Court explained that while a state may accommodate a group's religious needs by alleviating special burdens, it stepped over the line, especially since the board could have offered an appropriate program at one of its public schools or at a neutral site near one of the village's religious schools.

Within days after the Supreme Court had struck down the statute, the New York state legislature amended the statute in an attempt to eliminate the Establishment Clause problem. Still, New York's highest court invalidated the revised law as a violation of the Establishment Clause insofar as it had the effect of advancing one religion (*Grumet v. Cuomo* 1997; *Grumet v. Pataki* 1999).

Conflicts have arisen when officials in public and non-public schools entered into cooperative arrangements. More than a decade after the Supreme Court of Michigan upheld a state constitutional amendment on shared time, officials in Grand Rapids created an extensive program. The program grew to the point where publicly paid teachers conducted 10 percent of classes in religious schools and many of them worked in the religious schools. After the Sixth Circuit invalidated the plan, in *School District of City of Grand Rapids v. Ball* (*Ball* 1985) the Supreme Court affirmed that the released-time program was unconstitutional because it failed all three prongs of the *Lemon* test.

On the same day that it resolved *Ball*, the Supreme Court addressed an arguably more significant case from New York City over whether public school teachers could provide remedial instruction under Title I of the Elementary and Secondary Education Act of 1965 (Title I) for specifically targeted children, who were educationally disadvantaged, on-site in their faith-based schools. In *Aguilar v. Felton* (*Aguilar* 1985), the Supreme Court affirmed earlier orders that the program was unconstitutional. Even though the New York City Board of Education (NYCBOE) developed safeguards to insure that public funds were not spent for religious purposes, the Court struck it down based solely on the fear that a monitoring system might have created excessive entanglement of church and state.

Twelve years later, in *Agostini v. Felton* (*Agostini* 1997), the Supreme Court took the unusual step of dissolving the injunction that it upheld in *Aguilar*. The Court reasoned that the Title I program did not violate the *Lemon* test since there was no governmental indoctrination, there were no distinctions between recipients based on religion, and there was no excessive entanglement. The Court thus ruled that a federally funded program that provides supplemental, remedial instruction and counseling services to disadvantaged children on a neutral basis is not invalid under the Establishment Clause when the assistance is provided on-site in faith-based schools pursuant to a program containing safeguards such as those that the NYCBOE implemented. Perhaps the most important dimension in *Agostini* was that the Court modified the *Lemon* test by reviewing only its first two parts, purpose and effect, while recasting entanglement as one criterion in evaluating a statute's effect.

Vouchers

Considerable controversy has arisen over the use of vouchers, with courts reaching mixed results in disputes over their constitutionality. Still, the only Supreme Court case on vouchers arose in Ohio. The Ohio General Assembly, acting pursuant to a desegregation order, enacted the Ohio Pilot Project Scholarship Program (OPPSP) to assist children in Cleveland's failing public schools. The main goal of the OPPSP was to permit an equal number of students to receive vouchers and tutorial assistance grants while attending regular public schools. Another part of the law provided greater choices to parents and children via the creation of community, or charter, schools and magnet schools while a third section featured tutorial assistance for children.

The Supreme Court of Ohio upheld the OPPSP but severed the part of the law affording priority to parents who belonged to a religious group supporting a sectarian institution (*Simmons–Harris v. Goff* 1999). Moreover, in deciding that the OPPSP violated the state constitutional requirement that every statute have only one subject, the court struck it down. The court stayed enforcement of its order to avoid disrupting the then current school year. The General Assembly of Ohio quickly re-enacted a revised statute.

After lower federal courts, relying largely on *Nyquist* (1973), enjoined the operation of the revised statute as a violation of the Establishment Clause, the Supreme Court agreed to hear an appeal. In *Zelman v. Simmons–Harris* (*Zelman* 2002), the Court reversed the judgment of the Sixth Circuit and upheld the constitutionality of the OPPSP.

Relying on *Agostini*, the *Zelman* Court began by conceding the lack of a dispute over the program's valid secular purpose in providing programming for poor children in a failing school system, and the Court examined whether it had the forbidden effect of advancing or inhibiting religion. The Court upheld the voucher program because as part of the state's far-reaching attempt to provide greater educational opportunities in a failing school system, the law allocated aid on the basis of neutral secular criteria that neither favored nor disfavored religion, that it was made available to both religious and secular beneficiaries on a nondiscriminatory basis, and that it offered assistance directly to a broad class of citizens who directed the aid to religious schools based entirely on their own genuine and independent private choices. The Court was not concerned by the fact that most of the participating schools were faith-based because parents chose to send their children to them insofar as surrounding public schools refused to take part in the program. In fact, the Court noted that most of the children attended the faith-based schools not as a matter of law but because they were unwelcomed in the public schools. The Court concluded that because it was following an unbroken line of cases supporting true private choice that provided benefits directly to a wide range of needy private individuals, its only choice was to uphold the voucher program.

CONCLUSION

As faith-based schools face the future, the one certainty is that litigation will continue over the status of aid to schools, their students, and parents. The extent to which aid may be available depends on a combination of legislative action and judicial interpretation by the Supreme Court. At present, the accommodations seem to hold a slim majority of the Court. Whether a majority of the Supreme Court is willing to continue to support aid to faith-based schools bears constant watching.

REFERENCES AND FURTHER READING

Agostini v. Felton, 521 U.S. 203 (1997).
Aguilar v. Felton, 473 U.S. 402 (1985).
Board of Education of Central School District No. 1 v. Allen, 392 U.S. 236 (1968).
Board of Education of Kiryas Joel Village School District v. Grumet, 512 U.S. 687 (1994).
Cantwell v. Connecticut, 310 U.S. 296 (1940).
Chapter 2 of Title I, now Title VI, of the Elementary and Secondary Education Act (Chapter 2), 20 U.S.C.A. §§ 7301–73 (2010).
Cochran v. Louisiana State Board of Education, 281 U.S. 370 (1930).
Committee for Public Education and Religious Liberty v. Nyquist, 413 U.S. 756 (1973).
Committee for Public Education and Religious Liberty v. Regan, 444 U.S. 646 (1980).

Engel v. Vitale, 370 U.S. 421 (1962).

Everson v. Board of Education, 330 U.S. 1 (1947), *reh'g denied*, 330 U.S. 855 (1947).

Grumet v. Cuomo, 659 N.Y.S.2d 173 (N.Y.1997); *Grumet v. Pataki*, 697 N.Y.S.2d 846 (N.Y.1999), *cert. denied*, 528 U.S. 946 (1999).

Individuals with Disabilities Education Act, 20 U.S.C.A. §§ 1400 *et seq.* (2010).

Lemon v. Kurtzman, 403 U.S. 602 (1971).

Levitt v. Committee for Public Education and Religious Liberty, 413 U.S. 472 (1973).

Meek v. Pittenger, 421 U.S. 349 (1975).

Mitchell v. Helms, 530 U.S. 793 (2000), *reh'g denied*, 530 U.S. 1296 (2000), *on remand sub nom. Helms v. Picard*, 229 F.3d 467 (5th Cir. 2000).

Mueller v. Allen, 463 U.S. 388 (1983).

Pierce v. Society of Sisters of the Holy Names of Jesus and Mary, 268 U.S. 510 (1925).

School District of Abington Township v. Schempp and *Murray v. Curlett*, 374 U.S. 203 (1963).

School District of City of Grand Rapids v. Ball, 473 U.S. 373 (1985).

Simmons–Harris v. Goff, 711 N.E.2d 203 (Ohio 1999).

Sloan v. Lemon, 413 U.S. 825 (1973).

Walz v. Tax Commission of New York City, 397 U.S. 664 (1970).

Witters v. State Commission for the Blind, 771 P.2d 1119 (Wash.1989), *cert. denied*, 493 U.S. 850 (1989).

Witters v. Washington Department of Services for the Blind, 474 U.S. 481 (1986).

Wolman v. Walter, 433 U.S. 229 (1977).

Zelman v. Simmons–Harris, 536 U.S. 639 (2002).

Zobrest v. Catalina Foothills School District, 509 U.S. 1 (1993).

46

Politics of Faith-Based Schooling

Steven L. Jones

At Theiss elementary school in Spring, Texas, where I attended kindergarten through fifth grade, the first five minutes of every school day began the same way. We started with the Pledge of Allegiance to the American flag, and often followed that with the singing of a patriotic song such as *My Country Tis of Thee*, or the more rousing and popular *This Land is Your Land*. I do not remember this being controversial in the least. It was simply part of the morning routine, as natural as hearing the announcements for the day over the loudspeaker or saying good morning to my teachers. It was not until years later that I came to see the purpose of these opening exercises. On the surface, we were learning a few basic facts about our shared history, but this was less about learning the words of the pledge than about nourishing a feeling of belonging and loyalty within us toward our country. We knew we lived in America, but these few minutes were where we learned to be Americans. Though the routines may vary, my experience is not unique. Many public and private schools seek to cultivate an appreciation for America in the hearts and minds of school children.

This effort is not accidental. In fact, it is part and parcel of the very purpose of American education, especially American public education. Public schooling rose to prominence during the latter half of the nineteenth century. Before that, the distinction between private and public was not always as clear as it is today. Many schools were initiatives of religious and ethnic groups or various civic organizations, and several of these received some form of public money. The mix of characteristics that we associate with public schooling evolved unevenly, but by the beginning of the twentieth century the earmarks of public, as opposed to private education, were more apparent. Public schools were tax supported, tuition free, open to all, and officially nonsectarian. The potential of these schools to break down the spirit of factionalism so worrisome to the architects of American public schooling was an oft-cited justification for why common schooling was superior to the private, often faith-based institutions that already dotted America's educational landscape. What began as a justification for public schooling transitioned into a more pointed criticism of the attempts by religious communities to build and maintain their own schools. Faith-based schooling was seen by some critics not just as competition for the burgeoning (and perennially in crisis) public schools, but as a threat to the very social order of the society. This entry will examine the democratic arguments for and against private, faith-based schooling.

By democratic arguments, I do not mean to imply those issues connected to education that resurface from time to time in American politics. I will not, for instance, be exploring vouchers, charter schools, or textbook selection. Rather, this entry focuses on the debate over the place faith-based schools occupy in American education and public life more broadly.

Though it is too much to say that the critics of faith-based schooling are all cut from the same cloth, one of the most intriguing aspects of this debate is how consistently the basic issues resurface. Although late-twentieth-century opponents of faith-based schooling would separate themselves from their predecessors who complained against Catholic schools in the nineteenth century, some of their basic concerns are remarkably similar. At issue is whether faith-based schools, as institutions that appeal to and reinforce particular communal identities, stoke factionalism in American society and therefore contribute to social disorder or are a necessary and vital part of America's commitment to freedom and pluralism. Additionally, critics of faith-based schooling have asked whether or not these schools can produce citizens with the necessary habits of mind, for example a commitment to tolerance and the ability to recognize the rights of others, to promote effective citizenship in a pluralist democracy.

EDUCATION AND POLITICAL LIFE

Catholic Parochial Schooling

The connections between education and political life are many and layered. On the broadest level it has long been recognized that a literate public makes a better voting public. Accordingly, any society that empowers ordinary citizens to manage not only their own affairs but also the corporate affairs of the populace has a vested interest in promoting at least a rudimentary education. Thomas Jefferson recognized as much, writing about the importance of an enlightened public in numerous letters and drafting the Bill for the More General Diffusion of Knowledge for his home state of Virginia. Other members of the founding generation agreed with Jefferson's sentiments if not his actual plans, and thus numerous programs to promote education were put forward and discussed, though the lack of infrastructure and the presence of more pressing concerns made their implementation spotty and incomplete. Noah Webster, too, believed that education was essential for the survival of the new nation. The desire to foster a common identity among the citizenry motivated him to produce his famous spelling texts, which were expressly designed to distinguish American linguistic patterns from those in Europe. His reader, likewise, contained selections designed not just to promote literacy, but to praise the ideals of American democracy (Tyack 1966, 31–36). Exactly what role the churches were to play in the educational arrangements that were put forward is not always clear, but for many Americans in the early decades of the Republic the connections between religious organizations and education were simply taken for granted. Intellectual and moral formation was seen as part of the same developmental process, and thus it was assumed that the churches, as the primary guardians of American moral life, would be involved to some degree in education. What we now think of as secular alternatives were not available to everyone, but even had they been more widespread many Americans would have seen an education divorced from religious life as incomplete, perhaps even suspect. Faith-based schooling was both a common-sense arrangement and a necessary component of building a new nation.

As the nineteenth century began, America's educational infrastructure was still largely undeveloped, at least by today's standards, but between 1800 and 1850 educational activity expanded dramatically. Two series of events took place that both figure prominently in the debate over faith-based schooling in America. In New York City, the Public School Society (originally the Free School Society) battled with the city's Catholic leadership for access to public monies to be spent on schooling, while in Massachusetts Horace Mann promoted his model of the Common School as an antidote to social discord.

In the opening decades of the nineteenth century the Public School Society emerged in New York City as a means of organizing and providing an education for those children not enrolled in religious or otherwise private school. These schools, which were largely Protestant in practice if not design, attracted many of the poorer children in the city and, since they served a public good, were eligible to receive money from the state education fund. At the time, private religious schools could also apply for funding from the state. As the Society gained leverage, however, it began to support the levying of a specific, city-wide tax that would be earmarked for public education, meaning its schools. At this point, the city's Catholic population entered the fray. Their schools also enrolled many of the city's poorest children, and thus they believed they were entitled to a share of the tax revenue. New York's colorful bishop, John Hughes, argued that if Catholics had to pay the tax just as everyone else, they should be just as entitled to the payout as everyone else. The issue bounced back and forth among the various levels of city government, ending up in the state legislature in Albany, where it was referred to John Spencer, Secretary of State for New York and the superintendent of common schools. Spencer, aware that the question of public money for parochial schooling was a volatile one, changed the nature of the debate by focusing not on specific questions of funding, but by painting the Public School Society itself as an inherently undemocratic institution. Its officers were self-appointed rather than elected and their schools were not really subject to any supervision aside from the Society itself. In essence, Spencer argued that the Society's "public" schools were not really public at all. He further argued that schools should reflect the communities that surround them, so if the citizens of New York, Catholic or otherwise, wanted sectarian religious instruction in their schools, then the schools should offer such instruction. Though there was much political maneuvering over the following months, many of Spencer's basic positions were eventually codified into policy. In the end the Public School Society lost much of its prestige, most of which was self-appointed to begin with, but public expenditures for faith-based schooling were also discontinued.

For the bishop and his followers, the issue was only partly a matter of finances. Hughes recognized that Catholics were seen as less than fully American, and that their opposition to the supposedly religiously neutral public schools reinforced that perception. Thus he linked his defense of Catholic schools to the rights of Catholics as citizens more than to the accomplishments of the schools themselves. Reminding his listeners that immigrant Catholics had, by virtue of coming to this country, chosen American citizenship was Hughes' way of asserting the essential loyalty of his parishioners to America. In public speeches, Hughes drew attention to the lack of appreciation for democratic citizenship employed by his opponents by asking if, given their propensity for pointing out that it was Catholics who were seeking access to public money, there was any crime in being a Roman Catholic (Ravitch 1974, 35–66).

While the state legislature's decision brought a measure of closure to the events in New York, it was hardly the last time Catholics would face questions about the democratic potential of their schools. In 1889 the National Education Association hosted a debate between critics and advocates of Catholic schooling, the various addresses of which neatly capture many of the major issues at stake in terms of religious schooling and public life. One of the critics of Catholic schooling to address the audience, Dr. Edwin Mead characterized the Catholic philosophy of education as connived and dishonest. Catholics, he claimed, essentially rejected the state's interest in cultivating loyal citizens through the schools while claiming to uphold parental prerogatives. The fact that the Catholic Church had required member families to support parochial schools was, in his view, a denial of the "liberty of conscience" upon which democratic living rests. Any institution that would act in this manner was undemocratic in its operation and thus could not be depended on to promote democratic virtues in the young. Mead repeated the claims made against Bishop Hughes several decades earlier, that Catholic policy was formulated in Rome under the direction of a foreign potentate and was thus not the result of democratic deliberation or legislation. Mead's contemporary, public school advocate John Jay, appealed even more directly to the nativist fears Catholics faced throughout the 1800s. Though he praised those Catholic parents that supported the public schools, he also warned his listeners of the supposed plot to make America a Catholic nation. Stoking decades of rumor and assertion, Jay held that only public schools could teach the virtues necessary for democratic living. These included responsibility, freedom of conscience, and love of country. Catholic schools, which were taught mainly by those with un-American sympathies if not by "foreigners" themselves, could at most pay lip service to these ideals while their true purpose was only to ensure the "preservation of foreignisms" (National Education Association 1889, 15–39, 58).

James Cardinal Gibbons and the Rev. John Keane (National Education Association 1889, 15) represented the Catholic position at the meeting. Both reflected on the essential need for a thoroughly moral and Christian education as the key to Catholic schooling, and both implied that other denominations should be as involved in the education of youth as were American Catholics. Keane defended the American character of Catholic schooling by assuring his audience that, if anything, denominational schools (as he called them) would compete with one another to see who could turn out the most loyal citizens. Though strategically conciliatory in tone, both Gibbons and Keane were also critical of the very idea of a secular education, if by that advocates of public schooling meant a watered-down morality stripped of authentically Christian teaching. They held that true education must be religious education, a claim that subsequent defenders of faith-based schooling from across theological and denominational lines have made time and again. Attempting to put his critics on the defensive, Keane concluded his remarks with the following: "On the one side, the Catholic church emphatically declares for Christian education; and with us side all those non-Catholics, whatever their denomination, who believe in Christian schools. . . . On the other side are the upholders and advocates of a national system of schools in which Christian truth and duty cannot be taught. Can anyone in his senses hesitate (*sic*) which of these two sides is for the real welfare of our country?" (National Education Association 1889, 14–15).

Any examination of the role of faith-based schools in democratic life has to reflect on the issues faced by nineteenth-century Catholics in America, but the debate over these schools was not limited to Catholic institutions, nor did it end with the dawn of the twentieth century. As the stereotypes to which Mead and Jay appealed suggest, at least a portion of the debate over Catholic schools was also due to the general suspicion of, and outright bigotry towards, Catholics in America. From the Know Nothings to the eager audience for the supposed insider accounts of Catholic scandals represented by the likes of Maria Monk, nineteenth-century America was often hostile to religious outsiders, chiefly Catholics. But not all of the concern about the implications of denominational schooling for national unity can be strictly attributed to simple anti-Catholicism. The architect of American common schooling, Horace Mann, was also concerned about the growing pluralism in America and saw the potential of "non-denominational" schools as a means of promoting national unity and patriotism. Like Webster, Mann believed that the American character was sufficiently different from the European character to require a different approach to education. Obedience and subservience may have been the order of the day for most Europeans, but such 'virtues' did not fit in the New World. The habits of mind necessary for self-government would have to be inculcated by education. More than that, though, Mann believed that the America of his day was threatened by the presence of unassimilated ethnic, nationalist, and religious communities. In Mann's view, such social discord had been ruinous in Europe and thus he sought to counteract it in America. Here again, schooling was a helpful antidote, but only if it could be organized so as to not to reinforce communal particularity. Any institution administered by and for specific communities, he believed, would inevitably turn out citizens more committed to the good of their own group than to the wider public, thus giving rise to factionalism. As secretary of the Massachusetts Board of Education, Mann wrote that England, for example, allowed "churchmen and dissenters, each according to his own creed, [to] maintain separate schools, in which children are taught, from their tenderest years to wield the sword of polemics with fatal dexterity" (Mann 1957, 33). Only the common schools, free as they were from denominational control, could avoid the "disastrous consequences" of social discord.

Mann believed that promoting public institutions in which students of different backgrounds could mingle together while developing the superior virtues of American democratic thought and practice would prevent the balkanization of his society. Accordingly, much of his professional and personal life was dedicated to building such institutions. By some measures, he was remarkably successful. By the beginning of the twentieth century, non-sectarian, open-to-all schools were the de facto establishment of American primary education. Approximately 90 percent of school-aged children attended public institutions in 1900, a figure that has remained fairly constant for more than a century. And yet neither Mann's fears about factionalism nor his faith in the schools to combat it have been put to rest. In fact, the institutional dominance achieved by the public school, not just in numbers of attendees but also their cultural significance and default status, prompted some even more aggressive attempts to use the schools as a means of enforcing national unity.

Pierce v. Society of Sisters

In 1922, for example, the citizens of Oregon voted, by a fairly slim margin, to require all children to attend public schools through the eighth grade or until they were 16 years of age. A mix of post-World War I patriotism, anti-Catholicism, and a progressive optimism about the ameliorative possibilities of education all combined to pass this law. Oregon's Catholics, as well as the Department of Education for the National Catholic Welfare Council (formerly the War Council), recognized immediately that this could serve as a precedent for other states and municipalities to adopt similar measures and thus mounted an aggressive campaign to prevent its enforcement and indeed to overturn the law itself. Two groups, the Sisters of the Holy Names of Jesus and Mary and representatives of the

Hill Military Academy, took legal action to prevent Oregon from enforcing the law and closing the private schools, including those that were not religiously aligned. After a series of legal skirmishes in lower courts, the case ended up in the United States Supreme Court, and in 1925 the Court upheld the plaintiff's injunction, thereby forbidding the state of Oregon from requiring attendance at public schools. In doing so, the Court in *Pierce* (1925) famously held that "[t]he fundamental theory of liberty upon which all governments in this Union repose excludes any general power of the state to standardize its children by forcing them to accept instruction form public teachers only. The child is not the mere creature of the state; those who nurture him and direct his destiny have the right coupled with the high duty to recognize and prepare him for additional obligations" (*Pierce* 1925, 535).

Pierce is among the most celebrated cases in twentieth-century Supreme Court jurisprudence, and no consideration of the political, social, and legal roles of faith-based schooling can slight its significance. Aside from serving as the controlling legal precedent for all subsequent cases it is a microcosm of the debate over the faith-based schooling in American democracy. Advocates of the original law had publicly assailed private schools as potentially subversive institutions and called on Oregonians to demonstrate their loyalty by casting a vote in favor of public education. And this reasoning was not limited to political rallies before the election. In arguments made before the Court itself representatives for the state noted that suspicion of seemingly foreign religious groups was part of the motivation for Oregonians supporting the law in the first place. Separating children from one another along religious cleavages would only fuel that suspicion, while dissolving the institutional boundaries religious schools reinforced would serve as an inoculation against future internal dissention.

Those who argued against the Oregon law were equally aware of the issues at stake. The fundamental principle of liberty upon which the United States rests, they held, required parents to be free to direct the education of their children. Turning the tables on their critics, defenders of private and faith-based schooling held that it was the attempt to restrict parental freedoms that was plainly un-American. In their rendering of the issues, faith-based schooling is based on liberty, not compulsion, and is therefore a quintessentially American act. They also pointed out that private schools predated public schools in America, and that the founders of this country had been educated in non-public institutions. They condemned what they perceived as the new idea that state had the ultimate authority over children and stressed the fact that their schools had a long and accomplished record of producing patriotic and eager citizens.

At least a portion of the anti-Catholic schooling sentiment in the nineteenth century was due to the more general anti-Catholicism characteristic of the time. This is not to say, however, that there were not genuine concerns about faith-based schooling and its consequences for American public life. There were, and those concerns resurfaced only a few decades after the Supreme Court's *Pierce* decision in 1925. This time, the focal point of the debate was on the Jewish day schools that exploded in both numbers and influence after World War II. While the issues raised in the day school controversy were in many ways much like those raised about Catholic schooling, there was one notable exception. Whereas the critics of Catholic schools had for the most part been non-Catholics, the day school controversy was largely an intra-community affair. That is, both the defenders and the critics of the growth of Jewish day schooling came from within American Judaism. Still, the general contours of the debate are familiar. At issue was the perception that the day schools would promote social division and stigma at the expense of assimilation and integration (Schiff 1966, 203–16).

The Jewish Day Schools

American Jews had, for the most part, eagerly embraced public education and augmented it with various after-school and weekend programs. It was in these supplementary programs that students were supposed to learn the how's and why's of Jewish living in America. From the start, though, there were those who thought these supplementary programs were doomed to failure, first because they simply lacked the time and resources to be effective, but second because they reinforced a split between American life, represented in the public schools, and Jewish life, represented in these various educational settings. The very idea of "supplementary" religious and cultural education was problematic for these early advocates of a more intensive Jewish experience. Institutionally, though, most of the early Jewish day schools failed for lack of support. They simply could not stand up against the competition from free public education available right down the street.

That changed after World War II and the destruction of European Jewry. In 1940 there were some 35 full-time Jewish day schools operating in the United States and Canada, enrolling approximately 7,700 students. Ten years later there were 139 such schools serving more than 23,000 students. By the middle of the 1960s the number of schools had more than doubled, while the number of students had nearly tripled to more than 65,000. Whereas Orthodox and Conservative Jewry embraced day schooling during the 1940s and 1950s, Reform was more cautious. It was not until 1963 that Reform leadership really welcomed the rise of day schooling within their branch of American Judaism.

Partly, this growth can be attributed to the institutionalization of Jewish life in America more broadly, a sign of social maturation welcomed by the various Jewish communities. Day schools, however, were perceived by some as more problematic. Though advocates of Jewish day schooling took pains to point out how their schools were different from Catholic parochial institutions (they were communally organized rather than controlled by the religious hierarchy), their critics raised the same basic concerns as anti-Catholic school activists had a few generations before. Mordecai Grossman (1945, 20), for example, argued that the effectiveness of the day schools at producing reinforcing Jewish living should be secondary to the "inclusive purposes" such as building a common culture and "cooperative society without the social cleavages based on class, religion, race, or ancestry." In a post-*Pierce* legal framework, day schools were constitutionally protected, but, the critics held, were not necessarily beneficial because they placed the concerns of the particular community over and against those of the nation in which that community was trying to forge a life. They were thus doubly dangerous, first to the nation collectively, but also to the religious community itself in that they stigmatized the entire group as wanting to keep itself separate from the whole. Defenders of the day schools, too, made arguments reminiscent of their Catholic counterparts. Their schools represented only a tiny fraction of the entirety of American education, and, voluntary as they were, posed no real threat to public education. Religious schooling, they claimed, was the primary institutional means of ensuring religious freedom and diversity. By strengthening the religious community, which even their critics acknowledged they would do, the schools ensured that the various religious communities would be prepared to make their unique contribution to American life. Sounding much like some of his Catholic predecessors, Nahum Goldman (1963, 67–71) condemned the idea that the state alone should be able to command the loyalty of citizens within a democratic framework. Likening this notion to totalitarianism, Goldman argued that religious identity was essential for the full development of the citizen, and thus the day schools were pro-democratic institutions.

Protestant Schooling

The next major move toward faith-based education occurred among conservative Protestants and began near the end of the twentieth century. Over the decade of the 1970s, the number of students in Christian day schools grew dramatically, such that by the middle of the 1980s there were as many as 11,000 schools serving more than one million students (Carper 1984, 110–29). This growth was largely defensive in that it was motivated by the sense that America's public schools had secularized to the point of hostility towards evangelical Protestants and their concerns. A series of social conflicts ranging from the constitutionality of prayer in public schools to the very public legal and political battles about the content of science lessons and children's readers resulted in the perception that the public schools had been taken over by secular humanists. Many conservative Protestant leaders encouraged their followers to support private, faith-based schools as a means of protecting the seeds of faith that parents are charged with implanting in their children. Though not all of these efforts were defensive, many observers saw them this way.

These schools attracted the attention of journalists and scholars alike, and several observers have sought access into particular institutions to examine daily life in these schools. Alan Peshkin's popular and influential book *God's Choice: The Total World of a Fundamentalist Christian School* (1986) is a case in point. Based primarily on ethnographic research, he painted a picture of a sheltered environment bent more on indoctrination than on opening minds. The overall mission of schools like Bethany Baptist Academy, the school he observed, was one of promoting certainty and commitment at the expense of curiosity. In Peshkin's view, this was due to both epistemological and institutional factors. Epistemologically, faith-based schools are committed to a certain set of truths, represented sometimes quite concretely in their statement of faith or other institutional documents, and thus they cannot embrace a spirit of open inquiry. Institutionally, these schools simply are not pluralistic and thus can be more of an echo chamber than an open marketplace of ideas. Of course, the fact that such schools are dependent upon a measure of pluralism in society for their existence did not escape Peshkin's notice, but he worried that fundamentalist institutions could not really appreciate or promote freedom and tolerance. More nuanced is Walter Feinberg's work entitled *For Goodness Sake: Religious Schools and Education for Democratic Citizenry* (2006). Extended observation in a number of schools—Christian, Jewish, and Muslim—led Feinberg to examine the implications these schools have on attitudes toward pluralism, religious commitment, and the requirements for living in a democratic society more broadly. Taking up everything from science education to the way various pedagogies either promote or inhibit discussion, he argued that a pluralist and democratic society must allow institutions like these to exist; but he also proposed ways these schools could promote the sort of civic virtues they themselves depend on, not least of all tolerance and a recognition of the rights of others to articulate and live out alternative visions of the good.

Conservative Protestant interest in alternatives to public schooling also led to a dramatic increase in the number of homeschoolers, those who are taught primarily by the family outside of formal institutions. Indeed, homeschooling emerged as one of the major stories in American education over the 1990s and into the twenty-first century (Stevens 2001,

10–29). In the 1970s there were between 10,000 and 15,000 homeschooled children in America. By 1983 their numbers had grown to somewhere between 60,000 and 125,000. By 1990 there were between a quarter of a million and 350,000. Seven years later estimates surpassed one million students receiving their education primarily in the home. (Lines 1998, 1) Estimates for 2010 go as high as two million students (Ray 2011). Though not all homeschooling is faith-based, the majority is, and it is the morally and religiously conservative aspects of this movement that captured the most attention. This practice, too, came under specific criticism for its democratic consequences, though some of the points could be made against any non-public schooling option. Chris Lubienski (2000, 207), for instance, holds that homeschoolers, in leaving public education, have limited the public schools' ability to act democratically. Recognizing that advocates of homeschooling have a list of grievances, real or perceived, against public schools, he claims that by structurally removing themselves from public institutions homeschoolers deny the possibility of a truly democratic dialogue about how to address their own, and others', grievances. Their departure closes possibilities for dialogue rather than opening them. Michael Apple (2000) sounds a similar note in his criticism of homeschoolers. Their mistrust of government, evidenced by their withdrawal from the public schools, could snowball into their refusal to support other government programs such as the building of roads or social welfare programs. For both Lubienski and Apple, homeschooling is essentially an undemocratic practice that could undermine the kind of social capital democracies depend upon. Popular media have even linked homeschooling to the anti-government domestic terrorism associated with the Oklahoma City bombing.

EDUCATION, DISSENT, AND THE LIMITS OF PLURALISM

While the debate over the place of faith-based schooling is often connected to the efforts of specific communities, a more general dialogue has emerged in the last 30 years or so among academics from various fields, including education, political theory, and legal studies. Historians and sociologists have also entered the fray. While many of the criticisms can and have been applied against specific historical cases, this broader dialogue has also emerged, taking as its starting point not a particular set of faith-based institutions, but the more general requirements of a liberal social order. Thus, the voices in this metalevel of the debate criticize not Catholic or evangelical schools in particular, but rather the spirit of separatism or practice of indoctrination that may be present in these institutions. The general debate focuses on a modified set of issues. More committed to pluralism than nineteenth-century critics of Catholic schooling, for instance, the concern here is that after graduation, faith-based students will have been too sheltered to effectively navigate working with people of different religious, moral, and political convictions. They will not have learned tolerance, nor will they have had many chances to practice it, something the public schools are institutionally designed to promote (whether they actually do or not may be a different question). Also in the contemporary period, several scholars have raised questions about the rights of children themselves to play a larger role in shaping their socialization and educational experiences. The arguments here vary as well, with some critics accusing religious schools of violating the rights of their students and others making a more nuanced claim to the effect that religious schools may be an instrument for denying children the opportunity to form their own values and goals, thus robbing those same children in their later years of the right to truly act as individuals.

Noted and influential political theorist Amy Gutmann (1987; 1995), for one, holds that "segregation academies," those designed to cultivate and promote a separatist identity, often undermine the very commitment to mutual respect they depend on. Democratic societies, she claims, support such schools at their peril. Acknowledging that parents inevitably, and rightly, have some influence over the socialization of their children, she believes that the purposeful segregation of children away from traditions other than their own may result in the child's inability to engage in the kind of rational deliberation that is at the heart of democratic experience. Robert Reich (2005) criticized homeschooling along these lines as well; pointing out that critical thinking requires that even the authority of parents be open to questions and criticism. If some children opt to leave the religious tradition embraced by their parents, then that is the necessary consequence of living in a free society. Legal theorist James Dwyer (1998) goes even further, advocating for a legal principle that recognizes the temporal interests of children as at least equal to parental rights, rights which he aggressively attacks. Religious schools come under fire for the harm they do to students, including limitations on physical liberties (they discourage sexual experimentation and dating, for example), and they limit freedom of thought and expression. Finally, Dwyer asserts that such schools may do incalculable psychological harm in that they promote guilt, anxiety, and low self-esteem for those students that fail to live up to the moral ideals upheld by the school.

Less focused on the rights of the child, but still critical of particularist education, is Stephen Macedo (1995). He holds that while liberal democracies must respect freedom and diversity, there is likewise a duty to recognize that peaceful coexistence and a tolerant social order are not natural occurrences. Liberal democracies must plan and implement strategies to ensure at least a minimal amount of commitment to civic virtue distributed throughout the citizenry. For Macedo, the burden of proof is on separatist schools to show how they can support the democratic imperatives that common schooling can be designed to promote. His larger project, the development of "liberalism with a spine," requires advocates to do more than ensure the autonomy and freedom of every member of society. An individual or group within the society may act in ways as to circumvent liberal social order, and thus while he knows full agreement is a utopian ideal, he holds out hope for a tough-minded consensus that, while open to some alternative visions of the good life, is willing to discount others that may violate certain tenets of the larger social order. That is, the positive liberalism Macedo espouses does not require one to entertain the moral and religious ideals of one's fellow citizens, but only to respect their right to hold them even while arguing against them in certain contexts.

The overall project of religious schooling has advocates and defenders as well, and they too have tried to explore the ramifications of church schooling for democratic practice. Charles Glenn (1995; 2003), for instance, has pointed out that the concern about whether or not religious schools undermine social harmony has been debated in this country for more than two centuries. For the entirety of this debate, religious schools have been present in America and they have not generally promoted discord or upset the social order. In Europe, too, religious schools exist alongside more religiously neutral institutions and those societies are not coming apart at the seams. Further, many religious schools in Europe receive public support to cover some of their operating expenses without discernible harm to the social order. In his influential examination of the common school movement (1988), Glenn argued that the assertion that public schools were inherently more democratic than private institutions is more belief than reality. In building public education in America, the interests and concerns of numerous religious groups and individual families were simply trumped by the assertion that social unity in a democracy could only be built on the basis of common, officially non-sectarian, schooling. It is assumed, rather than proven, that public schools are more diverse or more liberal-minded than their private school counterparts.

Elmer Theissen (2001) has also defended religious schools from their critics who find them undemocratic. For Theissen, parents have a right to direct the education of their children, and those critics that oppose this right in the name of the best interests of the child fail to recognize that parents are often motivated not by some desire to completely control their children but rather by a genuine and sincere belief that education should reinforce basic truths about the world. Theissen also argues that religious schools are not, as their critics often claim, more focused on indoctrination than on education. Calling for a broader understanding of education, he advances the notion that education is not just a rational consideration of various propositions (some of which, the criticism goes, might be presented unfairly by religious voices), but a form of initiation into the community. Children, he argues, learn by doing and by imitating what they see. In this sense, all education moves toward indoctrination, and there is no reason to think that religious schools are more guilty than any other kind of institution in this regard. Not content to simply respond to the various criticisms made against religious schooling, Theissen also argues that a pluralist educational system would actually enhance democratic practice and better prepare students for life in a complex society.

Though the debate over the place of private religious schooling in America shows no signs of abating anytime soon, there are ways to move it forward. Most importantly, partisans on both sides should remember that appeals to tolerance are more credible when they come from civil and tolerant voices. Implying that advocates of church schooling are agents of some subversive force, foreign or domestic, intent on overthrowing democratic practice, or accusing critics of such schooling as trying to eradicate the bond between parent and child is inappropriate and should be roundly rejected by more constructive voices on both sides of the divide. The cultivation of humility would also be a welcome addition to the debate. Advocates on both sides should remember that visions of the true and good have changed over time, as has educational theory and practice. No one model for how to educate the children in a society as complex and diverse as ours will stay in vogue for long. Finally, activists on both sides of the "school question" would do well to examine their own understandings of pluralism, commitment, and democratic practice. Critics of religious schooling have a legitimate point when they worry about the balkanization of our public life, but so too do the advocates of church schools when they point out that a genuinely pluralist society must make room for alternative institutions. It would be a great irony if, in the name of promoting individual freedom and democratic vitality, our society were to mandate a one-size-fits-all model of education.

REFERENCES AND FURTHER READING

Apple, Michael. *Cultural Politics and Education*. Buckingham: Open University Press, 1996.
Apple, Michael. "The Cultural Politics of Home Schooling." *Peabody Journal of Education* 75 (2000): 256–71.
Billington, Ray. *The Protestant Crusade 1800–1860: A Study of the Origins of American Nativism*. New York: Macmillan.

Carper, James. "The Christian Day School." In *Religious Schooling in America*, edited by James Carper and Thomas Hunt, 110–29. Birmingham: Religious Education Press, 1984.

Carper, James, and Thomas Hunt. *The Dissenting Tradition in American Education*. New York: Peter Lang Publishers, 2007.

Dwyer, James G. *Religious Schools v. Children's Rights*. Ithaca: Cornell University Press, 1998.

Glenn, Charles. *The Myth of the Common School*. Amherst: University of Massachusetts Press, 1988.

Goldman, Nahum. "Jewish Education and the Future of Jewish Life in the Diaspora." *Jewish Education* 33 (Winter 1963): 2ff.

Gutmann, Amy. "Challenges of Multiculturalism in Democratic Education," http://www.ed.uiuc.edu/eps/PES-Yearbook/95_docs/gutmann.html (accessed November 5, 2010).

Gutmann, Amy. *Democratic Education*. Princeton: Princeton University Press, 1987.

Lannie, Vincent P. *Public Money and Parochial Education: Bishop Hughes, Governor Seward, and the New York School Controversy*. Cleveland: The Press of Case Western Reserve University, 1968.

Lines, Patricia. "Estimating the Home School Population." Washington DC: US Department of Education Office of Educational Research and Improvement, 1991.

Lubienski, Chris. "Whither the Common Good: A Critique of Home Schooling." *Peabody Journal of Education* 75 (2000): 207–32.

Mann, Horace. "Ninth Annual Report." In *The Republic and the School: The Education of Free Men*, edited by Lawrence Cremin. New York: Teachers College Press, 1958.

Mead, Edwin. "Has the Parochial School Proper Place In America?" *Denominational Schools*. New York: Kansas Publishing House, 1889.

National Education Association. *Denominational Schools*. New York: Kansas Publishing House, 1889.

Peshkin, Alan. *God's Choice: The Total World of a Fundamentalist Christian School*. Chicago: University of Chicago Press, 1986.

Pierce v. Society of Sisters, 268 U.S.510 (1925).

Ravitch, Diane. *The Great School Wars*. New York: Basic Books, 1974.

Ray, Brian D. "2.04 Million Homeschool Students in the United States in 2010." www.nheri.org (accessed January 11, 2011).

Rose, Susan D. *Keeping Them Out of the Hands of Satan: Evangelical Schooling in America*. New York: Routledge, 1988.

Ryan, James. *Catechism of Catholic Education*. Washington DC: Bureau of Education, National Catholic Welfare Council, 1922.

Schiff, Alvin Irwin. *The Jewish Day School in America*. New York: Jewish Education Committee, 1966.

Stevens, Mitchell. *A Kingdom of Children*. Princeton: Princeton University Press, 2001.

Theissen, Elmer J. *In Defence of Religious Schools and Colleges*. Montreal: McGill-Queens University Press, 2001.

Tyack, David B. "Forming the National Character: Paradox in the Educational Thought of the Revolutionary Generation." *Harvard Educational Review* 36 (1966): 29–41.

Tyack, David B. "The Perils of Pluralism: The Background of the Pierce Case." *American Historical Review* (1968): 74–98.

47

School Choice and Faith-Based Schools

Charles L. Glenn

In the United States, in the twenty-first century, millions of parents exercise their right to choose faith-based schools for their children. In a sense, then, the relationship between such schools and "school choice" as a matter of public policy seems entirely straightforward. In fact, however, it is complicated and ambiguous. Parents who send their children to faith-based schools do not necessarily think of themselves as exercising "choice" in the sense of consumerist behavior. They may base that decision on a fundamental life-orientation anchored in a religious tradition from which they have never departed or one arising from a life-changing decision as adults; it may follow automatically that their children will attend a certain school, just as they will go to a certain summer camp and be part of a certain youth group. They are likely to know the parents of their child's classmates, helping to create the "functional community" that sociologist James Coleman contended leads to the positive academic effects of faith-based schools (Coleman and Hoffer 1987).

Other parents (who may in some cases be equally committed religiously) send their children to public schools that they have chosen through an arduous process and perhaps at considerable sacrifice, such as moving to a community that has a desired school. A recent federal government report found that, from "1993 to 2007, the percentage of children enrolled in assigned public schools decreased from 80 percent to 73 percent," with 24 percent of Black students attending public schools that their families had chosen. About half of students in public schools "had parents who reported that public school choice was available, and 32 percent had parents who considered other schools," while "27 percent had parents who reported that they moved to a neighborhood for the school" (Grady, Bielick, and Aud 2010, iv–v).

In other words, "school choice" and "private schools" (including those with a religious character) do not necessarily go together in American policy discussions. While it is true that the great majority of American schoolchildren are assigned to particular public schools on the basis of where they live, those residential decisions are themselves—for those who can afford it—commonly a form of school choice. Apart from residential choices, state and local government policies allow millions of American families to exercise choice among public schools. More than 1.5 million pupils attend more than 5,000 charter schools by the choice of their parents, and the number should increase significantly as a result of recent changes in state laws under pressure from the Obama Administration. There are thousands of public magnet schools, often established to promote racial integration through voluntary attendance based on a distinctive and attractive curriculum. There are inter-district and intra-district public school choice programs in hundreds, perhaps thousands, of communities.

In short, school choice (public as well as private) is a widespread phenomenon in American life. Our concern, however, is not so much with the sociological realities of school choice as with the policy framework within which it is exercised and frequently debated. It is characteristic of almost all of these policies that they discriminate unfairly against those parents whose motivations for choice of a school are religious rather than simply social or pedagogical. A financial penalty is imposed upon these families, limiting their freedom to live out their religious convictions, which families making school choices for other reasons are not required to bear. This also restricts the growth of a vigorous alternative system of schooling serving all social classes of the sort that exists in other Western democracies.

APPROACHES TO SCHOOL CHOICE AS A POLICY ISSUE

Support for school choice by public funding that follows each child to the school that his or her parents select can be advocated for three entirely distinct reasons. One argument, based upon the efficiency of markets compared with systems of bureaucratic control, contends that K–12 schooling in the United States cannot be fundamentally improved by spending and regulating and testing more, but requires instead a dramatic increase in accountability "from below" through school-level competition in an open market. This "efficiency" argument was advanced most notably by the late Milton Friedman, Nobel-prize-winning economist at the University of Chicago.

A second argument is based upon the evident injustice that poor and moderate-income parents—disproportionately Black and Latino—have less opportunity than other American families to choose the schools their children will attend through moving to the suburban communities with the best reputations or through paying tuition to private schools. This equity argument led to the development of magnet schools, intra-district and inter-district transfer programs, and to the voucher programs in Milwaukee and Cleveland, discussed below.

The third argument is based upon educational freedom, the right of parents to make decisions about the religious up-bringing of their children, a right incorporated into a number of international human rights treaties since World War II and recognized by the Supreme Court of the United States in 1925. This right has two policy implications: one is that government must not forbid faith-based schools or so regulate them that their distinctive mission is compromised, and the other is that government should ensure that parents are not prevented from exercising this right by their financial limitations. Compared with other Western democracies, American public policy does notably well on the first, but notably badly on the second implication of educational freedom.

This entry focuses primarily on the third dimension of school choice, that concerned with freedom, rather than the efficiency and equity dimensions, though of course educational freedom is meaningless for the poor unless the equity dimension is addressed as well so that they can exercise the freedom to which they have a right.

HISTORICAL OVERVIEW

The distinctive American pattern of extensive parental choice of every sort of school except those with a religious character developed over two centuries of political choices, and cannot be understood without some knowledge of that history.

The distinction that seems in current discourse so fundamental and immutable between tuition-free "public" and tuition-charging "private" schools did not become clear in the United States until the decades before and after the Civil War. In the early Republic, "nonpublic" schools (to use an anachronistic term), for profit or operated by benevolent foundations, existed side by side with "public" schools without the perception of a significant difference. Such schools were not generally established as religious alternatives to public schooling, as were the later parochial schools, although religious motivations were commonly at work in their founding. Religious goals were taken for granted in education and characterized most "public" schools as well; the terms "public" and "private" had not acquired the specific and morally-freighted significance that would develop in subsequent education debates.

Education was provided largely by local initiatives, including many schools sponsored by churches and many others operated by individual entrepreneurial teachers. Public schools in most states required parents to pay tuition, either directly or through a supplemental tax, while many private schools received state or local funds. Despite the warnings about social-class sorting expressed by Horace Mann and others, "there was also no absolute class differentiation between the private and the public school populations" (Nasaw 1979, 34).

Nonpublic schools were a primary means of providing education at all levels in communities where population growth had outstripped the colonial arrangements. When the Boston School Committee carried out a ward-by-ward census in 1817, they found that public school enrollment amounted to 2,365 students, with over 4,000 students attending free or tuition-charging private schools (Schultz 1973, 32).

In the mid-Atlantic states, in particular, it was the churches that provided most schooling well into the nineteenth century. Competition among religious denominations stimulated the provision of schooling. As historian Carl Kaestle has pointed out: "In 1830, 217 of Pennsylvania's 274 Lutheran churches operated day schools." In fact, Protestants and not Catholics were the first to provide extensive systems of what could be called "parochial schools," and

> immigrant resistance to common schooling was not restricted to Catholics or to cities. In southeast and central Pennsylvania, German Lutherans, Reformed Protestants, and Mennonites in small towns and rural districts resisted the introduction of free schools in the 1830s and 1840s. . . . German Pietists and other immigrant Protestants of Pennsylvania had supported their own schools long before the creation of public schools, and they had withstood efforts in the eighteenth century to assimilate their children through English-language charity schools.
>
> Kaestle 1983, 164

Catholic leaders were insistent that the education of Catholic children should be guided by the Church. Already in 1852, the First Plenary Council of Baltimore directed that a Catholic school should be established in every parish and the teachers should be paid from parochial funds. Similarly, the Second Baltimore Council, in 1866, mandated that teachers belonging to religious congregations should be employed whenever possible in parochial schools, which should be present in every parish, and the Third Plenary Council, in 1884, stressed the "absolute necessity" of parochial schools and the obligation upon pastors to establish them, and if possible to make them tuition-free. Catholic parents were expected to send their children to Catholic schools.

On the frontier, the first California school law allowed religious schools to share in the state school fund, though it was repealed several years later as a result of nativist Protestant agitation. The Texas legislature in 1856 designated all schools to which parents sent their children as "free public schools," entitled to receive a share of the state school fund. Public funds were provided to church-sponsored schools in Pennsylvania and elsewhere: to Catholic schools in Lowell, Massachusetts, in the 1830s and 1840s; in Milwaukee in the 1840s; in several Connecticut cities and in New Jersey in the 1860s; and in New York State even later. In one community in New York State made up of members of the Shaker religious sect, for example, the public school was staffed by a member of the group and—consistent with its communitarian radicalism—the state funds were paid into the community's treasury (Justice 2005, 74).

Since the settlement pattern in most cities created ethnically identifiable neighborhoods, public authorities sometimes found it expedient to enter into arrangements with a local Catholic pastor to take over a parochial school and operate it as part of the public system, under an agreement that the pastor would approve the teacher employed by the school district and the books used in the school, but that explicitly religious instruction would be provided only outside of regular school hours.

Nor were such arrangements considered in violation of the First Amendment, though they were often deplored on political and anti-immigrant grounds. A review of the records of the New York State education office found that "not a single resident of Elmira, Poughkeepsie, Utica, Corning, or any other city challenged . . . plans" under which local government provided financial support to parochial schools (Justice 2005, 209).

Such arrangements were fairly common until education reformers began to insist that schooling of future citizens should be provided under state authority, although that view gained wide support only gradually. The generation of elite education reformers that included Horace Mann and Henry Barnard deplored nonpublic schools. Advocates of a system of schooling controlled entirely by local and state government were unenthusiastic about and sometimes openly hostile to the semi-public academies, which they saw as dangerous rivals. It appears, indeed, that much of the energy of the education reformers of the "common school revival," at least in the East and the longer-settled areas of the Midwest, had less to do with the unavailability of schooling—it was in fact widely available through local initiatives—than it did with opposition to the availability of such schooling under private or religious auspices (Glenn 1988).

A strong impulse was given to the efforts of the proponents of the common public school under state government control by growing concern about the assimilation of immigrants, especially those settled in urban centers where they were highly visible. The fact that most, in the 1840s and 1850s, were Irish and German Catholics gave a new and threatening significance to non-government schooling, increasingly Catholic schools came under what was perceived as alien direction.

Catholic schools, according to Protestant leader Horace Bushnell, were a menace to society, and their religious justification was in fact no justification at all. In such schools, the children of immigrants "will be instructed mainly into the foreign prejudices and superstitions of their fathers, and the state, which proposes to be clear of all sectarian affinities in religion, will pay the bills!" Bushnell, like many others, found it "a dark and rather mysterious providence, that we have thrown upon us, to be our fellow-citizens, such multitudes of people, depressed, for the most part, in character, instigated by prejudices so intense against our religion." It was his hope, however, that through the common school "we may be gradually melted into one homogeneous people" (Bushnell 1880, 303).

This would not be the case in the 1850s in Chicago, where the Catholic and public school systems grew up in parallel, and the establishment of parochial schools in immigrant neighborhoods was pressed much earlier and more vigorously than in eastern cities (Gallenson 1998, 26–31). A large proportion of the Chicago immigrants in this period were German, with an interest in instruction in their own language provided by some parochial schools. Whereas in Boston, New York, and other cities in the East, immigrants were mostly impoverished and their children were seen as an unwelcome problem for public schools, in the Midwest public and Catholic schools competed for the patronage of immigrant families.

It was in New York City that the most notable conflict arose. The Public School Society, a charitable organization with Quaker leadership, had been founded to provide schooling for poor children and received state funds for that purpose, as did charity schools operated by Baptist, Catholic, Methodist, and Episcopalian groups. The Society had begun by urging that church-sponsored schools be allowed to enroll only children from their own congregations, but soon escalated its position to argue that no public funds should go to any school associated with a particular denomination. By 1825 the Society was arguing that "it is totally incompatible with our republican institutions, and a dangerous precedent" to allow any portion of the public money to be spent "by the clergy or church trustees for the support of sectarian education" (Katz 1971, 299).

Gradually, most denominational charity schools were turned over to the Society, relieving the churches and voluntary associations that had founded them of a financial burden. The Society was permitted to levy a local tax to support its schools, and Catholics and other religious groups sought public funding for their own schools in the name of fairness. In 1822, 1832, and in 1840 religious groups challenged the effective monopoly, which the Society achieved on state funding for schooling, with Protestants as well as Catholics joining in the challenges. Catholic Bishop John Hughes charged, in 1840, that the administration of the Public School Society was such that "parents or guardians of Catholic children cannot allow them to frequent such schools without doing violence to their rights of conscience." Parents should not be forced "to see their children brought up under a system of free-thinking and practical irreligion," and in fact it is reported that only a few hundred of some 12,000 Catholic children in New York City in the late 1830s attended the Society's schools (Cohen 1974, 1126–27).

Governor William Seward attempted to head off sectarian conflict by recommending to the Legislature, in his 1840 Annual Message, that state funds be provided to support schools with "teachers speaking the same language with themselves, and professing the same faith" (Welter 1962, 85). Horace Mann and other crusaders for the common public school were deeply disturbed and publicly opposed this measure. Protestant denominations that previously had sought and accepted public funding for their own charity schools suddenly discovered a principled objection to such subsidies.

It was, above all, the perceived need to achieve uniform and effective socialization (what a later generation would call "Americanization") of the children of immigrants that would lead to the creation of bureaucratically organized and centralized urban school systems, in stark contrast to the typical American pattern of dispersed and rather informal schooling initiatives that Tocqueville had admired. Over time, through political decisions at the state and local levels, "public education" was defined as exclusively that provided by schools under direct government control, and the religious content of that education was reduced to a generic Protestantism and, eventually, to nothing at all.

EFFECTIVE FREEDOM FOR FAITH-BASED SCHOOLS

And what of faith-based schools belonging to civil society organizations rather than to the State? To Horace Bushnell and many other influential Americans, they were a threat to national unity and to the development of civic virtue. "Americanizers" insisted it was necessary that the immigrant child be "weaned away from the standards and traditions of its home" that faith-based schools tended to perpetuate. Although "many of the ethnic parochial schools claimed that they Americanized children even more effectively than the public schools, in part because they built on rather than destroyed family, religious, and ethnic traditions, the heightened fear of foreign influences aroused by the First World War led to efforts to drive them out of existence altogether" (Tyack 1974, 237, 242).

In Oregon a referendum backed by the Ku Klux Klan and other anti-immigrant groups required that all children between 8 and 16 attend public schools. Only in this way, the proponents urged, could social unity be achieved. The public schools would serve to blend Americans into a single people with shared loyalties and would minimize the effects of religious and other differences. A constitutional amendment had also been on the ballot in Michigan in 1920 that would have required all children between the ages of 5 and 16 to attend public schools. The sponsors suggested to voters that almost all the residents of homes for wayward girls in Michigan had attended parochial schools, and that passage of the amendment was necessary because parochial schools perpetuated foreign languages, customs, and creeds. Unlike Oregon, Michigan voted down the constitutional amendment, which created a government monopoly of education, and did so again in 1924. Despite their victory, though, advocates of educational freedom were alarmed that hundreds of thousands of voters—more than 421,000 in the second vote—supported the ban (Ross 1994).

The freedom to operate nonpublic schools—and of parents to choose such schools—was firmly established in American law when, in 1925, the Supreme Court ruled in the Oregon case that "the fundamental theory of liberty upon which all governments in this Union repose excludes any general power of the state to standardize its children by forcing them to accept instruction from public teachers only. The child is not the mere creature of the state; those who nurture him and direct his destiny have the right, coupled with the high duty, to recognize and prepare him for additional obligations." This freedom was not unlimited, however; the Court also stressed that

> the power of the state reasonably to regulate all schools, to inspect, supervise, and examine them, their teachers and pupils; to require that all children of proper age attend some school, that teachers shall be of good moral character and patriotic disposition, that certain studies plainly essential to good citizenship must be taught, and that nothing be taught which is manifestly inimical to the public welfare.
>
> *Pierce v. Society of Sisters* 268 U.S. 510, 535 (1925)

Compared with the situation in other Western democracies, government oversight of nonpublic schools since the *Pierce* decision has generally been superficial. In an important case, the Ohio Supreme Court ruled that the state's mandated "standards [for approval of nonstate schools] are so pervasive and all-encompassing that total compliance with each and every standard by a nonpublic school would effectively eradicate the distinction between public and nonpublic education, and thereby deprive these appellants of their traditional interest as parents to direct the upbringing and education of their children" (*The "State of Ohio v. Whisner" State of Ohio v. Whisner*, 351 N.E.2d 750, at 768 (1976)). *Pierce* protected freedom—for those who could afford it.

EFFECTIVE FREEDOM FOR PARENTS THROUGH VOUCHERS?

Even if faith-based schools are allowed to express their distinctive convictions freely, many parents who want an education for their children based on those convictions may not be able to obtain it if their resources are insufficient for tuition—or if faith-based schools in their area are unable to enroll a sufficient number of tuition-paying pupils to survive financially. The policy instrument of vouchers (used extensively to distribute other government-funded benefits like housing and groceries) has seemed, to many reformers frustrated with the slow pace of improvement in American public schools, a way to address this injustice.

Although something like vouchers was proposed by Tom Paine in the late eighteenth century, by John Stuart Mill in the mid-nineteenth century, and by reformers in France in 1872, the contemporary debate is usually traced to a proposal advanced by economist Milton Friedman of the University of Chicago, over 50 years ago (Friedman 1955; 1962). Unlike some Libertarians who have urged that government cease funding schools altogether, Friedman argued for continued government funding combined with parental choice among schools subjected to government oversight.

It is because of the especially disadvantaged position of religious schools and religiously motivated school choices under American court decisions that the rather complicated mechanism of vouchers has been proposed, in response to the distinctive—indeed almost unique—jurisprudence on public funding for schooling with a religious character. Legal scholar Michael McConnell points out that:

> Vouchers are used, without serious legal controversy, at the preschool level and the college level, at religious as well as public and other secular schools. . . . An estimated 40 percent of the kindergarten and preschool placements are under religious auspices; poor children attending these programs are eligible for government assistance under federal and state child care programs. . . . Out of all the many contexts in which religiously affiliated groups participate, on equal terms, in publicly supported educational, health, and social welfare functions, only aid to church-related primary and secondary education seems to raise eyebrows.
>
> McConnell 2000, 369; Glenn 2000

The Supreme Court has made a series of rulings placing strict limits on public funding of instruction (though not necessarily other services) in schools considered "pervasively religious"—basically, any school with a religious identity, however discretely expressed. Most of the states also have constitutional prohibitions against funding of such schools. Pressure has been building up to find some way around this judicial and statutory limitation. During a period when expenditures for public schools increased rapidly without reducing significantly the achievement gap between black and white youth, a number of researchers have found that Catholic schools, in particular, are notably successful in educating at-risk black pupils (Bryk, Lee, and Holland 1993). Ironically, this bit of good news has been accompanied by the bad news that many of these schools have been forced to close because they can no longer be supported by the modest tuitions that low-income parents can afford.

The idea of vouchers was thus picked up by social progressives concerned to empower poor parents in relation to unresponsive bureaucracies. In an influential study of the achievement gap between black and other pupils, the authors urged that diversity itself, in response to the varied needs of students and desires of parents, was a desirable reform:

> We will have to accept diverse standards for judging schools, just as we do for judging families. Indeed, we can even say that diversity should be an explicit objective of schools and school systems. No single home-away-from-home can be ideal for all children. A school system that provides only one variety of schooling, no matter how good, must almost invariably seem unsatisfactory to many parents and children. The ideal system is one that provides as many varieties of schooling as its children and parents want and finds ways of matching children to schools that suit them. Since the character of an individual's schooling appears to have relatively little long-term effect on his development, society as a whole rarely has a compelling interest in limiting the range of educational choice open to parents and students. Likewise, since professional educators do not seem to understand the long-term effects of schooling any better than parents do, there is no compelling reason why the profession should be empowered to rule out alternatives that appeal to parents, even if they seem educationally 'unsound.' . . . The list of competing objectives is nearly endless, which is why we favor diversity and choice.
>
> Jencks and others 1973, 25–57

This equity argument lies behind the voucher programs adopted for Milwaukee and Cleveland. Each of them is explicitly designed to provide an alternative to children attending public schools which are severely underperforming; thus they respond to the equity argument rather than to the freedom argument for school choice. A study on the relationship between eighth grade enrollments and high school completion four years later, for example, found that Cleveland had the worst record of any of the 50 largest school districts in the country, with only 28 percent graduating.

Milwaukee's publicly funded school voucher program, responding to another failing urban system, was enacted by the Wisconsin Legislature in April 1990, as the result of an initiative led by state Representative Annette "Polly" Williams, an African American Democrat. In alliance with the Republican Governor, Williams filed a bill to provide vouchers worth $3,100 for each of 3,000 low-income children from Milwaukee, a predominantly black urban district, to attend non-religious private schools. Although opposed by the powerful teacher unions, by "progressive" groups, and by Wisconsin's chief state school officer, the bill was enacted as "the Milwaukee Parental Choice Program."

It was clear that the scope of the program, open to public school pupils from families with an annual income less than 175 percent of the official poverty level, would remain very limited so long as faith-based schools, which make up the overwhelming majority of non-elite private schools, were excluded from participation. The legislature lifted this restriction in 1995, while increasing the funding substantially. Within days, 72 additional schools had indicated their intention of participating. By the 2001–2002 school year, 10,882 students were receiving vouchers to attend 106 private schools located in Milwaukee, up from 341 students at 7 schools in 1990–91. In 2000–2001, 62.4 percent of the pupils participating in the voucher program were African American.

A similar voucher program was enacted by the Ohio state legislature for low-income pupils living in Cleveland. In its historic decision of June 27, 2002, the United States Supreme Court reviewed the evidence and the legal arguments about the state-funded voucher program in Cleveland and concluded that it was "entirely neutral with respect to religion" and as a result "does not offend the Establishment Clause" of the First Amendment to the Federal Constitution. The Court noted that "there is no dispute that the program challenged here was enacted for the valid secular purpose of providing educational assistance to poor children in a demonstrably failing public school system." Although almost all of the families receiving vouchers were using them in religious schools, the Court noted that those families had a number of other options that were not religious, and that therefore the Cleveland voucher program fell within the category of "programs of true private choice, in which government aid reaches religious schools only as a result of the genuine and independent choice of private individuals" (*Zelman v. Simmons-Harris*, 536 U.S. 639 [2002]).

In her concurring opinion, Justice O'Connor noted that

> although just over one-half as many students attended community [charter] schools as religious private schools [at state expense], the State spent over $1 million more—$9.4 million—on students in community schools than on students in religious private schools.... Moreover, the amount spent on religious private schools is minor compared to the $114.8 million the State spent on students in Cleveland magnet schools.
>
> *Zelman v. Simmons-Harris*, 536 U.S. 639 (2002)

In short, considered within the overall context of the state-funded educational options, the program providing vouchers to attend religious schools was by no means indicative of state favoritism toward those schools.

Despite this green light from the Supreme Court, attempts to enact legislation that would provide publicly funded vouchers have generally failed; in each case the teachers' unions have made massive and ultimately successful efforts to block the voucher initiatives through advertising that played upon the public's fears that children would be grievously harmed by schools teaching witchcraft or worse. In California in 1993, for example, the state Teachers Association vowed to defeat a voucher proposition and spent $13 million on efforts to do so. Proposition 174 would have provided parents with vouchers worth at least half the amount spent on each public school student in the state, or about $2,500, to help pay for tuition at any "scholarship-redeeming school," including secular and religious private schools; it was defeated 70 percent to 30 percent. A second California initiative, in 2000, would have provided state-financed vouchers of at least $4,000 per child to offset tuition at private schools, including religious schools. Like the first, it was fiercely opposed by the teacher organizations and was defeated overwhelmingly. Other voucher initiatives have been defeated in Michigan (twice), Washington State, Colorado, Pennsylvania, and Maryland. The Opportunity Scholarship Program in the District of Columbia, which, since 2004, has provided scholarships of up to $7,500 per eligible low-income student, was shut off by Congress to new admissions in 2009 despite positive evaluations and strong support from District residents. Early in 2011, the new Republican Speaker of the House joined with Independent Senator Joe Lieberman to introduce a bill to revive this program, a move opposed by Mayor Vincent Gray, whose election campaign had attacked recent reforms of the District's schools.

There have been dozens of studies of public attitudes toward vouchers and other school-choice measures in the United States. Political scientist Terry Moe provided a careful and balanced account of public opinion on the subject, based upon a nationally representative sample of 4,700 adults. Moe found significantly stronger support for vouchers among poor and minority respondents than among those with incomes sufficient to live in affluent suburbs or to pay private school tuition. He also found higher support among those living in poorly performing school districts, as might be expected:

> Among public parents, vouchers are supported by 73 percent of those with family incomes below $20,000 a year, compared to 57 percent of those with incomes above $60,000. . . . 75 percent of black parents and 71 percent of Hispanic parents, compared to 63 percent of white parents. . . . 72 percent of parents in the bottom tier of districts favor vouchers, while 59 percent of those in the top tier do.
>
> Moe 2000, 212

He noted that government funding of tuition in religious schools, the most controversial aspect of voucher proposals as reflected in elite commentary, is apparently not a serious issue for the public in general. In fact, Moe pointed out that

> virtually everyone agrees that religious schools ought to be included. Overall, 79 percent think parents should be able to choose both religious and nonreligious schools with their vouchers, while only 11 percent think that choice should be restricted to nonreligious schools. . . . what we find is a complete disjunction between what is happening at the elite level and what is happening among the general public. For ordinary Americans, the inclusion of religious schools is *not* a controversial issue.
>
> Moe 2000, 295–97

Not a belief in market forces but a concern to extend educational opportunities is the real energy behind the current demand for vouchers in the United States, and the Supreme Court's decision in the Cleveland case permitting them was clearly based upon that consideration. In his concurring opinion, Clarence Thomas, the only black Justice, began by quoting black abolitionist Frederick Douglass, who told his audience in 1894 that "[e]ducation . . . means emancipation. It means light and liberty." "Today," commented Justice Thomas, "many of our inner-city public schools deny emancipation to urban minority students. . . . urban children have been forced into a system that continually fails them."

Opponents of vouchers, including the four dissenting justices, Thomas argued, "wish . . . to constrain a State's neutral efforts to provide greater educational opportunity for underprivileged minority students." Dismissing the charge that the Cleveland voucher program was an unconstitutional "establishment of religion" on the part of government, Thomas pointed out that it "does not force any individual to submit to religious indoctrination or education. It simply gives parents a greater choice as to where and in what manner to educate their children. This is a choice which those with greater means have routinely exercised." Similarly dismissing the ideological nature of the opposition to vouchers, Thomas pointed out that "[w]hile the romanticized ideal of universal public education resonates with the cognoscenti who oppose vouchers, poor urban families just want the best education for their children" (*Zelman v. Simmons-Harris*, 536 U.S. 639 [2002]).

EFFECTIVE FREEDOM FOR PARENTS THROUGH CHARTER SCHOOLS?

Vouchers face both political obstacles as a result of the concentrated opposition of the teacher unions and also legal obstacles in the anti-aid provisions of most state constitutions. While the latter are being challenged, and popular frustration with the educational status quo could change the political calculus, vouchers do not at present hold out much promise of correcting the unjust treatment of religious motivation in school choice or of rescuing thousands of faith-based schools that face financial extinction.

There is another dimension of the school choice movement that could be more promising for faith-based schools, while representing at the same time a major threat to their survival. Although the teacher unions tend to oppose charter schools, they have not been as successful in blocking their spread as they have with vouchers. Unfortunately, it appears that much of the growth of charter schools has been at the expense of nonpublic schools, since the former seem to promise, without tuition cost, the same independence as distinctiveness as the latter.

In response to financial pressures, a number of inner-city Catholic schools have converted to public charter schools. This could be a positive move for faith-based schools, *if they can retain their religious distinctiveness*. It would require amendment of many of the state laws authorizing charters (and of state constitutional provisions in many cases) to permit existing faith-based schools to "opt in" to the public system, as has occurred in New Zealand and in Alberta, Canada, without abandoning their distinctive character. It would also require that those working in and managing faith-based schools become mindful in a disciplined way about what makes the education that they provide distinctive. Loss of clarity and of nerve—"pre-emptive capitulation"—in response to professional norms and to cultural pressures can be more damaging to the mission of a faith-based school than government interference (Glenn 2000).

Conversion of parochial to charter schools is occurring already in various parts of the country, most notably in the District of Columbia, and it will be interesting to see to what extent, as the outer symbols of religious identity and practice are removed, a faith-based understanding of the requirements of human flourishing can be maintained and expressed as the same staff teach and give leadership in a "secular" context. Much will depend on how clearly such an understanding has been articulated and learned through teacher preparation programs.

A different sort of approach is that of the Brothers of the Christian Schools, founded by Jean-Baptiste de la Salle in 1680 and now operating Catholic schools around the world. In response to the "Renaissance 2010" initiative of the Chicago Public Schools to stimulate creation of 100 high-performing inner-city schools, the Brothers established two "Catalyst" charter schools for grades K-8. While these are public schools and their mission statements emphasize character rather than faith, they are informed by and grew out of the network of private and explicitly faith-based Nativity Miguel schools, whose website states that "Our schools' mission is explicitly faith based & addresses the spiritual, moral, and emotional development of students as well as academic, physical, and social needs" (http://www.nativitymiguelschools.org accessed December 5, 2010). Significantly, the website of the Chicago branch states that "San Miguel Schools Chicago has two 'sister' schools which operate as public schools within the Chicago Public Schools. The Catalyst Schools were founded with the same mission and are rooted in the same LaSallian tradition as the San Miguel Schools" (www.sanmiguelchicago .org/about-san-miguel.html accessed December 5, 2010).

Those who guide and who work in such schools, unless they retreat into timidity, will be on thin ice as they seek to remain true to their understanding of the requirements of a good education (as contrasted with mere instruction), but they should take encouragement from the Supreme Court's warning against "viewpoint discrimination" (*Rosenberger v. Rector and Visitors of the University of Virginia*, 515 U.S. 819 [1995]). No doubt the extent to which a charter school can be distinctive in ways that have a religious flavoring will be a source of extensive controversy and litigation (Weinberg 2007).

Absent such efforts to find a way for charter schools to respond to the wish of many parents for schooling that reflects their own deepest convictions, it seems likely that the ever-expanding educational choices in public schooling will have a negative rather than a positive effect on faith-based schools, and not only on those that continue valiantly to serve low-income families.

REFERENCES AND FURTHER READING

Bryk, Anthony S., Valerie E. Lee, and Peter B. Holland. *Catholic Schools and the Common Good*. Cambridge, MA: Harvard University Press, 1993.

Bushnell, Horace. *Life and Letters*. New York: Harper and Brothers, 1880.

Cohen, Sol, ed. *Education in the United States: A Documentary History*. Vol. 2. New York: Random House, 1974.

Coleman, James S., and Thomas Hoffer. *Public and Private High Schools: The Impact of Communities*. New York: Basic Books, 1987.

Friedman, Milton. *Capitalism and Freedom*. Chicago: University of Chicago Press, 1962.

Friedman, Milton. "The Role of Government in Education." In *Economics and the Public Interest*, edited by Robert A. Solo, 123–44. New Brunswick: Rutgers University Press, 955.

Galenson, David W. "Ethnic Differences in Neighborhood Effects on the School Attendance of Boys in Early Chicago." *History of Education Quarterly* 38 (Spring, 1998): 17–35.

Glenn, Charles. *The Ambiguous Embrace: Government and Faith-based Schools and Social Agencies*. Princeton, NJ: Princeton University Press, 2000.

Glenn, Charles. *The Myth of the Common School*. Amherst: University of Massachusetts Press, 1988.

Grady, Sarah, Stacey Bielick, and Susan Aud, *Trends in the Use of School Choice: 1993 to 2007*. Washington, DC: Institute of Education Sciences, U.S. Department of Education, 2010.

Jencks, Christopher, Marshall Smith, Henry Acland, Mary Jo Bane, David Cohen, Herbert Gintis, Barbara Heyns, and Stephen Michelson. *Inequality: A Reassessment of the Effect of Family and Schooling in America*. New York: Harper Colophon, 1973.

Justice, Benjamin. *The War that Wasn't: Religious Conflict and Compromise in the Common Schools of New York State, 1865–1900*. Albany: State University of New York Press, 2005.

Kaestle, Carl F. *Pillars of the Republic: Common Schools and American Society, 1780–1860*. New York: Hill and Wang, 1983.

Katz, Michael B. "From Voluntarism to Bureaucracy in American Education." *Sociology of Education* 44 (Summer 1971): 297–332.

McConnell, Michael W. "Legal and Constitutional Issues of Vouchers." In *Vouchers and the Provision of Public Services*, edited by C. Eugene Steuerle, Van Doren Ooms, George Peterson, and Robert Reischauer, 368–93. Washington, DC: Brookings Institution and Committee for Economic Development and the Urban Institute, 2000.

Moe, Terry M. *Schools, Vouchers, and the American Public*. Washington, DC: Brookings Institution, 2000.

Nasaw, David. *Schooled to Order: A Social History of Public Schooling in the United States*. Oxford University Press, 1979.

Ohio v. Whisner, 351 N.E.2d 750 (1976).

Pierce v. Society of Sisters of the Holy Names of Jesus and Mary, 268 U.S. 510 (1925).

Rosenberger v. Rector and Visitors of the University of Virginia, 515 U.S. 819 (1995).

Ross, William G. *Forging New Freedoms: Nativism, Education, and the Constitution, 1917–1927*. Lincoln: University of Nebraska Press, 1994.

Schultz, Stanley K. *The Culture Factory: Boston Public Schools, 1780–1860*. New York: Oxford University Press, 1973.

Tyack, David. *The One Best System: A History of American Urban Education*. Cambridge: Harvard University Press, 1974.

Weinberg, Lawrence D. *Religious Charter Schools: Legalities and Practicalities*. Charlotte, NC: Information Age, 2007.

Welter, Rush. *Popular Education and Democratic Thought in America*, New York: Columbia University Press, 1962.

Zelman v. Simmons-Harris, 536 U.S. 639 (2002)

48

Outcomes of Faith-Based Schools

David Sikkink

The critics and supporters of faith-based schools agree that these schools make some kind of difference. Both sides expect that faith-based elementary and secondary schools offer a unique environment, organization, or culture that affects educational success, stable families and communities, social harmony, civic engagement, or the viability of participatory democracy. What is the evidence that faith-based schools actually do matter for student outcomes?

The research interest in school sector effects would lead us to expect a large and definitive body of empirical work on the outcomes of faith-based schools. The religious school sector has provided a crucial comparison for educational researchers interested in the impact of differences in school governance, organizational culture, and various structural characteristics, such as relationships with parents, congregations, and community (Coleman and Hoffer 1987; Haertel, James, and Levin 1988). Public-religious school comparisons have been central to understandings of best schooling practices and to the development of sociological theory, especially the concepts of social capital and intergenerational network closure (Coleman 1988; Bryk, Lee, and Holland 1993).

Despite the considerable interest in student outcomes of faith-based schools, definitive empirical work is hard to find. That is due to the difficulty of gaining adequate nationally representative data on a minority population. In the United States approximately 87 percent of K–12th grade students attend public schools; private nonreligious schoolers account for about 2 percent of the 10 percent of students enrolled in private schools (Broughman et al. 2009; Snyder and Dillow 2010). Another intractable problem of student-outcome research is empirically demonstrating school effects without random assignment of students to schools (Morgan 2001).

Most of the research available on faith-based schools focuses on student outcomes, such as volunteering or test scores during the elementary and secondary years or longer-term outcomes such as educational attainment and adult civic participation. On most dimensions outlined below—religious, academic, and civic—the empirical literature is unsettled and often inconsistent, plagued by a lack of quality data and divergent schemes for categorizing differences within the private school sector.

That said, the general conclusion at this stage of research on student outcomes is that most faith-based schools have a positive effect on some aspects of religious and spiritual formation of their students (Sikkink and Hill 2005). Similarly, the weight of the evidence remains in favor of some religious school advantage in academic achievement, at least for some subjects and for most types of faith-based schools. And the literature on school sector and civic socialization reveals that faith-based schools have neutral to positive effects on most dimensions of civic virtue and engagement. Before turning to the findings on student outcomes at faith-based elementary and secondary schools, the next section outlines the various reasons that critics and supporters are right to expect that faith-based schools matter for student outcomes.

WHY FAITH-BASED SCHOOLS MATTER

Most critics expect that faith-based schools influence student outcomes because they embed students in a social enclave, which is often grounded in a congregation or group of congregations and draws significant social boundaries with public life and mainstream American culture. Religious schools may provide a protected environment—a religious hothouse, some would say—that may improve religious socialization. Fundamentalist schools have been described as "total institutions" (Goffman 1961), which follows from their absolutist claim to ultimate truth (Peshkin 1986). They more strongly enforce student behavior and expectations through formal and informal means of social control. Fundamentalist Protestant schools are marked by strict rules, including clothing and grooming restrictions and expectations of students for positive attitudes and courteous and respectful behavior toward authority (Peshkin 1986; Rosen 2005). Some argue that student identities are narrowly defined and maintained through socialization in these religious schools (Ammerman 1987).

Social boundaries and strong collective identities in schools are not inherently bad. The structural enclave of a faith-based school may combine with religious ideals to reduce delinquency and promote prosocial behavior. James Davison Hunter argues that moral cultures are the most important determinant of children's behavioral dispositions. Schools mediate moral understanding to children—both formally or informally. If a religious school is able to avoid and overcome larger cultural influences toward therapeutic understandings of morality, it may strongly influence the behavioral outcomes of their students (Hunter 2000, 169). We would expect that faith-based schools provide a disciplined environment and a strong moral order, which creates effective socialization of students, especially regarding individual moral behavior. More generally, this social enclave may generate the kind of disciplinary environment that influences student outcomes related to academic achievement. Focusing on black and Hispanic students' academic achievement, for instance, Andrew Greeley (1982) argued that the disciplinary environment combined with the academic emphasis of Catholic schools improves academic outcomes for the disadvantaged.

A social enclave may improve school climate in a way that produces prosocial behavior, respect for school and teacher authority, and a meaningful collective identity for students and others connected to the school community. Non-public schools, according to analysis of the highly regarded 1988 National Education Longitudinal Study (NELS), offer a generally better social climate than their public counterparts. As Steven Vryhof stated: "Student misbehavior is milder and less frequent. Instruction is less often interrupted by fighting, verbal abuse, or indifference. The non-public schools enjoy less truancy, greater school spirit, and better cooperation. Students are more likely to encounter acceptance, inclusion, support, and caring. They sense the importance of the school and its work; they share a sense of purpose. They are less likely to be lost in the 'system,' left to just get by in undemanding courses with little oversight and with little connection to larger educational goals" (Vryhof 2004, 136).

Social Capital

Much of the debate on school sector differences has turned on whether faith-based schools generate social capital—the social networks marked by trust and reciprocity—that would influence student outcomes. According to the social capital research, parents of Catholic school students are more likely to know one another, which contributes to inter-generational network closure (e.g., parents know the parents of their children's friends) and facilitates information exchange and social control (Coleman and Hoffer 1987). Therefore, students with low human capital (minority and other disadvantaged students) benefit from the higher social capital of the community that is served by Catholic schools. In this work, the effect of religion on school effectiveness is primarily through its effect on social capital.

Organizational Differences

The seminal work by Anthony Bryk and colleagues links student outcomes to the organizational cultures of faith-based schools. One central aspect of an effective school is a mission that is clear and widely supported by the school community. Religion provides an inspirational ideology that animates the school mission and provides common symbols and assumptions that bind the school community. The Catholic school effect on student outcomes depends on a communal rather than a bureaucratic organization, which includes a focus on the dignity of the person within the community and a high degree of shared values among teachers and students as well as shared activities (Bryk, Lee, and Holland 1993). Thus faith-based schools may be focused more clearly on student outcomes, rather than programs and procedures (Hill, Foster, and Gendler 1990).

The communal organization also influences student outcomes by shaping the academic organization of the school. For example, the constrained academic structure of Catholic schools minimizes initial student differences, in contrast to the comprehensive and highly differentiated public school organization that accentuates them. Learning opportunities in a communal organization are enhanced since higher-level academic courses are required of all students and a constrained curriculum ensures relatively similar and demanding content for students at every level (Bryk, Lee, and Holland 1993; Hill, Foster, and Gendler 1990).

The commitment to a curriculum that avoids the pernicious effects of tracking is rooted in religious conceptions of persons as created in the image of God (Bryk, Lee, and Holland 1993). It is a relatively short step to see these differences in organizational culture at other types of faith-based schools as well. We would expect that faith-based schools influence student outcomes through increasing time-on-task; maintaining a common core of academic work; a supportive, communal style of organization; decentralized governance; and an inspirational ideology.

These organizational characteristics may lead faith-based schools to have a distinctive approach to students that shapes student outcomes. Religious commitments of school personnel infuse relationships in the schools with an ethic of caring (Bryk, Lee, and Holland 1993; McCloskey 2008). The Catholic philosophy of education—which likely extends to other faith-based schools—promotes not only community values but also a high regard for the development of the whole person, including body, mind, and spirit. School personnel may effectively parent students rather than limiting their role to imparting technical skills and information. Faith-based schools may have clearer expectations and may generate reciprocal obligations for students as well as other members of the school community (Hill, Foster, and Gendler 1990). Collective identities and respect for school authority built in a communal organization increase the ability of teachers to keep students on task in the classroom (Bryk, Lee, and Holland 1993).

Finally, decentralized governance has an important impact on the ability of faith-based schools to maintain their distinctive vision (Chubb and Moe 1990; Salganik and Karweit 1982). Faith-based schools attract staff members who accept the school's premises and socialize new staff members into the school culture (Hill, Foster, and Gendler 1990). According to some researchers, teachers in faith-based schools are therefore "more willing to go out of their way to help students despite being paid far less than their public school counterparts. They are absent less. They create fewer problems for administrators. Students tend to respect them" (Vryhof 2004, 136).

WHY FAITH-BASED SCHOOLS MAY NOT MATTER

For other researchers, the strengths of faith-based schools are also weaknesses. The social enclave may reduce bridges to alternative views and information important for academic success. Following concerns that high levels of social capital can be stifling, some would say that faith-based schools generate norm-reinforcing rather than horizon-expanding social capital, which may limit educational attainment. As Morgan and Sorensen argue, intergenerational network closure (e.g., when parents know the parents of their children's friends) is *negatively* associated with mathematics test scores in the public sector (Morgan and Sorensen 1999). According to other researchers, school authority can be overbearing. Susan Rose found that the pedagogy of fundamentalist schools often leaves little room for teacher-student interaction and the exploration of ideas (Rose 1988).

A communal organization, which depends on reasonably high social boundaries with outsiders and with mainstream culture, may have a downside as well. Although lauding the discipline and caring relationships he found between students and teachers, Alan Peshkin expressed concern that the tension in faith-based schools between school culture and practices and broader values of a liberal democracy may hinder democratic education, especially the formation of civic virtues necessary for participating well in our democratic institutions (Peshkin 1986). Others have questioned whether communal organization is sufficient to improve student academic outcomes (Phillips 1997). This research would lead us to ask whether all faith-based schools embody essential characteristics necessary for student academic success: high academic press, including demanding curricular materials and high teacher expectations for academic success.

A further potential obstacle comes from the market pressures on faith-based schools. Melinda Bollnar Wagner frames conservative Protestant schools not as "total institutions" but as sites that meld dominant streams of American culture with elements from conservative Protestant worldviews. She points out that many conservative Protestant schoolteachers rely heavily upon secular pedagogical techniques and materials, and students are hardly oblivious or dismissive of "worldly" teenage lifestyles. Wagner concludes that these compromises are all part of a long process of adaptation that, in the face of market pressures to maintain adequate enrollments, ensures the continued existence of these schools (Wagner 1997). Under the influence of market pressures, conservative Protestant schools broaden their theological umbrella in order to appeal to religious conservatives within several religious traditions, including Catholicism.

Research has not addressed the effect of market pressures, especially as these are channeled through parent expectations, on the ability of a faith-based school to maintain its distinctive organizational culture and communal practices. But some research argues that Catholic schools are being transformed in response to market pressures favoring college preparatory schools (Baker and Riordan 1998; Youniss, Convey, and McLellan 2000; Youniss and McLellan 1999). Market pressures, combined with an increasingly privatized view of education that strongly connects schooling with social mobility, may make it difficult for faith-based schools to have a strong influence on student religious and civic outcomes.

Finally, faith-based schools may be less distinctive given broader cultural pressures to conform to what it means to "do school." The role of athletics in the school community, the concern with a practical education that contributes to social mobility, a focus on teacher professionalism, autonomy, and career, and decisions on whether and how the curriculum is aligned with state requirements and widely used standardized tests may draw on cultural models rooted in public schools and university schools of education, thereby limiting the distinctive character of faith-based schools. The neoinstitutionalist theorists would lead us to question whether religious schools are really that different organizationally than public schools, raising questions about whether faith-based schools would have strong effects on student outcomes compared to public or nonreligious private schools (Meyer 1977; Meyer and Rowan 1977).

RESEARCH ON FAITH-BASED SCHOOLS IN THE UNITED STATES

Although hampered by data and measurement limitations, there is notable work on the outcomes of faith-based schools, particularly regarding student outcomes in the areas of religion, academic achievement, and civic life. These works inform the following conclusions about the effects of faith-based schools on student outcomes.

Religion

Many of the distinctive characteristics of faith-based schools—a strong collective identity, a clear moral order, a mission to educate the whole person, and norms that sanction a parent role for teachers and administrators—are likely to have an impact on religious socialization of students. These organizational strengths combine with educational structures that connect religious instruction and practice with daily student life. About 80 percent of private school students—which accounts for nearly all religious school students—report that they were required to study religion, which included courses on the Bible (The Gallup Organization 2005). In addition, religious schools bring students together with religious peers. A critical mass of religious peers within an organizational culture that supports religious and spiritual formation may provide the social context that generates greater religious commitment. We would expect, then, that faith-based schools matter for religious and spiritual outcomes of students both in adolescence and young adult years.

According to one review, however, methodological problems plague studies of the religious outcomes of Catholic and Protestant schools, making any conclusions difficult (Hood, Hill, and Spilka, 2009, 121–23). Though the research literature provides mixed results, there is considerable evidence that conservative Protestant schools do influence the religious and spiritual outcomes of their students. The Catholic school effects are less certain, but significant studies support the role of Catholic schools in religious socialization as well.

Studies that have strong methodologies but which ignore the religious tradition of the school provide indirect evidence for school effects on religious outcomes of teenagers. One study found that adolescent religious service attendance and self-reported importance of religion is positively associated with average levels of student religiosity in a student's school. This school-level peer effect increases adolescent religiosity through the high school years. Beyond the peer effect, there is no additional direct effect of attending a religious school (defined as a Protestant or Catholic school) on teenage religiosity (Regnerus, Smith, and Smith 2004). However, we would expect that most Catholic and nearly all conservative Protestant religious schools have higher average levels of religiosity among their students, which provides a pathway to higher religiosity for individual students attending these schools.

Another study that also used data from the well-regarded National Longitudinal Study of Adolescent Health (Add Health) found that religious school norms shape both public religious expressions and private devotional activities (Barrett et al. 2007). Attending a Catholic school tends to increase participation in religious services and youth groups during high school and increases the frequency of prayer and the self-reported importance of religion. Greater increases were found for students attending non-Catholic religious schools—a category that would consist mostly of conservative Protestant schools. Interestingly, this study finds that these religious school effects operate through average levels of religiosity of school peers as well as through the importance of religiosity to student social status in the school (Barrett et al. 2007). Each of these factors is likely to be high in conservative Protestant schools.

An additional finding may help us understand when and how religious schools influence religiosity of their students: Students whose religious denomination matched the dominant religious denomination of students in their school were more likely to increase their public and private religiosity during the high school years (Barrett et al. 2007). Again, we would expect that conservative Protestant schools would have a student body with higher levels of religious homogeneity, which would then lead to increases in student religiosity.

Other studies that consider religious tradition differences have shown more mixed results, which may be explained by the particular religious outcome being considered. Greeley and Rossi (1966) found that Catholic school attendance influences adult religious participation but only if the students came from very religious homes and did not have an irreligious spouse. Early studies of Jewish school attendance found stronger effects on various aspects of adult religious participation and devotion, and found that these effects are strengthened when combined with at least a moderately religious home and a religious spouse (Himmelfarb 1979). Older surveys of Catholics in the United States and Canada reveal a positive effect of Catholic education on student religiosity, net of parental controls (Fee et al. 1981).

A more recent study found evidence of an association between Catholic school attendance, traditional Catholic beliefs and practices, and higher levels of some religious practices, such as Bible study and prayer group participation. These relationships, however, appeared to be limited to Catholics with more than 12 years of Catholic schooling, which would include some Catholic college experience (Davidson 1997). Other research found Catholic school effects on prayer, belief in life after death, and retaining a Catholic religious identity in adulthood—effects that were especially pronounced for those with more than nine years of Catholic schooling (Sander 2001). Another recent study found that more than three years of attendance in a Catholic high school protects against disaffiliation from

Catholicism in adulthood. This study also found that attending a Catholic high school increases adult religious service attendance among those who were raised Catholic (Perl and Gray 2007).

One recent study, that took advantage of school religious tradition information available in Wave 1 of the National Survey of Youth and Religion (NSYR), found that the impact of faith-based schools on student religious outcomes varies by Protestant and Catholic schools: "Catholic schoolers attend religious services more frequently and value their faith more highly than public schoolers, but attend religious education classes and youth group less often. Protestant schoolers' involvement in their local congregation is similar to public schoolers, but their faith plays a more salient role in their life and they are more active in private religious activities" (Uecker 2008, 563). Analyzing longitudinal data, Jeremy Uecker found that Protestant schoolers were far more religious as young adults than public schoolers, and this relationship is partly explained by the schools' religious environment (Uecker 2009). Young adults who attended Catholic schools report levels of religiosity that are similar to those educated in a public school on most religious outcomes and lower on some religious outcomes. These effects do not appear to be due to friendship networks, network closure, or adult mentors (Uecker 2008).

Other studies with regional samples offer more-detailed religious outcomes, which are worth considering despite the methodological limitations of many of these studies. There is evidence, for example, that Protestant schools have an impact on knowledge of the Bible. A study of Arkansas evangelical schools found that these schools tend to increase the biblical literacy of their students (Simpson 2002). Another study, based on data from seven evangelical schools, did not find that years of evangelical schooling influenced whether students adopted a clear biblical worldview (Meyer 2003).

Clearly, there is a lack of consistency in these findings. But the more recent and stronger studies, along with several older studies, support the conclusion that faith-based schools have a short- and longer-term influence on the religiosity of their students. There is not enough evidence on the more detailed aspects of religious and spiritual formation, but on various forms of participation in religious organizations, such as religious service attendance, faith-based schools appear to make a positive difference. This conclusion is stronger for conservative Protestant schools but extends to Catholic schools as well.

Academic Outcomes

Religious schools may have the kind of organizational culture and social capital that would support academic growth. But questions remain about whether all types of faith-based schools have a strong commitment to academic success, given the holistic mission of these schools, which may create some competition between academic and other goals. A lack of resources may also impede the ability of many religious schools to foster academic achievement, especially in areas that may benefit from equipment, facilities, and experienced teachers, such as science.

This tension may be reflected in the research findings. Research on academic achievement tends to find important religious school effects, but the small size and inconsistency of these effects raise doubts. Again, part of the problem may be due to the lack of careful measures of the various types of faith-based schools (Hood, Hill, and Spilka 2009, 121–23).

A descriptive analysis of public–private school differences in academic achievement is available from a study that draws on data from the National Assessment of Educational Progress (NAEP), which conducts standardized tests in a random sample of schools in the United States. The National Center for Education Statistics (NCES) report of these data reveals that, in general, religious schools—similar to nonreligious private schools—do better on NAEP standardized tests than public schools in each subject area and at each grade level tested (4th, 8th, and 12th grade) (National Center for Education Statistics 2005).

Interestingly, there is evidence of relatively small differences *within* the religious school sector. By classifying schools according to whether they are Catholic, are affiliated with a Lutheran schooling organization, or are affiliated with one of the major conservative Protestant schooling organizations, such as the Association of Christian Schools International, the NCES report reveals some differences by type of religious school. In the 2000 NAEP, Catholic school 12th graders were somewhat stronger in science than Lutheran school graduates. And Catholic school 12th graders were more likely to score in the "proficient" range than those in conservative Protestant schools. In the lower grades, the differences between religious schools are relatively small, but there was some evidence that conservative Protestant schools do less well than Catholic and Lutheran schools in 8th-grade reading skills. In 8th-grade mathematics performance, a slight edge goes to the Lutheran school students compared to the Catholic or conservative Protestant school students. In 4th-grade science, the Lutheran school students did better than the conservative Protestant school students. Writing scores in 4th grade favored Catholic and Lutheran schools over conservative Protestant schools (National Center for Education Statistics 2005)

This NAEP-based report, however, is not conclusive because the data is cross-sectional and does not control for family-background differences by sector. A follow-up report, which includes some controls for family background and various school characteristics, found several important differences among faith-based schools. The analysis included math and reading scores for a random sample of fourth and eighth graders. For the fourth graders, after controlling for some school and student characteristics, Catholic and Lutheran school students were slightly behind public school students in math—as were all private schools as a whole. In contrast, Catholic and Lutheran eighth-graders were doing better in reading, but conservative Protestant eighth-graders were no different than public school students. In math, the eighth-grade Lutherans were the only group doing better than public schoolers, and the conservative Protestant schools were doing significantly worse (Braun, Jenkins, and Grigg 2006).

These results may point to academic strengths in Lutheran and Catholic schools that are not found in conservative Protestant schools. But the results are not consistent across grade levels. In addition, we must keep in mind that the "Lutheran" category is dominated by the Missouri and Wisconsin Synod Lutheran schools, which are usually considered conservative Protestant. The theoretical task, then, is limited to the question of why conservative Protestant schools in the Lutheran tradition differ from other conservative Protestant schools. The answer may be that more evangelical schools are stronger academically than schools of the more fundamentalist variety, but this claim requires support from more careful research.

An evangelical-fundamentalist difference in academic achievement receives some support from a study based on NELS 1988. This study provides evidence that some types of conservative Protestant schools have a positive impact on academic achievement. Students in schools affiliated with Christian Schools International, the more evangelical and reformed variety of Protestant schools (Sikkink 2001), were found to perform better in reading, mathematics, science, and social studies than their peers in both public and Catholic schools (Vryhof 2004). This work has two methodological contributions to make: it investigates a faith-based school sector not considered in U.S Department of Education studies and it uses panel rather than cross-sectional data.

An overall assessment of research on religion and academic achievement is available in the work of William Jeynes, who conducted a meta-analysis of more than 60 research studies examining the effects of religious schools or personal religious commitment on the academic achievement of students. Limiting our focus to the impact of religious high schools, Jeynes's meta-analysis found that writing, vocabulary, social studies, math, and reading-achievement test scores were significantly higher for students in religious high schools than for those in public high schools. But this religious school advantage did not extend to science test scores. He also found that students at religious high schools had higher GPAs than students from public high schools, though it is difficult to know whether this indicates more than school differences in grading standards (Jeynes 2003).

Jeynes's meta-analysis draws on the many studies of faith-based schools spawned by vigorous debates over the so-called Catholic school advantage. The well-known works of James Coleman, Andrew Greeley, and Anthony Bryk and colleagues have found that Catholic schools compared to public schools improve the academic success of their students. Whether through informal social control provided by intergenerational network closure, high academic expectations for all students, a constrained academic core that is more demanding for all students, or a disciplined environment that increases time on task and deference to pro-schooling norms, Catholic schools are able to improve academic achievement of students as measured by standardized test scores (Coleman, et al. 1982; Greeley 1982; Jencks 1985). Although the size of the Catholic school effects has been challenged (Alexander and Pallas 1983; Jencks 1985), Catholic school effects on math scores have been confirmed using sophisticated statistical methods to deal with problems of self-selection (Morgan 2001). Catholic school academic effects remain controversial; recent research has not found Catholic school effects on academic outcomes at elementary school levels (Carbonaro 2006). Recent data on elementary school students shows little Catholic school advantage but a significant conservative Protestant school advantage in fostering reading achievement in early childhood education—a finding that may reflect the disciplined environment and emphasis on reading Scripture in the conservative Protestant churches and schools (Sikkink 2010).

Do religious schools have a particular academic advantage for the disadvantaged? There is some evidence that the religious school academic advantages extend to and are stronger for racial and ethnic minority and lower socioeconomic status students. According to Jeynes's meta-analysis, racial minorities who attended religious high schools scored higher on math and reading achievement tests and overall achievement tests than their public school counterparts (Jeynes 2003, 159). Other studies have found a strong common school effect for the disadvantaged in Catholic schools, which may be due to more rigorous courses and higher levels of homework (Greeley 1982). Bryk, Lee, and Holland (1993) found that ethnic minorities and students from disadvantaged backgrounds performed better at Catholic schools than at public high schools and that drop-out rates for minorities were lower in Catholic schools.

Other solid studies have confirmed a Catholic school advantage for the disadvantaged. After controlling for differences between public and Catholic school students, Catholic school students have higher math and reading test scores. And this Catholic school advantage appears to be particularly large for students from disadvantaged backgrounds, including lower socioeconomic status, Hispanic, and black students (Morgan 2001). Data from the respected National Longitudinal Study of Youth (NLSY) support longer term benefits of Catholic schools for minorities in urban areas. Blacks and Hispanics in urban areas are much more likely to graduate from high school and college if they attend Catholic schools (Neal 1997; Sander 2001).

The research literature provides evidence that faith-based schools make a difference for academic achievement, but there are contradictory findings. Based on the strength of the large meta-analysis and a strong recent study (Jeynes 2004; Morgan 2001), it does appear that Catholic schools positively influence student academic growth. Among faith-based schools, there is evidence that Catholic and Lutheran schools have a positive effect on academic achievement, while conservative Protestant schools have a neutral to negative effect, especially in science.

Deviance Outcomes

While the effects of religious schools on educational achievement are mixed, one would expect that strengths of the organizational culture in religious schools would influence levels of student deviance. But there are some discrepancies in the existing findings.

There is some evidence that private religious schools reduce delinquency among their high school students. Religious school attendance reduces teenage delinquency, and this is especially the case for conservative Protestants in religiously homogenous schools (Regnerus 2003). Older work using NELS shows that religious private schools reduce the likelihood of sexual activity, arrests, and use of cocaine but do not affect drinking, smoking, gang involvement, or marijuana use (Figlio and Ludwig 2000; Sander 2001). Other research using Add Health shows more equivocal results when focusing on Catholic schools: Catholic school attendance appears to reduce the use of cocaine and likelihood of having sex among females but increases the likelihood of selling drugs among males. No other effects on various forms of delinquency were found (Mocan, Scafidi, and Tekin 2002).

Additional research is necessary to confirm the exact relationship between faith-based schools and deviance outcomes. There are hints in the current research that conservative Protestant schools matter more strongly in limiting deviance, and that religious schools matter only for the more extreme forms of deviance.

Civic Outcomes

Religious tradition differences must be accounted for when considering the relationship between faith-based schools and civic virtues as well as academic outcomes. In general, the literature supports the view that religious schools matter for volunteering and strengthen civic virtues, though Catholic schools seem to have a stronger positive effect on most civic outcomes than conservative Protestant schools (Wolf 2007; Sikkink 2004).

There are important research findings that support the claim that religious schools foster student volunteering and community service. Even after stringent controls, religious school students are more likely to volunteer than public school students (Nolin et al. 1997). Some research shows that during high school years volunteering is generated by private religious schools but not private nonreligious schools (Niemi, Hepburn, and Chapman 2000; Wolf 2007). When considering religious tradition, research shows that Catholic schools increase the level of volunteering of their students, in part through service learning experiences

(McLellan and Youniss 2003; Smith 1997). In contrast, after rigorous controls, the average level of volunteering for *non*-Catholic religious schools is no different than public school students (Campbell 2001; Sikkink 2009). One regional study, however, found that fundamentalist schools surpass public schools on volunteering in the community and placing other values ahead of trying hard to succeed (Godwin, Ausbrooks, and Martinez 2004).

Since volunteering in high school increases the likelihood of civic engagement in young adult years (McFarland and Thomas 2006; Musick and Wilson 2008), we would expect that high school volunteering through a faith-based school would create the networks and commitments that would lead to greater civic participation in young adult years. One study, however, did not find that young adults who graduated from Catholic schools were more likely to volunteer than public school graduates (Dee 2005). The methods and controls in this study may have led to an overly conservative estimate of Catholic schooler volunteering (Wolf 2007).

The rapid expansion of public schools in the mid-to-late nineteenth century was mobilized through evangelical Protestantism, which rallied to a significant extent over concerns about the civic virtues of Catholic immigrants (Meyer et al. 1979; Jorgenson 1987). The growth of the Catholic parish schools that followed raised further questions about whether Catholics would be educated for participation in democracy. In the twentieth century, concerns about democratic education were directed at the growing number of evangelical and fundamentalist Protestant schools (Blacker 1998; Gutmann 1987; Macedo 2000; MacMullen 2007). Alleviating these concerns are studies that show important contributions of religious schools to democratic education, though there are some mixed results for conservative Protestant schools.

There is evidence, for example, that in terms of support for democratic principles faith-based schools do fairly well. Greeley and Rossi (1966) found that Catholic school students were no worse than public school students on measures of community involvement, interaction with non-Catholics, and attitudes toward other non-Catholic groups, such as Jews, blacks, and Protestants (Greeley and Rossi 1966). Wolf, Greene, Kleitz, and Thalhammer (2001) use a sample of college students in introductory courses on American government to examine political tolerance. They conclude that private school students (both religious and secular) score higher on their measures of political tolerance. The effect is even greater for those that spent most or all of their previous education in private schools.

That religious schools generate civic skills and virtues receives mixed support in other research. Catholic schools do better than public schools in generating student community service, civic skills, civic confidence, political knowledge, and political tolerance. Non-Catholic religious schools, however, score higher in civic confidence but lower in political tolerance (Campbell 2001). Catholic schools have been shown to produce graduates who are very supportive of free speech principles (Campbell 2001, Williams et al. 2010). There is evidence that non-Catholic religious school students are less supportive—at least when it comes to the question of whether a book that advocates the use of illegal drugs should be kept in the library (Campbell 2001). In other research, evangelical private schooling compared to public schooling does not affect support for democratic norms (Godwin, Ausbrooks, and Martinez 2001). Still, the lack of a negative effect of evangelical schools would surprise some critics.

Other studies of political tolerance find high levels of tolerance among college students that have spent their elementary and high school years in a religious school (Wolf et al. 2001). Data from NELS has been used by Jay Greene (1998) to argue that private schools are better racially integrated within the classroom, have more racially tolerant attitudes, and encourage more volunteering. Private schools are more likely to promote friendship across racial and ethnic lines and less likely to have fighting in the school among racial or ethnic groups.

There is evidence that non-Catholic religious school students score lower on standard political knowledge questions (Sikkink 2009). Again, there is some conflicting evidence. Fundamentalist schools, as measured in one study of schools that teach biblical inerrancy, creationism, salvation by faith alone, the sinfulness of homosexual behavior, and that women should submit to their husbands, would not be expected to offer a strong democratic education even in comparison to evangelical schools. Yet a greater number of years in fundamentalist high school compared to public schools appear to increase political knowledge, tolerance, and higher-stage moral reasoning. These schools do reduce support for marginalized groups and for the need for governmental action to address inequality. They also are lower on situational tolerance (Godwin, Godwin, and Martinez-Ebers 2004). But overall the study found surprisingly positive effects on civic virtues in fundamentalist schools.

Whether differences between students of different types of schools matter for later civic engagement has received less attention. Analyzing longitudinal data provided by NELS, an important study found evidence that non-Catholic religious schools compared to public schools (but not private nonreligious schools) influence their graduates toward voting in elections. There is also limited evidence that non-Catholic religious schools generate higher levels of volunteering among young adults than public schools. Catholic school effects, however, were not found (Dill 2009).

Altogether, the research leads Charles Glenn to conclude that faith-based schools are not a threat to social harmony: "The concern that children and youth who attend confessional schools will be anti-social, intolerant, or disloyal has no serious empirical basis and has been discredited by both current research and historical experience" (Glenn 2009, 247). Certainly he is right to emphasize that there does not appear to be strong and consistent negative effects of faith-based schooling for civic participation, skills, and virtue. The positive effects of faith-based schools are somewhat inconsistent—less so for Catholic school students—but there is significant evidence that faith-based schools improve democratic education at least on some dimensions.

CONCLUSION

Despite conflicting evidence on the impact of faith-based schools on religious, academic, and civic outcomes, the weight of the evidence favors a benign to positive view of faith-based school outcomes. The conservative Protestant schools make the strongest impact on the religiosity of their students, with the Catholic effects somewhat less certain. But on academic achievement, the Catholic and Lutheran schools appear to have an advantage. The religious school advantage extends to the disadvantaged as well. Regarding democratic or civic education, the volunteering and support for democratic principles among the Catholic schoolers is encouraging. Though the conservative Protestant schoolers may be less involved in volunteering and civic engagement than the Catholic schoolers, it is important that, outside of views on tolerance, there is some evidence of conservative Protestant civic education advantages.

The general conclusion is that the distinctive organizational cultures of faith-based schools matter for student outcomes. Despite challenges from market pressures, laicization (in Catholic schools) and professionalization of school personnel, and expectations that schools contribute to career and social mobility, faith-based schools are making a difference in broad terms. But specifics about what type of faith-based schools make a significant difference on what dimension of religious, academic, and civic outcome is less clear. More conclusive findings await research with more careful theories and methods that address not only the various dimensions of religious, academic, and civic outcomes but also carefully consider religious tradition differences within the faith-based school sector.

REFERENCES AND FURTHER READING

Alexander, Karl L., and Aaron M. Pallas. "Private Schools and Public Policy: New Evidence on Cognitive Achievement in Public and Private Schools." *Sociology of Education* 56 (October 1983): 170–82.

Ammerman, Nancy Tatom. *Bible Believers: Fundamentalists in the Modern World*. New Brunswick: Rutgers University Press, 1987.

Baker, David P., and Cornelius Riordan. "The 'Eliting' of the Common American Catholic School and the National Education Crisis." *Phi Delta Kappan* 80 (September 1998): 16–23.

Barrett, Jennifer B., Jennifer Pearson, Chandra Muller, and Kenneth A. Frank. "Adolescent Religiosity and School Contexts." *Social Science Quarterly* 88 (December 2007): 1024–37.

Blacker, David. "Fanaticism and Schooling in the Democratic State." *American Journal of Education* 106 (February 1998): 241–72.

Braun, Henry, Frank Jenkins, and Wendy Grigg. *Comparing Private Schools and Public Schools Using Hierarchical Linear Modeling*. Washington, DC: U.S. Government Printing Office, 2006.

Broughman, Stephen P., Nancy L. Swaim, and Patrick W. Keaton. *Characteristics of Private Schools in the United States: Results from the 2007–08 Private School Universe Survey—First Look*. Washington, DC: National Center for Education Statistics, 2009.

Bryk, Anthony S., Valerie E. Lee, and Peter Blakeley Holland. *Catholic Schools and the Common Good*. Cambridge, MA: Harvard University Press, 1993.

Campbell, David. "Making Democratic Education Work." In *Charters, Vouchers, and Public Education*, edited by Paul Peterson and David Campbell, 241–67. Washington, DC: Brookings Institution Press, 2001.

Carbonaro, William. "Public-Private Differences in Achievement among Kindergarten Students: Differences in Learning Opportunities and Student Outcomes." *American Journal of Education* 113 (November 2006): 31–67.

Chubb, John E., and Terry M. Moe. *Politics, Markets, and America's Schools*. Washington, DC: Brookings Institution, 1990.

Coleman, James S. "Social Capital in the Creation of Human Capital." *American Journal of Sociology* 94 (1988): 95–120.

Coleman, James S., Thomas Hoffer, and Sally Kilgore. "Cognitive Outcomes in Public and Private Schools." *Sociology of Education* 55 (April–July 1982): 65–76.

Coleman, James S., and Thomas Hoffer. *Public and Private High Schools: The Impact of Communities*. New York: Basic Books, 1987.

Davidson, James D. *The Search for Common Ground: What Unites and Divides Catholic Americans*. Huntington, IN: Our Sunday Visitor Pub. Division, 1997.

Dee, Thomas S. "The Effects of Catholic Schooling on Civic Participation." *International Tax and Public Finance* 12 (September 2005): 605–25.

Dill, Jeffrey S. "Preparing for Public Life: School Sector and the Educational Context of Lasting Citizen Formation." *Social Forces* 87 (March 2009): 1265–90.

Fee, Joan L., Andrew M. Greeley, William C. McCready, and Teresa A. Sullivan. "Young Catholics in the United States and Canada: A Report to the Knights of Columbus." New York, NY: William H Sadlier, 1981.

Figlio, David, and Jens Ludwig. "Sex, Drugs, and Catholic Schools: Private Schooling and Non-Market Adolescent Behaviors." In *Working Paper*, 44. Cambridge, MA: National Bureau of Economic Research, 2000.

Godwin, Kenneth, Carrie Ausbrooks, and Valerie Martinez. "Teaching Tolerance in Public and Private Schools." *Phi Delta Kappan* 82 (March 2001): 542–46.

Godwin, Kenneth, Jennifer W. Godwin, and Valerie Martinez-Ebers. "Civic Socialization in Public and Fundamentalist Schools." *Social Science Quarterly* 85 (December 2004): 1097–111.

Greeley, Andrew M. *Catholic High Schools and Minority Students*. New Brunswick, NJ: Transaction Books, 1982.

Greeley, Andrew M, and Peter H. Rossi. *The Education of Catholic Americans*. Chicago: Aldine Publishing Company, 1966.

Gutmann, Amy. *Democratic Education*. Princeton, NJ: Princeton University Press, 1987.

Haertel, Edward, H. Thomas James, and Henry M. Levin. *Comparing Public and Private Schools*. New York: Falmer Press, 1988.

Hill, Paul T., Gail Foster, and Tamar Gendler. "High Schools with Character." In *RAND Publication Series*, 1–13. Santa Monica, CA: RAND Corporation, 1990.

Himmelfarb, Harold S. "Patterns of Assimilation-Identification among American Jews." *Ethnicity* 6 (September 1979): 249–67.

Hood, Ralph W., Jr., Peter C. Hill, and Bernard Spilka. *The Psychology of Religion: An Empirical Approach*. 4th ed. New York: The Guilford Press, 2009.

Hunter, James Davison. *The Death of Character: Moral Education in an Age without Good or Evil*. New York: Basic Books, 2000.

Jencks, Christopher. "How Much Do High School Students Learn?" *Sociology of Education* 58 (April 1985): 128–35.

Jeynes, William. *Religion, Education, and Academic Success*. Greenwich, CT: Information Age Publishing, 2003.

Jorgenson, Lloyd P. *The State and the Non-Public School, 1825–1925*. Columbia: University of Missouri Press, 1987.

Macedo, Stephen. *Diversity and Distrust: Civic Education in a Multicultural Democracy*. Cambridge, MA: Harvard University Press, 2000.

MacMullen, Ian. *Faith in Schools?: Autonomy, Citizenship, and Religious Education in the Liberal State*. Princeton, NJ: Princeton University Press, 2007.

McCloskey, Patrick. *The Street Stops Here: A Year at a Catholic High School in Harlem*. Berkeley: University of California Press, 2008.

McFarland, Daniel A., and Reuben J. Thomas. "Bowling Young: How Youth Voluntary Associations Influence Adult Political Participation." *American Sociological Review* 71 (June 2006): 401–25.

McLellan, Jeffrey A., and James Youniss. "Two Systems of Youth Service: Determinants of Voluntary and Required Youth Community Service." *Journal of Youth and Adolescence* 32 (February 2003): 47–58.

Meyer, John W. "The Effects of Education as an Institution." *American Journal of Sociology* 83 (July 1977): 55–77.

Meyer, John W, and Brian Rowan. "Institutionalized Organizations: Formal Structure as Myth and Ceremony." *American Journal of Sociology* 83 (September 1977): 340–63.

Meyer, John W, David Tyack, Joane Nagel, and Audri Gordon. "Public Education as Nation-Building in America: Enrollments and Bureaucratization in the American States, 1870–1930." *American Journal of Sociology* 85 (November 1979): 591–613.

Meyer, Raymond Keith. "A Comparative Analysis of the Factors Contributing to the Biblical Worldview of Students Enrolled in a Christian School." PhD diss., Southern Baptist Theological Seminary, 2003.

Mocan, H. Naci, Benjamin Scafidi, and Erdal Tekin. "Catholic Schools and Bad Behavior." National Bureau of Economic Research Working Paper 39. Cambridge MA: National Bureau of Economic Research, 2002.

Morgan, Stephen L. "Counterfactuals, Causal Effect Heterogeneity, and the Catholic School Effect on Learning." *Sociology of Education* 74 (October 2001): 341–74.

Musick, Marc A., and John Wilson. *Volunteers: A Social Profile*. Bloomington: IN: University Press, 2008.

National Center for Education Statistics. "Student Achievement in Private Schools: Results from NAEP 2000–2005." Washington DC: U.S. Department of Education. Institute for Education Sciences, 2005.

Neal, Derek. "The Effects of Catholic Secondary Schooling on Educational Achievement." *Journal of Labor Economics* 15 (January 1997): 98–123.

Niemi, Richard G., Mary A. Hepburn, and Chris Chapman. "Community Service by High School Students: A Cure for Civic Ills?" *Political Behavior* 22 (March 2000): 45–69.

Nolin, Mary Jo, Bradford William Chaney, Chris Chapman, and Kathryn Chandler. "Student Participation in Community Service Activity. 1996 National Household Education Survey." In *Statistical Analysis Report*, 49. Washington, DC: National Center for Education Statistics, 1997.

Perl, Paul, and Mark M. Gray. "Catholic Schooling and Disaffiliation from Catholicism." *Journal for the Scientific Study of Religion* 46 (June 2007): 269–80.

Peshkin, Alan. *God's Choice: The Total World of a Fundamentalist Christian School.* Chicago: University of Chicago Press, 1986.

Phillips, Meredith. "What Makes Schools Effective? A Comparison of the Relationships of Communitarian Climate and Academic Climate to Mathematics Achievement and Attendance During Middle School." *American Educational Research Journal* 34 (Winter 1997): 633–62.

Regnerus, Mark D. "Moral Communities and Adolescent Delinquency: Religious Contexts and Community Social Control." *The Sociological Quarterly* 44 (Fall 2003): 523–54.

Regnerus, Mark D, Christian Smith, and Brad Smith. "Social Context in the Development of Adolescent Religiosity." *Applied Development Science* 8 (June 2004): 27–38.

Rosen, Christine. *My Fundamentalist Education: A Memoir of a Divine Girlhood.* New York: Public Affairs, 2005.

Salganik, Laura Hersh, and Nancy Karweit. "Voluntarism and Governance in Education." *Sociology of Education* 55 (1982): 152–61.

Sander, William. *Catholic Schools: Private and Social Effects.* Boston: Kluwer Academic Publishers, 2001.

Sikkink, David. "Conservative Protestants, Schooling, and Democracy." In *Evangelicals and Democracy in America*, edited by Steven Brint and Jean Reith Schroedel. 276–303. New York: Russell Sage Foundation, 2009.

Sikkink, David. "School Sector and Achievement Gains in Early Childhood." Department of Sociology Working Paper. South Bend, IN: University of Notre Dame, 2010.

Sikkink, David. "Speaking in Many Tongues: Diversity among Christian Schools." *Education Matters* 1 (Summer 2001): 36–45.

Sikkink, David. "The Hidden Civic Lessons of Public and Private Schools." *Journal of Catholic Education* 7 (June 2004): 339–65.

Sikkink, David, and Jonathan Hill. "Education." In *Handbook on Religion and Social Institutions* edited by Helen Rose Ebaugh, 41–66. New York: Kluwer Academic/Plenum Publishers, 2005.

Simpson, Jeffrey S. "An Analysis of Biblical Literacy of High School Students in Conservative Evangelical Schools." PhD diss., Southern Baptist Theological Seminary, 2002.

Smith, Tom W. "Factors Relating to Misanthropy in Contemporary American Society." *Social Science Research* 26 (June 1997): 170–96.

Snyder, Thomas D., and Sally A. Dillow. *Digest of Education Statistics, 2009.* Washington DC: National Center for Education Statistics, 2010.

Uecker, Jeremy E. "Alternative Schooling Strategies and the Religious Lives of American Adolescents." *Journal for the Scientific Study of Religion* 47 (December 2008): 563–84.

Uecker, Jeremy E. "Catholic Schooling, Protestant Schooling, and Religious Commitment in Young Adulthood." *Journal for the Scientific Study of Religion* 48 (June 2009): 353–67.

Vryhof, Steven C. *Between Memory and Vision: The Case for Faith-Based Schooling.* Grand Rapids, MI: W.B. Eerdmans Publishing Company, 2004.

Wagner, Melinda Bollar. *God's Schools: Choice and Compromise in American Society.* New Brunswick: Rutgers University Press, 1990.

Williams, Frank E., Eddie Dennessen, Chris Hermans, and Paul Vermeer. "Citzenship Education in Religious Schools." *Journal of Beliefs and Values* 31 (August 2010): 215–29.

Wolf, Patrick J. "Civics Exam: Schools of Choice Boost Civic Values." *Education Next* 7 (Summer 2007): 67–72.

Wolf, Patrick J, Jay P. Greene, Brett Kleitz, and Kristen Thalhammer. "Private Schooling and Political Tolerance." In *Charters, Vouchers, and Public Education*, edited by Paul E. Peterson, 268–89. Washington, DC: Brookings Institution, 2001.

Youniss, James, and Jeffrey A. McLellan. "Catholic Schools in Perspective." *Phi Delta Kappan* 81 (October 1999): 105–6, 108–13.

Youniss, James, John J. Convey, and Jeffrey A. McLellan. *The Catholic Character of Catholic Schools.* Notre Dame, IN: University of Notre Dame Press, 2000.

49

American Faith-Based Schools in Comparative Perspective

Charles L. Glenn

PUBLIC FUNDING OF FAITH-BASED SCHOOLS

International comparison of educational policies is often confusing. Americans take particular arrangements for granted and are startled to find that they may be quite different in other countries that seem culturally similar. This is the case even with Canada; Ontario's two public school systems, one of them explicitly Catholic and serving one in three of elementary and one in four of secondary students, would be unthinkable across the border in Michigan or New York State. Thus some distinctions need to be made.

In the United States, faith-based schools are in every case "private" and in no cases receive basic tuition support from government, though they often receive public funds for supplemental services of various kinds. In some cases (notably the Milwaukee and Cleveland voucher programs) faith-based schools receive public funds from parents rather than directly from government, a distinction that was decisive in the Supreme Court's well-known decision allowing such support (*Zelman v. Simmons-Harris*, 536 U.S. 639 (2002)).

There are also a few charter public schools in the United States that are accused, by "strict separationists," of having a concealed religious identity. This includes the Ben Gamla School in Hollywood, Florida, which is intended to be the first of a nationwide string of schools that offer "bilingual, bi-literate, and bi-cultural curriculum" in Hebrew and English, but denies that it is a Jewish day school. Similarly, the Tarek ibn Ziyad Academy in Minnesota requires Arabic and teaches from a distinctive cultural perspective but insists that it is not an Islamic day school. Both schools, as well as the Hellenic charter schools, which are closely associated with the Orthodox Church, and some of the Catholic schools, which have become charter schools out of financial necessity, are the target of suspicion and opposition from those who oppose public schools that express a distinctive worldview and are based in a community that distinguishes itself in some way from the American mainstream.

The situation is very different in most other Western democracies. Through a succession of political struggles and compromises over the past two centuries (Glenn 2011), some countries provide *public* schools that are religiously distinctive; this is the case in some German *laender* and in England, where about 3-percent of "local authority" schools are Anglican, Catholic, or in a few cases Islamic, Jewish, or Methodist. There are separate public Catholic systems in Northern Ireland and, as noted above, in Ontario. In other cases many public schools have a residual religious character, as in Scandinavia (Lutheran), Italy (Catholic), Greece (Orthodox), and Germany's Bavaria (Catholic).

In addition to public schools with a religious character, it is well-established in most of these countries that the government will fund nonpublic schools that meet various requirements (of which more below) on the basis of parental choice and generally at the same rate as public schools. Often, this practice has been embedded in constitutions. Some examples, in no particular order:

- According to the Constitutional Council of *France*, freedom of education—being one of the fundamental principles recognized by the laws of the Republic and laid down in the 1958 Constitution—justifies the provision of state aid to nonpublic schools under contract with the State. Similar arrangements exist in *Spain* and *Portugal*. Almost all schools participating are Catholic.
- According to the *Irish* Constitution, nonpublic schools are to be granted public funding. The Education Act provides a statutory basis for the funding of recognized schools by the State. Most elementary schools are Catholic, but the Protestant minority also has schools.
- In the *Netherlands*, the Constitution provides that nonpublic schools are fully financed from public funds, and some 70 percent of pupils attend such schools.
- The Private School Act of *Austria* provides for subsidizing of nonpublic schools with state recognition.
- The basic legal framework for the funding and operation of nonpublic schools in *Belgium* is set out under the School Pact Law, with public and non-governmental schools treated similarly. Some 73 percent of pupils in the Flemish and 63 percent of those in French-German Community attend such schools, most of which are Catholic.
- In *Luxemburg*, the Government grants subsidies to nonpublic schools on an annual basis.
- In *Italy*, a number of regions, including Lombardy, provide vouchers to enable pupils from families with moderate incomes or pupils with special needs to attend nonpublic schools.
- Nonpublic schools in *Denmark* are eligible for public financial support.
- *Sweden* provides vouchers for pupils to attend approved nonpublic schools.
- In *Finland*, public funding is provided for some nonpublic schools.
- Under the Private School Law of *Norway*, nonpublic schools are granted funding, with a preferential claim to schools that are founded to offer a distinctively religious and ethical, or pedagogical, education, provided that they either follow the curriculum of the public system or offer an alternative curriculum that is approved by the Ministry.
- The Compulsory School Act and Upper School Act in *Iceland* provide for funding of nonpublic schools.
- Under the Education Act, registered nonpublic schools receive public funding in *Australia*, where about a third of schoolchildren attend publicly funded but nonpublic schools (nearly one in five are in Catholic schools) and enrollment in this sector has been growing considerably more rapidly than it has in public schools
- In *New Zealand*, nonpublic schools that choose integration into the state system receive full public funding of teacher salaries. Integrated schools remain the property of their sponsor, known as the "proprietor," which may be the Catholic bishop or another—usually denominational—entity. Nonpublic schools that do not choose integration may receive partial government subsidies.

- The *Canadian* situation varies from province to province, with Ontario retaining the dual system established under the British North America (now the Constitution) Act, while British Columbia, Alberta, and other provinces have accommodated religious diversity in publiclyfunded schooling in various ways.
- The Constitutional Court of *Germany* decided that the right to establish a nonstate school includes a right of financial subsidies by the state.
- According to the Constitutional Court of *South Africa*, the state can subsidize nonpublic schools, and it does so.

While these arrangements are in every case the result of political settlements peculiar to each country, they have been protected politically by the influence of international covenants that are largely ignored in the United States. The possibility of setting up schools outside the network of state-operated institutions was recognized by these covenants as necessary to educational freedom, as is the right to entrust one's children to a nonstate school. The Universal Declaration of Human Rights (1948) states that "parents have a prior right to choose the kind of education that shall be given to their children" (Article 26, 3), while the International Covenant on Economic, Social and Cultural Rights (1966) states that

> the States Parties to the present Covenant undertake to have respect for the liberty of parents . . . to choose for their children schools, other than those established by public authorities, which conform to such minimum educational standards as may be laid down or approved by the State and to ensure the religious and moral education of their children in conformity with their own convictions.
>
> Article 13, 3

Similarly, the First Protocol to the European Convention for the Protection of Human Rights and Fundamental Freedoms provides that "in the exercise of any functions which it assumes in relation to education and teaching, the State shall respect the right of parents to ensure such education and teaching in conformity with their own religious and philosophical convictions" (Article 2).

In none of these cases does the right of parents to nonpublic schooling for their children carry with it an obligation on the part of government to fund that alternative schooling through providing subsidies and assistance equal to that which it provides to its own educational institutions. Put another way, the allocation of financial resources to government-operated schools but not to alternative schools does not, under international legal norms, constitute unlawful discrimination.

On the other hand, the question of equitable financing of nonpublic schools has arisen in many countries, once other providers of education are recognized by the government as equivalent to its own schools, and the diplomas issued by them are accorded official status, on the basis that the education provided meets appropriate standards. After all, if a school is providing a public service for which funds are appropriated by the government, should it not receive a just share of those funds, based upon the number and type of pupils served?

When the state chooses—whether in the name of freedom of conscience or in the name of social justice—to extend subsidies to independent educational institutions, it ought not to discriminate unfairly among them. Differences in the nature and extent of subsidies granted to independent institutions are permissible if based on relevant, rational, and *bona fide* criteria. These might, for example, include giving preferential treatment to schools that make special efforts to include pupils from minority, immigrant, or low-income families.

While there is an issue of equitable treatment of *schools*, there is also an even more pressing issue of equitable treatment of *parents* who wish to exercise their right to make decisions about the schooling of their children. The accusation is often brought against private schools that they are schools for the rich, but in fact the decision about which families can afford to make use of these schools is often made by the State, in choosing to subsidize its own schools but not alternatives to them.

Obviously, exercising the right to education in other than government-operated schools will be made financially impossible for many families if they must pay the full cost of that education. In addition to this question of social injustice, the government fails in its obligation of neutrality toward religious and philosophical positions if it so organizes the educational system that there are strong incentives for parents to choose secular over religious education. The principle of strict neutrality insists that government should not be in the business of making distinctions between religious and secular expression, and should confine itself to ensuring that neutral rules are enforced upon each.

A government committed to strict neutrality would fund equally qualified schools without regard to their religious character, and would demonstrate that it was strictly fair by favoring neither religion nor secular ideologies . . . nor the lack of all convictions. We could call this position "secularity," in distinction from the secularism that lurks behind the strict separationist position. While secularism is an ideology which seeks to make converts, secularity is a posture of even-handedness, an insistence that government should be neutral between competing beliefs.

STRINGS ATTACHED TO PUBLIC FUNDING

Public funding often comes with requirements that may be especially troublesome for faith-based schools that are seeking to express a distinctive vision of education for human flourishing. While few oppose "health and safety" requirements, there may be others that affect such sensitive aspects of school functioning as curriculum content, teaching methods, admission of pupils, and—most sensitive of all—the selection and evaluation of staff.

Advocates of educational freedom argue that government fails in its obligation of neutrality when it imposes conditions upon religious schools that make it impossible for them to offer a distinctive alternative to a secular education. There thus should be limits to the reach of government in seeking to promote, for example, its social agenda through regulating civil society institutions. In recognition of the principle that the State should be philosophically neutral, in some countries the national Constitution seeks to establish equality or *quasi* equality among all schools "recognized as legitimate" because they meet all the objective standards, without regard to their particular methods or philosophy and whether they are operated by government or not.

Whether or not nonstate schools are publicly subsidized—the argument goes—they should not be treated differently by public authorities, unless the treatment is based on objective standards. Above all, government should resist its characteristic temptation to seek to impose uniformity upon all schools, as it usually does (unfortunately) upon the schools that it operates and controls directly.

Since the State has an obligation to respect the religious or philosophical convictions of parents and children in its actions in the field of education, the argument goes, and to facilitate the existence of non-public schools by providing procedures and standards for the recognition of these schools, it should support the pluralism of choices within the education system as a whole. The European Court for Human Rights, in its interpretation of the First Protocol to the *European Convention for the Protection of Human Rights and Fundamental Freedoms*, stipulated that "the second sentence of Article 2 is binding upon the Contracting States in the exercise of each and every function . . . that they undertake in the sphere of teaching, including that consisting of the organising and financing of public education" (*Kjeldsen, Busk Madsen and Pedersen*, Series A, nr. 23 §50). In other words, European governments were required to respect the religious and philosophical convictions of parents, whether their children were in public or non-public schools. Article 2 aimed "at safeguarding the possibility of pluralism in education, which possibility is essential for the persuasion of the 'democratic society,' as conceived by the Convention" (*Kjeldsen, Busk Madsen and Pedersen*, Series A, nr. 23 §50).

Pluralism fosters the co-existence of groups within the society with different religious, philosophical, or other convictions and develops the autonomy and thus the responsibility of each citizen as a tangible democratic principle.

Of course, as the European Court for Human Rights pointed out in *Kjeldsen*, "the right to education by its very nature calls for regulation by the State, regulation which may vary in time and place according to the needs and resources of the community and the individuals." But how this regulation is exercised has serious implications for the extent to which faith-based schools can be truly distinctive, and thus for the rights of both educators and parents to educational freedom.

The following examples, taken from Glenn and De Groof (2004), are intended to illustrate some of the forms that government oversight of nonpublic faith-based schools can take in countries where they routinely receive public funding.

The Netherlands

The Dutch Constitution guarantees the distinctiveness of faith-based schools, but leaves the door open to extensive government regulation. Article 23, after expressing the general responsibilities of the state for the educational system and guaranteeing the freedom of education, states:

- The standards required of schools financed either in part or in full from public funds shall be regulated by Act of Parliament, with due regard, in the case of nonstate schools, to the freedom to provide education according to religious or other belief.
- The requirements for primary education shall be such that the standards both of nonstate schools fully financed from public funds and of public-authority schools are fully guaranteed. The relevant provisions shall respect in particular the freedom of nonstate schools to choose their teaching aids and to appoint teachers as they see fit.
- Private primary schools that satisfy the conditions laid down by Act of Parliament shall be financed from public funds according to the same standards as public-authority schools. The conditions under which private secondary education and pre-university education shall receive contributions from public funds shall be laid down by Act of Parliament.

Article 23 guarantees these rights only within the sector of primary education, but legislation has extended them to all other sectors, including higher education. In both primary and secondary education, school buildings are financed by the municipalities, which survey the need for facilities for all publicly funded schools within their territories and are expected to treat public and nonpublic schools on an equal basis. Other costs, for example personnel and instructional materials, are paid directly to the schools by the state. In secondary education this subsidy is a lump sum, while in primary education the subsidies are linked to three specific categories of costs (personnel, operational costs, and accommodations).

Nonpublic schools in the Netherlands may be owned and operated by an association or a foundation. The right to operate, and to select, a nonpublic school has been based upon the concept of *richting*, corresponding to religious or philosophical worldview, even though it is not necessary that a school be linked to a religious organization or community, much less a "recognized" denomination. Elementary enrollment is divided roughly evenly three ways among Catholic, municipal, and Protestant schools, with under 10 percent attending an assortment of other independent schools with a pedagogical or religious distinctiveness. Postma lists 17 religious types represented among publicly funded Dutch schools: Catholic, Protestant, four varieties of more conservative Protestant, Anthroposophic (Steiner), Orthodox Jewish, Liberal Jewish, Platonic, Rosicrucian, Orthodox Muslim, Liberal Muslim, Orthodox Hindu, Liberal Hindu, Evangelical, and Hernhutter (Postma 1995, 128).

This does not count the distinctions among pedagogical types, which may also serve as the basis for parent choice: Montessori, Dalton, Freinet, and so forth. There are currently 250 schools following the pedagogical ideas of Peter Peterson (Jenaplan), 160 Montessori schools, 60 Waldorf (Steiner) schools, 10 Freinet schools, and about 25 schools based on other alternative pedagogies. The demand for such schools increased their number from about 200 in 1975 to about 600 20 years later (Jach 1999, 139).

Any conditions attached to funding independent schools must "respect in particular the freedom of private schools to choose their teaching aids [that is, materials] and to appoint teachers as they see fit" (section 6 of article 23 of the *Netherlands Constitution*).

In exchange for the full financial support that they receive from government, privately run schools in the Netherlands are restricted by many requirements laid down in statutes and regulations. As noted above, however, government is required to take the distinctive character of the school into account in enforcing these requirements. The instrument for reconciling these competing demands, at the elementary level, is the school work-plan, in which the administration and board of a school set out in extensive detail how all of the government requirements will be met, and how the distinctive mission of the school will find expression.

While the constitutional protections for the distinctive character of an independent school were clearly concerned with denominational distinctions, there was from the beginning in 1917 a recognition that other forms of distinctiveness would be protected. There was discussion of the possibility of anarchist, humanist, or socialist independent schools, though in fact the great majority of schools founded were either Catholic or Protestant.

There has, however, been a significant shift in recent years to stressing pedagogical distinctiveness. No doubt this has been caused by the growing secularization of Dutch society and the weakening of its traditional "pillars," but it also shows the effect of demands by increasingly sophisticated parents for a range of distinctive approaches to education. One scholar has noted:

> The complicated arguments that must be constructed to make credible the differences between denominations within Protestantism, Islam and Buddhism (for supporters of different movements within these religions have already claimed to represent independent movements) ensure that the concept of denomination will have to play a decreasingly important

role in the planning of schools. . . . It can, therefore, be expected that an approach based on numbers will begin to dominate: if a sufficient number of parents want a particular school (in the sense of: can guarantee a sufficient number of pupils), Government will no longer need to know which denomination the school represents.

Akkermans 1996, 240

Another step in this development is that some public schools are now managed by foundations, thus acquiring in effect the independent status of independent schools. "A foundation is a legal person in private law; it is not, therefore, subject to public law and need not be democratically elected" (Akkermans 1996, 239). In effect, they are something like American charter schools.

There is constant discussion, in independent school circles in the Netherlands, about how to protect and express the distinctive character of the school in the face of government, financial, and cultural pressures. "Identity" is seen as a key factor in school quality, and there is even a debate over the extent to which it is legitimate for individual public schools to develop a distinctive profile so as to compete more effectively with independent schools (Braster 1996).

The history of the two primary alternatives to public schools has led to their standing in somewhat different relations to their formal identities. The sponsoring authority for Catholic schools was until recent years always church authorities, and as a result the identity of the schools was for many years not in question. Even in this case, there were signs of a "loss of nerve" as early as the 1960s. Sociologist Van Kemenade found that many teachers in Catholic schools did not share the high regard of the parents for Catholic education as such; only one in five of the teachers reported deliberate efforts to stress the religious and ethical dimensions of the material taught (Van Kemenade 1968, 229).

Protestant schools, by contrast, have been sponsored, not by the churches, but by independent associations. As a result, they have differed greatly in their faithfulness to their religious character, some working at it assiduously while others paying it little attention. As long ago as 1933, the government concluded that the right of conscience to choose a school required that several varieties of Protestant schools be recognized and funded, even if they were in close proximity (Postma 1995, 118). One of the results of the lack of institutional anchor is that Protestant school boards that wish to retain the religious character of their school must work at that quite deliberately, with the result that, arguably, there are more really distinctive Protestant than Catholic schools (Marwijk Kooy-von Baumhauer 1984).

The increased secularization of Dutch society has led to some calls for the abandonment or sharp reduction of the place of denominational schools (over 60% of total enrollment at the elementary level), especially in view of the declining enrollments, which forced a very significant reduction in the number of schools. Surveys have found, however, that many parents who are themselves not believers wish to send their children to a school with a religious character—in part because of their reputation as more flexible and child-centered than public schools and as being better at teaching about values. There appears to be a political consensus to maintain the present system largely intact (Glenn 2011).

England

Whether or not an English school receives state funding depends on the local need for school places in general, regardless of the religious or philosophical character of the school. Compromises made 100 years ago to preserve the extensive provision of schooling by denominational groups while greatly expanding provision by local government have continued in effect, with some 7,000 publicly funded religious schools. The Elementary Education Act of 1870 is usually regarded as the first comprehensive government measure in England to ensure the universal availability of schooling. This was by no means the inception of popular education; much had been accomplished by voluntary (mostly denominational) efforts. The Newcastle Commission of 1861 found that "the Church of England had provided, through voluntary contributions, twice as much money as the State for its schools since 1833," and by 1890 there were 14,479 "voluntary" denominational schools (Chadwick 1997, 9, 13). Subsequent legislation has continued to make a place for faith-based schools within the public education system.

Parliament provided its first grant to subsidize denominational schools in 1833, and such provisions have continued in one form or another ever since. They were codified in the Education Act of 1944, under which

> the financial settlement was made more generous to the voluntary bodies. Church schools could choose 'Aided' or 'Controlled' status. 'Aided' schools were to receive grants to cover teachers' salaries and other maintenance charges; a grant of 50 percent toward the cost of alteration of buildings; the cost of all internal repairs and half the cost of external repairs. Other grants at 50 per cent (increased to 75 per cent in 1959) were payable in respect of new school building when a school was transferred to a new site because the existing premises could not be brought up to standard, or where a new school was to be built in substitution for one or more existing schools. [In 1967 this became an across-the-board grant of 80 per cent on all approved Aided school buildings.] In Aided schools, the appointment of staff remained in the control of the Governors or Managers, the majority of whom were to be nominated by the Voluntary [denominational] body. As for Controlled schools, their governing bodies were to include a majority of L.E.A. representatives but denominational instruction was permitted to continue. Their schools became the financial responsibility of the L.E.A.
>
> Maclure 1986, 222

While Roman Catholic schools (9.8% of all government-supported schools) chose the more independent "aided" status, the majority of the Church of England schools that make up 21.3 percent of government-supported schools are "controlled" (12.5% vs. 8.8% "aided"). Much depends, for "voluntary controlled" schools, upon whether the representatives of the local education authority are willing to support the denominational character of the school in curriculum and other decisions (Chadwick 1997, 62).

Voluntary schools, mostly church-owned, are funded by local education authorities, though those with a greater degree of autonomy are required to contribute at least 15 percent of the cost of maintaining the premises. All state-funded schools must comply with regulations regarding curricula, collective worship, and religious instruction (though the schools with a religious character may express that in their instruction), while respecting the convictions of parents and pupils. The principle of neutrality of the state in England therefore has a rather specific meaning: publicly established or financed schools may be of a "generally Christian" character, but the religious beliefs of parents are to be respected.

France

The basis for financial support to nonpublic schools in France is an act of parliament in 1959, the so-called *Loi Debré*. This act offers nonstate schools a number of possibilities to obtain public funding. The first of those is for a private school to become fully integrated into the state school system. Since state schools in France are strictly neutral from a religious and philosophical point of view, such a school could no longer express its religious or philosophical basis. Some Protestant and Jewish schools took advantage of this opportunity, but Catholic schools did not.

Nonstate schools may also sign a contract with the state to obtain public funding. There are two types of contracts: the "*contrat simple*" and the "*contrat d'association.*" Each contract attaches specific conditions to the subsidies it grants. The "*contrat d'association*" offers the widest range of subsidies, but also imposes more conditions on the schools in question. Besides these contracts with the state, local authorities can, and sometimes must, contribute to the financing of specific costs of non-public schools.

According to a sociological study of the motivations of parents, it is frustration with what is perceived as the rigidity and the high failure rate of the public school system, rather than religious factors as such, that influences most who choose non-public schools. The Catholic schools are by no means an elite system, attracting many pupils from farming and artisan families and evidencing less social-class selection in access to the higher grades than do the public schools. Families may choose a Catholic school, perceived as more flexible about responding to individual needs, when a child has experienced difficulty in a public school, then switch back to a public school when the child is doing well again (Georgel and Thorel 1995, 91).

The parity of funding for non-public schools under contract has made them seem, to many parents, a haven from the strikes and disorder that sometimes afflict the public schools. In addition, the non-public schools are less subject to the disruptions caused by periodic efforts to use the educational system as an instrument of policy initiatives to transform French society. These and other factors have led to "a growing attachment on the part of a great number of families to the existence of a double network of schooling" (Langouet and Leger 1991, 53n, 29, 38).

Non-public schools may be created and administered by an individual, an association, or a society, which may have a religious or philosophical basis. Their sponsors may sign a contract entitling them to a public subsidy in exchange for a considerable measure of state control. The great majority have done so; there are only some 60,000 pupils in the country attending non-public schools that are not subsidized through a government contract.

Some authors have contended that private schools under contract are obligated to observe the same religious and philosophical neutrality as public schools (Durand-Prinborgne 1998, 241), but this view has not prevailed. In a 1977 case, the Constitutional Court ruled that "safeguarding the distinctive character of a school under contract . . . is simply to put into practice educational freedom." This also has the effect, the Court found, of protecting the freedom of the pupil, the right to attend a school providing a differently oriented education. It was with the intention of protecting this right against restriction in the name of *laïcité* that the legislators inserted into the *Loi Debré* the provision that schools under contract would provide the state-required instruction in a way that respected their distinctive character (Monchambert 1983, 172).

But is the distinctive character expressed, as some believe, only in the overall ambience of the school, in its supplemental activities, and not in the actual instruction? Must the instruction itself be *laïque*? Or can the school seek to translate its religious (or other) ethos into everything that it does? Catholic or Protestant theories of education deny that a clear boundary can—or should—be made between the transmission of information and the communication of values. Aren't parents, in choosing a confessional school, expecting that it will provide education in a distinctive spirit?

Of course, by no means all parents are motivated by that concern; many simply believe that the discipline, the focus, and the relationships in a confessional school are better for their child. But the rationale for publicly funding non-public schools is, at least in part, to make it possible for those parents who are seeking precisely the confessional dimension for their children to find it, consistently and without apology. Hence the on-going debate over what significance to attach to the distinctive character of the school.

The French government (unlike, for example, those in Belgium and the Netherlands) has refused to deal with the Catholic educational system as such, or with other groups that sponsor and organize schools; contracts are explicitly with individual schools. This means that the burden of maintaining religious or other distinctiveness rests upon the individual school and its leadership. In entering into a contract with the State, the school has a right to insert language that defines its distinctive character (Monchambert 1983, 174).

A further opportunity to define a distinctive character that determines aspects of the program of the school is provided by the recent emphasis upon the "educational project" that each school is expected to have. The *lois d'orientation* of 1989 and of 2005 laid a requirement upon schools at all levels to create a representative school-based management structure and, through it, to set out the educational goals and means of that particular school. The intention is to create a shared vision and a practical course of action to carry it out, and it rests upon an acceptance that all schools do not have to be alike in order to ensure national unity and equal opportunity (Bernède, Palauqui, and Barrault 1998, 290–93).

While the *projets éducatifs* are not typically of a religious or ideological character, but bear upon program elements responding to local needs or the interests of the staff and students, they create a strong precedent for diversity among schools that are recognized as providing an equivalent, but no longer identical, education:

> The elaboration of an educational project for the school—taking into account the social environment, the pupil intake, the types of instruction provided, the means available, and reflection on the most appropriate pedagogical methods—has as its goal to specify the goals and determine the stages to their accomplishment.
>
> Durand-Prinborgne 1995, 197

Schools may also seek approval to implement an experimental approach to the curriculum, which must be well-justified on pedagogical grounds. Before implementing such an approved approach, they must notify the parents of pupils presently enrolled, and assist any who object to enroll their children in another school (Monchambert 1983, 175).

Although schools under contract are expected to follow the national curriculum and sequence of instruction (unless an exception is granted), they are free to select their own textbooks to present the material. Even though the State may wish to promote certain attitudes, loyalties, and values through all of the schools, public and private, it leaves both free to select from among textbooks that are produced independently and without government approval (Durand-Prinborgne 1994, 97).

Germany

The German Constitutional Court has made it clear that anything like a monopoly of schooling on the part of the State would be unconstitutional, and that the philosophically neutral secular state may not promote a viewpoint through education in the way that private schools may legitimately do so. Indeed, the State must guarantee "educational diversity even from itself" (Avenarius and Heckel 2000, 198).

Private schools, while they must provide an education equivalent to that in state schools, are not required to do so in a similar way and are free to choose curriculum materials and teaching methods. Those with a religious character can decide not to provide the state-proscribed sex education (Avenarius and Heckel 2000, 209–10).

Public confessional schools (*Bekenntnisschule*) continue to serve about one-third of the elementary pupils in North Rhine-Westphalia, the largest state. These are operated by local school authorities and are subject to essentially the same controls as non-confessional public schools. In several other states, private confessional schools can be accepted into the public system. The confessional identity of the Catholic, and even more of the remaining Protestant, public schools may be limited to their periods of religious instruction. Clerical influence, in particular, is strictly limited. Despite the continuing existence of denominational public schools, then, they have tended to differ little if at all from other public schools (Ramm 1990, 48).

Most states in Germany now consider their elementary schools either inter-denominational Christian common schools (*Christliche Gemeinschaftsshulen*) or common schools without a specifically Christian identity, though with some variations on these choices. The states that choose to identify their schools as Christian are Baden-Württemburg, Bavaria, Rhineland-Palatinate, and Saarland. Berlin, Brandenburg, Hamburg, Mecklenburg-Vorpommern, Saxony, Saxony-Anhalt, Schleswig-Holstein, and Thüringen identify their schools as simply *Gemeinschaftsshulen*. Public schools in Bremen are *Gemeinschaftsshulen* "on a general Christian basis," those in Hesse "resting on a humanist and Christian tradition," those in Lower Saxony "on the basis of Christianity, of European Humanism, and of the ideas of liberal, democratic and social freedom movements," while North Rhine-Westphalia includes in its public system, as noted, confessional schools as well as *Gemeinschaftsshulen* "on the basis of Christian educational and cultural values in openness to Christian beliefs and to other religious and philosophical convictions" (Avenarius and Heckel 2000, 103–5).

Canada

While the Canadian federal government has no responsibility for education, each of the provinces exercises some form of oversight over nonpublic schools. Catholic schools in Alberta, Ontario, and Saskatchewan (and, formerly, Protestant schools in Quebec) enjoy a special status that includes full funding by local property taxes and by provincial governments, under the direction of elected boards representing the Catholic Community; vestiges of a parallel arrangement for Protestants remain in Alberta and Saskatchewan. The reason is historical: an effort on the part of British authorities after they gained control of Canada in the 1760s to conciliate and win the loyalty of the predominantly French Catholic population. In the case of Newfoundland, which officially joined Canada in 1949, the entirely denominational educational system that had evolved over many decades was left intact until 1997.

To a substantial extent, then, the desire for a Catholic education was accommodated within the structure of public education in Canada, by setting up separate and parallel systems for Protestant and Catholic education.

Over time, the official Protestant schools have become secularist (ostensibly religiously neutral, though believers of various stripes would disagree) with the result that Protestant parents seeking schooling that corresponds to their convictions must seek it in one of the hundreds of evangelical and other private schools, some of which are funded more or less adequately by government and others are not, depending upon each province's policies.

The publicly funded Catholic schools in the provinces that accord them a special status are not generally considered "private" but rather "separate" public systems. Thus Catholic schools are part of separately run public school systems in those provinces and enroll 21 percent of all pupils in Saskatchewan, 23 percent in Alberta, and 30 percent in Ontario. There are also "separate" Protestant schools serving 1.2 percent of the pupils in Alberta and 0.1 percent of those in Saskatchewan (Robson and Hepburn 2002, 12).

In the other provinces, Catholic schools are classified as "independent," along with Protestant, Jewish, and other schools. In five provinces, these independent schools are eligible for public funds, while in others they are not, though Ontario has adopted a refundable tax credit to offset independent school tuition costs. That the private or independent school enrollment is relatively low is explained by the classification of most Catholic schools as separate public schools. While in most Western nations, Catholic schools represent half or more of the non-state sector, they make up well under 20 percent of the independent sector enrollment in Canada.

In Newfoundland, the entire educational system was organized along denominational lines (with Pentecostal, Seventh-Day Adventist, and Catholic school systems and an "integrated" system representing five other denominations, all publicly funded) until a constitutional amendment and a referendum in 1997. The system, which had been in existence for over 150 years, has been replaced by a single system with religious instruction provided at the request of parents.

Other provinces make a variety of arrangements to support nonpublic schooling: "British Columbia, Manitoba, Alberta, and Quebec all provide partial funding to support independent schools that meet certain conditions. These provinces differ in their treatment of Roman Catholic schools, with British Columbia and Manitoba treating such schools on the same basis as Seventh-Day Adventist or Dutch Reformed schools, while Alberta and Quebec have fully funded Roman Catholic systems as well as partially supported religious and secular [independent] schools" (Holmes 1998, 31). As noted above, this is no longer true in Quebec; under a law adopted in 1987 and upheld by the Supreme Court in 1993, schooling in Quebec is now divided along linguistic rather than confessional lines.

Policies allowing and supporting parent choice of schools are broadly popular. A poll published in the *National Post* on September 4, 2001, found that 57 percent of Canadian respondents supported introduction of vouchers to allow choice of schools. There is in fact publicly funded school choice in one form or another in Canada, although, as noted above, the situation is extremely varied from province to province; there is "no logical policy in most provinces to determine the dividing line between fully supported, partially supported, and unsupported schools" (Holmes 1998, 31).

A point of major controversy in Ontario has been the inequity of providing full public funding for Catholic but not Protestant, Jewish, Muslim, Sikh, and Hindu schools (the public system in the province evolved out of the former Protestant system, but has lost any religious character). Unsuccessful efforts have been made to include other schools under the funding scheme that Catholic schools enjoy. A commission appointed by provincial premier William Davis and chaired by Bernard Shapiro reported, in 1985, that there were 535 private schools in Ontario representing a dozen religious affiliations and serving 87,000 students, of whom 80 percent attended schools with a religious character. What is more, this private sector was experiencing dynamic growth, having increased from

2.3 percent to 4.7 percent of total enrollment in a single decade. The commission's report pointed out that "many such schools also contribute to the fulfillment of public purposes in ways substantial enough to make the label 'private' somewhat misleading" (Shapiro 1985, 43).

Despite this acknowledgment of the public function of private schools, however, no action was taken at the time. Lois Sweet observes that "every government in Ontario since . . . 1984 has promised to examine the issue of school funding for members of religious minorities. . . . And thus far every government has managed to sidestep it" (Sweet 1997, 123)

The provision of public funding only to Catholic schools was challenged successfully, however, before the United Nations Human Rights Committee, which ruled, in November 1999, that the existing arrangement violated Article 26 of the International Covenant on Civil and Political Rights. The text of the decision, with summaries of arguments by the plaintiff and by the Province of Ontario, may be accessed online (at www1 .umn.edu/humanrts/undocs/session67/view694.htm). The plaintiff, Arieh Hollis Waldman, complained that he was paying tuition for his children to attend a private Jewish day school while Catholic parents were able to make use of publicly funded Catholic schools, and that "these provisions create a distinction or preference which is based on religion." The Human Rights Committee concluded that the plaintiff had "sent his children to a private religious school, not because he wishes a private non-Government-dependent education for his children, but because the publicly funded school system makes no provision for his religious denomination, whereas publicly-funded religious schools are available to members of the Roman Catholic faith." Providing only a secular public education was consistent with the International Covenant on Civil and Political Rights, but "if a State party chooses to provide public funding to religious schools, it should make this funding available without discrimination." As a result, "the State party is under the obligation to provide an effective remedy, that will eliminate this discrimination." To date, however, it has not done so.

CONCLUSION

In almost every Western democracy except the United States (Greece is an exception, and Italy a partial exception) the government funds the cost of nonpublic schools, and especially faith-based schools. This public funding is seldom justified on the basis of the merits of competition and "markets," but rather of the right of parents to choose schools that reflect their religious and philosophical convictions. Education is recognized as an enterprise that inevitably engages a worldview, and the experience of government misuse of the power of schooling to impose an official doctrine has created a strong support for educational pluralism, even in societies with advanced secularism.

In recent decades, however, the desire on the part of governments across the political spectrum to use schooling as an instrument of social and economic change has led to increased interventions that threaten the distinctive character of schools. At the same time, the increased professionalization of teaching and school management has promoted norms that tend to make schools more similar, even if they claim to rest on distinct ways of understanding education (Glenn 2000).

Comparison between the Netherlands, for example, and the United States suggests certain advantages on each side. The Dutch commitment to funding the schools that parents choose for their children means that there is no penalty for choosing a faith-based school;

this is clearly more consistent with religious freedom than the American situation. This has the effect that poor and moderate-income families have the same opportunities and are treated with the same respect as agents exercising choice on behalf of their children as are more affluent families. Perhaps the most striking evidence of this is that the government has approved and funded some 50 Islamic schools in response to demand on the part of immigrant families. Some of these have struggled, it is true, because of the shortage of experienced and educated leadership in that community, but this leads to interventions by the government Inspectorate and observers are optimistic that the situation will improve over time.

In the United States, by contrast, there is a constant struggle to maintain those faith-based schools that serve low-income communities, and in fact they have closed by the hundreds in recent years. Short of some change in public policy and in constitutional jurisprudence, it seems likely that the ability to choose a school with a religious character will become more and more limited to the upper half of the middle class and above. On the other hand, compared with Dutch faith-based schools, those in the United States are subject to less government oversight and are in general freer to be distinctive. Whether they always take wise advantage of this freedom is another question.

REFERENCES AND FURTHER READING

Akkermans, P. W. C. "Education: A Persistent Constitutional Problem in the Netherlands." In *Education under the new Constitution in South Africa*, edited by Jan De Groof and Elmene Bray. Leuven (Belgium): Acco, 1996.

Avenarius, Hermann, and Hans Heckel. *Schulrechtskunde*. 7th ed. Kriftel (Germany): Luchterhand, 2000.

Bernède, Georges, Michelle Palauqui, and Éric Barrault. *Administrer l'école primaire*. Paris (France): Hachette Éducation, 1998.

Braster, J. F. A. *De identiteit van het openbaar onderwijs*. Groningen (The Netherlands): Wolters-Noordhoff, 1996.

Chadwick, Priscilla. *Shifting Alliances: Church and State in English Education*, London (United Kingdon): Cassell, 1997.

Durand-Prinborgne, Claude. *L'éducation nationale*. Paris (France): Nathan, 1994.

First Protocol to the European Convention for the Protection of Human Rights and Fundamental Freedoms. http://www.echr.coe.int/nr/rdonlyres/d5cc24a7-dc13-4318-b457-5c9014916d7a/0/englishanglais.pdf.

Georgel, Jacques and Anne-Marie Thorel. *L'enseignement privé en France*. Paris (France): Dalloz, 1995.

Glenn, Charles L. *Contrasting Models of State and School: A Comparative Historical Study of Parental Choice and State Control*. New York and London: Continuum, 2011.

Glenn, Charles L. *The Ambiguous Embrace: Government and Faith-based Schools and Social Agencies*. Princeton, NJ: Princeton University Press, 2000.

Glenn, Charles L., and Jan De Groof. *Balancing Freedom, Autonomy, and Accountability in Education*, I–III. Nijmegen (The Netherlands): Wolf Legal Publishing, 2004.

Glenn, Charles L., Jan De Groof, and Cara Stillings Candal. *Balancing Freedom, Autonomy, and Accountability in Education*, I–IV. Nijmegen (The Netherlands): Wolf Legal Publishing, 2011.

Holmes, Mark. *The Reformation of Canada's Schools*. Montreal (Canada): McGill-Queen's University Press, 1998.

International Covenant on Economic, Social and Cultural Rights http://www.un.org/millennium/law/iv-3.htm

Jach, Frank-Rüdiger. *Schulverfassung und Bürgergesellschaft in Europa*. Berlin (Germany): Duncker and Humblot, 1999.

Kemenade, J. A. van. *De Katholieken en hun onderwijs*. Meppel (The Netherlands): Boom, 1968.

Kjeldsen, Busk Madsen and Pedersen v. Denmark, European Court of Human Rights, Strasbourg (France), 7 December 1976

Langouet, Gabriel and Alain Leger. *Public ou privé?* Nanterre (France): Publidix, 1991

Maclure, J. Stuart. *Educational Documents: England and Wales 1816 to the present day.* 5th ed. London (United Kingdom): Methuen, 1986.

Marwijk Kooy-von Baumhauer, Liesbeth. *Scholen verschillen: een verkennend vergelijkend onderzoek naar het intern functioneren van vijfentwintig schoolgemeenschappen vwo-havo-mavo.* Groningen (The Netherlands): Wolters Noordhoff, 1984.

Monchambert, Sabine. *La liberté de l'enseignement.* Paris (France): Presses universitaires de France, 1983.

Netherlands Constitution http://www.servat.unibe.ch/icl/nl00000.html.

Postma, Andries. *Handboek van het nederlandse onderwijsrecht.* Zwolle (The Netherlands): W.E.J. Tjeenk Willink, 1995.

Ramm, Thilo. "Die Bildungsverfassungen." In *Vergleich von Bildung und Erziehung in der Bundesrepublik Deutschland und in der Deutschen Demokratischen Republik.* edited by Oskar Anweiler and others. Cologne (Germany): Verlag Wissenschaft und Politik, 1990.

Robson, William, and Claudia Hepburn. *Learning from Success: What Americans Can Learn from School Choice in Canada.* Indianapolis, IN and Vancouver, BC: Milton & Rose D. Friedman Foundation and the Fraser Institute, 2002.

Shapiro, Bernard J. *The Report of The Commission on Private Schools in Ontario.* Toronto (Canada): The Commission, 1985.

Sweet, Lois. *God in the Classroom: The Controversial Issue of Religion in Canada's Schools,* Toronto (Canada): McClelland & Stewart, 1997.

Universal Declaration of Human Rights http://www.un.org/en/documents/udhr/index.shtml.

Appendix I

U.S. Supreme Court Decisions
and Faith-Based Schools

John Witte, Jr.

U.S. Supreme Court Cases and Faith-Based Schools

#	Issue	Case	Citation	Year	Ratio	Author	Holding
1	Building Grants; First application of Disestablishment Clause	Bradfield v. Roberts	175 U.S. 291	1899	9-0	Peckham, J.	Upheld, against disestablishment clause challenge, the allocation and distribution of federal funds to build religious hospital.
2	Religious School Funding; Indian Trust Disbursement	Quick Bear v. Leupp	210 U.S. 50	1908	9-0	Fuller, C. J.	Upheld federal distribution of funds (under an Indian treaty) to Catholic schools that offered education to Native Americans.
3	Religious School Curriculum	Meyer v. Nebraska	262 U.S. 390; dissent attached to Bartels v. Iowa, 262 U.S. 412	1923	7-2	McReynolds, J.	State statute mandating English-only instruction in all grade schools held unconstitutional, as applied to private religious school.
4	Religious School Attendance	Pierce v. Society of Sisters	268 U.S. 510	1925	9-0	McReynolds, J.	Invalidated state law mandating attendance at public schools as violation of rights of private schools and of parents.
5	Religious School Regulation	Farrington v. Tokushige	273 U.S. 284	1927	9-0	McReynolds, J.	States may not impose unduly intrusive and stringent accreditation and regulatory requirements on religious and other private schools.
6	Religious School Subsidization: Textbooks	Cochran v. Louisiana Board of Education	281 U.S. 370	1930	9-0	Hughes, C. J.	Upheld state policy of furnishing textbooks to public and religious school students over objection of taxpayer that this constituted a taking of his private property in violation of the Fourteenth Amendment due process clause.
7	Licensing; Free Exercise Clause Incorporated	Cantwell v. Connecticut	310 U.S. 296	1940	9-0	Roberts, J.	Free exercise clause expressly applied to the states through the Fourteenth Amendment; city licensing law, requiring religious groups to procure a license in advance but giving discretion to local administrators to deny such licenses, held unconstitutional.

#	Topic	Case	Citation	Year	Vote	Justice	Holding
8	Flag Salute	*West Virginia State Board of Education v. Barnette*	319 U.S. 624	1943	6-3	Jackson, J.	Overruled *Minersville School Board v. Gobitis*, 310 U.S. 586 (1940); First Amendment provides exemption from mandatory participation in rituals that parties conscientiously oppose—including saluting the flag in a public school classroom.
9	School Transportation; Disestablishment Clause Incorporated	*Everson v. Board of Education*	330 U.S. 1	1947	5-4	Black, J.	Expressly applied disestablishment clause to the states through the Fourteenth Amendment; but it is not establishment of religion for states to provide school bus transportation to religious and public school children alike.
10	Standing	*Flast v. Cohen*	392 U.S. 83	1968	8-1	Warren, C. J.	Federal taxpayer has standing to challenge appropriation of federal funds for religious schools under the disestablishment clause.
11	Religious School Subsidization: Textbooks	*Board of Education v. Allen*	392 U.S. 236	1968	6-3	White, J.	Upheld state law requiring that textbooks of "secular subjects" be provided to all students in the state, whether attending public or private (religious or other) schools.
12	Tax Exemptions	*Walz v. Tax Commission*	397 U.S. 664	1970	8-1	Burger, C. J.	Upheld state property tax exemption for church property against disestablishment clause challenge.
13	Religious School Subsidization: Textbooks	*Lemon v. Kurtzman (I)*	403 U.S. 602	1971	6/1/1-0	Burger, C. J.	Disestablishment clause requires laws to have (1) a secular purpose; (2) primary effect that neither advances nor inhibits religion; and (3) no excessive entanglement of church and state—statute that reimbursed religious schools for costs of teaching secular subjects violates (3).
14	Compulsory Education	*Wisconsin v. Yoder*	406 U.S. 205	1972	6-1 (but dissenting opinion concurred in part)	Burger, C. J.	Granted free exercise exemption to the Amish, which exempted them from full compliance with compulsory school attendance law.

#	Topic	Case	Citation	Year	Vote	Author	Holding
15	Religious School Subsidization	*Lemon v. Kurtzman (II)*	411 U.S. 192	1973	4/1-3	Burger, C.J. (for the plurality)	*Lemon v. Kurtzman (I), 403 U.S. 602 (1971)*, should not be applied retroactively.
16	Religious School Subsidization: Textbooks	*Norwood v. Harrison*	413 U.S. 455	1973	7/2-0	Burger, C.J.	State may loan textbooks on secular subjects to religious schools, but not if those schools discriminate on racial grounds.
17	Religious School Subsidization	*Levitt v. Committee for Public Education and Religious Liberty*	413 U.S. 472	1973	5/3-1	Burger, C.J.	States may not reimburse religious schools for most costs incurred to administer standardized tests and to prepare mandated state records.
18	Religious School Subsidization	*Committee for Public Education and Religious Liberty v. Nyquist*	413 U.S. 756	1973	Pluralities	Powell, J. (opinion of the Court)	Disallowed state reimbursement for low-income parents for part of religious school tuition; disallowed tax deduction for low-income parents whose children attended religious schools; disallowed direct grants to private schools; disallowed direct grants to private schools serving low-income students for maintenance and repair costs.
19	Religious School Subsidization	*Sloan v. Lemon*	413 U.S. 825; additional opinions attached to Committee for Public Education and Religious Liberty v. Nyquist, 413 U.S. 798, 813 (1973)	1973	6-3	Powell, J.	Disallowed state reimbursement to parents for portion of religious school tuition.
20	Title I; Religious School Subsidization	*Wheeler v. Barrela*	417 U.S. 402	1974	6/1/1-1	Blackmun, J.	State receiving Title I funds must provide "comparable" but "not identical" services to disadvantaged students in both public and private schools, or forfeit Title I funds.
21	Religious School Subsidization: Textbooks	*Meek v. Pittenger*	421 U.S. 349 overruled by *Mitchell v. Helms, 530 U.S. 793 (2000)*	1975	Pluralities	Stewart, J. (for the plurality)	State may loan textbooks to religious schools, but not other various supplies and film, nor various counseling and other personnel, even if those were mandated by state policy.

			Pluralities		
22	Religious School Subsidization	*Wolman v. Walter*	433 U.S. 229, overruled by *Mitchell v. Helms, 530 U.S. 793* (2000)	1977	Blackmun, J. (for the plurality)	State may provide various personnel, diagnostic services, and standardized testing but may not loan instructional materials to private schools or to parents or provide transportation for field trips by private schools.
23	Religious School Subsidization	*New York v. Cathedral Academy*	434 U.S. 125	1977	6-3	Stewart, J.	Disallowed reimbursement of religious schools for state-mandated record keeping.
24	Labor Law	*National Labor Relations Board v. Catholic Bishop of Chicago*	440 U.S. 490	1979	5-4	Burger, C. J.	Denied jurisdiction to the NLRB over a Catholic school's teachers, based on the rights of a religious group to function separately from the state.
25	Religious School Subsidization	*Committee for Public Education and Religious Liberty v. Regan*	444 U.S. 646	1980	5-4	White, J.	Upheld reimbursement of religious schools for "actual costs" of state-mandated tests and reporting.
26	Religious Schools and Unemployment Compensation Taxes	*St. Martin Evangelical Lutheran Church v. South Dakota*	451 U.S. 772	1981	8/1-0	Blackmun, J.	The word "church" in the Federal Unemployment Tax Act exempting service performed in the employ of a church applies to schools that have no separate legal existence from a church.
27	Tax Exempt Status	*Bob Jones University v. United States &Goldsboro Christian Schools, Inc. v. United States*	461 U.S. 574	1983	7/1-1	Burger, C. J.	Upheld IRS decision to remove federal tax-exempt status from religious schools that engaged in racial discrimination, on the basis of its religious convictions, in matriculation and employment decisions.
28	State Income Tax Deduction	*Mueller v. Allen*	463 U.S. 388	1983	5-4	Rehnquist, J.	Upheld state law that allowed parents of private school children to claim state income tax deductions for the costs of "tuition, transportation, and textbooks."

#	Category	Case	Citation	Year	Vote	Justice	Decision
29	Religious School Subsidization: Shared Time Programs	*Grand Rapids School District v. Ball*	473 U.S. 373	1985	Pluralities	Brennan, J. (opinion of the Court)	States may not lend public school personnel to teach remedial and enrichment courses in religious schools.
30	Title I Remedial Services	Aguilar v. Felton	473 U.S. 402, overruled by Agostini v. Felton 521 U.S. 203 (1997)	1985	5-4	Brennan, J.	States may not use public school teachers to hold remedial educational programs to indigent children in classrooms leased from religious schools.
31	Federal Jurisdiction	*Ohio Civil Rights Commission v. Dayton Christian Schools*	477 U.S. 619	1986	5/4-0	Rehnquist, J.	Federal District Courts should abstain from adjudicating pending state proceedings as long as federal plaintiff has opportunity to litigate his/her constitutional claim.
32	Employment Discrimination	*Corporation of the Presiding Bishop of the Church of Jesus Christ of Latter-Day Saints v. Amos*	483 U.S. 327	1987	5/2/1/1-0	White, J.	Upheld exemption of religious school from Civil Rights prohibition against religious discrimination; religious employer not required to retain employee who has lapsed from its faith.
33	Religious School Subsidy: Interpreter	*Zobrest v. Catalina Foothills School District*	509 U.S. 1	1993	5-4	Rehnquist, C. J.	State's provision of an interpreter to disabled student at religious high school does not violate disestablishment clause.
34	Title I Remedial Services	*Agostini v. Felton*	521 U.S. 203	1997	5-4	O'Connor, J.	Overturned *Aguilar v. Felton*, (1985); the mere presence of a state employee in a religious institution is not per se unconstitutional, and thus the state may provide Title I remedial services to students at religious schools.
35	Religious School Subsidy: Interpreter	*Mitchell v. Helms*	530 U.S. 793	2000	4/2/3	Thomas, J.	Federally funded state policy to lend educational materials directly to public and private schools does not violate the disestablishment clause simply because many of the private schools receiving aid are religiously affiliated; *Meek v. Pittinger* (1975) and *Wolman v. Walter* (1977) overruled.

36	Religious School Subsidy: Voucher	*Zelman v. Simmons-Harris*	536 U.S. 639	2002	5-4	Rehnquist, C. J.	School voucher program, enacted for valid secular purpose of providing educational assistance to poor children in demonstrably failing public school system, does not violate the disestablishment clause, because program was neutral toward religion and government aid to religious schools was the result of parents' "true private choices."
37	Standing/ Disestablishment Clause	*Arizona Christian School Tuition Organization v. Winn*	563 U.S. ___	2011	5-4	Kennedy, J.	Taxpayers lack standing to make an establishment clause claim under *Flast v. Cohen* because their challenge involved an education tax credit not a government expenditure.
38	"Ministerial Exception"	*Hosanna-Tabor Evangelical Lutheran Church and School v. EEOC*	565 U.S. ___	2012	9-0	Roberts, C. J.	"Ministerial exception" applies to a teacher at a religious elementary school. The First Amendment religion clauses prohibit the government from interfering with the personnel decisions of religious organizations.

Appendix II

State Supreme Court Decisions and Faith-Based Schools

Charles J. Russo

In this, the companion appendix to the chapter "Leading Supreme Court Decisions on Faith-Based Schools," it is important to begin by addressing the relationship between the United States Constitution and state constitutions. Simply put, subject to the supremacy of the Federal Constitution, state constitutions are the basic law of individual states.

State constitutions typically address many of the same topics as the Federal Constitution, particularly with regard to aid to faith-based schools, even if the results of litigation interpreting these provisions vary dramatically. More specifically, consistent with the equal protection analysis of the Fourteenth Amendment, states may place more, but not fewer, limits on governmental aid to faith-based schools than the Federal Constitution ordinarily permits. In fact, the First Amendment did not even apply to the states until the Supreme Court so ruled in *Cantwell v. Connecticut* (1940), wherein the Justices invalidated the convictions of Jehovah's Witnesses for violating a statute against the solicitation of funds for religious, charitable, or philanthropic purposes without prior approval of public officials. States may thus grant more, but not fewer, rights than required by the Federal Constitution. Moreover, as issues relating to faith-based schools and their students evolve, individual states have typically placed greater limitations on aid to these institutions than under the Federal Constitution.

This appendix focuses on state, rather than federal, case law. Still, it is important to recognize that despite the relative dearth of litigation on aid to faith-based schools, developments at both levels often overlap. In other words, while cases may arise under state law, such as vouchers in Cleveland, Ohio, they are often ultimately resolved on the basis of the Federal Constitution (*Zelman v. Simmons–Harris*, 2002). As noted, then, it is worth recalling that the Federal Constitution is more open to some forms of aid to religious schools than its state counterparts, a distinction that emerged during the latter part of the nineteenth century.

The movement for separation between church and state advanced on December 7, 1875, when President Grant, in his final State of the Union address, called for a constitutional amendment "forbidding the teaching [of religion in public schools] . . . and prohibiting the granting of any school funds, or school taxes or any part thereof, either by legislative, municipal, or other authority, for the benefit or in aid, directly or indirectly, of any religious sect or denomination. . . ." (Grant 1875, 175). Grant added that "[n]o sectarian tenets shall ever be taught in any school supported in whole or in part by the State, nation, or by the proceeds of any tax levied upon any community" (181).

Following the lead of President Grant, Congressman, later Senator, James K. Blaine of Maine introduced a constitutional amendment in 1875 designed to prevent aid from going to schools "under the control of any religious sect," code for Roman Catholic schools. Under this proposed amendment:

> No State shall make any law respecting an establishment of religion or prohibiting the free exercise thereof; and no money raised by taxation in any State for the support of public schools, or derived from any public fund therefore, nor any public lands devoted thereto, shall ever be under the control of any religious sect, nor shall any money so raised or lands so devoted be divided between religious sects or denominations.
>
> Blaine 1875, 205

The Amendment failed to win passage in 1876. Still, 37 states adopted Blaine-type provisions that place substantial limits on the relationship between religious institutions and state governments (http://www.blaineamendments.org/states/states.html). Despite this early concern over the relationship between religion and education, more than 50 years would pass before the Supreme Court would address a case from a state court in this contentious arena, initially reviewing disputes under the Fourteenth Amendment, and it did not accept a case on the merits of such a claim until *Everson* in 1947.

STATE AID TO STUDENTS IN FAITH-BASED SCHOOLS

The following sections examine the primary topics and cases involving state aid to faith-based schools and their students under the headings of early litigation, transportation, textbooks, income tax issues, auxiliary services, shared facilities, and vouchers. The appendix rounds out with a brief conclusion.

Early Litigation

The first state case on faith-based schools to make its way to the Supreme Court was *Cochran v. Louisiana State Board of Education* (*Cochran* 1930), a dispute involving a statute that provided free textbooks for all students in the state, regardless of where they attended school. After the Supreme Court of Louisiana rejected a challenge to the law (*Cochran* 1928), the Supreme Court unanimously affirmed its constitutionality under the Due Process Clause of the Fourteenth Amendment rather than the First Amendment's Establishment Clause (*Cochran* 1930). In so doing, the Justices set the stage for the onslaught of litigation that would follow, in federal and state courts, over the constitutionality of aid to faith-based schools and their students.

Transportation

Everson v. Board of Education (*Everson* 1947) was the first Supreme Court case on the merits of the Establishment Clause and education. In *Everson* the Justices upheld a law from New Jersey permitting parents to be reimbursed for the cost of transporting their children to faith-based schools. Following *Everson*, state courts must evaluate whether publicly funded transportation to students who attend faith-based schools is acceptable under their own constitutions.

State courts reached mixed results on the permissibility of providing transportation for students in faith-based schools. Courts in Alaska (*Matthews v. Quinton*, 1961, 1962), Idaho (*Epeldi v. Engelking*, 1971, 1972), Missouri (*McVey v. Hawkins*, 1953), Oklahoma (*Board of Education for Independent School District No. 52 v. Antone*, 1963), and Washington (*Visser v. Nooksack Valley School District No. 506*, 1949) agreed that providing transportation violated their constitutions. In a different dimension with regard to transportation, a state trial court in New York agreed that the commissioner of education could prohibit a local school board from providing free transportation to children who attended private pre-kindergarten classes (*Board of Education of Lawrence Union Free School District Number 15 v. McColgan*, 2007). The court held that the law on student transportation to school did not authorize local boards to provide it to children in private pre-kindergarten classes.

On the other hand, the Supreme Court of Pennsylvania (*Pequea Valley School District v. Commonwealth of Pennsylvania Department of Education* 1979a, b) allowed students from faith-based schools to be transported beyond district lines. Later, the Supreme Court of Kentucky affirmed the constitutionality of a statute that allocated funding for students who attended faith-based elementary schools (*Neal v. Fiscal Court, Jefferson County*, 1999). The court found that the plan did not unconstitutionally aid faith-based and other non-public schools.

Textbooks

Following the lead of *Cochran*, under the First, rather than the Fourteenth, Amendment, in *Board of Education of Central School District No. 1 v. Allen* (*Allen*, 1968) the Supreme Court affirmed the constitutionality of a statute from New York that required local school boards to loan books to children in grades 7 to 12 who attended faith-based schools. However, state supreme courts in California (*California Teachers Association v. Riles*, 1981), Illinois (*People ex rel. Klinger v. Howlett*, 1973), Kentucky (*Fannin v. Williams*, 1983), Massachusetts (*Bloom v. School Comm. of Springfield*, 1978), Michigan (*In re Advisory Opinion* 1975), Missouri (*Paster v. Tussey*, 1974, 1975), Nebraska (*Gaffney v. State Department of Education*, 1974), and South Dakota (*Matter of Certification of a Question of Law from U.S. Dist. Ct., Dist. of S.D.*, 1985) vitiated similar plans under their own constitutions.

Income Tax Issues

After the Supreme Court upheld a statute from Minnesota granting all parents state income tax deductions for the actual costs of tuition, textbooks, and transportation associated with sending their children to all K–12 schools, including those that were faith-based, in *Mueller v. Allen* (*Mueller* 1983) the one state court case on point agreed while the second did not address the merits of the claim.

In Illinois, an appellate court upheld a tax credit of up to $500 for educational expenses spent on behalf of students in grades K-12 in public or faith-based schools that met established criteria. The court rejected arguments that the credit had the effect of advancing religion not only because the majority of non-public schools are faith-based but also since 82 out of the state's 102 counties did not have any non-sectarian schools (*Griffith v. Bower*, 2001a, 2001b). The Supreme Court of Oregon later held that since a draft title of a ballot initiative that was designed to grant state income tax credits to parents for children in grades K–12 was inadequate because it failed to address its goal adequately, it had to be modified before it could be submitted to voters (*Terhune v. Myers*, 2007).

Auxiliary Services

Zobrest v. Catalina Foothills School District (*Zobrest* 1993), allowing the on-site delivery of special education services to children in faith-based schools, heralded a significant shift in the Supreme Court's Establishment Clause jurisprudence. Even so, in the one state case most closely related to *Zobrest*, admittedly not involving K–12 schools, the Supreme Court of Washington interpreted its constitution as prohibiting the use of public funds in faith-based institutions; the Supreme Court refused to hear an appeal (*Witters v. State Commission for the Blind*, 1989a, b).

A year later, the Supreme Court, in *Board of Education of Kiryas Joel Village School District v. Grumet* (1994), invalidated the creation of a school district in New York with the same boundaries as those of a religious community in an attempt to accommodate the needs of parents of children with disabilities who wished to send them to a nearby school that would have honored their religious practices on the ground that it violated the Establishment Clause. Shortly after the Court announced its judgment, the state legislature amended the law in an effort to correct the constitutional defect. Yet, New York's highest court struck down the revised statute for violating the Establishment Clause insofar as it had the effect of advancing one religion; the Supreme Court refused to intervene (*Grumet v. Cuomo*, 1997; *Grumet v. Pataki*, 1999a, b).

Shared Facilities

A fair amount of litigation ensued once officials in public and faith-based schools entered into cooperative arrangements. The extent to which the shared use of facilities is permissible is an open question because jurisdictions differ on whether public and non-public schools can use the same buildings or operate dual-enrollment programs under state law. The key issues in these disputes are whether public funds are used for religious purposes and whether religious influences are present in public schools.

When dealing with the use of public funds in faith-based schools, disputes occur when school boards lease part or all of church-owned buildings. In a pair of cases, the Supreme Court of Nebraska invalidated a leasing program where part of a building was used by a religious school due to the garb and devotional attitude of the nuns who taught there, the instructions and services that the local priest offered in the chapel and classrooms, and the insignia around the building created an environment reflecting Catholic beliefs (*State ex rel. Public School District No. 6, Cedar County v. Taylor*, 1932). In the second case, decided 40 years later, the court decided that a public school board may use or lease classrooms in a church or other building affiliated with a religious organization for public school purposes if the property is under the control of public school officials and the instruction is secular (*State ex rel. School Dist. of Hartington v. Nebraska State Board of Education*, 1972a, b). The Supreme Court of New Mexico also forbade prohibiting the use of facilities where direct and indirect religious influences were present in schools (*Zellers v. Huff*, 1951).

Relying on language in the latter case from Nebraska, the Supreme Court of Georgia affirmed that an arms-length contract under which a public school system leased classroom space from a church did not violate the state constitution (*Taetle v. Atlanta Independent School System*, 2006). The court pointed out that since the purpose of the lease was to permit the public school system to establish and operate a kindergarten in a nonsectarian environment, the payments did not constitute an unconstitutional form of monetary aid to the church.

Disputes relating to shared time or dual enrollment depend largely on the wording of state laws. In perhaps the earliest case, the Supreme Court of Pennsylvania posited that a student who attended a faith-based school could not be denied the opportunity to enroll in a manual training course in a local public school (*Commonwealth ex rel. Wehrle v. School District*, 1913). More than 50 years later, an appellate court in Illinois upheld an experimental program that allowed students who otherwise would have been eligible for full-time enrollment in public high schools to attend classes there on a part-time basis and take other courses in faith-based schools (*Morton v. Board of Education*, 1966). Avoiding the First Amendment issue, the court indicated that the local board could experiment in an educational program that applied to all non-public schools, not just ones that were faith-based. The court concluded that state law failed to specify that all classes had to take place in one location.

In the same year, the Supreme Court of Missouri reached the opposite result (*Special District for Education and Training of Handicapped Children v. Wheeler*, 1966). The court questioned procedures whereby public funds were used to send speech teachers into faith-based schools to provide speech therapy and to allow some of these students to go to public schools to receive speech therapy during the regular class day. The court prohibited public school personnel from going into faith-based schools and invalidated the practice of permitting their students to travel to public schools. The court interpreted state law as requiring the school day to be of a set length and that it had to be spent entirely in one type of school.

The Supreme Court of Michigan considered shared time in response to a state constitutional amendment prohibiting financial aid to students or their faith-based schools. The court upheld the program in clarifying that if teaching took place on leased premises or in faith-based schools, services had to be provided only under conditions appropriate for public schools (*In re Proposal C.*, 1971). The court explained that ultimate and immediate control of subject matter, personnel, and premises had to be under the control of public school officials, and the courses had to be open to all eligible students.

A dozen years later, officials in another district in Michigan created a far-reaching program that grew to the point where publicly paid teachers conducted 10 percent of classes in faith-based schools while many of them worked in the religious schools. After the Sixth Circuit invalidated the plan as violating the Establishment Clause (*Americans United for Separation of Church and State v. School District of City of Grand Rapids*, 1983), in *School District of City of Grand Rapids v. Ball* (1985), the Supreme Court affirmed that the released-time program failed all three prongs of the *Lemon v. Kurtzman* (1971) test, discussed in the chapter entitled "Leading Supreme Court Decisions on Faith-Based Schools." Moreover, the Court invalidated a community education after-school program in which teachers from faith-based schools worked part-time for the local public school board, instructing students in their own buildings.

Vouchers

Considerable controversy has arisen over the use of vouchers, with courts reaching mixed results in disputes over their constitutionality. The Supreme Court of Wisconsin upheld a voucher program that allowed students to attend faith-based schools (*Jackson v. Benson*, 1998a, 1998b). Yet, Maine's highest court upheld a law including non-sectarian schools but specifically excluding faith-based schools from participating in a tuition vouchers program (*Bagley v. Raymond School Dep't*, 1999a, b). The same court subsequently upheld a statute prohibiting the use of either state (*Anderson v. Town of Durham*, 2006a, b) or municipal (*Joyce v. State of Maine*, 2008) general funds to pay tuition for children who attended faith-based schools. Earlier, the Supreme Court of Vermont affirmed the unconstitutionality of a state law that would have allowed taxpayer support to reimburse parents for tuition for faith-based schools (*Chittenden Town School Dist. v. Department of Education*, 1999). Still, it was not until a dispute from Ohio made its way to the Supreme Court that vouchers assumed center stage.

In an initial challenge to a statute that provided aid to children in Cleveland's failing public schools, the Supreme Court of Ohio upheld the statute but severed the part of it affording priority to parents who belonged to a religious group supporting faith-based schools. In invalidating the law as a violation of the state constitutional requirement that every statute have only one subject, the court stayed enforcement of its order to avoid disrupting the then current school year (*Simmons–Harris v. Goff*, 1999). The General Assembly of Ohio quickly re-enacted a revised statute that the Supreme Court upheld in *Zelman v. Simmons–Harris* (*Zelman* 2002).

Post-*Zelman* litigation challenging vouchers focuses on state constitutional grounds because, as noted, they are typically more restrictive than their federal counterparts. In a case that began before *Zelman* reached the Supreme Court, an appellate court in Florida initially upheld vouchers for students who attended faith-based schools (*Bush v. Holmes*, 2000, 2001). Following *Zelman*, the Supreme Court of Florida affirmed that a voucher system that would have provided indirect benefits to "sectarian" schools violated the state constitution's requirement of a uniform system of free public schools (*Bush v. Holmes*, 2006).

The Supreme Court of Colorado affirmed that a program that required school boards to pay a portion of locally raised tax revenues to parents with children who were performing at an unsatisfactory level in public schools, which in turn required the parents to pay those funds to faith-based schools with special programs designed for those children, violated the local control provisions of the state constitution (*Owens v. Colorado Congress of Parents, Teachers and Students*, 2004). Conversely, the Supreme Court of Arizona upheld a voucher program for children with disabilities who were in foster care because the funds were earmarked for those students, thus making them the true beneficiaries under the law (*Cain v. Horne*, 2009).

The Supreme Court of Utah, in a case that did not reach the merits of the issue, refused to grant a writ to sponsors of both a voucher law and a referendum on the statute that challenged the ballot title of the referendum (*Snow v. Office of Legislative Research and General Counsel*, 2007). In reasoning that the referendum ballot title was neither patently false nor biased, the court refused to modify its wording. Eventually, voters rejected a law that would have enacted the most comprehensive voucher program in the United States (Robelen 2007).

CONCLUSION

Perhaps the only certainty in reviewing litigation in state courts is that since state constitutions generally place greater restrictions on the types and amount of aid that can be provided to faith-based schools and their students, there will be a steady stream of cases for years to come. As such, it bears watching to see whether states choose to follow the lead of the Supreme Court and Federal Constitution by allowing more aid to students in the faith-based schools that continue to contribute so much to the success of the United Sates.

REFERENCES AND FURTHER READING

Advisory Opinion, In re, 228 N.W.2d 772 (Mich.1975).

Americans United for Separation of Church and State v. School District of City of Grand Rapids, 718 F.2d 1389 (6th Cir. 1983).

Anderson v. Town of Durham, 895 A.2d 944 (Me. 2006a), *cert. denied*, 549 U.S. 1051 (2006b).

Bagley v. Raymond School Department, 728 A.2d 127 (Me. 1999a), *cert. denied*, 528 U.S. 947 (1999b).

Blaine Amendments, http://www.blaineamendments.org/states/states.html (last accessed Feb. 6, 2011).

Blaine, J. K. Proposed Constitutional Amendment, 4 CONG. REC. 205 (1875).

Bloom v. School Committee of Springfield, 379 N.E.2d 578 (Mass. 1978).

Board of Education for Independent School District No. 52 v. Antone, 384 P.2d 911 (Okla. 1963).

Board of Education of Central School District No. 1 v. Allen, 392 U.S. 236 (1968).

Board of Education of Kiryas Joel Village School District v. Grumet, 512 U.S. 687 (1994).

Board of Education of Lawrence Union Free School Dist. Number 15 v. McColgan, 846 N.Y.S.2d 889 (N.Y. Sup. Ct. 2007).

Bush v. Holmes, 767 So. 2d 668 (Fla. Dist. Ct. App. 2000), *review denied*, 790 So. 2d 1104 (Fla. 2001); 919 So. 2d 392 (Fla. 2006).

Cain v. Horne, 202 P.3d 1178 (Ariz. 2009).

California Teachers Association v. Riles, 632 P.2d 953 (Cal. 1981).

Cantwell v. Connecticut, 310 U.S. 296 (1940).

Chittenden Town School District v. Department of Education, 738 A.2d 539 (Vt. 1999).

Cochran v. Louisiana State Board of Education, 123 So. 664 (La. 1928), 281 U.S. 370 (1930).

Commonwealth ex rel. Wehrle v. School Dist., 88 A. 481 (Pa. 1913).

Epeldi v. Engelking, 488 P.2d 860 (Idaho 1971), *cert. denied*, 406 U.S. 957 (1972).

Everson v. Board of Education, 330 U.S. 1 (1947), *reh'g denied*, 330 U.S. 855 (1947).

Fannin v. Williams, 655 S.W.2d 480 (Ky. 1983).

Gaffney v. State Department of Education, 220 N.W.2d 550 (Neb. 1974).

Grant, U.S. (1875) (annual message of the president of the United States). 4 CONG. REC. 175 (1875).

Griffith v. Bower, 747 N.E.2d 423 (Ill. App. Ct. 2001), *appeal denied*, 755 N.E.2d 477 (Ill. 2001).

Grumet v. Cuomo, 659 N.Y.S.2d 173 (N.Y.1997).

Grumet v. Pataki, 697 N.Y.S.2d 846 (N.Y.1999), *cert. denied*, 528 U.S. 946 (1999).

Jackson v. Benson, 578 N.W.2d 602 (Wis.1998a), *cert. denied*, 525 U.S. 997 (1998b).

Joyce v. State of Maine, 951 A.2d 69 (Me. 2008).

Lemon v. Kurtzman, 403 U.S. 602 (1971).

Matter of Certification of a Question of Law from U.S. District Court, District of S.D., 372 N.W.2d 113 (S.D.1985).

Matthews v. Quinton, 362 P.2d 932 (Alaska 1961), *cert. denied*, 368 U.S. 517 (1962).

McVey v. Hawkins, 258 S.W.2d 927 (Mo. 1953).

Morton v. Board of Education, 216 N.E.2d 305 (Ill. App. Ct. 1966).

Mueller v. Allen, 463 U.S. 388 (1983).

Neal v. Fiscal Court, Jefferson County, 986 S.W.2d 907 (Ky. 1999).

Owens v. Colorado Congress of Parents, Teachers and Students, 92 P.3d 933 (Colo. 2004).

Paster v. Tussey, 512 S.W.2d 97 (Mo. 1974), *cert. denied*, 419 U.S. 1111 (1975).

People ex rel. Klinger v. Howlett, 305 N.E.2d 129 (Ill. 1973).

Pequea Valley School District v. Commonwealth of Pennsylvania Department of Education, 397 A.2d 1154 (Pa. 1979a), *appeal dismissed for want of a substantial federal question*, 443 U.S. 901 (1979b).

Proposal C. In re, 185 N.W.2d 9 (Mich. 1971).

Robelen, E. W. (2007, Nov. 14). "Utah's Vote Raises Bar on Choice: Voucher Program's Defeat May Lead to Strategy Shift," *Education Weekly*, November 14, 2009, 1.

School District of City of Grand Rapids v. Ball, 473 U.S. 373 (1985).

Simmons–Harris v. Goff, 711 N.E.2d 203 (Ohio 1999).

Snow v. Office of Legislative Research and General Counsel, 167 P.3d 1051 (Utah 2007).

Special District for Education and Training of Handicapped Children v. Wheeler, 408 S.W.2d 60 (Mo. 1966).

State ex rel. Public School District No. 6, Cedar County v. Taylor, 240 N.W. 573 (Neb. 1932).

State ex rel. School District of Hartington v. Nebraska State Board of Education, 195 N.W.2d 161 (Neb.1972a), *cert. denied*, 409 U.S. 921 (1972b).

Taetle v. Atlanta Independent School System, 625 S.E.2d 770 (Ga. 2006).

Terhune v. Myers, 154 P.3d 1284 (Or. 2007).

Visser v. Nooksack Valley School District No. 506, 207 P.2d 198 (Wash.1949).

Witters v. State Commission for the Blind, 771 P.2d 1119 (Wash.1989a), *cert. denied*, 493 U.S. 850 (1989b).

Zellers v. Huff, 236 P.2d 949 (N.M. 1951).

Zelman v. Simmons–Harris, 536 U.S. 639 (2002).

Zobrest v. Catalina Foothills School District, 509 U.S. 1 (1993).

Index

Jewish day schools: charter schools, 444–47; community day schools, 227–35; Conservative day schools, 237–46; curriculum, 244, 268, 280, 286, 287–88; dual-curriculum program, 286; enrollment by type, 230, 272, 285; Hebrew cultural charter schools, 444–47; history, 13–14, 18, 22, 24, 238–39, 480–81; non-denominational approach, 227–35, 271; Orthodox day schools, 247–55; politics and, 479, 480–81; Reform day schools, 258–69; special education, 272, 285; student outcomes, 504; teachers, 244, 254, 287

Jewish Education Services of North America (JESNA), 271

Jewish homeschooling, 132

Jewish population: demographics, 245; geographic dispersion, 232–33

Jeynes, William, 507

Jim Joseph Foundation, 254

John Paul II (pope), 332

Johnson, George, 309, 310

Johnson-Reed Act of 1924, 433

Johnson, T. E., 154

Johnstone Report of 1966, 18–19

Joyce v. State of Maine (Me. 2008), 544

Judaism: Conservative Judaism, 242; Orthodox Judaism, 247–48, 284; patrilineal descent, 266; Reform Judaism, 258–59, 260, 266, 267. *See also* Jewish day schools; Jewish population

Junior Academy, 193

Justice, Benjamin, 12

Kaestle, Carl, 488

Kafer, Krista, 338

Kaiser, Roy, 158, 167

Kaminetsky, Joseph, 284

Kane, Kathryn, 371

Karff, Rabbi Samuel, 264

Kashatus, William, 7, 13

Katzer, Archbishop of Milwaukee, 306

Kaufman, Rabbi Jay, 263

Kealey, Robert, 388

Keane, Rev. John, 477

Kennedy, Anthony (Supreme Court Justice), 23

Kennedy, John F., 312

Kenrick, Francis (Bishop of Philadelphia), 4

Kent School (Connecticut), 85

Kentucky: Amish schools, 36; Catholic schools, 384; Old Order Mennonite schools, 48; state case law, 454, 541

Kentucky State Board v. Rudasill (Ky. 1979), 454

Kerfoot, John Barrett, 81

Kern, Andrew, 118

Kettle Moraine Lutheran High School (Wisconsin), 181

Keyworth, Karen, 426

Kienel, Paul, 107, 108, 109

King's College (New York), 77

Kingsley, Charles, 83

Kiryas Joel (New York), 444–45, 470–71, 542

Kleitz, Brett, 509

Klicka, Christopher, 129–30

Knight, George R., 10, 190

Know-Nothing Party, 301

Koehler, E. W., 168

Kolbe Academy (California), 352, 384–85, 387

Kolbe Homeschool Academy, 385

Koloze, Lou, 107

Komer, Richard D., 337

Koob, C. Albert, 325, 396

Kozol, Jonathan, 447

Kraemer, William A., 166–67

Kramer, Marc N., 228, 284

Kuiper, Henry, 72

Kuiper, Klaas, 71, 72

Ku Klux Klan (KKK), 12, 13

Kuyper, Abraham, 63, 65

Labor law legal case, *National Labor Relations Board v. The Catholic Bishop of Chicago, et al.* (1979), 21, 535

Lacey, Paul, 209, 210

Lakeside Lutheran High School, 181

Lancaster Mennonite School (Pennsylvania), 57

Lane, Pastor Alex, 175

Lange, Paul, 162

Langhorne, Mary, Lady Astor, 85

Lankenau, F. J., 156

La Salle, Jean-Baptiste de, 496

Latinos, Catholic schools, 318–19, 320

About the Editors and Contributors

THE EDITORS

James C. Carper is Professor of Social Foundations of Education at the University of South Carolina, where he has been a faculty member since 1989. He earned his B.A. in American history from Ohio Wesleyan University and his doctorate in foundations of education at Kansas State University. His research interests include the history of American education, education and religion, and private schools. He has published in numerous journals, including *Journal of Church and State*; *Religion and Education*; *Kansas History*; *History of Education Quarterly*; *Educational Leadership*; *Register of the Kentucky Historical Society*; *Kappa Delta Pi Record*; *Educational Forum*; and *Educational Policy*. He and Thomas C. Hunt are the coeditors of the *Praeger Handbook of Religion and Education in the United States* (2009) and coauthors of *The Dissenting Tradition in American Education* (2007).

Thomas C. Hunt received his PhD from the University of Wisconsin-Madison in 1971 in the Educational Policy Studies Department. He joined the faculty at Virginia Tech that year, where he served until 1996. While at Tech he received numerous awards in teaching, research, and service, including its highest teaching award. In 1996 he joined the faculty at the University of Dayton, where he received the Alumni Award for Scholarship in 2002. This book will be the 25th book he has authored or edited in his professional career, and it will be the 16th book he has authored or edited during his years at Dayton, all but one on religion and education. He served as coeditor of *Catholic Education: A Journal of Inquiry and Practice*, at the time the only refereed journal exclusively devoted to Catholic schools in the nation, from 1998 to 2008. In 2007 he was named a Fellow in the Center for Catholic Education at the University of Dayton.

THE CONTRIBUTORS

Larry D. Burton has spent his teaching career in Seventh-day Adventist schools. He taught 13 years at the elementary and junior academy levels in Ohio, Arkansas, Louisiana, and Michigan. As a multi-grade specialist, he never taught a single-grade classroom. After completing his PhD in 1995 he joined the faculty of Andrews University, where he served as faculty member, program director, and department chair for teacher education. Since 2005 he has been Professor of Curriculum and Instruction while simultaneously directing the graduate programs in Curriculum and Instruction and serving as editor for the *Journal of Research on Christian Education.*

Effie N. Christie is Assistant Professor and Chair of the Educational Leadership Department at Kean University, Union, New Jersey, where she has taught since 2005. Her research interests include gender issues in leadership and educational reform in urban schools. She co-authored a book with Sideris Bastas, *Teens and Technology: What Makes Your Teen Tick and How to Keep Them Safe.* Her short story, "The Red Pen," was published by Kappa Delta Pi in *So to Teach: Inspiring Stories that Touch the Heart.* Her work has also appeared in *The Journal of Reflective Practice, The Encyclopedia of Educational Reform and Dissent,* and *NCPEA Educational Leadership Review.*

William D. Cochran is the Director of School Ministry, The Lutheran Church Missouri Synod. He received a bachelor of science degree upon graduation from Concordia Teacher's College, Seward, Nebraska, in 1968. He received a master's degree and Administrative Certificate from Southern Illinois University in Edwardsville, Illinois. In 1984 became the founding principal of Good Shepherd Lutheran School in Collinsville. In 1992 he received a call to be the Superintendent of Lutheran Schools in the Eastern District of the Lutheran Church Missouri Synod. In 1998 God called him to be the principal of Christ Community Lutheran School in Kirkwood, Missouri.

Elaine R. Shizgal Cohen is the Director of the Schechter Day School Network at the United Synagogue of Conservative Judaism, where she has served since 2003. She is a former head of school and educational director of Jewish day schools in Montreal and New Jersey. She earned her doctorate from Rutgers University in Education and Counseling Psychology, received her B.A. from McGill University, and holds master's degrees from Harvard University and Boston College. She has served as a board member of the New Jersey Association of Independent Schools and as a mentor in the Day School Leadership Training Institute at the Jewish Theological Seminary.

Bruce S. Cooper is Professor of School Leadership and Policy at Fordham University's Graduate School of Education, in New York City. He is editor of the *Private School Monitor* and co-author of *Blurring the Lines: Charter, Public, Private and Religious Schools Come Together.* He has a long-term interest in private and religious education, and he was a founder and president of Associates for Research on Private Education, a Special Interest Group of the American Education Research Association. He has published numerous articles on politics of education, private schools, and school choice.

Eileen J. Councill is the Principal at Houston Christian High School. Her two decades of educational experience include work in the public and private sector in the United States and internationally, most notably at the United Nations International School. A national leader, she has presented at conferences around the world and has a passion for hands-on learning and technology integration in the classroom. She received her BS from Geneva College, her MS from Western Connecticut State University, her MSEd from Baruch College, and her EdD from Fordham University.

Mark W. Dewalt is Professor of Educational Research at Winthrop University. His research and writing interests include Amish education and culture, Old Order Mennonite education and culture, effective teaching, working with students of poverty, and children's literature. He has published several books, including *Amish Education in the United States and Canada, The Life and Times of Thomas Jefferson*, and *South Carolina People and Places*. He has also published in numerous journals, including the *Journal of College Student Retention, Virginia Quarterly Review, Journal of Research in Rural Education, The Lutheran Educator*, and *Anthropology and Education Quarterly*.

R. Guy Erwin is the Gerhard & Olga J. Belgum Professor of Lutheran Confessional Theology at California Lutheran University, where he has taught since 2000. His research interests are in the areas of Luther studies, Reformation history, and the history of Lutheranism in the early modern period. He is currently completing (in collaboration with L. DeAne Lagerquist of St. Olaf College) *An Introduction to World Lutheranism*, to be published in 2012 by Cambridge University Press. He also works in the area of Lutheran higher education and speaks widely in ELCA circles about the role of the church in education.

Susan M. Ferguson received her master's degree from the University of Dayton in 1983. From 1984 to 1989 she served as a school psychologist in the Darke County Ohio schools. In 1990 she joined the faculty of the University of Dayton as an adjunct professor in educational psychology. She was appointed to the position of First Year Experience Coordinator for the Department of Teacher Education in 1998 and Undergraduate Coordinator for the Department of Teacher Education in 2002. In 2007 she became the executive director of the Center for Catholic Education at which she continues today. She has conducted many professional development sessions for public and Catholic school educators.

James M. Frabutt is a faculty member in the Mary Ann Remick Leadership Program in the Alliance for Catholic Education and Concurrent Associate Professor of Psychology at the University of Notre Dame. With colleagues in the Remick Leadership Program, he has co-authored three books: *Research, Action, and Change: Leaders Reshaping Catholic Schools; Faith, Finances, and the Future: The Notre Dame Study of U.S. Pastors;* and *Action Research in Catholic Schools: A Step-by-Step Guide for Practitioners*.

Lyndon G. Furst is Professor Emeritus of Educational Administration at Andrews University. He recently retired from Andrews as Dean of the School of Graduate Studies. Prior to that position he served as Professor of Educational Administration. He also worked in the Seventh-day Adventist school system for 21 years as elementary teacher and principal, high school principal, and educational superintendent for a two state region. Furst holds an EdD in educational administration from the University of the Pacific. His research interests include the legal aspects of education, nonpublic schools, and the intersection of those two topics.

Charles L. Glenn has been Professor of Educational Leadership and Development at Boston University since 1991; from 1970 to 1991 he was the Massachusetts state official responsible for educational equity and urban education. His books include *The Myth of the Common School* (1988); *Educational Freedom in Eastern Europe* (1995); *Educating Immigrant Children* (1996); *The Ambiguous Embrace: Government and Faith-based Schools and Social Agencies* (2000, with Jan De Groof); *Balancing Freedom, Autonomy, and Accountability in Education* (2004); *Contrasting Models of State and School* (2011) and histories of the schooling of African-American and American Indian pupils (2011).

Brother John R. Habjan, S. M., is a member of the Society of Mary (Marianists). He was a high school administrator and teacher in Marianist-sponsored schools. For six years, he was Assistant Director of Education for the Marianist Province of the United States. He is currently Assistant Archivist for the Marianist Province. He previously published "Society of Mary: Marianists," *Catholic Education: A Journal of Inquiry and Practice*, 11, 2, pp. 198–217.

Daniel R. Heischman is Executive Director of the National Association of Episcopal Schools. Previously he served as Chaplain and Head of the Religion Department at Trinity School in New York, Executive Director of the Council for Religion in Independent Schools, Assistant Headmaster and Head of the Upper School at St. Albans School in Washington, D.C., and Chaplain at Trinity College in Hartford CT. In 2009 he authored the book, *Good Influence: Teaching the Wisdom of Adulthood*. He also serves as Adjunct Instructor in the Doctor of Ministry program at Virginia Theological Seminary and as Secretary of the Board of the Council for American Private Education.

John C. Holmes is the Director of Government Affairs for the Association of Christian Schools International (ACSI), an office he founded in Washington, DC in 1985. Holmes previously served as the superintendent of four Christian schools in the Los Angeles area, where he completed a doctorate at Pepperdine University. He has served as an ordained minister of the Foursquare Gospel Church for over 40 years. In 2006, he was given the Distinguished Pepperdine University Graduate School of Education and Psychology Alumnus Award. He has written for publications by ACSI, the Foursquare Church, and the Associates for Research in Private Education, plus several chapters in books.

Anthony C. Holter is a faculty member in the Mary Ann Remick Leadership Program at the University of Notre Dame where he teaches research methods in the Master of Arts in Educational Administration program and Education, Schooling, and Society minor for undergraduates. Holter has published and presented on Catholic education, interpersonal forgiveness, moral education and development, and research methods. His current research interests focus on community based action research for school leaders and the development of the Catholic School Identity Inventory (CSII).

Steven L. Jones is Associate Professor of Sociology at Grove City College in Pennsylvania. He is the author or editor of four books, including *Religious Schooling in America* (Praeger 2008). He has been the recipient of fellowships from the Center on Religion and Democracy; the Center for Children, Families, and the Law; and the Institute for Advanced Studies in Culture. His current work focuses on the limits of parental rights in democratic societies.

Karen E. Keyworth is the Co-founder and Director of Education for the Islamic Schools League of America (founded in 1998). She has worked for over 20 years as faculty member and administrator at the college/university and K-12 levels. In 1996, she was the founding principal of the Greater Lansing Islamic School. Her research interests include all aspects of Islamic schools/schooling and Islamic identity. She has published in several journals, including *Islamic Horizon*, and books, including *Educating the Muslims of America* and *The Praeger Handbook of Religion and Education in the United States*.

Robert F. Klindworth was educated at the undergraduate level at Dr. Martin Luther College in New Ulm, MN; Robert F. Klindworth received his Master's in Education from St. Mary's University and his doctorate in Educational Policy and Administration from the University of MN-Twin Cities in 2008. He has taught and served as principal of Lutheran schools at the elementary, middle school, and high school levels. In 2003 he joined the faculty of Martin Luther College in New Ulm, MN. Klindworth has written education articles for several professional journals and has authored a book on non-public school leadership. He has spoken at various educational conferences and has presented at numerous educational conferences.

Marc N. Kramer is the Executive Director of RAVSAK: The Jewish Community Day School Network. In addition to his work with RAVSAK, he is an educational consultant and group facilitator for the Jewish Board of Family and Children's Services of New York. He is the author of several major studies on Jewish day school education and develops psychotherapeutic programs that explore the interface of traditional Jewish texts, civic engagement, and normative mental health issues. Kramer is the former head of the Beit Rabban School in New York, New York, and the Director of Judaic Studies for the El Paso Hebrew Day School. He is the recipient of the 2006 Covenant Award.

George J. Lisjak received his EdD in Educational Leadership from Duquesne University in 1998. He has been in Catholic education for over 30 years, most of that as a teacher and principal at North Catholic High School in Pittsburgh, Pennsylvania. In 2005, he became Director of Marianist Educational Studies and Partnerships. He is engaged in research and programming in support of Mission Integration for the three universities and 18 secondary schools of the Marianist Province of the United States.

Regina A. Lloyd holds her BS degree, summa cum laude, and her MS degree from the University of Dayton in Dayton, Ohio. She taught third grade for seven years in the public school system before taking time off to raise her children. After completing graduate studies in education, and realizing the importance of Catholic schools in our society, she joined the dedicated team of professionals in the Center for Catholic Education at the University of Dayton where she is able to contribute to the work of fostering excellence in Catholic schools.

Jan W. Lohmeyer is an Adjunct Professor at Concordia University of Texas, where he has been a faculty member since 1999. He is also Director of Curriculum at Lutheran High North of Houston, Texas. His research interests include Christian Apologetics, the history of Lutheran education, teacher training, Classical Education, and private schools. He has published in numerous journals, including *Lutheran Education Association, The Spirit of*

Southern, The Lutheran Portal, and *The Southern District Educator*. He has served on 15 educational committees and task forces for the Lutheran Church–Missouri Synod. He received his PhD in Education from the University of New Orleans.

Arthur Maloney received his EdD from Teachers College, Columbia University in 1989. From 1970 to 2001 he was a teacher and high school principal at several schools in the metropolitan New York City Area. Moving to Pace University in 2001, he served as Department Chair from 2004 to 2010 and was the co-founder of Pace University High School and Director of the Distinguished Educators Lecture Series. He received the Pace University Award for Distinguished Service in 2004. His most recent publication is *Blurring the Lines, Charter, Public, Private and Religious Schools Coming Together*.

Ralph Mawdsley is Professor of Educational Administration and The Roslyn Z. Wolf Endowed Chair in Urban Educational Leadership at Cleveland State University, Cleveland, Ohio. He holds a JD from the University of Illinois and a PhD from the University of Minnesota and is licensed to practice law in Illinois and Minnesota. In addition, he was awarded an honorary doctorate (DEd - honoris causa) from the University of Pretoria, South Africa, in 2010 for his contribution to education law and his work with doctoral students. He has been the recipient of two Fulbright Awards to South Africa and Australia in the area of education law and has over 500 publications to his credit in that field. Prior to his tenure at Cleveland State University, he was a county prosecutor, a religious K-12 school teacher and administrator, and a religious university's in-house legal counsel.

Amy S. McEntee received her bachelor of science degree in education from the University of Dayton in 2003. She taught in the public schools in Maryland and Florida for several years before moving into Catholic education. McEntee has worked in parish ministry in the area of faith formation for children, youth, and adults, and she served as the co-ordinator of Lalanne, a Catholic teacher-service program. She currently is an assistant director in the Office of Evangelization and Catechesis for the Archdiocese of Cincinnati.

Irene McHenry is the Executive Director of Friends Council on Education, President of the Council for American Private Education board and member of Haverford College board. She was a founding faculty member for Fielding Graduate University's doctoral program in education, founding Head of Delaware Valley Friends School, co-founder of Greenwood Friends School and adjunct faculty at Lincoln University. She co-authored *Governance Handbook for Friends Schools*, co-edited *Tuning In: Mindfulness in Teaching and Learning*, and published articles in *SCT in Action*, *A Passion for Teaching*, *Journal of Negro Education*, *Phi Delta Kappan*, and *Journal of Education for Students Placed At-Risk*.

Janet Mulvey received her doctorate from Fordham University. She holds three master's degrees in education and has taught at the elementary, middle, and high school levels. She served as a Principal at the elementary level for 13 years in the Lakeland School District, New York. Currently she is an Assistant Professor at Pace University in New York City where she teaches subjects in Educational Leadership and Research and Literacy. Dr. Mulvey has published two books, contributed to articles in the *School Administrator*, participated in a debate on faith-based charter schools for Sage, and is currently under contract with Palgrave MacMillan for a book focusing on the intersection of health, education, and welfare.

Ronald J. Nuzzi is a Catholic priest of the Diocese of Youngstown, Ohio and currently serves as Senior Director of the Mary Ann Remick Leadership Program in the Alliance for Catholic Education (ACE) at the University of Notre Dame. He has served as editor of *Catholic Education: A Journal of Inquiry & Practice*, and a variety of scholarly reference works including: *Handbook of Research on Catholic Education, Catholic Education in the United States: An Encyclopedia*, and *Moral Education: A Handbook*.

Walter L. Prehn, is an Episcopal priest and Headmaster of Trinity School of Midland-Odessa in West Texas. He studied under Jennings Wagoner at the University of Virginia and received the Ph.D. in the History of American Education in 2005. His dissertation was a history of the national school-making movement initiated by William Augustus Muhlenberg (1796–1877) and his three principal disciples, a mission in education that produced some of America's finest schools. Prehn was prepared at historic Chamberlain-Hunt Academy in Mississippi, earned a BA degree in history from Texas A&M, and graduated Master of Divinity from Nashotah House Episcopal Seminary (Wisconsin) in 1985.

Brian D. Ray is president of the National Home Education Research Institute in Salem, Oregon, and internationally known for his research on homeschooling (home-based education). He has published in journals such as *Peabody Journal of Education, Educational Leadership*, and *Academic Leadership Journal*. He has served as a professor at the undergraduate and graduate levels, a classroom teacher in public and private schools, and an expert witness before many courts and legislatures. Ray holds a BS in biology from the University of Puget Sound, an MS in zoology from Ohio University, and a PhD from Oregon State University.

Karen M. Ristau became NCEA's ninth president in July 2005. Dr. Ristau has worked as a teacher and administrator in Catholic schools for over a decade in California. In subsequent years, she was a faculty member and director of programs in education at the University of St. Thomas in Minnesota. She held administrative positions at Saint Joseph College in Connecticut and then at St. Mary's College, Notre Dame, Indiana. Dr. Ristau is published in many scholarly educational journals and is a frequent speaker at educational gatherings. She has received the Neil D'Amour Award from NCEA, the Murray Medallion from the University of St. Thomas, an outstanding service award from the University of San Francisco and has been awarded two honorary doctorates.

Charles J. Russo is the Joseph Panzer Chair in Education in the School of Education and Allied Professions and Adjunct Professor in the School of Law at the University of Dayton (Ohio). The 1998–99 President of the Education Law Association and 2002 recipient of its McGhehey (Achievement) Award, he has written and spoken extensively about education law in the United States and overseas.

David Sikkink is Associate Professor of Sociology at the University of Notre Dame and a fellow in the Institute for Educational Initiatives and the Center for the Study of Religion and Society at Notre Dame. His research interests include issues of religion in public life;

specifically religious school sector effects, religion and schooling attitudes and practices, and religion and civic participation. His work has been published in *Social Forces, Social Problems, Journal for the Scientific Study of Religion*, and *Review of Religious Research*. He is currently a principal investigator for the Cardus Education Study, a national study of Catholic and Protestant schools in the U.S. and their impact on the everyday lives of graduates.

Moshe Sokolow is the Fanya Gottesfeld-Heller Professor of Jewish Education at Yeshiva University's Azrieli Graduate School of Jewish Education and Administration. He publishes on the history and philosophy of Jewish education, and on comparisons between Jewish and Muslim educational philosophies. His major research interest is in the utilization of classical Jewish sources (both literary and documentary) to promote Jewish values and identity. He is the author of *Studies in the Weekly Parashah Based on the Lessons of Nehama Leibowitz*, and co-editor of *Between Rashi and Maimonides* and *The Azrieli Papers: Dimensions of Orthodox Day School Education*.

Donovan D. Steiner is Director of the Master of Arts in Education program at Eastern Mennonite University, Harrisonburg, Virginia, where he is the Jesse T. Byler Professor of Education. Along with administrative duties he teaches courses in literacy, social and ethical issues, and Anabaptist-Mennonite education. He received a PhD in education at Southern Illinois University at Carbondale.

Steven C. Vryhof, a former high school teacher, received his PhD from the University of Chicago. His dissertation was published as *Between Memory and Vision: The Case for Faith-Based Schooling*. An adjunct professor at Calvin College, he has taught, written, and consulted widely on faith-based schooling and the Effective Lifelong Learning Inventory (ELLI) from England. He was instrumental in founding Daystar School in Chicago and is the founder and executive director of the Daystar Center, offering educational, cultural, and professional development opportunities.

Jane West Walsh is a Jewish education practitioner and independent scholar in the fields of adult education and inter-religious learning. She current serves the Union for Reform Judaism as Day School Consultant and Executive Director of PARDeS: Progressive Association of Reform Day Schools, an international network of schools affiliated ideologically with Reform Judaism and the Reform movement.

Judylynn Walton is Executive Assistant of the American Association of Christian Schools (AACS). Previously she taught in AACS-member schools in Florida and Wisconsin and worked for the Old Dominion Association of Christian Schools, the AACS state affiliate in Virginia.

John J. White was educated in Catholic schools in Boston and at the University of Massachusetts, Boston. White received his PhD in history from Boston College in 2000. He came to the School of Education and Allied Professions at the University of Dayton in 2007, where he is assistant professor of social studies education and (by courtesy) history. He has published articles and book chapters on curriculum in international education and on the history of Catholic schools.

John Witte, Jr. is the Jonas Robitscher Professor of Law, Alonzo L. McDonald Distinguished Professor, and Director of the Center for the Study of Law and Religion at Emory University Law School in Atlanta. He specializes in legal history, religious liberty, and marriage and family law. His publications include *Religion and the American Constitutional Experiment*; *Modern Christian Teachings on Law, Politics, and Human Nature*; *God's Joust, God's Justice: Law and Religion*; and *The Reformation of Rights: Law, Religion, and Human Rights in Early Modern Calvinism*.

Michael Zeldin is Professor of Jewish Education and Director of the Rhea Hirsch School of Education at Hebrew Union College-Jewish Institute of Religion in Los Angeles. He is principal author and co-editor of *Touching the Future: Mentoring and the Jewish Professional*. He is also Senior Editor of the *Journal of Jewish Education*, the premier academic and scholarly journal in Jewish education. and a member of the Editorial Board of the URJ Press, the Executive Committee of the Commission on Lifelong Jewish Learning of the Union for Reform Judaism, and the Executive Steering Committee of the Consortium for Applied Studies in Jewish Education.

Angela Ann Zukowski, **MHSH,** received degrees from the University of Dayton and United Theological Seminary. She is currently a Professor in the Department of Religious Studies, Director of The Institute for Pastoral Initiatives, and an adjunct professor in the School of Education at the University of Dayton (UD). She joined the UD faculty in 1978. She served as the World President for Catholic Communications (UNDA) and on many international and national educational boards and committees. She is the Executive Editor of the UD Catechist Formation Series (Peter Li, Inc), Chair of the Catholic Schools of Tomorrow Award for Innovations in Education, and member of the Executive Board for the Catholic Education Collaborative. She has co-authored several books and copious articles. Zukowski is recognized as an international and national conference speaker. Widely recognized as a leader in Catholic Education, having received a number of national and international awards and recognitions, she is an entrepreneur and pioneer for discovery learning.